Cooperstown Symposium on Baseball and the American Culture

Baseball and American Society
Series ISBN 0-88736-566-3

1. Blackball Stars
   John B. Holway
   ISBN 0-88736-094-7   CIP 1988

2. Baseball History, Premier Edition
   Edited by Peter Levine
   ISBN 0-88736-288-5   1988

3. My 9 Innings: An Autobiography of 50 Years in Baseball
   Lee MacPhail
   ISBN 0-88736-387-3   CIP 1989

4. Black Diamonds: Life in the Negro Leagues from the Men Who Lived It
   John B. Holway
   ISBN 0-88736-334-2   CIP 1989

5. Baseball History 2
   Edited by Peter Levine
   ISBN 0-88736-342-3   1989

6. Josh and Satch: A Dual Biography of Josh Gibson and Satchel Paige
   John B. Holway
   ISBN 0-88736-333-4   CIP forthcoming, 1991

7. Encyclopedia of Major League Baseball Team Histories
   Edited by Peter C. Bjarkman
   Volume I: American League
   ISBN 0-88736-373-3   CIP forthcoming, 1991

8. Encyclopedia of Major League Baseball Team Histories
   Edited by Peter C. Bjarkman
   Volume 2: National League
   ISBN 0-88736-374-1   CIP forthcoming, 1991

9. Baseball History 3
   Edited by Peter Levine
   ISBN 0-88736-577-9   1990

10. The Immortal Diamond: Baseball in American Literature
    Peter C. Bjarkman
    ISBN 0-88736-481-0 (hardcover)   CIP forthcoming, 1991
    ISBN 0-88736-482-9 (softcover)   CIP forthcoming, 1991

11. Total Latin American Baseball
    Peter C. Bjarkman
    ISBN 0-88736-546-9   CIP forthcoming, 1992

12. Baseball Players and Their Times: A History of the Major Leagues, 1920–1940
    Eugene Murdock
    ISBN 0-88736-235-4   CIP forthcoming, 1991

13. The Tropic of Baseball: Baseball in the Dominican Republic
    Rob Ruck
    ISBN 0-88736-707-0   CIP 1991

14. The Cinema of Baseball: Images of America, 1929–1989
    Gary E. Dickerson
    ISBN 0-88736-710-0   CIP forthcoming, 1991

15. Baseball History 4
    Edited by Peter Levine
    ISBN 0-88736-578-7   CIP forthcoming, 1991

16. Baseball and American Society: A Textbook of Baseball History
    Peter C. Bjarkman
    ISBN 0-88736-483-7 (softcover)   CIP forthcoming, 1992

17. Cooperstown Symposium on
    Baseball and the American Culture (1989)
    Edited by Alvin L. Hall
    ISBN 0-88736-719-4   CIP 1991

18. Cooperstown Symposium on
    Baseball and the American Culture (1990)
    Edited by Alvin L. Hall
    ISBN 0-88736-735-6   CIP forthcoming

Cooperstown Symposium on Baseball and the American Culture (1989)

Sponsored by
The State University of New York
College at Oneonta

Alvin L. Hall
Editor

Meckler
in association with
The State University of New York
College at Oneonta

FIRST EDITION

Jacket art: John Hull, "Spectator: Wytheville," 1988, acrylic on canvas. Art-work courtesy of the Grace Borgenicht Gallery, New York, New York.

Library of Congress Cataloging-in-Publication Data

Cooperstown Symposium on Baseball and the American Culture (1st : 1989
: Cooperstown, N.Y.)
    Cooperstown Symposium on Baseball and the American Culture, 1989 /
sponsored by the State University of New York, College at Oneonta ;
Alvin L. Hall, editor.
        p.   cm. — (Baseball and American society ; 17)
    Papers of the first symposium held June 8–9, 1989.
    Includes bibliographical references (p.   ).
    ISBN 0-88736-719-4 : $
    1. Baseball—Social aspects—United States—Congresses.
2. Baseball—United States—History—Congresses. 3. United States—
Social conditions—Congresses. I. Hall, Alvin L.   II. State
University of New York College at Oneonta. III. Title. IV. Series.
    GV863.A1C635   1991   90-21289
    796.357'0973—dc20   CIP

British Library Cataloguing in Publication Data

Cooperstown symposium on baseball and the American culture
    (1989).
Cooperstown symposium on baseball and the American culture
(1989) — (Baseball and American society)
1. United States.   Baseball related to culture
1. Title   II. Hall, Alvin L.   III. Series
306.483

    ISBN 0-88736-719-4

State University of New York College at Oneonta, Oneonta, NY 13820.

Meckler Publishing, the publishing division of Meckler Corporation,
    11 Ferry Lane West, Westport, CT 06880.
Meckler Ltd., 247-249 Vauxhall Bridge Road, London SWIV 1HQ, U.K.

Printed on acid free paper.
Printed and bound in the United States of America.

Contents

Introduction

by Alvin L. Hall

> Our . . . highland lake can lay no claim to grandeur; it has no
> broad expanse, and the mountains about cannot boast of any great
> height, yet there is a harmony in the different parts of the picture
> which gives it much merit, and which must always excite a lively
> feeling of pleasure. The hills are a charming setting for the lake at
> their feet, neither so lofty as to belittle the sheet of water, nor so low
> as to be tame and commonplace; there is abundance of wood on
> their swelling ridges to give the charm of forest scenery, enough of
> tillage to add the varied interest of cultivation; the lake, with its
> clear, placid water lies gracefully beneath the mountains, flowing
> here into a quiet little bay, there skirting a wooded point filling its
> ample basin, without encroaching on its banks by a rood of marsh
> or bog.
>
> And then the village, with its buildings and gardens covering
> the level bank to the southward, is charmingly placed, the waters
> spreading before it, a ridge of hills rising on either side, this almost
> wholly wooded, that partly tilled, while beyond lies a background,
> varied by the nearer and further heights. The little town, though an
> important feature in the prospect, is not an obtrusive one, but quite
> in proportion with surrounding objects. It has a cheerful, flourish-
> ing aspect, yet rural and unambitious, not aping the bustle and
> ferment of cities, and certainly one may travel many a mile without
> finding a village more prettily set down by the water-side.
>
> Susan Fenimore Cooper
> *Rural Hours*

Such was the description of Cooperstown, New York, and the
surrounding countryside by the daughter of its most famous
resident on the morning of Saturday, June 9, 1848, one hundred
forty-one years before the dates of the "First Cooperstown Symposium on Baseball and the American Culture," June 8 and 9, 1989.

Twentieth century Cooperstown resembles the nineteenth century version in many ways—small, rural, pastoral, dominated by Lake
Otsego. Yet there is one major difference. Each summer, hundreds of
thousands of visitors invade this small, upstate New York village,
drawn in part by these very characteristics. The larger magnet, however, is a relatively new attraction, the National Baseball Hall of Fame
and Museum, Inc., located right on Main Street in the heart of the
village.

Born in 1939, conceived by the triple desires of providing a suitable depository for the relics of the national pastime, a shrine to its heroes, and a boost to the local economy, the Hall of Fame celebrated its fiftieth anniversary in June of 1989. Cooperstown marked the occasion in typical American fashion with a parade, speeches and an Old Timers' Game featuring some of the sport's greatest names, Bob Feller and Warren Spahn among them.

The State University of New York College at Oneonta chose to add another dimension to the celebration. What more appropriate setting existed in which to examine the role of baseball in shaping the American culture than Cooperstown, a small, rural village surrounded by rolling hills and open fields, a backdrop long associated with this quintessential American game in both myth and fact.

The evolution of the First Cooperstown Symposium on Baseball and the American Culture is both simple and amazing. As one who is neither a particularly devoted fan nor a scholar whose research interests extend to baseball, the opportunity would probably have passed me by were it not for two rather innocent conversations one week apart in the fall of 1988.

The first took place in my office. Ron Feldstein, the director of the Hunt College Union at SUNY-Oneonta, and I were talking about future program ideas. He observed, rather casually, that the fiftieth anniversary of the Baseball Hall of Fame was coming up the following summer. "Wouldn't it be nice for the college to do something in connection with that?" My initial response was noncommittal and somewhat less than enthusiastic, "I'll think about it."

The next week, I journeyed to Cooperstown for the first time with my primary mission no more significant than getting to know some people I needed to know to do my job as dean of continuing education in a public university. One of the people on my list was Tom Heitz, librarian at the National Baseball Library. I dropped in unannounced, but Tom found time to see me. In the course of our conversation, Tom mentioned his desire to use the fiftieth anniversary as the opportunity to invite a few scholars to Cooperstown during the celebration to discuss the role of baseball in the American culture. Because the Hall of Fame has a relatively small full-time staff, Tom simply did not have time to devote to the project. It took me about two seconds to put the two conversations together, and I asked if he thought there would be any objection to the college's organizing such an event in conjunction with the anniversary. Team player that he is, Tom referred me to Howard Talbott, director of the Hall of Fame and his boss. Following that meeting, and armed with Talbott's blessing and the board of directors' consent, we were off.

As one who had never dealt with the subject, I was amazed at the response to the idea. When I issued the call for papers in October, 1988, I prayed for twelve submissions. With twelve papers, I thought we could hold a credible conference. We received nearly one hundred proposals, from all over the United States and Canada, from faculty in institutions ranging from community colleges to the most prestigious research universities, in disciplines from art history to sociology. We even received one original musical composition. Of these, we selected eighteen to be presented over the two days.

At the suggestion of Tom Heitz, I called James Vlasich, an associate professor of history at Southern Utah University, to invite him to deliver the keynote address. There are better known scholars of baseball, but none had research interests as appropriate to this symposium on this occasion. Jim had just completed a manuscript for a book on the origins of the Hall of Fame based on the personal papers of Alexander Cleland, one of the key, but least known, figures in the movement to establish that institution. Jim accepted with delight. I next called on Marty Appel, an alumnus of the college, author of eight popular books on baseball, and executive producer of New York Yankee baseball for WPIX-TV in New York City, to ask if he would open the second day of our meeting. He also was delighted. The rest is history.

The First Cooperstown Symposium attracted nearly one hundred participants. We spent two days together at the Otesaga Hotel overlooking Lake Otsego. We listened to colleagues present their papers and then we talked about baseball and art, baseball and history, baseball and literature, baseball and geography, baseball and sociology and anthropology, baseball and language, baseball and philosophy, baseball and ethnicity. To me, a relative outsider, this gathering was amazing and somewhat incongruous. Here was a group of scholars, each well grounded in his or her discipline based at a college or university, yet at the same time, an avid fan of the game of baseball. This symposium gave them an opportunity to combine their two passions, according to all who attended, in a way unique among other meetings they had attended. Before the first symposium adjourned, we scheduled the second for June, 1990.

With the second as well received as the first and now safely behind us, the college will continue to sponsor the Cooperstown Symposium on Baseball and the American Culture every year. The Third Symposium is scheduled for June 10, 11, and 12, 1991 at the Otesaga Hotel in Cooperstown. There is no better place for it.

Alexander Cleland and the Origin of the Baseball Hall of Fame

by James A. Vlasich

In the last half century, the Baseball Hall of Fame has grown from humble beginnings to an internationally recognized organization. For players, induction into the Baseball Hall of Fame has come to symbolize the highest achievement of the national pastime. Every fan of the game recognizes the connection between greatness in the sport and enshrinement at Cooperstown. Few people, however, realize how the institution was initiated and who was responsible for its beginnings. The concept of honoring individuals for reaching the pinnacle of their professional achievement was, after all, a modern innovation. Before the twentieth century no institution had initiated the idea of a hall of glory, but in 1900 New York University started the idea with the inception of the Hall of Fame for Great Americans. This organization was specifically designed to honor people who had made major contributions to the establishment and growth of the nation.[1] Although the original hall in New York City achieved a certain degree of success, nobody thought to apply it to specific fields of endeavor. The idea of enshrining heroes came more than a quarter of a century after the foundation was laid for the alleged time, place and inventor of the national pastime.

The man who was responsible for determining the beginning of baseball was Albert G. Spalding, the quintessential baseball entrepreneur of the late nineteenth century. He established a self-appointed committee and promised that it would collect every shred of evidence in order to ascertain the origin of the game. The chairman of the group was A. G. Mills, who had served as National League president from 1882–1884. Mills wrote the final decision of the special investigating committee. He stated without hesitation "that 'Base Ball' had its origin in the United States" and "that the first scheme for playing it, according to the best evidence obtainable to date, was devised by Abner Doubleday at Cooperstown, N.Y., in 1839." His conclusion was based on letters written by Abner Graves, a former resident of Cooperstown.[2]

No action of any consequences resulted in the immediate aftermath of the Mills committee decision. Doubtless, few people were surprised at the conclusion that baseball was American, and many fans simply viewed the decision as being more intuitively based than scientifically formulated. However, the committee's second major finding concerning the Doubleday–Cooperstown connection was viewed with skepticism, curiosity or surprise. Previously, Doubleday was known only for his service in the Union Army during the Civil War.

Because there was no link between the upstate New York village and the Mills commission, the people of Cooperstown did not make any immediate plans to capitalize on their newly discovered national claim to fame. The location of the first contest cited by Graves had not yet become sacrosanct ground, and for almost a decade no action was taken to develop it as such. In 1917, however, local citizens began fund-raising activities to improve the property as a public playground. Gradually, enough money was raised to officially open Doubleday Field in September 1920. Three years later, city taxpayers approved legislation to allow the village to purchase the area, and some construction work was done to expand the property and build a wooden grandstand.

Because of the depression, nothing was done to improve the land until the fall of 1933, when work was resumed through a New Deal program. Under the Work Relief Program, the entire field was graded, a new diamond was constructed, the area was fenced and the entrance was landscaped. When work ended the following summer, Lt. Governor M. William Bray of New York formally reopened Doubleday Field.[3]

The ideas of the original planners had been realized, and perhaps everyone felt that the dream of recognizing the village's contribution to baseball and American history had also become a reality. However, it would soon become apparent that Cooperstown's celebrity status was just beginning to be understood. In order to gain further recognition, two important items were necessary—financial support on a large scale and a grand idea on which promoters could capitalize.

The first item would be supplied by the village's leading family—the Clarks. Descendants of patriarch Edward W. Clark, they had accumulated a fortune through his association with sewing machine inventor Isaac M. Singer. As the wealth of the Clark family grew, so did its holdings in Cooperstown. Edward first bought property there in 1854, and gradually the family became solely responsible for many important community projects. Thus they had established a reputation for civic responsibility that helped to set the village apart from other communities.

Concerning economic development in Cooperstown, none of the family members was more important than Edward's grandson, Stephen Carlton Clark. A graduate of Yale and Columbia law schools, he had served in the New York State Assembly, as a director in the Singer Company and as a trustee of the Metropolitan Museum of Art. As a nationally known philanthropist, Stephen Clark was ideally suited to become the leading developer of the village. His creation of the Clark Foundation led to the financing of the hospital, recreation center, and college scholarships for local high school graduates. Concerned about the economic self-sufficiency of the region, he began to focus on the promotion of tourism as a means of attracting money into the community while preserving its charm and unspoiled character.[4]

While Stephen Clark would eventually become the financial backer of the Baseball Hall of Fame, the idea for its inception belonged to one of his employees—Alexander Cleland. Like his boss, Cleland didn't follow the sport, and in fact, he didn't even move to the United States until he was 26 years old. Leaving his native Scotland where he was a coal salesman in Glasgow, he lived in England for about a year and then came to America in 1903. His professional calling was in the area of social work, and his first job (1904–06) in Chicago involved work as industrial secretary for the central Y.M.C.A.

Being an immigrant himself, Cleland gradually got involved in work with new arrivals to America. From 1906 to 1913, he served as investigator for the Dillingham Federal Immigration Commission, the North American Civic League and the State Immigration Commission of New York. He was also employed as superintendent of Emergency Lodging House in Chicago and the executive secretary of the New Jersey Immigration Commission. In the 1920s he worked in the empire state as financial agent and assistant superintendent of the Broad Street Hospital, and as secretary of the Bowling Green Neighborhood Association.

While Cleland's work record was laudable both in its effort and his service to mankind, it hardly seemed to be a background that would qualify him for a position connected with the sport of baseball. Because of his work experience, however, he became acquainted with people in high places and demonstrated a sincere concern for the welfare of others. Both of these characteristics would prove valuable when he encountered his new employer in 1931.

Cleland's association with Stephen Clark began that year when he became director of the Clark House in New York City which was founded by the Clark Foundation. Like similar organizations throughout the country at this time, this settlement house provided for immigrants services such as temporary housing and aid in obtaining employment. Located on the lower east side of New York, Clark House introduced Cleland to a variety of people and served as an outlet for his humanitarian zeal. He established a personal reputation for efficiency, fairness, and ethical principles. In many ways Clark was the same kind of person, and it was not surprising that a mutual admiration developed between the two.[5]

The WPA project designed to expand and improve Doubleday Field was in full swing in the spring of 1934. On Saturday, May 6, Cleland and Clark met in Cooperstown to discuss some Clark House matters. Having finished with business affairs, the 57-year-old director decided to take a walk through the pleasant environment of the village. As he passed the field under construction, a number of men were grading and filling in the property. Cleland was greeted by a young, enthusiastic worker who asked what he thought of the construction project. He also mentioned that the village was becoming very excited about plans for celebrating baseball's 100th anniversary in five years.

On the train back to New York City, Cleland began to ponder the young man's remarks. Always capable of recognizing the business side of things, he wondered if a large number of people might be enticed to visit the village before the celebration took place. He began to formulate a plan that would attract a great deal of publicity for the project and wrote a memorandum to Clark concerning this subject. This was not a mundane proposal, and Cleland knew that the idea had great potential.

Cleland's plan centered around the construction of "a building on Doubleday Field where a collection of all past, present and future historical data of the game could be shown." He felt that there must be a large selection of baseball memorabilia throughout the country "that would make an interesting museum." Addressing the issue of financing the project, he explained that the cost of construction and maintenance could be paid by the governing bodies of both leagues. He also suggested that a special game played by representatives of the National and American Leagues could help finance the proposed museum. Cleland believed that the village would simply donate the site for the project.

Cleland pointed out the intrinsic historical nature of his proposal. He stressed that numerous fathers "would be interested to stop at Cooperstown and show the building to their sons and perhaps throw a baseball or two on the field." He was adamant in his belief that if the concept he visualized could receive proper publicity (perhaps through the Baseball Writers Association), then "hundreds of visitors would be attracted to the shopping district right in the heart of Cooperstown." Cleland had certainly struck all the right notes— nostalgia plus publicity equals profit. Not only would the village benefit, but baseball clubs could profit "from a publicity point of view"; therefore, he concluded, they should be willing to finance the scheme.[6]

If Cleland doubted his boss would find merit in his plan, he shouldn't have. Clark was quite the entrepreneur himself, and he quickly recognized the possibilities of his employee's idea. After all, the concept was simple, straightforward, and appealed to the business instincts of both men. About two months later, Cleland again wrote to his employer with some more suggestions for him to consider concerning the project. Realizing the limitations of a one-man plan, he proposed the formation of a committee "to formulate a policy and plan of action for the furthering of the Memorial plan."

Clark's interest in the project was growing, and he began to discuss with village elders the field's development and a site for the new museum. He also encouraged his employee to make every effort to contact baseball's commissioner, Judge Kenesaw Mountain Landis. By this time the story of Abner Doubleday had become fact in the minds of many Americans, and the centennial celebration of his alleged invention was drawing near. Major league officials had already set up a commission to organize the 100th anniversary of the national pastime and Clark realized the necessity of coordinating Cleland's idea with a national program.[7]

By October, 1934, the trustees of Cooperstown had officially appointed Cleland as their representative in New York City for the purpose of promoting a memorial at Doubleday Field that would become a national shrine for the game. Cleland sent a memorandum to Landis; to National League president, Ford Frick; and to his American League counterpart, William Harridge. He pointed out that concerning the museum (which would show the growth of the game since 1839) the planners were not actually seeking any financial assistance from the major leagues. Rather, they sought only "the approval of the project in order to give it standing and dignity in the eyes of the baseball public." Frick would prove to be Cleland's most ardent supporter. He emphatically stated that Alexander not only had the league's approval but also their "fullest cooperation in any project you may evolve."[8]

In the spring of 1935, two events took place which would have a major impact on the future of Cooperstown's most renowned facility. On April 10, the first meeting of the Doubleday Field Association was held at the Alfred Corning Clark Gymnasium. A number of village elders attended. Among them was the editor of the local newspaper, Walter R. Littell. As Cleland had predicted in the initial plan for the museum, one man was simply not enough to promote such a formidable scheme. Officers for the group were chosen, including Clark as vice president and Cleland as the executive secretary. From this point on, Cleland would have the most authoritative position in helping to establish the museum in the village. Since the secretary lived in New York City, Littell would serve as his link with the local community. As a longtime resident of Cooperstown and a knowledgeable source on all of the village's activities and the people within, the editor was ideally suited for this job. He would also be in direct contact with Clark, who was often away on business.[9]

The connections that Clark and Cleland made with Frick and Littell would prove to be significant in the early development of baseball promotion in Cooperstown. While the editor served as the most important communications link with the village, the new league president helped to attract the interest of baseball's highest authorities. America was in the grips of its worst economic crisis and baseball attendance was suffering because of this decline. Frick was willing to promote any scheme that might enhance the game's revenues. There was a brief attempt by Cleland to garner support from baseball's commissioner, but Landis never really committed himself to the project until it was completed.[10]

The second important occurrence involved the initiation of the Hall of Fame concept. Up until this point, Cleland had merely suggested a museum to display artifacts of the game. While he may have considered a scheme to enshrine the greatest players, he didn't write about it at this time. The idea first took form in the spring of 1935 at a meeting between the museum's executive secretary and the National League president. During their conference, Cleland informed Frick that the village wanted publicity for their part in the baseball celebration of 1939, and he suggested an all-star game for Cooperstown to attract newspapermen. Frick, however, claimed to have had a more expansive idea that went far beyond a museum display. As he later recalled, he suggested a grandiose plan whereby the superstars of the game could be enshrined in a Hall of Fame that would be part of the museum complex.

This proposal was monumental in terms of baseball history, but it was also significant in that it embraced the concept of honoring those who had excelled in a particular field of endeavor. The plan was based on the Hall of Fame for Great Americans and since the league president had resided in New York City for 14 years, he was probably aware of the original shrine and may simply have adapted the concept to baseball. As simple as this explanation may be, it should not diminish the genius behind the idea. More than a promotional scheme, Frick believed that it would keep the continuity of baseball flowing from one generation to the next and allow fans to compare old stars with new ones. Recognizing the importance of history to the game, he wanted to make a permanent record of what happened in the past.[11]

After the dedication of the Hall of Fame in 1939, Frick was always given credit for initiating the concept of the shrine. Before he died, he reflected on his life in baseball and claimed that his proudest achievement was his role in starting the Hall. "That is my baby," he claimed, "I started it. This was in 1936 when I was president of the National League." He recalled the meeting with Cleland and the secretary's suggestion of an all-star game as part of the village's celebration. However, Frick added, "Hell, why do that? If you're going to do that, why not start a baseball museum, a Hall of Fame, and have something that will last."[12]

Without question, Frick was initially the only authority from organized baseball to endorse the project, and he continued to support Cooperstown's recognition. He can't take credit, however, for all of the developments in the village, and his recollection of dates certainly wasn't accurate. For one thing, the museum definitely was not his idea; it was originated by Cleland in 1934, and his first correspondence with the league president took place the next year. While most sources also credit Frick for the Hall of Fame concept, this act is not without some disclaimer. In a letter to some friends in Brooklyn at the beginning of the 1939 season, Cleland recalled that in the past, they had "rather smiled when I mentioned the Hall of Fame and the Baseball Museum." He added that Doubleday Field had been "entirely reconstructed since I had my idea of the Hall of Fame." This was the only occasion when Cleland took credit for the concept.

Generally reserved and unassuming, it was uncharacteristic for Cleland to seek glory whether he deserved it or not. However, the possibility that it was he and not Frick who originally proposed the Hall of Fame idea has some merit. When the secretary first heard from the league president in early February 1935, the correspondence was concerned only with the museum component. In mid-May Cleland wrote to some radio officials and this was the first time that the term "Hall of Fame" appeared in his letters. Frick did not publicly use the phrase until August, when the official announcement of the shrine took place. According to Don Cleland of Las Vegas, Nevada, his grandfather was the person who originated the plan to recognize the greats of the game through enshrinement.

Actually, both men may have contributed to the idea. Cleland's original concept included the induction of ten players—five from each century. Apparently he did not set up a system whereby members could be added later on. However, Frick was concerned with the possibility that future stars would come along who would surpass the original members, and he therefore suggested a perpetual system that would allow them to be included. This was the league president's real contribution, and together with the secretary's plan, the actual Hall of Fame concept emerged.[13]

With the election of Cleland to a leadership position and the proposal of the hall and museum complex, the stage was set for a national announcement. Cleland had already explained the details of the plan to the members of the Doubleday Field Association, and the concept received the wholehearted support of the village. No one expected it to be launched nationally until after the baseball season was over, but the idea was so appealing that Frick decided to reveal it on August 15, 1935. He invited Cleland to his office to meet with baseball officials concerning the proposal and the next day the village of Cooperstown was advertised across the country as the future home of the Hall of Fame and Baseball Museum.[14]

Since Frick's announcement came during the middle of the season, little more attention was focused on Cooperstown during the rest of the summer. The league president had merely planted the seed for the Hall of Fame and it was up to Cleland, Clark, and Littell to follow up on its growth and promotion. Other aspects also had to be considered, including the construction of a building for the museum collection, the gathering of historical items and the selection of those to be enshrined. Following the Cubs–Tigers World Series, Cleland met with Frick to make concrete plans for future developments in Cooperstown.[15]

There was nothing novel about the idea of establishing a museum, but it was unique in that its focus was baseball items. While not a baseball fan himself, Cleland understood that these artifacts would hold a certain fascination for fans young and old. Displaying them in a museum would only tend to increase their value both monetarily and historically. The local village club had been cleared out for use as a temporary museum. The secretary's major problem was how to find significant material and to convince their owners that they deserved a fitting place in the baseball museum.

Cleland soon discovered that the pursuit of baseball artifacts could be very frustrating. Typically, he would get a lead on an item from an acquaintance and then try to track it down. Even if eventually he made a discovery, some people were not willing to part with their keepsake. Nevertheless the secretary continued to pursue the former greats of the game, often by contacting their closest living relative and sometimes utilizing intermediaries to overcome the resistance of donors. Cleland assured them that they needn't be concerned about the safekeeping of their artifacts; the local historical society had acquired adequate experience in this area through their housing of the permanent James Fenimore Cooper collection.[16]

The reluctance of collectors to part with memorabilia inspired Cleland to utilize a pamphlet that had been put together to advertise the museum. The brochure contained the history of baseball's progress in Cooperstown complete with photographs of Doubleday Field, the Doubleday baseball, the famous general himself and a brief account of the Mills commission.[17] Over the next four years, different versions of the brochure were published and gradually more information was added. Cleland mailed it out to publishers, league officials and all possible donors.

The first year's attempt to gather artifacts had resulted in little more than frustration for the museum's first secretary. Undaunted, Cleland continued to press forward in spite of the complications involved. His perseverance would pay off and he must have been surprised by the variety of items that eventually were offered to the museum. No single item was donated more than the baseball itself. Most of these balls had a unique historic significance, including one from the first game where people paid an admission to view an 1858 contest. Another popular item was books. Most of them were nineteenth century publications containing statistics, scoring instructions, league rules and bylaws of early clubs. Other items included old bats, gloves, paintings, scorecards, a statute of John McGraw, a bust of Christy Mathewson, pamphlets, World Series buttons, and shoulder straps from the army uniform of General Doubleday.[18]

As time for the 1939 centennial celebration drew near, the museum was overwhelmed with contributions. By then interest in the complex was becoming widespread through a variety of promotional campaigns. Even *Spalding's Official Base Ball Guide* encouraged its readers to contact Cleland if they had any contributions. Frick also encouraged fans from around the country to become part of the celebration by giving baseball heirlooms to the museum's collection. Since each item received would bear the name of its donor, he reminded individual contributors that they would have their names in the Hall of Fame displays. The league president assured the fans that their artifacts would become part of a permanent setting in the Cooperstown display.[19]

The majority of donations focused on the early days of the game. Although these memorabilia had obvious historic significance and served as physical reminders of the game's development, they may not have aroused as much curiosity as the planners had hoped. In order to attract the interest of younger or more recent fans of the game, the museum needed to acquire items from contemporary stars. Especially important in this regard were contributions from those who had already been elected to the Hall of Fame.

Even before any inductees had been chosen for enshrinement, Cleland began to pursue items associated with some of the game's greatest stars. As early as April, 1935, he contacted the wife of Christy Mathewson, whose husband had died of tuberculosis following service in World War I. Enclosing the museum's new pamphlet, he asked the great pitcher's widow if she would cooperate with the Cooperstown effort by contributing some of her husband's materials from his playing days. Hoping to overcome any fears she might have of exploitation, he reassured her of the credentials of the museum and its backers. Eventually she sent Christy's favorite mitt and one of her husband's uniforms. They represented the first objects gathered from a major league star. Cleland also hoped that they would encourage other players who may have been hesitant to make a donation.[20]

Unfortunately, Cleland's effort to garner memorabilia from modern-day baseball figures met with failure in 1936. He made an effort to contact Walter Johnson directly, but there was no response to his inquiry. However, these dismal returns only served to strengthen the secretary's resolve to turn the situation around. Following the disclosure of the second election results in January, 1937, he sent similar letters directly to Babe Ruth, Honus Wagner, Napoleon Lajoie, Ty Cobb, Tris Speaker and Cy Young. Like the Johnson correspondence, this message expressed the urgency on the part of the museum officials to gather personal effects that would certainly attract a great deal of attention and publicity for the Cooperstown repository. Although the major leagues would furnish plaques for the inductees, Cleland emphasized the museum's desire to garner items for display that would demonstrate the historic aspects of the game.

This extensive letter writing campaign produced mixed results. Neither Ruth, Cobb nor Lajoie sent an immediate response to the museum although the latter two would eventually respond during the year. Ruth, the game's most popular star, probably never realized that he was threatening the museum's success through his own inaction. Often oblivious of situations around him, the Babe was simply unconcerned with the historical process. More than anything else, Ruth's lack of correspondence could possibly be attributed to the fact that he was hardly a man of letters. Eventually the museum did receive a donation from Ruth's career just before the centennial celebration. The gifts, however, didn't come from the home run king. Rather, a collector from the Hillerich and Bradsby bat company donated some of Ruth's former equipment.[21]

The first of the Hall of Fame members to respond to Cleland's call for memorabilia was Cy Young, who sent a handwritten note to the secretary. Not only did the renowned pitcher possess these kinds of items, but he was quite willing to donate them. Young cautioned Alexander that it would take some time to get his collection packaged and sent off, but the secretary hoped to have the Ohioan's donation by May so that it would be on display for the summer tourist season. Wanting to make the delivery as easy as possible for the aging pitcher, Cleland offered to visit him in the spring to pick up the donations. Frustrated by the disappointing results of the collection process, Cleland had already decided that a personal touch was necessary. Therefore he made plans for an automobile trip from New York City to Washington D.C. (to visit John B. Foster of the Spalding Company), then on to Germantown, Maryland (to see Walter Johnson), and finally to Young's home. Following this visit he planned to continue on to Cleveland to visit with Lajoie and Speaker. Later, the secretary received word from Wagner in Pittsburgh that he was willing to make a donation and the former shortstop was added to the list of stops.

Since Ty Cobb retired in Menlo Park, California, it was impossible for the secretary to see him personally. And since the irascible Tiger great was known for his mood swings, Cleland proceeded very carefully in order to coax him to make a contribution. Catering to Ty's ego, Cleland reminded the former outfielder that he was the first choice among the baseball writers in the Hall of Fame poll. Because of his number one ranking, the museum was extremely anxious to receive some personal contribution. Over a year passed before Cobb finally responded, but he explained his procrastination by stating that he had given away any fitting items for the museum to souvenir sellers. Later he was able to find some clothes from his playing days, and on a trip to Georgia he also discovered a highly prized bat for the museum.[22]

Before he left on his sweeping travels, Cleland decided to ensure his success by obtaining letters of recommendation. John T. Doyle, publisher of the *Guide,* helped him out by sending letters to various officials of A. G. Spalding Brothers. They must have helped because by the end of the summer of 1937, the secretary was receiving correspondence from his previous contacts. For example, Lajoie responded with a promise to forward personal items, and eventually he sent a complete uniform and a ball that he batted for his 3,000th hit in 1915. Speaker had been injured in a car accident and this delayed his search, but he promised to forward appropriate souvenirs after a visit to his native state of Texas.[23]

As the museum's collection increased, its officials became more aware of the problem of housing the mementos. Originally, the display items were kept with the exhibits of the Otsego County Historical Society on the second floor of the Village Club. The space at the club, however, was limited, and the museum authorities had no real control over the club building. The collection had grown beyond all predicted bounds and there was some concern over how to protect this expanding national treasure. In July, 1937, the local Cooperstown newspaper proudly announced the plan to develop a new fireproof museum specially designed to house the national baseball collection.

When initial plans for developing Cooperstown's baseball heritage unfolded, a separate building was discussed; but the idea was abandoned as premature. However, the overwhelming response by organized baseball, sportswriters, fans, and the general public caused the originators to reconsider their proposal. Of primary importance was the need to guarantee the safety of the priceless donations that were being received. There were, in fact, a number of inquiries concerning this point from people who were considering a valuable contribution to the museum. Cleland also hoped that a secure building could expedite the entire program's development. Finally, fans would be pleased that a unique building had been designed and constructed for the sole purpose of housing baseball artifacts.[24] The Clark family was responsible for financing the building's construction and it was opened in time for the 1938 tourist season.

Another important aspect of Cleland's work as executive secretary involved the promotion of the hall, museum and the 100th anniversary activities in Cooperstown. The best method for attracting attention turned out to be the annual election of members to the shrine, which was conducted from 1936 to 1939. Each year the election results produced considerable controversy and gradually more people joined the debate.[25] The response to the election process surpassed all expectations and represented a major coup for the shrine's innovators.

In their attempt to gather mementos and select baseball people for recognition, the hall's promoters were augmenting the entire project with a promotional scheme on the national level. However, these were not the only attempts to spread the word of the museum-hall development, for the originators explored every possible means to inform the entire country of their plans. Indeed, they felt that the success of their project was directly tied to advertising. Cleland's efforts in this area were aided by the fact that the state of New York was already promoting the 1939 World's Fair in the nation's largest city, which would coincide with Cooperstown's baseball celebration. The Bureau of State Publicity contacted Cleland in the spring of 1935 and correspondence between the two groups continued through the centennial year.[26]

This was just the beginning of the promotion. Articles continued to appear in national magazines and major newspapers and Cleland would often forward these items to Littell so that he could inform people in the village of the publicity they were receiving. As the word of the Hall of Fame spread, he confided in Littell his belief that they were well on their way to making the project a big success. As these stories on Cooperstown's role in baseball's development increased, the village gained recognition as the "Birthplace of Baseball."[27]

A number of magazines and newspapers covered these events including the foremost sports publications. One of the first to jump on Cooperstown's bandwagon was *Baseball Magazine*, which published an article on the village in the spring of 1936. However, the most important coverage came from the two renowned publications of the day— *The Sporting News* and the Spalding *Guide*. Starting in the 1936 edition of the latter, editor John B. Foster discussed the creation of the Hall of Fame and the people who had been elected. For every year that followed, the *Guide* published an article on the developments in Cooperstown, the artifacts that had been gathered and the inductees. *The Sporting News*, a weekly publication, contained much more detailed information. Their first article included a story on the museum developments, plans for the 1939 celebration, and a history of events leading to Cooperstown's recognition.[28] Long recognized as the baseball bible, its articles continued to be a major source of information for fans throughout the country.

The Hall of Fame story was not confined to sporting publications. Following the 1938 election, *Time* magazine began to cover the results. The piece described how Cooperstown gained its recognition, the upcoming centennial celebration, the new museum building, and the procedure to elect members. Both Cleland and Littell were impressed that one of the nation's major publications had given such a thorough coverage of these activities. The local newspaper editor included a lengthy article on the coverage given the Hall of Fame in the next issue of *The Otsego Farmer*. Shortly after the centennial celebration, *Newsweek* featured Doubleday on the cover of their magazine with a caption proclaiming him the father of the game.[29]

As 1938 came to a close, an air of great satisfaction and anticipation rippled through the community of Cooperstown and with good reason. A year that began with many doubts and anxieties had finished with resounding confidence. In an editorial on the day before New Year's Eve, Littell addressed both the frustrations of the past and the hope of the future. He recognized that 1939 was destined to be one of the most significant years in the history of the village. Indeed, he opined that "the eyes of the whole nation are upon this little village." The celebration, which originally focused on Doubleday Field, was now being promoted by organized baseball on a national level. Even though the direct publicity campaign by the major leagues was still more than a month away from being initiated, people throughout the country were well aware of the connection between Cooperstown and the birth of baseball. Baseball's officialdom also recognized this relationship and had decreed that the village was to be the hub of the anniversary observance.

Littell was aware of the countrywide recognition. He had recently received a number of articles touting the birth and development of baseball which had appeared in the Christian Science *Monitor,* the New York *Herald Tribune,* the Detroit *Free Press* and various papers on the Pacific coast. Littell doubted that the World's Fair, in spite of the millions of dollars spent advertising it, was better known than the centennial and the Hall of Fame. The editor was very specific as to why this situation had developed. In his mind, nobody deserved more credit for this recognition than Alexander Cleland, who had undertaken the task four years earlier.

While the record ascribing the honor of the invention of the game had long ago been given to Doubleday by the Mills commission, little had been done to capitalize on it. In fact, few people in the village ever recognized the amazing appeal that came with this historic connection. Even Cleland had no definite concept at the very beginning, but gradually it developed into a national program thanks to his experience, perseverance, and masterful diplomacy. These attributes, coupled with the intrinsic appeal of the hall-museum complex and the generous support of the concerned people of Cooperstown, had resulted in national recognition of the centennial celebration. Littell felt that the success Cleland had achieved went "far beyond the hopes of the most sanguine friends of the project."

The editor also believed that there was a lesson to be learned from Cleland's experience. He recognized that even the most ardent supporters had witnessed many discouragements, delays and exasperations in the past few years. In spite of the numerous causes for concern, Cleland had never wavered. Littell felt that his success was a direct consequence of his ability, courage and optimism and that Cooperstown should remember that what made him successful in the past could also achieve the same thing for them in the future. If the people of the community copied the determination of the executive secretary, the village would be rewarded historically, culturally and economically. As Littell saw it, the year 1939 was not the end in sight but rather the beginning of Cooperstown's history "as the shrine of baseball which will last for a long time."[30]

Following the dedication of the Hall of Fame in June, 1939, Cleland's role as the first executive secretary of that organization became less demanding. He retired from his position in 1941, but he always kept in touch with the organization. He died in Whippany, New Jersey, in 1954 at the age of 77. It is unfortunate that he never received the national recognition he deserved for his role in helping to start the most highly recognized organization of its kind in the world. Certainly, he served well the people of Cooperstown, the baseball public and American society.

Notes

1. Thomas C. Jones, ed., *The Halls of Fame* (Chicago: J. G. Ferguson Publishing Company, 1977), p. 5.

2. *Spalding's Official Base Ball Guide*, 1905, pp. 9–13; *Spalding's Office Base Ball Guide*, 1908, pp. 36–37, 41–42, 47–48.

3. *The Sporting News*, June 22, 1939; Ken Smith, *Baseball's Hall of Fame* (New York: Grosset & Dunlap, 1980), pp. 41–43; William Guifoile, "Plaque to Commemorate Doubleday Field's Origin," National Baseball Hall of Fame Library (NBHFL), June 27, 1986.

4. Robert Wernick, "The Clark Brothers Sewed Up a Most Eclectic Collection," *Smithsonian Magazine* (April, 1984), 123–126; *The Sporting News*, September 28, 1960.

5. New York *Herald Tribune*, July 8, 1954; David Houser, "Treasures

Found in Grandmother's House," *Baseball Hobby News* (February 1984), 20; *The Otsego Farmer,* July 16, 1954.

6. Alexander Cleland to Stephen C. Clark, Alexander Cleland Collection (ACC), May 8, 1934.

7. Alexander Cleland to Stephen Clark, ACC, July 18, 1934; Stephen Clark to Alexander Cleland, ACC, June 25, 1934.

8. Alton G. Dunn to Alexander Cleland, ACC, October 18, 1934; Alexander Cleland to Walter Carter, ACC, November 15, 1934; Walter Carter to Alexander Cleland, ACC, November 23, 1934; Alexander Cleland to Walter Carter, ACC, January 10, 1935; Alexander Cleland to Ford Frick, ACC, January 30, 1935; Ford Frick to Alexander Cleland, ACC, February 7, 1935.

9. Walter Littell, Notes on Meeting of Doubleday Field Association, ACC, April 10, 1935; W. R. Littell to Stephen Clark, ACC, April 11, 1935; *Freeman's Journal,* November 16, 1935; *The Otsego Farmer,* April 17, 1935.

10. Alexander Cleland to Kenesaw M. Landis, ACC, May 8, 1935; Kenesaw M. Landis to Alexander Cleland, ACC, June 6, 1935.

11. *The Sporting News,* February 19, 1977; *The Otsego Farmer,* January 24, 1936.

12. *The Sporting News,* April 22, 1978.

13. Alexander Cleland to Henry C. Yoxall, ACC, April 20, 1939; Interview with Don Cleland, September 25, 1987.

14. *Glimmerglass,* Cooperstown, New York, August 16, 1935; Alexander Cleland to Walter Littell, ACC, August 16, 1935; *The Otsego Farmer,* August 30, 1970; *New York Times,* August 16, 1935.

15. Alexander Cleland to Walter R. Littell, ACC, October 10, 1935.

16. Alexander Cleland to Clark Griffin, ACC, June 4, 1935.

17. *National Base Ball Museum,* ACC, n.d.

18. Alexander Cleland to W. R. Littell, ACC, February 4, 1935; *The Otsego Farmer,* July 21, 1939; *Spalding's Office Base Ball Guide,* 1937, pp. 22–23; *The Otsego Farmer,* April 28, 1939.

19. *Spalding's Official Base Ball Guide,* 1937, p. 23; *Spalding's Official Base Ball Guide,* 1939, p. 30.

20. Alexander Cleland to Mrs. Christy Mathewson, ACC, April 15, 1935; *Spalding's Official Base Ball Guide,* 1937, p. 22.

21. Alexander Cleland to Walter Johnson, ACC, February 26, 1936; Alexander Cleland to Babe Ruth, ACC, February 18, 1937; Alexander Cleland to Napoleon Lajoie, ACC, February 18, 1937; Alexander Cleland to Cy Young, ACC, February 18, 1937; Alexander Cleland to Honus Wagner, ACC, February 18, 1937; Alexander Cleland to Tris Speaker, ACC, June 18, 1937; *The Otsego Farmer,* February 17, 1939.

22. Cy Young to Alexander Cleland, ACC, February 28, 1937; Alexander Cleland to Cy Young, ACC, March 5, 1937; Cy Young to Alexander Cleland, ACC, April 4, 1937; Alexander Cleland to Cy Young, ACC, April 13, 1937. J. Honus Wagner to Alexander Cleland, ACC, n.d.; Alexander Cleland to Ty Cobb, ACC, June 14, 1937; Ty Cobb to Alexander Cleland, ACC, August 18, 1938; Ty Cobb to Alexander Cleland, ACC, April 29, 1939.

23. John T. Doyle to M. B. Reach, ACC, May 13, 1937; John T. Doyle to John B. Foster, ACC, April 13, 1937; N. Lajoie to Alexander Cleland, ACC, August 23, 1937; Tris Speaker to Alexander Cleland, ACC, August 30, 1937.

24. Smith, *Baseball's Hall of Fame,* pp. 44–46; Walter L. Littell to Alex-

ander Cleland, ACC, March 5, 1937; *The Otsego Farmer,* July 9, 1937; William Beattie to Alexander Cleland, ACC, March 31, 1939.

25. *Jersey Journal,* December 31, 1938; Smith, *Baseball's Hall of Fame,* pp. 54–55.

26. K. R. Thatcher to Alexander Cleland, ACC, June 4, 1935.

27. Alexander Cleland to Walter R. Littell, ACC, December 27, 1935; Alexander Cleland to Walter Littell, ACC, January 16, 1936; New York *Sun,* February 13, 1936.

28. Frank Graham, "Coming Events Cast Their Shadows," *Base Ball Magazine* (March, 1936), 43–44; *Spalding's Official Base Ball Guide,* 1936, pp. 30–33; *The Sporting News,* May 21, 1936.

29. *Time,* January 31, 1938; *The Otsego Farmer,* February 4, 1938; *Newsweek,* June 19, 1939.

30. *The Otsego Farmer,* December 30, 1938.

Opening Address

by Marty Appel

Thank you, Ron, for your kind introduction. I was originally going to have my family here, but my son's Little League team with their 0–18 record plays its final game tomorrow, and you can imagine how Brian would feel if he skipped it and they won.

I've coached the team through this brilliant season, so I can recall my days in the Yankee front office, and feel George Steinbrenner watching my every move. He did assure me I'd finish the season no matter what, however, and we all know how those promises work out.

Despite the 0–18 record, many of the games have been close and, in fact, downright exciting, which has caused me to once again appreciate the beauty of the game on the field. I, perhaps more than anyone, love the peripherals surrounding baseball—the books, the statistics, etc. But when you watch an amateur game, and you know there will be no newspaper story tomorrow, no records kept, no television production to go with it, you are reminded that it is the game itself, far above anything, that is so perfect, and so pure. Despite our perfect record this year, I have loved every minute of working with the kids and watching them learn the game. I only wish we used wooden bats.

I want to especially thank Dr. Hall, whose efforts went into making this such a grand, memorable and meaningful occasion. I'm especially appreciative of the invitation to be here today; very honored in fact, because I consider any invitation to speak in Cooperstown, in this 50th anniversary year, to be very special indeed.

I would very much like to extend special thanks to a very good friend here today, Bill Guilfoile, Associate Director of the Hall of Fame, who, together with Bob Fishel, broke me in as a pup in the fan mail department of the Yankees back in 1968. Bill and I both know this is also the 50th anniversary of the greatest scandal in baseball history, the Sox Scandal of 1939. This is not to be confused with the Black Sox Scandal of 1919. I speak of the photo taken at the dedication of the Hall of Fame fifty years ago, with the greatest players seated as a group, legs crossed, socks in various stages of being rolled up or torn. They really could have dressed better for the occasion.

And speaking of that famous photo, the caption as we know, always reminds us that Ty Cobb, delayed en route, missed the photo by minutes. I mean, this was Ty Cobb! They couldn't reshoot the photo?

I also see my friend Ed Stack here today, the President of the Hall of Fame. Ed and I were speaking recently about his desire to find an automobile to place in the baseball Museum; perhaps an old Chalmers, which went to the batting champ. Ed had been informed that Cobb's car was for sale. But the obvious solution, at least to me, seems to come out like this—Jose Canseco's Jaguar!

Some of you may know that I have spent the last 21 seasons involved in baseball, and for those unfamiliar with me, I will tell you of some of my fortunate stops along the way to this microphone today. But I must begin by explaining that I was a member of the Class of 1970 at Oneonta State, and it is that connection that made logic out of my invitation. That, plus Joe DiMaggio was booked, and Choo Choo Coleman was already speaking at a similar symposium at the State University campus in Fly Creek. For four years, only two people at Oneonta State received subscriptions to *The Sporting News*—myself and my roommate. I know this because on Saturdays we would go to the mail room early to see if it had arrived, so that we wouldn't have to waste the day on homework and things like that.

I was also considered the most boring date during the wild 1960s at Oneonta State. While everyone else was discovering sex and drugs and rock and roll, I would have the nerve to take dates to the Hall of Fame. Even met Lee Allen. You would be surprised to know how few antiwar demonstrations took place on Main Street in Cooperstown. It was as wild and crazy a town back then as it is today.

I should mention, and I think it is historically significant, that baseball was very much out of fashion in the '60s with young people. True fans like myself didn't quite believe this, but I well remember being ousted from the dorm television set because I wanted to watch the World Series of 1967, while the overwhelming majority preferred a regular season Giants football game. I don't think the full impact of this hit me for several years, when I did in fact acknowledge to myself that baseball had very much hit a major slump with America's youth. I must say that there were very few people among the student body at Oneonta who were at all impressed when I announced that I had gotten a summer job with the Yankees in 1968.

Baseball *was* in the doldrums though. Talent, for one thing, was drying up. The great sluggers of the '50s and '60s were winding down their careers, and exciting young players were simply not coming along to take their places. While Mays and Mantle and Banks and

Colavito and Clemente and Aaron and Mathews and Maris were nearing the end, the Rookies of the Year had names like Blefary, Helms, Sizemore, Bahnsen and Agee. The All-Star Game of 1970 had names like Merritt and Wright, Peterson and Menke, Alomar and Hickman, Grabarkewitz and Dietz, Fosse and Harper. It was a time of transition for baseball, but there were no guarantees that new superstars were on the horizon. The game was considered slow by contemporary standards. Attendance was stagnant; teams had not yet developed any marketing strategies; old ballparks were rich with tradition but uncomfortable and inconvenient; and alas, there were no strong teams in New York or Los Angeles. Even the "voice of the Game of the Week," the magnificent Curt Gowdy, was probably the wrong man for those times, given his laid back style at a time when baseball needed a kick in the seat.

The excitement of the Mets victory in 1969, and the emergence of the Seavers, Benches and Jacksons were a step in the right direction. The end of the war brought the attention spans of young people back toward more pastoral pleasures. Teams learned that winning alone did not ensure attendance; you had to market the game, and there was no sin in doing it. Vida Blue was "sold" to the American public and everyone noticed. By 1975, the thrilling Red Sox–Reds World Series had the nation talking baseball. In '76, the Yankees returned to the World Series and a guy named Mark Fidrych had come along—wow, was he fun. And fun seemed to be the word. We had the Baseball World of Joe Garagiola, colorful uniforms, two networks showing baseball, Hank Aaron breaking the home run record on a prime time national telecast, and attendance records falling. The Game, with a capital G, was back. How blind many of us were in hindsight to see what sad shape it had momentarily slumbered into. So let us not forget that we can never become too complacent about this. Those of us who make up the so-called "hard-core fans;" those of us who will always live and die on every pitch, should never forget that the game needs more than us to grow and prosper—it needs the casual, twice a year fan, and it needs the continued interest of young people. More than anything, there is competition for their attention spans. And if baseball forgets to grab their interest early, it may never get them back. In a small way, I think one of the great things of the last decade has been the popularity of team mascots like the Phillie Phanatic and the San Diego Chicken. Clever marketing like that has brought fans to baseball games at ages like five and six. And for many people, one day at the ballpark is a memory for life, and probably a lifetime ticket to the love that is baseball. Another positive development in this area has been the acknowledgment by the past three commissioners that baseball people had better make their ballparks more pleasant as family surroundings. The crackdowns on drunken fans, the institution of alcohol- and smoke-free sections, and the enforcement of drug laws in ballparks were overdue and very welcome. Too many people have had unpleasant experiences in their first visits to ballparks, and at last, the teams are concentrating on getting a handle on this. This is, of course, not a problem unique to our times. If you look at the old baseball guides, which incidentally are being reprinted and sold by a wonderful gentleman in St. Louis named Ralph Horton, you discover that the problem of crowd control due to alcohol consumption is as old as the professional game itself.

But getting back to the gray days that were the late '60s, one of my first recollections of my years with the Yankees was the outrage of a small but loyal group of Yankee fans who were beside themselves when the Yankees traded Andy Kosco—ANDY KOSCO—to the Dodgers for Mike Kekich. It's hard to believe, but Andy Kosco was briefly a hometown hero in the House that Ruth Built.

I had the odd sense to write a letter to the Yankees in 1967, while sitting in Golding Hall in Oneonta. I addressed it to a man named Bob Fishel, the head of their public relations department. I introduced myself as a lifelong Yankee fan, now sports editor of the campus newspaper in Oneonta, and interested in any summer job for the following season that might be available. I never expected a response.

But Bob Fishel was a very classy guy, and good timing was with me. He got the letter on a day he was thinking about the problems of keeping up with Mickey Mantle's fan mail, and he invited me in for an interview.

Needless to say, that àlone would have been enough. To actually be in Yankee Stadium on a day the team was off—the empty stadium . . . the Yankee offices! I went, had my interview, snuck a peek past a door that said "NO WOMEN BEYOND THIS POINT" (it wasn't, alas, the clubhouse), and a few weeks later was hired to handle the fan mail. That was during the summers of 1968 and 1969, and the man I reported to was Bill Guilfoile, a wonderful man who taught me how to fill out a W-4 tax form, answer the mail, and learn public relations. Bill was Bob Fishel's assistant . . . in 1970 he became PR director of the Pittsburgh Pirates and in 1979, associate director of the Hall of Fame right here. Small world, is baseball, and I'm very proud today, 21 years later, to still call Bill Guilfoile a friend and a mentor.

When Bill left for Pittsburgh, Bob Fishel offered me his position, and I left college on a Friday and reported for work on Monday. You don't get any happier than I was on my first day at Yankee Stadium. And for the last 21 years, I've had a love affair with baseball that has never faded.

I worked for the Yankees from 1968 to 1977, spanning the CBS–Mike Burke years and into the George Steinbrenner–Billy Martin–Reggie Jackson years. In that span we had the rebuilding of Yankee Stadium, the two-year hiatus to Shea Stadium, the signings of Catfish Hunter and Reggie Jackson, the Mickey Mantle retirement, the block-buster sale of the club, the return to the World Series, the return from exile of Casey Stengel and Mel Allen, and even the scandal of two left-handed pitchers named Peterson and Kekich trading families.

I left the Yankees in 1977 and pursued a writing career. The first book I did was called *Baseball's Best: The Hall of Fame Gallery,* which featured lengthy biographies of each member of the Hall of Fame. I'm still very very proud of that book, which was the first of its kind to offer detailed and lengthy biographies of the 19th century and Negro League players, as well as the umpires and club executives who have been installed in the Hall of Fame. That was followed by collaborative books with Thurman Munson, Tom Seaver and Commissioner Bowie Kuhn. Munson's became a belated best seller following the tragedy of his death in a private air crash in 1979. To this day I'm very proud of having my name linked with his through his autobiography.

The Kuhn book was a labor of love. I had worked on his staff for two years after leaving the Yankees, and then when he left office in 1984, he sought me out to serve as an editorial assistant on his memoirs. The opportunity to work so closely with a man who WAS baseball history for 16 turbulent years was as fascinating an experience as any fan could hope for. And the final product is a book I'm enormously proud of—a detailed record for all time of the behind-the-scenes workings of baseball as told by its chief executive. Judge Landis died in office and never did a memoir. Ford Frick wrote a memoir that did not get into the details of governing the sport. I am pleased to note that at the age of 90, Happy Chandler, in 1989, has written a memoir, and I hope we can look forward to one by Peter Ueberroth.

Commissioner Giamatti, I suspect, is already at work on his. Books are the permanent record, the stuff we leave the future historians to ponder. I hope you have all had a chance to visit the wonderful library here at the Hall of Fame, and I encourage each of you to lobby your local libraries to include books of historic significance in their permanent collections. I'm sure Tom Heitz, the librarian at the Hall of Fame, who is also with us today, would agree.

I am at work now on a book quite on the other end of the spectrum from Bowie Kuhn. Whereas Commissioner Kuhn came from an Ivy League/Wall Street/law firm background, my current effort involves a black man from the worst section of the Philadelphia ghetto, a section known as The Bottom. His brother is doing 20 years in state prison on armed robbery and drug charges. His sister was found dead of a drug overdose. His father was an alcoholic wife-beater who deserted the family after tormenting them for years.

This man, at the age of 15, was watching the Game of the Week, and heard Curt Gowdy say "Be a major league umpire. Earn $30,000 a year. For information contact Umpire Development School, St. Petersburg, Florida." A young Eric Gregg, said "that's my ticket out of here," and is today a veteran, if somewhat overweight, National League umpire, full of wonderful stories and the joy of life. Oh, what baseball did for this man. It's a very inspirational story.

I've also been privileged to have worked with Lee MacPhail on his memoirs, just recently published, and to have written a children's book called "The First Book of Baseball," which was inspired by the questions of my own young son, such as "why is the ball so hard?"

In 1980, I joined WPIX television in New York, where I currently am employed as Executive Producer of Yankee telecasts. This season, that placed before me the matter of Bill White's departure, and the search for replacements, which led to Tom Seaver and George Grande. Bill White is one of the finest people I've ever known in my life, and I feel like a prideful little brother in seeing him achieve the success he has found as National League president. But I must say, when he first mentioned it to me, all I could think of was Bill White, wearing Brooks Brothers suits, sitting at a desk, living in Manhattan, and going on those awful "politic lunches" he always despised. Bill White was always a man who enjoyed fishing in the morning and taking in a game with Rizzuto in the evening, and putting on his WPIX blazer for the two minutes he was on camera.

When I called him a few days after his press conference to see how he was doing, he said, "what do you think? I just left Brooks Brothers and spent $3,000 on 4 suits." He didn't sound all that happy about that part of it, but he's adjusting. And he's going to be one of the best things that ever happened in the National League.

One month ago, we brought Bill White back into the booth for one last time. I hope some of you saw the game. It was a final opportunity to say thanks to the fans for their support over his 18 seasons, and to wish Phil Rizzuto and his successors, Seaver and Grande, good luck. Now Bill is not a very emotional guy, but when his inning in the booth ended, we turned the camera towards Phil and Bill . . . they stood, shook hands, embraced, and then Bill left the booth for the last time. It was a very, very touching moment, one of those great little moments in time that baseball can provide, even in the remoteness of the broadcast booth. I will never forget it.

As for Rizzuto, he's the only man I know who uses WW in his scorebook—for "wasn't watching."

Let me talk to you for a moment about something I feel very strongly about. It has to do with the preservation of the baseball history we are now living through, and that which was passed on to us by our parents, and by the great sportswriters and historians of their times.

Not too many months ago, Bill Terry and Carl Hubbell passed away. They received proper obituary notices in the newspapers, but I searched in vain for more—some well written column in someone's sports section, to bid them a proper farewell in the city they carried their fame through, New York.

But alas, it wasn't there. For indeed, in recent years, we have also said goodbye to Red Smith, Milton Richman, Dick Young and others who knew how to send off these greats of the game. So I began to pester my friend Ira Berkow, the sports columnist of the *New York Times,* and biographer of Red Smith. And I kept saying "Ira, this mantle has fallen to you. You are the heir apparent. You have to deliver the eulogy and recapture the greatness, or today's younger fans will never understand the impact of these immortals."

Ira demurred. He acknowledged the need, but said as he didn't know them personally, he couldn't do it.

And then Lefty Gomez died. And a few days later, there in the Sunday *Times,* was a lovely column about Lefty, written by Ira. He had called Lefty's widow and had called Bill Dickey, and had gotten enough material for a nice personal column. And Ira also tore out the column from that paper and wrote on the bottom *You're to blame,* and sent it to me. And as memorabilia go, that's a very special piece for me. I think that, in a small way, I made a statement about the preservation of the game.

Fantasize with me for a moment. Think about an America that still exists 500 years from now. There are a lot of things about the society of that time—the 25th century—that one could wonder about.

But how about our beloved little game of bat and ball? Will there always be baseball? Professional baseball?

Of greatest importance to me in pondering this is the matter of baseball today. You know, we tend to disregard all records set in the 1800s. . . . We simply assume that record keeping was sloppy and the game was too different to compare to today. And so many record books simply say that "modern baseball" records begin with the year 1900.

Is that the fate that awaits us 500 years from now? Will all of what we are witnessing be dismissed as part of baseball's primitive early days? Will we be an asterisk?

That would be most unfortunate. But I *don't* think that will be the case. By and large, this has been a time of *enormously* accurate record keeping, both on the page and through the magic of videotape. This is very much a golden age for the historical tracking of baseball. Part of this is the growth of SABR [Society for American Baseball Research]; part the flourishing of baseball publishing and events like this one. We have today a barrage of more statistics than we need, but maybe they will emerge as the essence of record keeping. So good for you, Bill James, John Thorn, Pete Palmer and the Elias Sports Bureau.

Think about how difficult it will be to do something that had never been done before by the time we get to, say, the 25th century. Mathematically, each passing year makes it harder and harder to do something that's never been done before. Do you think anyone will surpass Hank Aaron in his most celebrated accomplishment? I'm not talking about home runs or runs batted in. I'm talking about the 1-in-13,000 chance that the game's all-time home run leader was also first in alphabetical order. Now *that's* amazing.

And how many people will it take to carry the *Baseball Encyclopedia,* or the fine new book, *Total Baseball,* 500 years from now? And when will Harold Seymour give us more of his great histories?

The key to making certain that all we are living through now remains vital and important to future generations is the preservation of the basic current rules—which ought not be a problem, although the DH will never go—and the maintenance of the present schedule of 162 games or so. If that is ever dramatically reduced, or even increased, everything will change statistically, and all that we now consider sacred will lose its meaning. Economic factors will dictate the future lengths of seasons, just as they have dictated the end of doubleheaders and the introductions of night baseball and expansion. Let us hope that the clubs' owners and league officials will always be able to come to grips with the volatile economic issues of the day and make their best efforts to hold on to the integrity of the traditional schedule. But I assure you, the tradition will be of much lesser importance than the economic realities.

Not that baseball isn't ever changing. But the cosmetic changes are fun to chart, and not harmful to the evolution. We've all adjusted comfortably to division play and the League Championship Series—and when are they going to give us a break and call them play-offs?

One of the little things I enjoy doing is observing the subtle changes that slip into baseball and quietly change the look of the game. For example, when Jerry Neudecker, the American League umpire, retired in 1985, with him went the last balloon chest protector worn by umpires. For a century, that was one of the traditions of *how baseball looked*.

I made notes in the early '60s of Willie Mays and Tito Fuentes, teammates on the Giants, who took their uniforms to a tailor and had them tapered into tight fitting garments. Don't tell me *that* didn't change the way baseball players looked. How easy it is to tell a pre-1960 photo from a post-1960 photo. You see black bats in the hands of hitters today, a very common sight, whereas we once had all light pine. How many here made note that it was Pat Kelly, a White Sox outfielder, who was the first to use a black bat in modern times.

How about the dirt path between home plate and the mound? That disappeared in the early 1950s for good, but it was Bill Wrigley, who always cared more about esthetics than other owners, who eliminated it.

And what about that ridiculous custom of players leaving their gloves lying on the field? That was finally legislated out in 1953. Did that require a rule change? How could that ever have become a custom in the first place?

One thing I'm watching now, and this is a small thing of course, is who will be the last batter to wear a helmet without an ear flap? Virtually all players today wear the ear flap helmets, which were invented for Little League. Only a few veterans who preceded the rule change wear the helmets without flaps. I note Dave Winfield, Mookie Wilson, Candy Maldonado, Keith Hernandez and Ernie Whitt as five such holdouts, and I'm on the lookout to see who will be the last to wear one. Did you know that Phil Rizzuto was the first in the American League to wear one? Branch Rickey sent him one after his helmet company designed them for the Pittsburgh Pirates. Do you remember the days when the Pirates wore them not only at bat but in the field? Even the pitchers wore helmets.

I enjoy charting the firsts and lasts in a lot of areas. Can anyone name the last players of the old franchises to retire, thereby, in a sense, marking the formal end of the franchises' life?

Here's what I mean: the last active player who wore a New York Giants uniform was Willie Mays. The Giants last season in New York was 1957, but Mays played until 1973.

The last "surviving" Brooklyn Dodger was Bob Aspromonte, who played until 1971.

The last Boston Brave was Eddie Mathews, 1968.

The last Milwaukee Brave was Phil Niekro, 1987.

The last St. Louis Brown was Don Larsen, 1967.

The last Philadelphia Athletic was Vic Power, 1965.

The last Kansas City Athletic was Reggie Jackson, 1987.

The last original Washington Senator—Jim Kaat, 1983.

The last expansion Senator was Toby Harrah (1986) whose name was spelled the same backwards and forwards. In fact, he wore uniform number 11, which was also the same backwards and forwards.

The last Seattle Pilot was Fred Stanley in 1982.

The last Los Angeles Angel was Jim Fregosi in 1978.

The last Houston Colt .45 was Rusty Staub in 1985.

I'm also watching another upcoming event—the first major leaguer to be born in the 1970s. It should be here this year or next. Ken Griffey Jr. missed by a few weeks. [Postscript added for this publication: the first was Texas pitcher Wilson Alvarez, born March 24, 1970, who debuted in 1989.] The first major leaguer who was born in the 1950s was John Mayberry. The first born in the 1960s was the pitcher Tim Conroy, one of those seven year veterans we seem to have trouble remembering.

And, of course, there is the every-present "four decade man" syndrome we will be hearing about next year. Players whose career spanned four decades, in this case the 1960s, '70s, '80s and '90s. I suppose with the big salaries today, the incentive is greater to keep playing. Carlton Fisk, Rick Dempsey, Tommy John, Bill Buckner, Jerry Reuss and Darrell Evans are those eligible to make it. And to think of an average journeyman player like Dempsey is also fairly amazing. By the way, did you hear of the time last season when Jamie Quirk pinch-ran for Buckner in Kansas City, and after the game, Bill told the KC writers that it was "the most embarrassing thing that's ever happened to me"? The *Boston Globe* picked up that quote and ran it under a headline the next day that simply said, "THINK HARDER BILL." They never forgive in Boston.

Digress with me for a moment if you will, into another area I've sometimes fantasized about. It involves the age-old question "who was the greatest player of all time?" I think most would vote for Babe Ruth, some for Ty Cobb, and you'll always get a scattering of votes for Bombo Rivera. But if we accept the premise that much of the talent in our greatest players is God-given . . . wouldn't it be interesting to find that God gave the most talent—perhaps the talent to bat .500 and hit 100 home runs a year—to someone born in a country where baseball is never played. I mean, isn't God capable of a sense of humor? Perhaps the greatest player in baseball history never picked up a bat. It's nice to see baseball played in so many countries today, and the chances of that happening becoming smaller and smaller.

Did any of you have a chance to see the wonderful new movie *Field of Dreams* with Kevin Costner? Wonderful, wasn't it? Please don't miss it.

Field of Dreams was a fantasy. Let me share with you for a moment something that happened during a rain delay at the old Yankee Stadium around 1971. To keep the crowd entertained during the long delay, Bob Fishel and I decided to flash the "all-time top 20 Yankee home run hitters," one by one, on the message board in the outfield. We had George Schmelzer, the electrician posted in the board, punch out the letters one by one: 20. Frank Crosetti 97, and so on, until we were hitting the really big names. Now the fans were getting into it, and great cheers would go up at the appearance of Berra, DiMaggio, Gehrig. Now we had Mantle and the place was going crazy as soon as we had 2. MICK . . . that was all that was needed. Now we're about 20 minutes into this, and it's really been a great thing, and everyone knows what's coming next. So up pops 1. Then comes B A B E and the place is going nuts. Then up goes the R and suddenly, with a torrential rain still falling, a bolt of lightning strikes the scoreboard and knocks it dead. And you never saw 15,000 screaming fans gasp and grow silent so fast. Now that was living a real-life fantasy. And I was there. And I think The Babe was too.

There is another note I would like to inject here, and that's the matter of free TV for baseball. Perhaps it was only a matter of time before baseball people realized that there is no money to be made from fans far removed from big cities and minor league towns. That's sad. But access to baseball has, as you know, become limited, not expanded. Throughout the history of baseball, every new form of communication that has come along has been used to increase the game's exposure. The telegraph, the radio and television all won countless new fans for baseball. Now, for the first time, baseball is turning to pay-TV in increasing number and *reducing* access to the games.

It is sad to see the end of the Game of the Week, a tradition which brought exposure to all teams into every home in the country. The mere 12 games to be shown on CBS next year is a sad development. The fact that many games will be shown nationally on cable hardly compensates for that—only half the homes in America have access to cable.

Many more homes, particularly in America's inner cities, may have access, but not the means to afford the $500 or $600 bill each year to get games. The tragedy is perhaps greatest in New York, where, beginning in 1991, cable television has the rights to every Yankee game. That means that for many taxpayers in the city, whose dollars rebuilt and maintain Yankee Stadium, it is shutout city. Broadway, fine restaurants and Lincoln Center are not available to everyone. For millions, the summer's lone form of entertainment was the enjoyment of free baseball on TV. In a society of haves and have nots, here's now another way to distinguish between them. It was a beautiful thing to be able to see cab drivers and stockbrokers talk about last night's game. Elevator operators and CEOs could share conversation about those Yankees or those Mets. In seeing a winding down of that aspect of American society, we are seeing a sad end to an era.

Well, I've probably gone on long enough, but there was one more point I wanted to make about preserving history and appreciating it while it unfolds before us. As I said, in years to come, it will be harder and harder to set records or establish "firsts." The more years the game goes on, the harder it is to stand out. So when we have before us players who may very well be the best of all time, I think it is important for us to savor each day that they are still playing, and make sure we have the proper appreciation for them.

When I was a child, *The Sporting News* book daguerreotypes ran an article on baseball's all-time all-star team, based on a poll of experts, and a man named Jimmy Collins—he's in the Hall of Fame—was voted the greatest third baseman ever. Well, that was the only place I ever saw that, and we all came to accept that it was really Pie Traynor. But as Brooks Robinson wound down his career, the accepted wisdom was that Brooks deserved the honor.

You could make a great case for Mike Schmidt, you know, and while I won't stand here and say he's the best third baseman who ever played the game, one could certainly make a good argument for it. So let's be sure we pay him his due and appreciate that he was ours—and perhaps the only current player to qualify for a greatest-ever list. The same could be said for Ozzie Smith, who may certainly be the greatest *defensive* shortstop of all time. No way he could hit with Honus Wagner, but look at Wagner's stats in daguerreotypes someday, and you'll notice something interesting. In all his years as a regular, there are no asterisks on any of his fielding statistics. Never once led the league in put-outs or assists. So let's give Ozzie his due and appreciate him while we can.

And Nolan Ryan. It's time to stop Ryan-bashing based on his won–lost record. His strikeout and no-hit records may live forever. And as every pitcher eventually gets a sore arm—and here's a guy who we thought wouldn't make it to the '70s because of finger blisters—when you look at Ryan you just want to say WOW.

And finally, Rickey Henderson, who will in short order pass Cobb and Hamilton and Brock and become baseball's all-time stolen base champion in less than a decade. Sometimes I watch the game today and wonder if the stolen base has become perhaps too easy. Might not the game be better if 50 percent of runners were caught stealing? Maybe. But as long as Henderson does what he does, let's be sure we savor those moments and appreciate the greatness he displays, lest it be gone all too quickly.

What is my greatest regret as a baseball fan? The fact that in the mid 1950s, I was too young to appreciate the greatness and magic that was the Brooklyn Dodgers, right in my backyard.

My greatest satisfaction? Whatever I did to preserve the Yankee tradition during the time I was there. I remember the day I was shown a potential road uniform that was navy with white pinstripes. I made a face and groaned so loudly that the road uniform was left unchanged. And I'm very proud of the fact that even at age 13 I rooted for Roger Maris—never booed him, and years later, found Sal Durante, the fellow who caught his 61st homer, and had him throw out the first ball, right from his old seat in the right field stands, on the 15th anniversary, to another #9, Graig Nettles, the first Yankee to lead the league in home runs since Maris. Things like that—things that connect traditions, give me a great deal of pleasure.

Incidentally, did you know that the Yankees—the Bronx Bombers, with that inviting porch in right field—have not led the American League in home runs since they hit the record 240 in 1961? That was 28 years ago. And did you realize that in six short years Maris' record will have lasted as long as Ruth's did?

Speaking of things that connect, here's one that I love: the ever replenishing of the game's talent, little by little, so that rookies can play side by side with veterans and learn all about where the game came from. Ken Griffey Jr. played in the same year as Tommy John, who was a teammate of Early Wynn's when he broke in. Wynn, who broke in in 1939, played in the league at the same time that Ted Lyons did. When Lyons broke in, Ty Cobb was still active. Cobb, as a rookie, found Willie Keeler on the diamond. Keeler played against Cap Anson. Griffey, John, Wynn, Lyons, Cobb, Keeler, Anson. Seven players and we've covered the major leagues since the day the National League began play in 1876.

That's it for me today, although I would welcome your questions and I know I'd enjoy talking baseball with you either from here or afterwards, because you know . . . I haven't thought of anything I'd rather talk about after all. Catfish Hunter, on his Day, said, "Thank you God for giving me strength and making me a ballplayer." Well, I would have enjoyed being one too; but I say thanks for that day in 1955 when my father took me to Ebbets Field and I first experienced the sight of those slivers of green as you walked up the ramps toward your seat, until at last the majesty of the entire expanse of grass would sit before you. And that day in 1967 when Bob Fishel hired me. It's been a great trip. It's been wonderful, every day of it. Thank you all very much for having me.

Baseball Novels from Gil Gamesh to Babe Ragland to Sidd Finch

A Bibliographical Survey of Serious Adult Baseball Fiction Since 1973

by Peter C. Bjarkman

In the twentieth century there is perhaps no more ubiquitous metaphorical backdrop
for the acting out of myth in America than baseball.
—John R. Cashill (1974)

Baseball's century-long-plus history has been chronicled with loving detail during the past decade, and increasing attention has also been paid by both professional academics and enthusiastic amateurs (members of the Society for American Baseball Research, in particular) to cataloguing the impact of America's pastime upon our nation's idiom, our folkways, and our booming popular culture. The same cannot be said for the history of baseball literature, however; while hundreds of titles have been devoted to every facet of the national game in recent years, little has been done to catalogue or critique this rich literature as serious American intellectual achievement. Baseball fiction especially has suffered in this regard: the baseball novel (the sports novel in general) has long been considered a mere pulp enterprise and thus shunned by serious academic critics. A single complete critical study of baseball literature has yet to appear, although at least one is now scheduled for imminent publication (Bjarkman 1992, in press). While several dozen Ph. D. dissertations have explored the cultural implications of baseball fiction and baseball history, only one serious academic article has critiqued this additional valuable store of baseball scholarship (Bjarkman 1988). At best, a handful of baseball novels are known to the general reading public (those of Malamud, Harris, and perhaps Kinsella), despite the fact that more than six dozen serious adult baseball novels have appeared since Bernard Malamud's *The Natural* (1952). Eric Rolfe Greenberg's *The Celebrant* (1983) may well stand as one of the finest historical novels of the recent epoch, yet few readers know it and most of these have likely dismissed as trivial the social import of its baseball-rich contents.

Baseball books—especially baseball novels—are exceptionally hot, however, among literary consumers, if not among academic critics, and this past decade has witnessed a remarkable creative outpouring of fiction set upon the real and imaginary diamonds of America's favorite summer pastime. Bill Kinsella's tandem—*Shoeless Joe* and *The Iowa Baseball Confederacy*—are perhaps the best known but hardly the most representative among dozens of recent baseball novels ranging from outrageous satirical anti-fictions to unparalleled imaginative fantasy and spellbinding, thickly plotted murder mystery. Within the brief history of "literary baseball" (as this phenomenon of baseball fiction might be labeled), 1973, however, was the truly momentous year. That summer brought publication of Philip Roth's bizarre and unprecedented comic burlesque—an outrageous extravagance of fiction which the author whimsically entitled *The Great American Novel.* This most mysterious of all our sports novels today continues to baffle countless critics and scholars with its unparalleled attempt to exploit baseball history in the guise of savage literary joke and to turn baseball legend and folklore on their ear in the service of ruthless political satire. Roth converts traditional elements of the national pastime into shameless slapstick, simultaneously creating both "counter-history" and a companion "counter-mythology" as well. Philip Roth's literary game is "demythologization" of our sacred national baseball mythology, and his unique novel is a memorable reflection of the irrational, unpredictable, humorous, and often violent scene that was America in the shameless 1950s and volatile 1960s—perhaps baseball's best and worst decades.

While critics continue to debate the meanings as well as the artistic merits of *The Great American Novel,* there is little doubt that baseball fiction has never been quite the same since Roth irreverently employed baseball's legends and lore to critique and condemn everything from contemporary American politics and deep-rooted sociocultural myths to the esteemed national literary establishment itself. Roth's novel seems as much a joke on *Moby Dick* as it is on the excesses of the nation's summer pastime. After Roth, baseball novels no longer found their subject matter restricted to "that simple boy's game" played professionally by grown men in concrete urban stadiums; it was no longer sufficient to reconstitute myths internal to the national pastime, or to repackage virtues personified by its real-life or fictional ballplayer heroes. Baseball novels were now more symbolic and sophisticated; they aimed to tackle the broader scope of our national life and our personal fantasies. The true-to-life diamond struggles of Mark Harris' Henry Wiggen (or Wiggen's boastful prototype, Lardner's Jim Keefe) were supplanted by the surrealistic adventures of Roth's ill-fated pitcher Gil Gamesh, Jerome Charyn's magical left-handed third baseman Babe Ragland, and (more recently) George Plimpton's Buddhist flamethrowing prospect Sidd Finch. And for all their whimsical fantasies, these more solipsistic novels seem somehow better at capturing those metaphysical complexities of baseball which have made this beloved American game so much more than just another sport—which have, in fact, elevated it to the status of unrivaled national institution. While pre-1973 baseball novels, for all their mythic overtones, focused on mundane big league events, the best of post-Roth baseball fiction has usually been magical in tone and even surrealistic in its luscious pastoral settings—a true escapist world of time-travel and ballpark fairy tale.

Baseball fiction itself certainly is not an exclusive phenomenon of the second half of the twentieth century. An established tradition of boy's novels and pulp fiction produced enough volumes on the national game to fill over forty pages of entries in Anton Grobani's first extensive bibliography of baseball literature (Grobani 1975). Yet the first serious adult baseball fiction—if one excludes perhaps Ring Lardner's dozen best stories and one major novel—did not appear until the early 1950s, first bursting upon the scene like an unseasoned rookie with Bernard Malamud's *The Natural* (1952) and Mark Harris' Henry Wiggen trilogy (1953, 1956). This was more than a full century after baseball had first been crowned the American national game. Why, then, such a lengthy embryonic period for the serious baseball novel? In part, the answer is simply that somehow we could not take our baseball fiction as "serious literature" until the arrival of the introspective 1960s, the age when TV would first separate us as fans from the games we watched, removing us electronically from intimate contact with actions and players on the field. Major novels of the 1960s and 1970s (i.e., those of Coover and Roth) thus began to treat baseball as highly symbolic metaphorical activity—focusing on archetypes of human behavior and on actions appropriate to the stylized worlds of magic and fantasy. From the rich historical ambience of Greenberg's *The Celebrant* (baseball's best novel) to the vapid plotting of Plimpton's *The Curious World of Sidd Finch* (it's most overrated novel), contemporary baseball novels are as rich in archetype as any competing brand of American fiction.

Malamud wrote the first serious adult baseball fiction and in the process engendered the mythic baseball novel. As most serious readers of baseball fiction are aware, *The Natural* is far more than simply a modern-day rendering of the popular theme of the Black Sox scandal, in which the star slugger is spurned by the penny-pinching owner (the Charles Comiskey prototype), tempted by evil women (the "terrible dark mothers" of Western myth), and in the end bought out by unscrupulous gamblers. Critic Michael Oriard argues that the history of serious sports fiction begins with *The Natural;* Malamud was the first American novelist to exploit seriously the potent mythic qualities of American sport, and his inaugural novel cleverly employs historical events and legendary feats from America's only true native folk mythology—baseball history. Critics already have extensively detailed Malamud's unprecedented blending of actual baseball incident with pervasive Western literary tradition (T. S. Eliot's "Wasteland," Jesse Weston's Percival Legend, and Sir James Frazer's vegetation myth of the Fisher King); they have also catalogued the novel's extensive parallels between fictional event (Roy Hobb's knocking the cover off the ball or launching a home run which shatters the scoreboard clock) and real-world baseball incident (Wasserman 1965; Turner 1968). All of the novel's most miraculous and improbable events, in fact, have firm precedent in baseball's own on-field history: e.g., Babe Ruth's colossal bellyache; Chuck Hoestetler's bizarre version of "Fisher's Flop"; Pete Reiser's own anticipations of Bump Bailey's life-threatening collisions with unyielding outfield fences; the New York Knights' slapstick imitations of the 1914 Miracle Boston Braves. No critic can fairly contend that any novelist knew baseball history more thoroughly, or exploited it with more savvy while creating the stuff of an indigenous American mythology.

Mark Harris followed on the heels of Malamud with his popular Henry Wiggen trilogy of "unedited autobiographical fictions"— *Bildungsroman* tales reportedly penned by a raw rookie southpaw hurler for the fictional New York Mammoths. Harris provided (with *The Southpaw* and *Bang the Drum Slowly*) the first important adult baseball novels in a naturalistic-realistic frame. These Henry Wiggen novels are, of course, quite reminiscent of the rustic and boastful "letters to home" authored by Ring Lardner's crude "Baseball Joes"; but *The Southpaw* in the end reads more like Harris' version of *The Adventures of Huckleberry Finn* than like any lesser attempt at duplicating Lardner's hackwork in *You Know Me, Al.* Harris' stories, like those of Hemingway and Faulkner, are clearly tales of initiation through blood and violence into manhood. But the symbolic violence here is the game action of the major league diamond, and the initiation comes to us in the form of the now time-tested baseball tale involving the talented young prospect who must realize life's inevitable lessons of aging and failure, lessons only earned through the epic cycles of the single summer's seemingly endless baseball season. Harris is, in fact, the first important novelist to exploit Roger Kahn's important notion of the ideal baseball fiction. "It is a harsh, jarring thing to have to shift dreams at thirty," wrote Kahn in 1957, "and if there is ever to be a major novel written about baseball, I think it will have to come to grips with this theme" ("Intellectuals and Ballplayers"). Henry Wiggen stands firm as our supreme prototype of the sainted, ingenuous ballplayer reworking his life's dreams at the crest of a diminishing baseball youth.

It was left for Coover and Roth, then, at the end of the 1960s and outset of the 1970s, to launch the popular baseball "fantasy-novel" now so familiar to the present generation of baseball readers. Coover's *Universal Baseball Association* provides a still unrivaled use of the notion of parallel universes of baseball action: protagonist Henry Waugh creates a fantasy baseball dice game (forerunner of APBA and Strato) which first blurs his (and then ultimately the reader's) perceptions of material and imaginative realities. Kinsella subsequently has brought such baseball novels of "magical realism"—invented by Coover—to their greatest imaginative heights during the past decade, especially with his less critically acclaimed *Iowa Baseball Confederacy*. Here Gideon Clarke wanders to the end of an abandoned railway spur and suddenly finds himself implausibly transferred across time and space into a baseball dreamworld of six decades earlier. Kinsella's are also novels that depend on a notion of the "parallel baseball universe" as the source for unlimited baseball fantasy, as are almost all the best baseball novels of the past two decades. Coover launched all such parallel baseball universes with Henry's *UBA,* where events in Waugh's dice game slowly merge with a humdrum everyday reality as milktoast accountant in the firm of Dunkelman, Zauber & Zifferblatt. Roth exploits a parallel notion with his bogus historical baseball league, discredited and expunged forever from the standard history books, yet a league reminiscent of the shadowy real-life Negro Leagues of the 1940s, while approximating mainstream major league baseball as well—in mythic overtones and legendary events. Kinsella opts for time-travel and the conjuring up of implausible baseball dreamworlds (those of Ray Kinsella and Gideon Clarke) while bringing his charming tales of baseball fantasies alive to everyday fans on the farmlands of Middle America.

Today's baseball novels seem to fall neatly into five readily identifiable types. First are the *realistic novels,* drawn in the tradition of Mark Harris' Henry Wiggen trilogy, in which stark everyday realities of big league baseball and locker room politics are of paramount interest. These are stories in which the players are recognizable true-to-life baseball prototypes, the on-field action is always believable and lovingly detailed, and the themes and issues always involve ballplaying heroes struggling for elusive fame and fleeting career survival. The *mythical baseball novels* of writers like Bernard Malamud *(The Natural)* and Robert Coover *(The Universal Baseball Association)* offer a genuine departure from the realistic mode, with their highly stylized and symbolic actions and the religious and archetypal importance in which ballplaying is cloaked. *Personal nostalgia novels*—the supreme examples being David Ritz's *The Man Who Brought the Dodgers Back to Brooklyn* and Robert Mayer's *The Grace of Shortstops*—focus on the humanizing role of baseball memories and personal baseball fantasies within the lives of middle-aged fans. Often they unmask the adult male anti-hero struggling to come to grips with inevitable aging and with personal failure. This third genre often focuses more on the fan of baseball than on actual ballplayer heroes, and the dozens of recent adult softball novels fall clearly within this mold. Another type is the "magical realism" or *fantasy baseball novel* practiced first by Jerome Charyn and Philip Roth and brought to new heights by W. P. Kinsella. Here the artistic intention is usually satirical, the baseball events are likely to be bizarre, magical, even otherworldly; and the thematic impact is far more often genuinely comic rather than intentionally tragic (as with mythic novels). Finally, there is a whole minor sub-genre of *baseball detective novels* where the local ballpark becomes the setting for murder and mayhem in the best tradition of our finest "who-done-it" action thrillers.

The best and most popular among baseball novels of the past two decades have ranged all across these several genre types. Three outstanding novels deserve special mention, however. Eric Rolfe Greenberg's *The Celebrant* (1983) is indisputably baseball's most accomplished historical novel and provides perhaps the seminal fictional portrait of baseball's role in the Americanization of the European Jewish immigrant family. Barbara Gregorich *(She's On First)* braves new ground with her story of female shortstop Lindy Sunshine while providing the best novel yet done on the risky theme of a first woman big-leaguer—an idea exploited far less successfully by several earlier novelists (Paul Rothweiler was perhaps first) in the service of cheap fictional stunt or exploitative and sensationalized literary motif. David Carkeet's *The Greatest Slump of All-Time* is the ultimate black humor baseball novel, an unforgettable satiric *coup de main* exposing the institutional foibles of American baseball right alongside the laughable excesses of our current national craze for pop psychology and its feeder cult of psychological pain.

The most notable fact about our baseball fiction of the past decade and a half has been its extensiveness. One hundred or more baseball novels (109 in the bibliography below) have appeared since 1973, many featuring baseball as main plot line or as subject of central thematic concern, some merely utilizing baseball backdrops as enriching thematic motif. Yet academic scholarship has not kept pace with such creative outpouring, and my own forthcoming scholarly study of baseball literature will surprisingly be the first true comprehensive book-length treatment on the topic. Mike Shannon, editor of the popular underground baseball literature journal *Spitball,* provides insightful essays on 100 baseball books within his new volume *Diamond Classics* (Shannon 1989), yet Shannon's treatment lacks thematic unity and his emphasis is never squarely on baseball fiction per se. Cordelia Candelaria has also recently published *Seeking the Perfect Game* (Candelaria 1989), a book touted as a comprehensive overview of contemporary baseball fiction. Yet Candelaria's study (revisions of her 1976 Ph. D. thesis) regrettably focuses on but seven pre-1975 novels (it is most useful for its essays on Jerome Charyn and Jay Neugeborn) and ignores altogether the modern baseball novel of the 1980s, offering no chapters at all on such important contemporary writers as Gregorich, Kinsella, or Eric Rolfe Greenberg.

Bibliographies are particularly sparse, and there is no available comprehensive published listing of baseball novels previous to this present study. James Mote recently released *Everything Baseball,* which pledges on its dust jacket to list "absolutely every baseball song, poem, novel, play, movie, TV and radio show, painting, sculpture, comic strip, cartoon, and more" (cf. Mote 1989). The promise itself is almost ludicrous, and Mote predictably leaves out a full third of the baseball fiction titles of the past two decades. Mote's eight-page section on fiction did provide several titles not included in previous drafts of this present survey; however, Mote's listing includes only 76 of the post-1979 baseball novels. Anton Grobani's much celebrated 1975 *Guide to Baseball Literature* is especially useful for tracking the juvenile fictions of the pre-World War II period, yet it is also hopelessly antiquated for today's dedicated scholar, having considerably predated the windfall in adult baseball fiction witnessed by the past two decades. Finally, Myron Smith, Jr. *(Baseball: A Comprehensive Bibliography)* provides an exhaustive reference of 22,000 titles—yet surprisingly ignores baseball fiction entirely in the bargain.

What follows here is a near-complete catalogue of baseball novels and baseball fiction anthologies from the past several decades; it is perhaps the only exhaustive list of its kind available for the baseball fiction enthusiast. Bibliographical listings have been divided here into five sections, for convenience of the novice reader and serious scholar alike. Each section boasts special features as outlined below:

1. *Baseball's Pre-1970s Adult Novels and Fiction Collections* (from early 1900s to the present), a list ranging from the first serious adult novels by Malamud and Harris, in the early 1950s, back to pioneering borderline adult–juvenile short stories from the second decade of the present century (Zane Gray, Charles Van Loan, and others). Baseball-related stories (those in which baseball is a secondary thematic interest) and baseball murder mysteries are here separately coded for easy reader reference. (44 entries)

2. *Baseball's Dozen Outstanding Contemporary (post-1973) Adult Novels,* including standbys like Greenberg's *The Celebrant* and Kinsella's beloved Iowa baseball fantasies, as well as lesser-known classics from Barbara Gregorich, Jerome Charyn, John Alexander Graham, and Canadian Paul Quarrington, etc. All dozen novels are cogently summarized in abstract form. (12 entries)

3. *Additional Recent Serious Adult Baseball Novels,* all from the 1970s and 1980s, with accompanying subjective ratings to tout fictional achievement and baseball interest-level for each individual novel. These works all have baseball as primary narrative interest and comprise a full inventory of baseball novels from the past two decades. (51 entries)

4. *Additional Baseball-Related Novels and Serious Adult Baseball Fiction,* fiction books which do not always merit strict classification as "baseball novels" but which exploit baseball locale for plot and setting, and in which baseball action is at least a minor plot feature or thematic motif. Selections here are classified by strict genre type, as detective thriller, softball novels, short story collections, and science-fiction stories. (51 entries)

5. *Selected Baseball Literature Anthologies and Baseball Literature Bibliographies,* including all major anthologies of earlier decades (e.g., Einstein's Fireside series) as well as the best of recent baseball fiction, prose and poetry collections. All available published baseball literature bibliographies are also inventoried (Grobani, Smith, Mote). (18 entries)

6. *Selective Bibliography of Important Critical Sources on Contemporary Baseball Fiction,* with special focus here on important academic and

scholarly essays that explicate the major baseball novels of the past two decades. (51 entries)

The final listing of baseball literature criticism features several university doctoral dissertations; this is not an exhaustive listing of academic dissertations and for a fuller inventory of this rarely explored scholarly resource on baseball fiction the reader is asked to consult my own earlier *SABR Review of Books* article (Bjarkman 1988). Taken as a whole, this partially annotated list of contemporary baseball novels and related criticism should prove extremely useful to any enthusiastic novice reader of baseball fiction, especially those readers wishing to survey the broad genre of adult baseball novels and to assess personally the weight of critical literary discussion which baseball currently generates.

References

Bjarkman, Peter C. "Bats, Balls and Gowns: Academic Dissertations on Baseball Literature, Culture and History," *The SABR Review of Books* 3 (1988), 89–104.

Bjarkman, Peter C. *The Immortal Diamond: Baseball in American Literature and American Culture*. Westport, CT: Meckler Books, 1992 (in press).

Candelaria, Cordelia. *Baseball in American Literature: From Ritual to Fiction*. Unpublished doctoral dissertation. South Bend, Indiana: The University of Notre Dame, 1976.

Candelaria, Cordelia. *Seeking the Perfect Game: Baseball in American Literature*. Westport, CT: Greenwood Press, 1989.

Grobani, Anton, Editor. *A Guide to Baseball Literature*. Detroit: Gale Research, 1975.

Kahn, Roger "Intellectuals as Ballplayers" in *American Scholar* 26 (1957), 342–349.

Mote, James. *Everything Baseball*. New York: Prentice Hall Press, 1989.

Oriard, Michael V. *Dreaming of Heroes: American Sports Fiction, 1868–1980*. Chicago: Nelson-Hall Publishers, 1982.

Shannon, Mike. *Diamond Classics: Essays on One Hundred of the Best Baseball Books Ever Published*. Jefferson, North Carolina: McFarland Publishers, 1989.

Smith, Myron J., Jr. *Baseball: A Comprehensive Bibliography*. Jefferson, North Carolina: McFarland Publishing Company, 1986.

Turner, Frederick W. "Myth Inside and Out: Malamud's *The Natural*," *Novel* 1:2 (1968), 133–139.

Wasserman, Earl R. *"The Natural:* Malamud's World Ceres," *Centennial Review of Arts and Sciences* 9:4 (1965), 438–460.

Bibliographical Survey of Baseball Novels and Baseball Fiction

1. Baseball's Pre-1970s Adult Novels and Fiction Collections
* denotes baseball-related stories; (MM) notation indicates a murder mystery.

*Alexander, Holmes. *Dust in the Afternoon.* New York: Harper and Brothers, 1940.

Asinof, Eliot. *Man on Spikes.* New York: McGraw-Hill Book Company, 1955.

Bagby, George. *Twin Killing.* New York: Doubleday and Company, 1947. (MM)

Ball, John. *Johnny Get Your Gun.* Boston: Little-Brown, 1969. (MM)

Beaumont, Gerald. *Hearts of the Diamond.* New York: Dodd, Mead and Company, 1920. (short story collection)

*Broun, Heywood. *The Sun Field.* New York and London: G. P. Putnam and Sons (Knickerbocker Press), 1923.

Coover, Robert. *The Universal Baseball Association, Inc., J. Henry Waugh, Prop.* New York: Signet New American Library, 1968.

*Davies, Valentine. *It Happens Every Spring.* New York: Farrar, Straus and Young, 1949.

*Edmunds, Murrell. *Behold, Thy Brother.* New York: Beechhurst Press, 1950.

Einstein, Charles. *The Only Game in Town.* New York: Dell Publishing Company, 1955.

Fenner, Phyllis R. (Editor). *Crack of the Bat—Stories of Baseball.* New York: Alfred A. Knopf, 1952. (short story collection)

*Fitzsimmons, Cortland. *Death on the Diamond.* New York: Frederick A. Stokes, 1934.

Graber, Ralph S. *The Baseball Reader.* New York: A. S. Barnes Publishers, 1951.

*Green, Gerald. *To Brooklyn With Love.* New York: Simon and Schuster, 1967.

Grey, Zane. *The Redheaded Outfield and Other Baseball Stories.* New York: Grosset and Dunlap Publishers, 1920. (short story collection)

Grey, Zane. *The Short-Stop.* New York: Grosset and Dunlap Publishers, 1914.

Grey, Zane. *The Young Pitcher.* London: John Long, Limited, 1924.

*Griffith, Peggy. *The New Klondike.* New York: Jacobs-Hodgkinson Publishers, 1926.

Harris, Mark. *The Southpaw (by Henry W. Wiggen, Punctuation Freely Inserted and Spelling Greatly Improved by Mark Harris).* Indianapolis: Bobbs-Merrill Publishing Company, 1953 (Lincoln, Nebraska: The University of Nebraska Press, 1984).

Harris, Mark. *Bang the Drum Slowly (by Henry W. Wiggen, Certain of His Enthusiasms Restrained by Mark Harris).* New York: Alfred A. Knopf, 1956 (Lincoln, Nebraska: The University of Nebraska Press, 1984).

Harris, Mark. *A Ticket for a Seamstitch (by Henry W. Wiggen, but Polished for the Printer by Mark Harris).* New York: Alfred A. Knopf, 1956 (Lincoln, Nebraska: The University of Nebraska Press, 1984).

Herskowitz, Mickey. *Letters from Lefty.* Houston, Texas: Houston Post Company, 1966.

Karlins, Marvin. *The Last Man Is Out.* Englewood Cliffs, New Jersey: Prentice-Hall Publishers, 1969 (republished, under pseudonym of Robert Browne, as *The New Atoms' Bombshell,* New York: Ballantine Books, 1980).

*Kennedy, Lucy. *The Sunlit Field.* New York: Crown Publishers, 1950.

Lardner, Ring. *You Know Me Al—A Busher's Letters.* New York: Curtis Publishing Company, 1914 (New York: Vintage Books, 1984).

Lardner, Ring. *Treat 'em Rough: Letters from Jack the Kaiser-Killer.* Indianapolis, Indiana: The Bobbs-Merrill Company, 1918.

Lardner, Ring. *The Real Dope.* Indianapolis, Indiana: The Bobbs-Merrill Company, 1919.

Lardner, Ring. *Lose With a Smile.* New York: Charles Scribner's Sons, 1933.

Malamud, Bernard. *The Natural.* New York: Farrar, Straus and Giroux Publishers, 1952 (New York: Avon Books, 1980).

*Michael, D. J. (pseudonym for Charles Einstein). *Win or Else!* New York: Lurton Blassingame Publishers, 1954.

*Molloy, Paul. *A Pennant for the Kremlin.* New York: Doubleday and Company, 1964.

Needham, Henry Beach ("Introduction" by Connie Mack). *The Double Squeeze.* Garden City, New York: Doubleday, Page and Company, 1915. (short story collection)

Quigley, Martin. *Today's Game.* New York: The Viking Press, 1965.

*Richler, Mordecai. *St. Urbain's Horseman.* New York: Alfred A. Knopf, 1971.

*Smith, H. Allen. *Rhubarb.* New York: Doubleday and Company, 1946.

Van Loan, Charles E. *The Big League.* Boston, Massachusetts: Small and Maynard, 1911. (short story collection)

Van Loan, Charles E. *The Ten-Thousand-Dollar Arm and Other Tales of the Big League*. Boston, Massachusetts: Small and Maynard, 1912. (short story collection)

Van Loan, Charles E. *The Lucky Seventh*. Boston, Massachusetts: Small and Maynard, 1913. (short story collection)

Van Loan, Charles E. *Score by Innings*. New York: George H. Doran, 1919. (short story collection)

*Wade, Robert. *Knave of Eagles*. New York: Random House, 1969. (MM)

Wallop, Douglass. *The Year the Yankees Lost the Pennant*. New York: W. W. Norton, 1954.

*Witwer, H. C. *From Baseball to Botches*. Boston, Massachusetts: Small and Maynard, 1918.

*Witwer, H. C. *A Smile a Minute*. Boston, Massachusetts: Small and Maynard, 1919.

*Witwer, H. C. *There's No Base Like Home*. New York: Doubleday, Page and Company, 1920.

2. Baseball's Dozen Outstanding Contemporary Adult Novels

Carkeet, David. *The Greatest Slump of All Time*. New York: Harper and Row Publishers, 1984 (New York: Viking Penguin, 1985).

An unprecedented parody of big league play and of the two dominant diversions of our times—major league baseball and the popular passion for psychotherapy and self-help pop psychology. Showcased here is Carkeet's ribald portrait of a wildly successful major league team that somehow manages to contend for a pennant despite its makeshift roster of big league basketcases, a starting nine who individually suffer every imaginable Freudian disorder and emotional complaint. Carkeet provides vivid and memorable portraits of "a stupendous bunch of eccentrics, oddballs, and general misfits"—a catcher who fantasizes about pitchouts so that he might "jump out of his claustrophobic tools of ignorance"; a chatterbox third sacker boasting total recall of myriad useless baseball statistics; a Dutch-Spanish outfielder whose fractured pronouncements suggest "a solution to it all." For students of American literature, this novel is distinguished by its subtle and ingenious echoes of Albert Camus' standard European existentialist classic, *The Stranger*.

Charyn, Jerome. *The Seventh Babe*. New York: Arbor House Publishers, 1979 (New York: Avon Books, 1980).

Remember the 1923 Boston Red Sox? This is the team that traded away Babe Ruth ("the First Babe") to those hated Yankees of Colonel Ruppert, a team considered universally to be the indisputed laughingstock of major league ball. "The outfielders couldn't catch a cold and the hitters couldn't run if they were stockings." But just when all seemed lost, these same Red Sox acquired an unknown rookie named Babe Ragland—a lanky left-handed third baseman (yes left-handed!) who gobbles up grounders, seduces beautiful women, yet also packs the fans in record numbers into quaint Fenway Park. At least, that is, until this new Babe ("the Seventh Babe") is framed in an all-too-predictable baseball betting scandal, is banned from baseball for life, and is thus forced to become the first barnstorming white ballplayer with the Cincinnati Colored Giants—a ragtag outfit roaming the countryside with seven Buicks and a team witch doctor, playing in cemeteries and backwoods swamps.

Graham, John Alexander. *Babe Ruth Caught in a Snowstorm.* Boston: Houghton Mifflin Company, 1973.
"Baseball players wanted . . . Ability not necessary . . . Only desire counts." This small notice is circulated throughout New York City and the line of applicants stretches for three city blocks! Slezak, a man who dreams of a baseball team built solely on his love for the game, forms his patchwork Wichita Wraiths from the strangest imaginable assortment of baseball "talent," ironically locates his team in Massachusetts, finds his club miraculously invited to join the majors, and then discovers his baseball fantasy mushrooming into something he is entirely unprepared to handle. A deftly crafted work, Graham's novel utilizes the metaphor of baseball to examine childhood dreams and what results when we try too hard to hang on to them. The central baseball symbol (Slezak's miniature snow-filled Babe Ruth paperweight) is the most ingenious device found within the entire baseball fiction genre.

Greenberg, Eric Rolfe. *The Celebrant.* New York: Everest House, 1983 (New York: Viking Penguin, 1986).
Greenberg weaves together those real-life chronicles of our first great national baseball hero (Christy Mathewson) with fictional accounts of a Jewish immigrant family of New York jewelers, passionately involved with the turn-of-the-century game of American baseball. The Kapp family has been selected to design team championship rings for the New York Giants of Mathewson and John J. McGraw, and while Jackie Kapp had once dreamed of being a great pitcher, he must now settle for lesser glory in the management of family business. That is,

until Kapp rediscovers his love for baseball and becomes a "true celebrant" and devoted personal disciple of the ill-fated dying Mathewson. Loss of innocence in American big business is here paralleled by the failure of innocence for American sport; the Kapps discover unpleasant realities lurking behind baseball's shiny illusions once the infamous Black Sox scandal shatters baseball's wholesome image and darkens all American life.

Gregorich, Barbara. *She's on First.* Chicago: Contemporary Books, 1987 (Toronto and New York: Paper Jacks Limited, 1988).
Lindy Sunshine is the hottest big league prospect in a dozen seasons—a crack shortstop with great range and shotgun arm, a clutch .300 hitter, a firebrand sparkplug who almost singlehandedly lifts the doormat Chicago Eagles back into the thick of a pennant race. But Lindy is also dogged by endless controversy and embroiled in riotous conflict: Sunshine's teammates threaten revolt if the much ballyhooed rookie remains in the lineup, and fans jeer Sunshine's every appearance in the field. Not since the fabled Jackie Robinson, in fact, has any rookie been greeted with such universal animosity and treated to such relentless indignities. Ms. Lindy Sunshine, star rookie shortstop for the Chicago Eagles, is, after all, a woman—the first female player to make it into the Bigs. And as the game's first female star, Sunshine provides—for teammate, fan, and reader alike—the ultimate assault on that last pure male bastion which masquerades as America's national pastime.

Harris, Mark. *It Looked Like Forever.* New York: McGraw-Hill Book Company, 1979 (New York: McGraw-Hill Paperbacks, 1984).
A final installment in the Henry Wiggen tetrology unfolds, as Author Wiggen faces retirement from baseball and wrestles with his life after his days of diamond glory. Wiggen is now thirty-nine, bogged down with a fading fastball, a troublesome prostate, and numerous other signs of his impending mortality. But when unceremoniously released after nineteen winning seasons with the New York Mammoths (boasting 247 victories as the twenty-seventh winningest pitcher of all time), Wiggen decides that he is not quite ready to hang up his spikes. Henry treks to California and then Japan, convinced that he has at least a few good innings left; but in the end a more mature Author Wiggen uncovers some important universal truths about life as well as baseball. As with Harris' three earlier baseball sagas, this novel is warmly human and wistfully humorous. Harris himself has termed this novel

the best of the Wiggen books, and poet and baseball essayist Donald Hall asserts that "If I had a vote, I would put Henry Wiggen up for Cooperstown."

Hays, Donald. *The Dixie Association.* New York: Simon and Schuster, 1984 (New York: Warner Books, 1984).
Donald Hays spins here a most unforgettable tale of the sustaining role of minor league baseball within the social fabric of the American south. This novel features a panoply of unforgettable and unprecedented baseball types—a beer-guzzling and lecherous old knuckleballer; half-Indian and ace spitballer Jeremiah Eversole; the first woman to play professional baseball; a couple of genuine Communists; several Cubans on loan from Fidel Castro; a few rawboned kids and salty old-timers; Black Muslim Genghis Mohamed, Jr., who "lets religion stand between him and a barbecued spare rib"; an ex-con power hitter; and a brilliant left-wing one-armed manager. Together they constitute the Arkansas Reds of the Dixie Association, a thinly disguised literary version of the Southern Association of two decades ago. The narrator of this raucous tale, Hog Durham, is himself a released cattle rustler and petty thief who fills out his narrative with bawdy witticisms, irreverent invectives, and probing self-analyses while at the same time playing a masterful first base for one of baseball's most irrepressible and truly unforgettable fictionalized teams.

Herrin, Lamar. *The Rio Loja Ringmaster.* New York: The Viking Press, 1977 (New York: Avon Books, 1978).
Richard Dixon was a star pitcher for the Cincinnati Brewmasters during their championship season, a relief-ace haunted by the dream of being a starting hurler. Now he takes the mound for a Mexican scrub league team from San Lorenzo and finds himself sweating out a no-hitter in the seedy town of Rio Loja. Confronted by the ruins of his failed marriage, the betrayal of an important friendship, and prospects for a new life away from the baseball metaphors through which he has lived his life, Dixon must make a final effort to "get right with his past." Herrin's first novel provides for one reviewer "a dazzling, funny, and richly evocative narrative journey." It also provides, as well, still another guise for the often repeated theme of the 1919 Black Sox World Series scandal and the recurring spectre of baseball's darkest hour. In the end, this is a novel of both *demythologization* (baseball destroys love) and *mythologization* (baseball's redemptive powers) and one of the richest treats of baseball literature. Herrin is perhaps the

most skillful prose master among today's baseball novelists and his baseball action is unparalleled in modern sports fiction.

Kinsella, W. P. *Shoeless Joe.* Boston: Houghton Mifflin Company, 1982 (New York: Ballantine Books, 1983).
Mysteriously, the voice of a ghostly baseball announcer informs Iowa farmer Ray Kinsella: "If you build it, he will come!" Ray somehow intuits that the "he" is the legendary Joe Jackson and the "it" is a stadium to allow "Shoeless Joe" and his ill-fated teammates of 1919 to continue playing out their endless dream-life of nightly baseball games. Ray, himself a hopeless dreamer, thus builds his stadium, wishes his ex-catcher father onto the playing field, sets out on a quest to bring reclusive author J. D. Salinger to Iowa to show him the wonder of this magical ballpark, and discovers dreams beyond even those he had so far been able to imagine. While overly saccharine and sentimental for some readers and critics, this novel nonetheless stands as the supreme achievement of Kinsella's very special brand of "magical realism" which is the hallmark of contemporary baseball fiction.

Kinsella, W. P. *The Iowa Baseball Confederacy.* Boston: Houghton Mifflin Company, 1986 (New York: Ballantine Books, 1987).
Like his father Matthew before him, Gideon Clarke is a man driven by a dark secret and obsessed with a bizarre mission. Gideon maintains sole memory (the complete history has been magically burned into his consciousness) of the long-lost Iowa Baseball Confederacy, an altogether forgotten amateur league once thriving in his home state after the turn of the century but irrevocably erased from all human memory during a cosmically significant 1908 exhibition game with the World Champion Chicago Cubs. After years of futile searching for some trace of this fateful game, Gideon and his aging bush league companion Stan follow an old railroad bed ("the Baseball Spur") leading them on to a most strange rendezvous with lost time and human destiny. What they discover is a titanic ball game played out over 2000 rainsoaked innings (2,614 precisely!), with a most surprising outcome. An unsurpassed allegorical fantasy about time travel, parallel universes, and a mythical endless game between the Chicago Cubs and a rag-tag collection of Iowa semi-pro players.

Quarrington, Paul. *Home Game.* Garden City, New York: Doubleday and Company, 1983 (Toronto, Ontario: Doubleday Canada Limited, 1983).
In a style mindful of Tom Robbins or John Irving, Quarrington

captures true incongruities of our human condition with genuine conviction and irrepressible humor. This is at one and the same time the story of a marooned circus sideshow troupe, an unforgettable former baseball hero, and a small Michigan village dominated by a fundamentalist religious sect that passionately wishes the expulsion of all immoral intruders. The organization and training of a baseball team, however, and the playing out of a crucial game through which the expulsion issue will ultimately be decided, surprisingly lead this cast of eccentric characters to an ultimate understanding of the humanity which makes them all members of a single, more universal human team. This is a funny, zany, yet also moving novel that negotiates a most precarious path between the poles of human absurdities and human compassion—and it is all done with "magical realism" that rivals the very best of Kinsella.

Roth, Philip. *The Great American Novel.* New York: Holt, Rinehart and
     Winston, 1973 (New York: Viking Penguin Books, 1981).
Easily the most sophisticated and satirical use of baseball as metaphor yet achieved, this landmark novel unfolds a sweeping parody of American life and literature at the zenith of the Cold War and the New Age of American letters. Ostensibly the novelistic account of the banished Patriot League of the Depression Era—supposedly penned by an exiled and eccentric retired sportswriter named Word Smith— what emerges is an exceptional study in literary irreverence. Roth employs his tale as an ingenious vehicle for parody of almost every major novel, personage, and literary device from the history of American fiction. Displaying an impressive knowledge of baseball lore and baseball history, Roth delights with his use of symbolic player names (Gil Gamesh is only the best of dozens of allusive comic baseball names), outrageously humorous baseball events, and ribald narrative style.

3. Additional Recent Serious Adult Baseball Novels

The novels below all fit into a category of "serious adult baseball fiction" and thus contain enough baseball to be considered *true baseball novels.* (MM) notation indicates a *murder mystery* or detective story using baseball as setting, backdrop, or primary theme. Rating Key: ***
Hall of Fame Fiction. ** Big League Novel. * Strictly Bush League Effort.

Ardizzone, Tony. *Heart of the Order.* New York: Henry Holt and Company, 1986.**

Babitz, Eve. *Slow Days, Fast Company.* New York: Alfred A. Knopf, 1977.**

Beckham, Barry. *Runner Mack.* New York: William Morrow and Company, 1972 (Washington, D.C.: Howard University Press, 1984).**

Bell, Marty. *Breaking Balls.* New York: Signet New American Library, 1979. (MM)*

Benjamin, Paul. *Squeeze Play.* New York: Avon Books, 1984. (MM)*

Bowen, Michael. *Can't Miss.* New York: Harper and Row Publishers, 1987.** (first woman in baseball theme)

Brady, Charles. *Seven Games in October.* Boston: Little, Brown and Company, 1979.**

Browne, Robert (pseudonym for Marvin Karlins). *The New Atoms' Bombshell.* New York: Ballantine Books, 1980 (previously published as *The Last Man Out,* Englewood Cliffs, New Jersey: Prentice-Hall Publishers, 1969, by Marvin Karlins).**

Burch, Mark H. *Road Game.* New York: The Vanguard Press, 1986.

Clifton, Merritt. *A Baseball Classic.* Richford, Vermont: Samisdat Press, 1978.** (first woman in baseball theme)

Craig, John. *All G.O.D.'s Children.* New York: William Morrow and Company, 1975 (New York: Signet New American Library, 1976).**

Craig, John. *Chappie and Me: An Autobiographical Novel.* New York: Dodd, Mead and Company, 1979.** (plot parallels Quigley's *The Original Colored House of David*)

Cronley, Jay. *Screwballs.* Garden City, New York: Doubleday and Company, 1980.**

DeAndrea, William L. *Five O'Clock Lightning.* New York: St. Martin's Press, 1982. (MM)**

Donohue, James F. *Spitballs and Holy Water.* New York: Avon Books, 1977.**

Everett, Percival L. *Suder.* New York: The Viking Press, 1983.**

Frank, Morry. *Every Young Man's Dream—Confessions of a Southern League Shortstop.* Chicago: Silverback Books, 1984.**

Geller, Michael. *Major League Murder.* New York: St. Martin's Press, 1988. (MM)**

Gethers, Peter. *Getting Blue.* New York: Delacorte Press, 1987.***

Gordon, Alison. *Dead Pull Hitter.* Toronto: McClelland and Stewart, 1988. (MM)***

Hemphill, Paul. *Long Gone.* New York: The Viking Press, 1979.**

Honig, Donald. *The Last Great Season.* New York: Simon and Schuster, 1979.**

Hough, John, Jr. *The Conduct of the Game*. New York: Harcourt Brace Jovanovich, 1986.***

Kahn, Roger. *The Seventh Game*. New York: Signet New American Library, 1982.**

Kluger, Steve. *Changing Pitches*. New York: St. Martin's Press, 1984.**

Kowet, Don. *The Seventh Game*. New York: Dell Publishing Company, 1977. (MM)**

Littlefield, William. *Prospect*. Boston: Houghton Mifflin Publishers, 1989.***

Mayer, Robert. *The Grace of Shortstops*. Garden City, New York: Doubleday and Company, 1984.*** (one of the best novels of baseball and the Jewish community)

Morgenstein, Gary. *Take Me Out to the Ballgame*. New York: St. Martin's Press, 1980.**

Morgenstein, Gary. *The Man Who Wanted to Play Centerfield for the New York Yankees*. New York: Atheneum Books, 1983.**

Neugeboren, Jay. *Sam's Legacy*. New York: Holt, Rinehart and Winston, 1974.***

Peuchner, Ray. *A Grand Slam*. New York: Harcourt Brace Jovanovich, 1973.*

Platt, Kin. *The Screwball King Murder*. New York: Random House Publishers, 1978. (MM)**

Plimpton, George. *The Curious Case of Sidd Finch*. New York: Macmillan Company, 1987 (New York: Ballantine Books, 1988).* (most overrated baseball novel of the decade)

Pomeranz, Gary. *Out at Home*. Boston: Houghton Mifflin Publishers, 1985.**

Quigley, Martin. *The Original Colored House of David*. Boston: Houghton Mifflin Company, 1981.*** (surprisingly promoted as juvenile fiction but also entertaining adult fiction)

Rice, Damon (pseudonym). *Seasons Past*. New York: Praeger Publishers, 1976.*** (actual authors were Svein Arber, Harold Rosenthal, and Ford Hovis)

Ritz, David. *The Man Who Brought the Dodgers Back to Brooklyn*. New York: Simon and Schuster, 1981.*** (second novel to feature a woman major leaguer as plot device)

Rothweiler, Paul R. *The Sensuous Southpaw*. New York: G. P. Putnam and Sons Publishers, 1976.** (pioneering yet second-rate novel about the first woman major leaguer)

Schiffer, Michael. *Ballpark*. New York: Simon and Schuster, 1982 (New York: Signet New American Library, 1983).*

Seaver, Tom and Herb Resnicow. *Beanball: A Novel of Baseball and Murder*. New York: William Morrow Company, 1989. (MM)*

Senzel, Howard. *Baseball and the Cold War (Being a Soliloquy on the Necessity of Baseball in the Life of a Serious Student of Marx and Hegel from Rochester, New York)*. New York: Harcourt Brace Jovanovich, 1977.*** (rare and delightful fictionalized personal history)
Small, David. *Almost Famous*. New York: W. W. Norton and Company, 1982 (New York: Avon Books, 1983).**
Snyder, Don J. *Veterans Park*. New York: Franklin Watts Publishing Company, 1987.**
Stansberry, Domenic. *The Spoiler*. New York: Atlantic Monthly Press, 1987. (MM)**
Stein, Harry. *Hoopla*. New York: Alfred A. Knopf, 1983 (New York: St. Martin's Press, 1983).*** (second best novel on the Black Sox 1919 World Series episode)
Tennenbaum, Sylvia. *Rachel, The Rabbi's Wife*. New York: William Morrow and Company, 1978.*** (one of the best novels on women and baseball)
Willard, Nancy. *Things Invisible to See*. New York: Alfred A. Knopf, 1984 (New York: Bantam Books, 1986).*** (one of the best novels on women and baseball)
Winston, Peter. *Luke*. New York: Manor Books, 1976.*
Wolff, Miles J. *Season of the Owl*. New York: Stein and Day Publishers, 1980 (New York: Stein and Day Paperback, 1984). (MM)**
Zacharia, Irwin. *Grandstand Rookie*. Canoga Park, California: Major Books, 1977.*

4. Additional Baseball-Related Novels/Serious Adult Baseball Fiction

The novels below utilize baseball (or softball) as background setting or occasional thematic thread (often containing single baseball scenes included for dramatic effect or symbolic richness) but are *not true baseball novels*. (MM) notation indicates a *murder mystery* or detective story employing baseball as setting, backdrop, or primary theme. (SS) indicates short story collections, and (SB) marks novels using softball as main motif or story setting. (SF) indicates baseball science-fiction story.

Andersen, Richard. *Muckaluck*. New York: Delacorte Publishers, 1980.
Bjarkman, Peter C., Editor. *Baseball and the Game of Life: Stories for the Thinking Fan*. Otisville, New York: Birch Brook Press, 1990. (SS)
Boyle, Thomas. *Only the Dead Know Brooklyn*. New York: Penguin Books, 1986. (MM)

Broun, Hob. *Odditorium.* New York: Harper and Row, 1983. (first woman in baseball theme)

Cairns, Bob. *The Comeback Kids.* New York: St. Martin's Press, 1989.

Clifton, Merritt. *Baseball Stories for Girls and Boys (Past Puberty).* Richford, Vermont: Samisdat Press, Volume 32:4, 1982. (SS)

Cohler, David Keith. *Gamemaker.* New York: Doubleday and Company, 1980. (MM)

Coomer, Joe. *A Flatland Fable.* Austin: Texas Monthly Press, 1986 (New York: McGraw-Hill Book Company, 1986).

Cooney, Ellen. *All the Way Home.* New York: G. P. Putnam and Sons Publishers, 1984. (SB)

Curtis, Richard. *Strike Three.* New York: Warner Books, 1975. (MM)

Dawson, Fielding. *A Great Day for a Ballgame.* Indianapolis: Bobbs-Merrill, 1973.

Doctorow, E. L. *Ragtime.* New York: Random House Publishers, 1975 (New York: Bantam Books, 1976).

Engleman, Paul. *Dead in Centerfield.* New York: Ballantine Books, 1983. (MM)

Fish, Bob and Henry Rothblatt. *A Handy Death.* New York: Simon and Schuster, 1972. (MM)

Foster, Alan S. *Goodbye, Bobby Thompson! Goodbye, John Wayne!* New York: Simon and Schuster Publishers, 1973.

Guthrie, A. B., Jr. *Wild Pitch.* Boston: Houghton-Mifflin, 1973. (MM)

Hegner, William. *The Idolaters.* New York: Pocket Books (Simon and Schuster), 1973.

Holton, Leonard. *The Devil to Play.* New York: Dodd, Mead and Company, 1974. (MM)

Johnson, Curt. *The Morning Light.* Pomeroy, Ohio: Carpenter Press, 1977.

Jordan, Pat. *The Cheat.* New York: Villard Books, 1984.

Katz, Steve. *Wier and Pouce.* Washington, D.C.: Sun and Moon Press, 1984.

Keifetz, Norman. *The Sensation.* New York: Atheneum Books, 1975.

Kennedy, William. *Ironweed.* New York: The Viking Press, 1984.

King, Frank. *Southpaw.* New York: Lynx Books, 1988. (MM/horror thriller)

Kinsella, W. P. *Shoeless Joe Comes to Iowa.* Ottawa, Canada: Oberon Press, 1980). (SS)

Kinsella, W. P. *The Thrill of the Grass.* Middlesex, England: Penguin Books, 1984. (SS)

Kinsella, W. P. *The Further Adventures of Slugger McBatt.* Boston: Houghton Mifflin and Company, 1988. (SS)

Klein, Dave. *Hit and Run*. New York: Ace Charter Books, 1982. (MM)

Klinkowitz, Jerry. *Short Season and Other Stories*. Baltimore: Johns Hopkins University Press, 1988. (SS)

Knopf, Mel. *The Batting Machine*. Great Neck, New York: Todd and Honeywell, 1981. (SF)

Lorenz, Tom. *Guys Like Us*. New York: Viking Press, 1980. (SB)

Magnuson, James. *The Rundown*. New York: Dial Press, 1977. (MM)

McAlpine, Gordon. *Joy in Mudville*. New York: E. P. Dutton Publishers, 1989.

McCormack, Tim. *Strictly Amateur*. New York: Pinnacle Books, 1982. (MM)

McManus, James. *Chin Music*. New York: Crown Publishers, 1985 (New York: Grove Press, 1987). (SF)

McSherry, Frank D., Jr., Charles Waugh and Martin H. Greenberg, Editors. *Baseball 3000*. New York: Elsevier-Dutton Publishing Company, 1981. (SS)(SF)

Newlin, Paul. *It Had to Be a Woman*. New York: Stein and Day, 1979.

Nighbert, David F. *Strikezone*. St. Martin's Press, 1989. (MM)

O'Connor, Philip F. *Stealing Home*. New York: Alfred A. Knopf, 1979.

Parker, Robert B. *Mortal Stakes*. Boston: Houghton Mifflin Publishers, 1975. (MM)

Paulos, Sheila. *Wild Roses*. New York: Dell Publishers, 1983. (SB)

Powers, Ron. *Toot-Toot-Tootsie, Good-Bye*. New York: Delacorte Publishers, 1981.

Rosen, R. D. *Strike Three, You're Dead*. New York: Walker and Company, 1984 (New York: Signet New American Library, 1986). (MM)

Rubin, Louis. *Surfaces of a Diamond*. Baton Rouge: Louisiana State University Press, 1981.

Sayles, John. *Pride of the Bimbos*. Boston: Little, Brown and Company, 1975. (SB)

Sheed, Wilfrid. *The Boys of Winter*. New York: Alfred A. Knopf, 1987. (SB)

Spencer, Ross H. *The Stranger City Caper*. New York: Avon Books, 1980. (MM)

Spencer, Ross H. *Kirby's Last Circus*. New York: Donald A. Fine, 1987. (MM)

Tapply, William G. *Follow the Sharks*. New York: Charles Scribner's Sons, 1985. (MM)

Vogan, Sara. *In Shelly's Leg*. New York: Alfred A. Knopf, 1981. (SB)

Williams, Philip Lee. *Slow Dance in Autumn*. New York: Peachtree Press, 1988.

5. Selected Anthologies and Baseball Literature Bibliographies

All listed anthologies feature large selections of baseball fiction, either as excerpts from novels or in the format of reprinted short stories. Greenberg's *On the Diamond* actually reprints Jerome Charyn's *The Seventh Babe* in its entirety. Kerrane and Grossinger's rare *Baseball Diamonds* (now out of print) is the "state of the art" baseball anthology, while Anton Grobani and Myron Smith, Jr. still supply the most comprehensive bibliographies of baseball literature. Smith's massive volume, however, largely ignores fiction while Anton Grobani's study is excellent for juvenile fiction but now hopelessly outdated.

Bjarkman, Peter C., Editor. *Baseball and the Game of Life: Stories for the Thinking Fan*. Otisville, New York: Birch Brook Press, 1990. (SS)

Einstein, Charles, Editor. *The Baseball Reader—Favorites from the Fireside Books of Baseball*. New York: McGraw-Hill Publishers, 1980.

Einstein, Charles, Editor. *The Fireside Book of Baseball*. Fourth Edition. New York: Simon and Schuster, 1987.

Fenner, Phyllis R., Editor. *Crack of the Bat—Stories of Baseball*. New York: Alfred A. Knopf, 1952. (classic juvenile fiction anthology)

Gardner, Martin. *The Annotated "Casey at the Bat": A Collection of Ballads About the Mighty Casey*. Chicago: The University of Chicago Press, 1982.

Graber, Ralph S. *The Baseball Reader*. New York: A. S. Barnes Publishers, 1951.

Greenberg, Martin H., Editor. *On the Diamond: A Treasury of Baseball Stories*. New York: Bonanza Books (Crown Publishers), 1987.

Grobani, Anton, Editor. *A Guide to Baseball Literature*. Detroit: Gale Research, 1975.

Grossinger, Richard, Editor. *The Temple of Baseball*. Berkeley, California: North Atlantic Books, 1985.

Grossinger, Richard, Editor. *The Dreamlife of Johnny Baseball*. Berkeley, California: North Atlantic Books, 1987.

Holtzman, Jerome, Editor. *Fielder's Choice: An Anthology of Baseball Fiction*. New York: Harcourt Brace Jovanovich, 1979.

Kerrane, Kevin and Richard Grossinger, Editors. *Baseball Diamonds—Tales, Traces, Visions and Voodoo From a Native American Rite*. New York: Anchor Books, 1980.

Kerrane, Kevin and Richard Grossinger, Editors. *Baseball I Gave You the Best Years of My Life*. Third Edition. Berkeley, California: North Atlantic Books, 1985.

Mote, James. *Everything Baseball*. New York: Prentice Hall Press, 1989.

Shannon, Mike, Editor. *The Best of* Spitball, *The Literary Magazine of Baseball*. New York: Pocket Books (Simon and Schuster), 1988.

Thorn, John, Editor. *Armchair Book of Baseball*. New York: Charles Scribner's Sons, 1985.

Thorn, John, Editor. *Armchair Book of Baseball 2*. New York: Charles Scribner's Sons, 1987,

Villani, Jim and Rose Sayre, Editors. *Pig Iron No. 9 (Baseball Issue)*. Youngstown, Ohio: Pig Iron Press, 1981.

6. Selective Bibliography of Important Critical Sources on Contemporary Baseball Fiction.

The fifty-one highly selective articles below highlight both the scope and flavor of recent serious academic and journalistic criticism of baseball fiction. While several of these articles deal with pioneering novels by Malamud, Harris and Coover (and are included here largely for their unmatched observations on the essence of baseball fiction and on the distinctive achievements of baseball novels per se) most selections below treat only novels or stories that have appeared since 1973. Generous reading from the selections below will provide baseball literature enthusiasts with extensive background on the "baseball novel" genre, unlocking reasons why this fictional form has prospered so remarkably in recent decades.

Angelius, Judith Wood. "The Man Behind the Catcher's Mask—A Closer Look at Robert Coover's Universal Baseball Association," *The Denver Quarterly* 12:1 (1977), 165–174.

Ardolino, Frank R. "The Americanization of the Gods: Onomastics, Myth, and History in Philip Roth's *The Great American Novel*," *Arete: The Journal of Sport Literature* 3:1 (Fall 1985), 37–59.

Berman, Neil S. "Coover's *Universal Baseball Association*: Play as Personalized Myth," *Modern Fiction Studies* 24:2 (1978), 209–222.

Bjarkman, Peter C. "Bats, Balls and Gowns: Academic Dissertations on Baseball Literature, Culture and History," *The SABR Review of Books: A Forum of Baseball Literary Opinion*. Edited by Paul D. Adomites. Kansas City: The Society for American Baseball Research, Volume 3 (1988), 89–104.

Bjarkman, Peter C. "Diamonds Are a Gal's Worst Friend—Women in Baseball History and Fiction," *The SABR Review of Books: A Forum of Baseball Literary Opinion*. Edited by Paul D. Adomites. Garrett Park, MD: The Society for American Baseball Research, Volume 4 (1989), 79–95.

Bjarkman, Peter C. "Major League Hits From Minor League Players—Small Presses and the Baseball Book Industry," *Small Press* 7:3 (June 1989), 26–27.

Bjarkman, Peter C. *The Immortal Diamond: Baseball in American Literature and American Culture*. Westport, CT: Meckler Books, 1992 (in press).

Boe, Alfred F. "Shoeless Joe Jackson Meets J. D. Salinger: Baseball and the Literary Imagination," *Arete: The Journal of Sport Literature* 1:1 (1983), 179–185.

Boe, Alfred F. "Street Games in J. D. Salinger and Gerald Green," *Modern Fiction Studies* 33.1 (Spring 1987), 65–72.

Caldwell, Roy C., Jr. "Of Hobby Horses, Baseball, and Narrative: Coover's *Universal Baseball Association*," *Modern Fiction Studies* 33.1 (Spring 1987), 161–171.

Candelaria, Cordelia. *Baseball in American Literature: From Ritual to Fiction*. Unpublished doctoral dissertation. South Bend, Indiana: The University of Notre Dame, 1976.

Candelaria, Cordelia. *Seeking the Perfect Game: Baseball in American Literature*. Westport, CT: Greenwood Press, 1989.

Cashill, John R. "The Life and Death of Myth in American Baseball Literature," *American Examiner: A Forum of Ideas*, Michigan State University, Volume 3 (1974), 24–37.

Cochran, Robert. "Bang the Drum Differently: The Southpaw Slants of Henry Wiggen," *Modern Fiction Studies* 33.1 (Spring 1987), 151–159.

Cochran, Robert. "A Second Cool Papa: Hemingway to Kinsella to Hays," *Arete: The Journal of Sport Literature* 4:2 (Spring 1987), 27–40.

Dodge, Tom. "William Kennedy's *Ironweed:* The Expiation of a Broken Ballplayer," *Arete: The Journal of Sport Literature* 4:2 (Spring 1987), 69–74.

Gilman, Richard. "Ball Five—A Review of *The Great American Novel*," *Partisan Review* 40 (1973), 467–471.

Golubcow, Saul. *Baseball as Metaphor in American Fiction*. Unpublished doctoral dissertation. Stony Brook: State University of New York at Stony Brook, 1975.

Grella, George. "Baseball and the American Dream," *Massachusetts Review* 16:3 (Summer 1975), 550–567.

Harris, Mark. "Bring Back That Old Sandlot Novel," *The New York Times Book Review* 42 (October 16, 1988), 1, 44–45.

Harris, Mark. "Horatio at the Bat, or Why Such a Lengthy Embryonic

Period for the Serious Baseball Novel?" *Aethlon: The Journal of Sport Literature* 5:2 (Spring 1988), 1–11.

Harrison, Walter Lee. "Six-Pointed Diamond: Baseball and American Jews," *Journal of Popular Culture* 15:3 (1981), 112–118.

Harrison, Walter Lee (1980). *Out of Play—Baseball Fiction from Pulp to Art.* Unpublished doctoral dissertation. Davis, California: University of California at Davis, 1980.

Higgs, Robert. *The Unheroic Hero—A Study of the Athlete in Twentieth Century American Literature.* Unpublished doctoral dissertation. Knoxville: University of Tennessee, 1967.

Hye, Allen. "*Shoeless Joe* and the American Dream," *The Markham Review* 15 (1986), 56–59.

Knisley, Patrick Allen. *The Interior Diamond—Baseball in Twentieth Century American Poetry and Fiction.* Unpublished doctoral dissertation. Boulder, Colorado: University of Colorado, 1978.

Kudler, Harvey. *Bernard Malamud's "The Natural" and Other Oedipal Analogs in Baseball Fiction.* Unpublished doctoral dissertation. New York: St. Johns University, 1976.

Lass, Terry Russell. *Discoveries of Mark Harris and Henry Wiggen.* Unpublished doctoral dissertation. Columbia, Missouri: University of Missouri, 1986.

O'Connor, Gerry. "Bernard Malamud's *The Natural:* 'Or, The Worst There Ever Was in the Game'," *Arete: The Journal of Sport Literature* 3:2 (Spring 1986), 37–42.

O'Donnell, James. "A Short History of Literary Baseball," *Crosscurrents* (Washington Community College Humanities Association Yearbook) 7:1 (1988), 4–6.

Randall, Neil. "*Shoeless Joe:* Fantasy and the Humor of Fellow-Feeling," *Modern Fiction Studies* 33.1 (Spring 1987), 173–182.

Reynolds, Charles Dewey Hilles. *Baseball as the Material of Fiction.* Unpublished doctoral dissertation. Lincoln, Nebraska: The University of Nebraska, 1974.

Roberts, Frederic. "A Myth Grows in Brooklyn: On Urban Death, Resurrection, and the Brooklyn Dodgers," *Baseball History* 2:2 (Summer 1987), 4–26.

Rodgers, Bernard T., Jr. "*The Great American Novel* and 'The Great American Joke'," *Critique* 16:2 (1974), 12–29.

Saposnik, Irving S. "Homage to Clyde Kluttz or the Education of a Jewish Baseball Fan," *Journal of American Culture* 4:3 (Fall 1981), 58–65.

Schwartz, Richard Alan. "Postmodernist Baseball," *Modern Fiction Studies* 33.1 (Spring 1987), 135–149.

Shannon, Mike. *Diamond Classics: Essays on One Hundred of the Best Baseball Books Ever Published.* Jefferson, North Carolina: McFarland Publishers, 1989.

Shelton, Frank W. "Humor and Balance in Coover's *The Universal Baseball Association, Inc.*" *Critique* 17:1 (1975), 78–89.

Smith, Leverett T., Jr. "Versions of Defeat: Baseball Autobiographies," *Arete: The Journal of Sport Literature* 2:1 (Fall 1984), 141–158.

Smith, Leverett T., Jr. "More Versions of Defeat," *Arete: The Journal of Sport Literature* 5:1 (Fall 1987), 97–114.

Solomon, Eric. "Jews, Baseball, and the American Novel," *Arete: The Journal of Sport Literature* 1:2 (Spring 1984), 43–66.

Solomon, Eric. "The Bullpen of Her Mind: Women's Baseball Fiction and Sylvia Tennenbaum's *Rachel, The Rabbi's Wife*," *Arete: The Journal of Sport Literature* 3:1 (Fall 1985), 19–31.

Solomon, Eric. "Counter-Ethnicity and the Jewish–Black Baseball Novel: The Cases of Jerome Charyn and Jay Neugeboren," *Modern Fiction Studies* 33.1 (Spring 1987), 49–64.

Solomon, Eric. "Diamonds Are the Girls' Best Friends—A Review of *Things Invisible to See* by Nancy Willard and *In Shelly's Leg* by Sara Vogan," *American Book Review* 9:2 (March–April 1987), 10.

Solomon, Eric. "The Boy of Summer Grows Older: Roger Kahn and the Baseball Memoir," *Baseball History* 2:2 (Summer 1987), 27–47.

Stein, Harry. "Baseball on Their Minds—The Lure of the Diamond, the Pace of the Plot," *The New York Times Book Review* 40 (June 1, 1986), 9, 56.

Turner, Frederick W. "Myth Inside and Out: Malamud's *The Natural*," *Novel* 1:2 (1968), 133–139.

Umphlett, Wiley Lee. "The Black Man as Fictional Athlete: *Runner Mack,* the Sporting Myth, and the Failure of the American Dream," *Modern Fiction Studies* 33.1 (1987), 73–83.

Wallach, Jeffrey. "Game Without Limits—Review of *The Iowa Baseball Confederacy* by W. P. Kinsella and *Every Young Man's Dream* by Morry Frank," *American Book Review* 9:2 (March–April 1987), 18.

Wasserman, Earl R. "*The Natural:* Malamud's World Ceres," *Centennial Review of Arts and Sciences* 9:4 (1965), 438–460.

Wineapple, Brenda. "Robert Coover's Playing Fields," *Iowa Review* 10:3 (1979), 66–74.

I am deeply indebted to SABR members Jim O'Donnell and Ralph Graber, whose earlier bibliographical work has provided the backbone of fiction bibliographies catalogued here. Also to Leverett

"Terry" Smith, Jr., for commentaries and criticism, as well as for his extensive knowledge of baseball fiction. And finally, to Robbie Plapinger and to Andy McCue, for clearing up some of the deepest mysteries surrounding the entangled orphan genre of baseball's "who-done-it" mysteries.

This article originally appeared in slightly altered form in *The Minneapolis Review of Baseball* 9:1 (1990), 32–54. The author wishes to thank the editor (Steve Lehman) and publishers (Wm. C. Brown) of that journal for permission to reuse these materials in the present volume.

A Swing and a Myth

The Persistence of Baseball in the American Imagination

by Thomas L. Altherr

E very few years or so, some pundits predict demise for American baseball and even chortle about the prospect. According to the premature epitaph, baseball is too slow, too boring, too expensive (given the players' astronomical salaries), and too predictable. Or, conversely, the game lacks enough glitziness, violence, sex, and scoring to hold the public's attention. Others castigate baseball for its alleged militarism and tribalism, undue emphasis on competition, racist exclusion of blacks and other nonwhite people from key administrative positions, and sexism. Yet others blame baseball for the reverse. It's too tepid a game compared to football, they say, to make boys into real men. Bigots complain that nonwhites have stolen the game from whites. All in all, baseball seems destined to die out or devolve into a studio sport on cable television with devotees numbering no more than those who worship roller derby.

Far from disappearing from its preeminence as the national pastime, American baseball continues its hold on the American imagination. The populace is less rural in perspective and habitation each year, and yet baseball, celebrated for its supposed rural origins, remains popular. Last season major league franchises enjoyed overall successes at the ticket windows and over the airwaves, including some record-breaking totals in numbers and dollars. "Farm" teams, the official minor leagues and the ersatz ones, the college circuits, held steady. Little leagues, American Legion ball, and "littler" leagues for T-ball all attracted numerous participants, some too young even to appreciate the game. Aging baby boomers may have turned to baseball's cousin, softball, as insurance costs and injuries would plague adult baseball, but team and regional loyalties for baseball persists. Baseball books crowd the sports shelves in bookstores and baseball movies proliferate on the screen. Players continue to garner much press, even if for the wrong reasons, as Wade Boggs, Steve Garvey, and Pete Rose discovered. Fans sport replica vintage caps and shirts. Baseball nostalgia, especially cards, command rising prices. Even people who claim to dislike the sport repeat unblinkingly baseball's linguistic contributions to American English. Old-timers' games, "fantasy" camps and cruises, rotisserie leagues, and the rise of saber-metrics, an interest in the statistical side of the game, all attest to an American refusal to relegate baseball to the refuse heap of past amusements.

Perhaps there are some obvious reasons for this persistence of baseball in the American mind. The general increase in population could account for some absolute numerical rise in attendance, lis-tenership, and watchership. Faced with stiffer entertainment competi-tion, franchises have become more aggressive in attempting to attract fans to the parks. Cable transmission has allowed greater numbers of people to see baseball games at all hours of the day. The relative absence of dynasty teams in the mold of Yankee and Dodger squads of yore has raised hopes for formerly sodden franchises. With the excep-tions of Seattle and Texas, each major league franchise has won, or flirted with winning, its division during the twelve years since the last expansion. Fans may sour more easily when anticipated victories don't come regularly, but the bulk doesn't desert its teams. Of course, some long-standing losing teams owned devoted followerships, but the demonstrated "parity" within the leagues in recent years convinces more marginal fans that a pennant or Series appearance by the local stumblebums is not out of the realm of possibility.

The rise in amateur participation may likewise have some predict-able causes. Renewed emphases on competition and athletic achieve-ment in team form, somewhat suspect in certain circles during the 1960s and 1970s, may have brought more players out to the diamond in the 1980s. Vicarious identification with glamorized professional players must account for some of the motivation. Migration to warmer sunbelt climates has permitted more people to play longer seasons. The overall increase in recreation, paradoxical to the point that many Americans now play harder than they work, may have pushed more individuals onto teams. More girls and women play softball (a few play baseball) and thus may have developed a more thorough appre-ciation for and understanding of baseball. But, in less welcome ways, the reemergence of masculine-oriented national arrogance, expressed in movies like *Top Gun* and *Rambo,* may have resulted in more displays of machismo on the playing field.

Other explanations for baseball's popularity may be harder to ascertain. Regarding the sport's rural connections, there may be more confusion than clarity. As baseball historians such as Harold Seymour, David Voigt, Stephen Riess, Warren Goldstein, and Allen Guttmann have demonstrated, baseball was hardly exclusively rural.[1] Early commercialism necessitated the presence of a steady paying audience. Barnstorming tours were predictably less lucrative than the setting up of urban franchises. Small towns and rural regions still contribute their share to the player pool, but increasingly baseball has become an urban or suburban game. And yet rural images possess great appeal. Dizzy Dean is gone from the broadcast booth, but sportcasters still pay homage to rural rhetoric with well-seasoned cliches. Despite some neologisms such as "velocity" and "location," baseball's terminology remains old-timey. Writers label stadia as "green cathedrals," "emerald refuges," and other pastoral tropes. Inner-city and suburban kids put a pinch of chaw (or, let us pray, gum) between their cheeks and gums and rehearse other rural rhythms. Perhaps as with country music, which holds strong against urban-oriented rock 'n' roll, baseball has been part of a national nostalgia, a combined yearning for and dismissal of the rural past.

But then, baseball has been figuratively a game for all seasons, has meant different things at different times. For all of the commentators who have cheered the rural qualities of the sport, there have been those who said it matched the hustle and bustle of the rising cities. Early on, some reformers chastised players and spectators for idleness and dissipation. Others, however, such as Philadelphia intellectual Charles King Newcomb, rhapsodized about baseball as the gentlemanly game.[2] Demographics of internal mobility and immigration undercut that claim by the 1880s, as less-than-gentlemanly players came to dominate the game. This trend elicited contrary estimates, as some moralists pronounced the game vulgar once again, and others defended it as democratic, at least for whites. Early progressive businessmen sponsored the sport for recreational benefits for workers; others saw the requisite teamwork on the field as valuable for the shop or office. To yet other thinkers, baseball expressed the militaristic and the mechanical. As David Lamoreux suggested in a provocative article, post-Civil War enthusiasts tended to promote the sport as emblematic of military organization so important in the recent war and the churning machines at work in the industrial surge.[3] Similarly, Steven Gelber and Warren Goldstein argued that workers found in baseball a confirmation of their work ethic and patterns rather than an idyllic retreat from them.[4]

Into the twentieth century, many of these trends continued apace, but the further saturation of media coverage accentuated the importance of the game to Americans. Newspapers had devoted some attention to baseball regularly, but by the 1920s the sportswriters were shaping public opinion more and more. Radio networks brought the sound of the game to the hinterlands and the homebound more effectively. Regional loyalties for certain teams strengthened, as farmers and small-town residents tuned in the frequent broadcasts. New heroes seemed to have changed the game overnight, particularly Babe Ruth with his gargantuan exploits and stunning home run totals. Who could doubt the limits of wealth and stock market speculation when Ruth seemingly topped his marks each year? Even when much of the optimism foundered in the 1930s, baseball filled in as a welcome distraction from the Depression. President Franklin Roosevelt sensed the therapeutic themes of baseball so well that once the next world war broke out, he gave baseball owners the proverbial green light to bolster the national morale. Many a soldier and sailor hungered for scores from home as sort of a cultural lifeline to America.

Postwar years brought yet another new role for baseball. As a laboratory for racial integration, the sport threw players and fans into the tense experiment of introducing black and Hispanic players into the leagues. For racial minorities, baseball became sometimes an actual, more likely a symbolic, ticket to equality. In the late 1950s and early 1960s, league expansion and franchise moves to California shattered the old familiar eight-team circuits. After a period of some doldrums at the gate, baseball recovered its vibrancy in the 1970s. Domed stadia, designated hitters, artificial turf, flashier uniforms, and contract disputes greeted these new generations of fans, but the game survived. Purists howled about the changes, but all it took were a few breathless World Series, such as in 1969, 1972, and especially 1975, to return the faithful to the fold. Clearly, baseball was entrenched in the American sentiment, surviving competition from football and arguments against its values. Shooting forth greenly every spring, constant summer companion (except in 1981), habitual harvest of play-off and Series games in the fall, and even simmering throughout the hot stove sessions of winter, baseball satisfied Americans more than any of the other major sports could hope to do.

Some analysts have made much of baseball's capacity to distract people from the turbulence or monotony of everyday life. Baseball, they conjecture, has the right amount of space and whimsy and airiness to vent the most claustrophobic of frustrations and angers. This catharsis could occur communally or individually. Several historians have speculated that the Detroit Tigers' successful run to the pennant in the summer of 1968 saved that city from a measure of expected racial violence. Blacks and whites, so the assumption goes, deflected their resentments to root for the racially mixed team. Seven

years later, on a blustery April Friday in Fenway Park, this smoothing
of troubled waters reappeared concerning the Vietnam War. Three
teenagers, two girls and a boy, stood up for the national anthem. One
girl vehemently refused to sing, and the two girls launched into an
argument. That week the United States was going through the death
throes of the prolonged military commitment in southeast Asia. The
anthem reminded her of the senseless violence in the war, said the
protesting girl, but her friend maintained that patriotism alone man-
dated they sing. The dispute lingered on past the end of the song,
whereupon the boy overrode both of their cases with an appeal to
baseball. In dulcet New England tones, he shouted "Shaddup, this is
Fenway Pahhk! This is baseball!" The political moralist would hold
that he should have engaged in one of the ideological positions. And
perhaps he should have, and perhaps he did outside of the park. But
there was a certain certitude in his pronouncement, sturdy and reso-
lute in the face of political agony. Typically, though, the Red Sox
dropped the game, 11–8, as the Orioles' Lee May powered two home
runs, and nearly a third. The game never guarantees victory, but it
does offer reprieve from weighty rigors, sitting in the sanctuary of the
stadium, listening to a broadcast along an interstate, or catching a
game on cable.

In yet another wrinkle of interpretation, historian Christopher
Lasch has suggested that baseball's charm lies ideally in its insistence
on strict, formalized rituals for essentially no tangibly earthshaking
reasons. No one lives or dies *per se* because of a baseball game, but that
does not diminish its importance. Lasch argues that baseball, and
other sports, are most satisfying when the audience suspends disbelief
and accepts the mythic constructs of the psychodrama before them.
Far from being the opiate of the people, sports such as baseball
rehearse the archetypal patterns of life, but don't do so in a life-or-
death manner, as does warfare. In his essay, "The Degradation of
Sport" in *The Culture of Narcissism,* Lasch chides modern jaded spectators for equating the game too closely with life and for de-
mythologizing players. He lambastes the owners for trivializing and
overcommercializing the game.[5] Lasch scores many a telling point,
but even he underestimates the resiliency of baseball as a potent
source of myth. Boys may not be able to recite the statistics on the
reverse of baseball cards as much these days as they know the monetary value of the cards, but enough still imitate stars on the sandlots.
The sport may never escape some of the new superfluous theatrics,
mascots, and exploding scoreboards, but beneath the hucksterish
hoopla are the pitcher, the batter, the runner, the fielders, the um-

pires, the diamond, the outfield. Sports journalism may tell us too much about the meaner side of players, their shortcomings and feet of clay, but time and again, as players they transcend their mere mortal status and dazzle the fans with hits and plays that take their breath away once again.

Possibly accounting for baseball's long-standing appeal may be its historical propensity to generate mythology of enduring attraction. Every sport, to be sure, has its share of hoary heroes, legendary exploits, sagas of grandeur, and fluke occurrences that devotees revere and recite for years on end. Baseball, of them all, seems more steeped in mythology. Football can boast of its bruisers, boomers, and busters and electrifying "fantastic finishes." Similarly, basketball can point to its own magical moments. Baseball bests them both, having sustained a panoply of myths over a longer time. Football and basketball memories tend to have a greater currency loyally in the franchise city; an unexpected home run from a hobbling hero in the bottom of the ninth lights up the whole nation. Even the Baseball Hall of Fame reflects this texturing of baseball myth. Compared to several other halls of fame, which rely on more modern architecture, the red brick structure in Cooperstown exudes a dignity approaching the sacrosanct.

Baseball myths have persisted in various forms in the American mind: fleeting flicker-frame memories of players and events caught in folklore, iconography in the visual and plastic arts, musical and literary expressions. Often these types intertwine, as a novel relies on the folk memory of certain players or incidents. Or a painting memorializes a situation which may never have happened in "real" baseball. Photographs may take on a sort of luminosity of epiphanous quality over time. Characters from a novel become as familiar as the actual players. Baseball mythology, thus, may be as flexible as it is ingrained.

Almost every baseball fan is privy to a long list of mythologized personages, events, and images: "King" Kelly sliding; "Wee Willie" Keeler hittin' 'em where they weren't; Connie Mack on the end of the bench; Honus Wagner gobbling up another grounder; Ty Cobb filing his spikes; Christy Mathewson reaching back for more; Tinker to Evers to Chance; John McGraw hands on hips; Walter Johnson smoking all those strikes; Babe Ruth launching another home run and even "calling his shot" in the Series; Grover Alexander striking out Lazzeri; Lefty Grove toiling through another inning; Pepper Martin, Dizzy Dean, and the other Gashousers running wild; Carl Hubbell mowing down the All-Star lineup; Hack Wilson knocking in another run; Lou Gehrig bowing out the luckiest man alive; "Rapid Robert" Feller blazing it past another luckless batter; Dimaggio patrolling center field and streaking for fifty-six games in 1941; Ted Williams nailing down .406 and socking Sewell's blooper pitch to the stars; Stan the Man slapping another double; Warren Spahn plunging on to another win; Jackie Robinson frantic off third and burrowing under Berra to steal home; the Whiz Kids and the Miracle of Coogan's Bluff; Willie Mays, cap flying, catching up to Wertz's drive; Mickey and the Duke trading Series homers; Mazeroski in the bottom of the ninth; Maris whacking Number 61 for an asterisk; Whitey slipping in another slider; Koufax snapping off another curve; Frank Robinson homering in all the ballparks; Yaz bringing home the pennant almost singlehandedly; Bob Gibson falling away and bearing down; Tom Terrific and the Amazin' Mets; Brooks vacuuming up everything in Cincinnati; Clemente swinging at everything in sight; Johnny Bench redefining catching; the Mustache Gang in green and gold winning three in a row; Henry Aaron hammering Number 715; Pudge Fisk waving the fly fair in Fenway in the bottom of the twelfth; Mr. October watching the third dinger of the night sail out; Stargell windmilling his big bat; Carew and Brett hot in pursuit of .400; Rickey Henderson swiping another base chest-first; Ryan and Rocket exploding the ball plateward; Pete dropping in Number 4,192; Darryl driving the nail into the Red Sox coffin; the Wizard of Oz redefining shortstop; José Canseco pummeling the ball and pounding down the base paths; and, most recently, Kirk Gibson stroking The Home Run. And surely this list has left out any number of favorites.

What other sport's enthusiasts remember and rue so many failures and flukes? Baseball lore abounds with inopportune bad hops, bad calls, pitchers throwing seventh games on too little rest, stumbles, falls, gopher balls, and second guesses. Several flubs are famous to many a fan: Merkle's Boner, Snodgrass's Muff; the 1919 Black Sox and "Say it ain't so, Joe"; three Dodgers on third; Hank Gowdy's mask; Lombardi's snooze; Mickey Owen's missed third strike; Kubek taking a bad hop in the throat; Bernie Carbo, Elrod Hendricks, and Ken Burkhart in the weirdest home plate ballet ever; and Bill Buckner as The Human Croquet Wicket. What other game gives its goats a fond form of fame, as Ralph Branca, Ralph Terry, and Mike Torrez have found? Baseball, with its unpredictabilities, complexities, and chances for mental lapses, turns inglorious gaffes into epics of defeat.

Nor does baseball mythology reside only on the major league level. Minor leagues celebrate their own demigods: Luke Easter ricocheting drives off the scoreboard in Buffalo; Joe Bauman and his seventy-plus homer season in New Mexico; last season's Salt Lake City

Trappers and their winning streak. Before baseball's reintegration racially, the Negro Leagues furnished many worthies such as Satchel Paige, Josh Gibson, "Cool Papa" Bell, and others to whom even white fans have granted national mythic stature retroactively. On a more personal plane, many ex-players cherish a memory or two, maybe magnified by time into a triumph. In the early 1960s, a fourteen-year-old catcher thrust a hip into an onrushing runner, flipped him head over heels, and tagged him out before he fell on the plate. Or families carry along the legends. One tells of a grandfather as a promising player in southern Ohio whom locals swear could jump up in the air and still hit a home run, so strong was he. Of course, other family legends could be less glamorous. In the same family there was the great-uncle who ended a town ball game one day by trying to steal third base with his team down, 12–2.

Baseball has persisted in the national imagination in more concrete forms beyond these verbal or fleeting memories. The pastime has attracted packs of those writers and artists who traffick in myth. As James Mote's massive compendium, *Everything Baseball,* displays, there have been hundreds of baseball movies, television shows, plays, songs, paintings, sculptures, poems, and miscellaneous expressions all employing baseball as a major theme. Mote's book doesn't include folklore variant stories and photography, but his book indicates that baseball has had a major impact on the national imagination. Many of these artistic products would not merit top-drawer prizes, but the cumulative effect of so many baseball-oriented efforts signifies the continued appeal of the sport.[6]

In that shadowy area between fiction and nonfiction, baseball writers have flourished. Roger Angell, frequent contributor to *The New Yorker,* is perhaps the most noteworthy of a large group of erudite columnists who have turned to baseball not just for material, but for its instant communicability with the readership. Whether he writes player profiles or the yearly summation of the season, Angell delivers prose odes that capture the texture of the game anew. Who else has reminded us so brilliantly of baseball's greenness, its timelessness in revolt against temporality, its perfect geometry of perfect distances, its ballet of teamwork and individual exertion, its long settling out of averages and short runs which buck those figures? Individual readers might vote for Roger Kahn, Peter Gammons, Tom Boswell, or Ira Berkow.

Over into the realm of writing which is more avowedly fiction, writers have delved repeatedly into baseball motifs for fictive material. The several anthologies of baseball fiction available, the journal *Arete,* and The Society for American Baseball Research's *Review of Books* all testify to this literary predilection. In the last fifteen years alone, eighty or so novels claiming to be serious fiction have centered on baseball. Maybe the best of these have been W. P. Kinsella's magical flights in Iowa, but other readers may prefer personal favorites. Previous to that period, Bernard Malamud's *The Natural* (1952), Robert Coover's *The Universal Baseball Association, J. Henry Waugh, Prop.* (1969), and Philip Roth's *The Great American Novel* (1973) demonstrated the flexibilities of baseball myth. Malamud was quite self-conscious about his mythic elaboration of baseball: "During my first year at Oregon State, I wrote *The Natural,* begun before leaving New York City. Baseball had interested me, especially its comic aspects, but I wasn't able to write about the game until I transformed game into myth, via Jessie Weston's Percival legend with an assist by T. S. Eliot's 'The Waste Land,' plus the lives of several baseball players I had read, in particular Babe Ruth's and Bobby Feller's. The myth enriched the baseball lore as feats of magic transformed the game."[7] Well might Mark Harris, himself the author of a quadrilogy of excellent baseball novels, lament the lack of "sandlot" novels which take less lofty literary aim, but his commentary undercuts his point and reinforces the serious mythic intent in even his own novels: "Earnest people devoted to the salvation of novelists have long been moved to insist that baseball novels are not at all about baseball, that they are really about the grander themes of life, death, God, theology, art, morals, or that they are, at the very least, mythical representations of legendary America. A serious writer, they say, forsakes lowly baseball for symbolic heights."[8] Not every baseball novel must aspire to treat those abstruse topics, but the fact that many writers argue a serious connection between game and myth shows the mythic persuasiveness of baseball. As Debra Dagavarian has shown in her dissertation on juvenile baseball fiction, even those "sandlot" novels evinced contemporary societal values for younger audiences.[9]

Although fewer poets have offered poems on baseball compared to the novelists' barrage, there have been a surprising number of poetic attempts. Many fall into the category of doggerel. No one will ever mistake Ernest Thayer's "Casey at the Bat" for a national epic, but its narrative has touched the hearts of millions of Americans. More recently, however, several serious poets have plumbed baseball. A recent anthology of sports-related poems and a dissertation which devoted a chapter to baseball poetry indicate that baseball poetry has attained a measure of respectability. Perhaps the Donald Halls will continue to affirm the poetic possibilities of the game.[10] In terms of plays and Broadway productions, baseball has not engendered a significant body of theater. *Damn Yankees* had a respectable run in the 1950s and August Wilson's *Fences* showed the promise of baseball themes for theater, but overall the stage remains an untapped arena.

Hollywood renditions of baseball have rarely been box office blockbusters or major advances in cinematic technique. Sentimentality tended to mark many of the early films. But from time to time, baseball films such as *Bang the Drum Slowly* have risen above the lot. More recently, with *The Natural* in 1984, *Bull Durham* in 1988, and this season's *Field of Dreams*, films have gone beyond the formulaic boundaries and visualize baseball myth. In the first, Malamud's knight-errant hero, wicked sirens, angelic savior, and slimy owners came to life eerily and ethereally on the screen (if only to set the backdrop for Kirk Gibson four years later). The second opted for more rollicking, albeit sexist humor, and yet it, too, paid homage to baseball as a collection of enduring myths. Annie Savoy's baseball shrine may have been a tinge parodic, but in the last scene, the camera played lovingly over the artifacts, resting on the photograph of Thurman Munson, the late great catcher. The third dwelled on father and son relationships, but incorporated bushels of baseball lore in depicting Kinsella's Iowa-based fantasy.

Visual artists who work in paint and plastic materials have also kept up an interest in the pictorial aspects of the game. Aside from Thomas Eakins and William Morris Hunt, most serious painters did not choose baseball as a subject. Mostly Currier and Ives-type prints and Norman Rockwell-type paintings formed the bulk of baseball art, cementing the game nostalgically with the past. Recently, however, more artists have "discovered" baseball, as the works in *Diamonds Are Forever* affirm.[11] Photographers, too, have trained their lenses on the game for a long time, not just for journalistic purposes, but for artistic reasons as well. The wonderful collection of Charles Martin Conlon photographs in *The Sporting News* archives reveals the potential for art. Conlon, who photographed many major leaguers over the decades, was responsible for the famous shot of Ty Cobb sliding into third base, dust flying, nearly upending the spraddle-legged baseman, a photograph that "took itself," as the amazed cameraman pushed the button instinctively.[12] Recent assemblages like John Thorn's *A Game for All America* and the Hall of Fame Library's ongoing exhibits suggest photographers will continue this symbiosis with baseball in the future. Songwriters have done their share to immortalize baseball, as Mote's extensive chapter on baseball songs shows. Many of the songs have been of ephemeral quality, but occasionally a gem like "Take Me Out to the Ballgame" transcends the others. The only art which has lagged seriously behind the others has been television. With the exception of some hour-length baseball dramas, a baseball movie or two made for television, and a couple of abortive series like "Ball Four" and "Bay City Blues," baseball has been unable to break into that medium. But neither has any other major sport, so perhaps the medium resists dramatizing sports, except in live coverage.[13]

On its own, baseball probably has engendered a sufficient number of folkloristic characters who could rank with the pantheon of former demigods. "Mighty Casey" has attained roughly the same stature as Davy Crockett over the last hundred years. Last summer's centennial celebration of the poem and Frank Deford's delightful recreation, "Casey on the Loose," bespeak Casey's popularity.[14] One could argue that Babe Ruth, Ty Cobb, and a few others have become folklore personages dwarfing their actual persons.[15] On occasion, baseball lore and more traditional folklore will fuse. One pleasing example is Wyatt Blassingame's 1971 children's tale *John Henry and Paul Bunyan Play Baseball*. In this book, the heroes retain their revered capabilities from previous stories, but now have picked up baseball skills. Bunyan hits balls out of sight with tree trunk bats. John Henry, forerunner to Plimpton's Sidd Finch, pitches faster than anyone had ever seen. In the inevitable showdown, Bunyan lets two strikes pass, as did Casey, and then takes a mighty swing at the third. No one can find the ball, and the awestruck spectators surmise that Henry had burned up the ball, he threw it so fast, and Bunyan swinging equally fast, had burned up his tree trunk. Although the author ducks the issue of racial confrontation, the climax is every bit as satisfying as Roy Hobbs hitting the cover off the ball.[16]

As a generator of mythologies, baseball has had the ability to excite in ways even beyond the more obvious apotheosizing of national and local heroes. Wavering between restrictive rules and temporary riot, the game has allowed audiences to resolve, or at least envision, the contrary pulls of chaos and orderliness. Every fan knows the exquisite pleasure of witnessing an outburst of base-running or a relay to home to nail the sliding runner. Often such occurs after a protracted period of control, wherein the pitcher and fielders strive to retire the batters or those hitters keep up the grim business of protecting the plate. Then comes the hit or overthrow or the wild pitch or the stretched double, punctuating and puncturing the tension and sending the defense into a frantic scramble to restore tranquility.

Like myths of old (and newer ones), baseball has been an accessible, repetitive ritual demonstrating the human condition caught between entropy and stasis. The day may come when some militaristic sport like rollerball replaces the more genteel pleasures of baseball, but let us postpone that day as long as possible and gather around some hearth and recite who was the best there ever was.

Notes

1. Harold Seymour, *Baseball: The Early Years* (New York: Oxford University Press, 1960); David Q. Voigt, *American Baseball*, 3 vols. (University Park, PA: Pennsylvania State University Press, 1983); Steven A. Riess, *Touching Base: Professional Baseball and American Culture in the Progressive Era* (Westport, CT: Greenwood Press, 1980); Warren J. Goldstein, "Playing for Keeps: A History of American Baseball, 1857–1876," unpub. Ph.D. dissertation, Yale University, 1983; and Allen Guttmann, *From Ritual to Record: The Nature of Modern Sports* (New York: Columbia University Press, 1978) and Guttmann, *A Whole New Ball Game* (Chapel Hill: University of North Carolina Press, 1988).

2. Thomas L. Altherr, " 'The Most Summery, Bold, Free, & Spacious Game': Charles King Newcomb and Philadelphia Baseball, 1866–1871," *Pennsylvania History*, v. 52, n. 2 (April 1985), 69–85.

3. David Lamoreux, "Baseball in the Late Nineteenth Century: The Source of Its Appeal," *Journal of Popular Culture*, v. 11 (1977), 597–613.

4. Steven M. Gelber, "Working at Playing: The Culture of the Workplace and the Rise of Baseball," *Journal of Social History*, v. 16, n. 4 (1983), 3–22; Goldstein, "Playing for Keeps," *passim*.

5. Christopher Lasch, *The Culture of Narcissism* (New York: Norton, 1979), ch. 5.

6. James Mote, *Everything Baseball* (New York: Prentice Hall Press, 1989).

7. Bernard Malamud, quoted in Mark Harris, "Bring Back That Old Sandlot Novel," *New York Times Book Review*, October 16, 1988, 45.

8. *Ibid.*, 1.

9. Debra Dagavarian, "A Descriptive Analysis of Baseball Fiction in Children's Periodicals: 1880–1950," unpub. Ed.D. dissertation, Rutgers University, 1987.

10. Emilie Buchwald and Ruth Boston, eds., *This Sporting Life: Contemporary American Poems About Sports and Games* (Minneapolis: Milkweed Editions, 1987); Patrick Allen Knisley, "The Interior Diamond: Baseball in Twentieth Century American Poetry and Fiction," unpub. Ph.D. dissertation, University of Colorado at Boulder, 1978.

11. Peter H. Gordon, Sydney Waller, and Paul Weinman, eds., *Diamonds Are Forever: Artists and Writers on Baseball* (San Francisco: Chronicle Books, 1987).

12. See the sampling of Conlon's photographs in *Baseball Immortals, 1905–1935* (St. Louis: The Sporting News, 1984); I am indebted to Dr. Steven Gietschier, archivist at *The Sporting News*, for information about Conlon and the Cobb photograph.

13. Mote, *Everything Baseball*, chs. 4 and 20.

14. Frank Deford, *Casey on the Loose* (New York: Viking, 1988).

15. Francis P. Bowles makes similar argument in his dissertation, "America at Bat: The Baseball Hero in Life and Letters," University of New Mexico, 1980.

16. Wyatt Blassingame, *John Henry and Paul Bunyan Play Baseball* (Champaign, IL: Garrard Publishing Co., 1971).

The Grand Game of Baseball: Baseball as Art—The Art of Baseball*

by Shelly Mehlman Dinhofer

Baseball, the great American national pastime, is a straightforward, lively game strenuously played in the warmth of the summer sun. It is a sandlot game in quiet backwaters, a game of stickball on the hard pavements of busy urban streets, a spectator sport in vast impersonal arenas. The game requires individual ingenuity and team interaction and has come to symbolize initiative, competition, and the enterprising, combative spirit of commercial success.

This vital, exciting, ever-evolving sport has enabled each succeeding generation to discover and establish its own cultural identity within the framework of the American experience. Its literary scope is impressive: novels, short stories, essays, poetry, and plays. Almost everyone who writes has written at some time about baseball. The English language has been expanded through baseball's special vernacular. Sportswriters provide the descriptive analyses; photographers, the visual documentation. Songs are written with fluid grace and staccato beat. "Take Me Out to the Ball Game" still vies with the "Star Spangled Banner" for first place. It is all a cultural feast for the baseball public.

The art of baseball occupies a separate place in the spectrum of cultural diversity. It brings forward in timeless imprint the artist's interpretation of the color and form, the physical interaction, the sheer energy of the game.

Baseball supplied nineteenth century American artists with provocative themes and icons that reflected the American experience. They were intrigued by its dramatic action and colorful atmosphere, its humor and frustration, and especially by the hordes of spectators, sometimes raucous and quarrelsome but more often simply content to be out in the summer sun, expressing fidelity to their team. The artists themselves were not simply passive viewers, removed from the tumult. Some were participants, others proved to be among baseball's foremost fans and most acute observers. With perception and esthetic judgment, they placed the game within the context of visual and cultural history.

*Many of the art works cited in this contribution can be found in the author's recently published book, *The Art of Baseball* (Harmony Books, 1990).

Portraiture provided financial support for professional and itinerant artists alike. A formal portrait by an unknown painter, *Boy with Ball and Bat* (1844), is a straightforward presentation of a solemn youngster, meticulously clothed, holding the necessary gear of the game. Undoubtedly a commission, the painting is a competent, disciplined portrayal. It is reflective of the concern for childhood and its accoutrements which prevailed at that time, but the firm reality of ball and bat, the determined demeanor, add a further dimension.

Still life paintings with their use of everyday objects lent an intimate, decorative touch to the warmth and intimacy of home and family life. An idealized evocation of youth's passage is David Gilmour Blythe's (1815–1865) *Youth* (1865). Included among the appurtenances of youth are a primer, a pocketknife, marbles, a firecracker, and, centrally focused, a baseball, larger than the other objects, a plausible symbol of play. In the background the United States Capitol dome emerges from the mist, a reflection of hope and ambition. O. W. Southard's (n.d.) *Still Life With Bat and Ball* (c.1895) juxtaposes a roustabout's crushed hat and a partially eaten banana with the bat and ball, evoking a more carefree, informal image.

Baseball's imagery was a handy political weapon, particularly for those directly involved in the power plays and civil chaos of the 1860s. The nuances were easily understood and appreciated. In response to the vitriolic dialogues and debates, the lithography firm of Currier and Ives produced an inexpensive print for mass distribution, *The National Game . . . Three Outs and One Run . . . Abraham Winning the Ball . . . (1860)*. The four presidential candidates, Abraham Lincoln, John Bell, Stephen Douglas, and John C. Breckenridge, were depicted as baseball players espousing the usual election year rhetoric. Its candor was well received.

The art of illustration developed dramatically during the years of the Civil War. Illustrators visited the scattered war fronts, creating sometimes poignant, sometimes horrific images of death and destruction. Otto Boetticher (b. about 1816—died after 1864), however, provided a leitmotif. Incarcerated in a Confederate prisoner of war camp, he portrayed a participatory activity, baseball, in his lithograph, *Union Prisoners at Salisbury, N.C.* (1863). The game is spirited and engrossing. Some spectators are watching intently; others are just lounging about. The peaceful village is seen just beyond the picket fence. It's a civilized scene and an excellent propaganda ploy for the Confederacy.

With the war over, the Industrial Revolution continued apace, expanding the middle class base. The game of baseball proceeded to regain its momentum as the premier American sport. Artists who could afford to do so were off absorbing European culture. Some enthusiasts remained abroad as expatriates; others eagerly returned to the American environment.

Thomas Eakins (1844–1916) is notable for effectively adapting the rigors of the academic studio to his own individual style. He studied in Paris with the highly acclaimed neoclassicist Jean-Leon Gérôme for three years, mastering his formal technique and factual precision. Eakins returned to Philadelphia with a significant interest in figure studies: figures in motion, engaged in the expressive performance of sporting events. Although he depicted boxers, scullers, and swimmers, *Baseball Players Practicing* (1875) is his unique depiction of baseball. The work is deceptively simple, concerned with the immediacy of a tense moment in the game. The stances of the players are rigid with anticipation, an urgency and suspense left forever unresolved. There is an airiness, an infusion of light which removes it from the academic formula. True to his insistence on accuracy, Eakins identified the Philadelphia Athletics as the club involved.

William Morris Hunt (1824–1879), another "American abroad," returned with a decidedly different perspective, a result of his studies with Jean-Francois Millet and the French Barbizon school. *The Ball Players* (1877), three men playing ball in an open field, captures the elusive mood and spirit of the game in true Barbizon perspective, leaving the details muted and indistinct.

While American artists were developing richer esthetic values, they continued to experiment with baseball imagery. John La Farge (1835–1910), a student of Hunt's, developed his own neoclassical vocabulary. His interests were enhanced by travels to the Orient and the South Seas. An intelligent, facile painter, La Farge combined the mythic grandeur of the ideal and the solid respectability of the representational scene. *Standing Dance Representing the Game of Ball* (1890–91) depicts classical figures playing baseball in an idyllic South Seas environment.

The strongest, most representative baseball figure of this period is Douglas Tilden's (1860–1935) bronze sculpture *The Baseball Player* (1890). An avid sports fan and college athlete, Tilden understood the importance of the game to the American psyche. The player's stance, left arm bent across the chest, upper torso thrust forward, accentuates the illusion of immediate action. Though based on classical canons of balance and weight, the figure epitomizes the idealized hero so relevant to his times. The original life-size work was exhibited in the Paris salon of 1890 and at San Francisco's Art Loan Exhibition of European

Masters the following year. Today, it is on permanent display in Golden Gate National Park, the donation of a private collector. In response to public demand, reduced replicas were produced by the original Paris foundry. One of these replicas is currently in the collection of the National Baseball Hall of Fame and Museum, Cooperstown, New York.

Artists used baseball's eclectic viewpoint to explore other stylistic areas. The sentimental, moral tone of genre painting with its pretty settings and happily engaged people appealed to an affluent, status-conscious middle class. The true reflections of the time, social displacement and economic inequity, were not considered appropriate themes for household decoration. John George Brown (1831–1913), one of the more influential genre painters, was in great demand. His *Put It There* (n.d.) portrays a young, ragged urchin pounding his mitt and grinning malevolently, while awaiting the ball. Inexpensive mass-produced chromolithographs and other prints of his work attest to Brown's remarkable popularity.

By the beginning of the twentieth century, the harsh reality of the industrial landscape was clearly apparent. The active, vibrant, visually exciting city life was on the teeming streets. European art's academic impact was diminishing and, in reaction, a purely American dynamic emerged, American Realism.

In Philadelphia, a group of newspaper illustrators, all of whom worked for the *Philadelphia Press,* became the nucleus of what has euphemistically been termed the Ashcan School. They painted the raw street scenes, the rowdy optimistic enthusiasm of city dwellers. Robert Henri (1865–1929) was their leader and teacher. Among his devoted adherents was George Luks (1866–1933), a rambunctious, outspoken man who worked at an easel, visited saloons and played ball, all with similarly ferocious intent. In an affectionate cartoon, *George Luks Playing Baseball* (1904) Henri portrayed Luks as paunchy and unkempt, but grinning broadly and anything but docile as he prepared to toss a baseball.

Attracted as Henri and his group were to dark-toned palettes, there were differences in approach; Luks's *Boy With Baseball* (c.1925) emerges fresh faced and cheerful from a somber backdrop, his bright pink cheeks a startling contrast. A baseball cap is turned rakishly around on his head and his baseball is carefully placed on the settee beside him, a provocative reminder of the out-of-doors.

The most notable of the second-generation realists, George Bellows (1882–1925), played competitive baseball in high school and college. He was a successful semiprofessional summer player when the Cincinnati Reds offered him a contract. Although the offer was sorely tempting, he decided that the heady art world of New York with its open, challenging atmosphere would provide the esthetic stimulation he required. He joined Henri's group, responding to the city with his own inimitable scenes of graphic action, boxers in the heat of battle, swimmers diving off the sweltering piers into the fetid East River and croquet players in the park. His painting was far removed from the ideal; reality was the dominating force. The baseball fans in his charcoal drawing *Take Him Out* (1906) are giving vent to their frustrations naturally and with unabashed vengeance, mouths agape, teeth bared, bodies in twisted tension.

There were others who saw the fan-filled stands as models of decorum and good taste. In *Everybody Up—Seventh Inning Stretch* (1913), Charles Dana Gibson's (1855–1919) well-bred threesome could just as easily have emerged from a box at the opera as from their stadium seats.

The growing ethnic diversity of the urban population persuaded artists to portray the inherent differences with sympathy as well as caricature. Maurice Sievan (1898–1981) drew his *Newsboy* (1914) racing down a tenement-lined street, holding aloft a newspaper which proclaimed the "Giants Win," as two elderly Jewish men in customary dress look on indulgently.

Although paintings of black ball players and spectators were rare, an unknown artist conceived a beautifully structured naive painting of an all-black baseball team in the midst of a suspenseful action. That the artist was not conversant with traditional composition and technique is clear, yet the painting conveys its own sense of immediacy. The numbered jerseys on the players indicate a 1920s time frame; however, the women's fashionable clothing appears to be of an earlier vintage.

As the twentieth century progressed, the expansion of cities, unexpected population growth and environmental disorder challenged urban life. Buildings soared, darkening the narrow streets. The speed and noise, the sheer nervous energy of the machine age became the dominant elements.

James Daugherty (1890–1974) was influenced by the Italian Futurists who painted the exploding city in whirling fragments and colors. His gouache *Three Base Hit* (1914) was reproduced in the *New York Herald* as *Futurist Picture of the Opening Game* and analyzed by the artist as follows: ". . . This is not a picture of a baseball game. It is a representation of the various sensations of the onlooker. The pitcher whirls about, a confusion of head, arms and legs. The ball flashes across the diamond in curves that make make a snake look like a curtain rod. The batter swings the stick in flashing semicircles, driving the ball like a comet over the first baseman's reach into the field. The runners tear around the diamond in a hurricane of flying legs and arms. The ball comes skyrocketing back from the field to the third baseman's mitt as he fails to block a famous slide. One side of the grandstand is a crazy quilt of waving hats and yelling mouths; on the other side the fans present a checkerboard of gloom—the losing bets . . ."

Modernist experimentation presaged an exultant optimism, a desire, finally realized, to break the bonds of tradition. Vaclav Vytlacil (1892–1984), a native New Yorker, had followed the time worn path to Paris and then to Munich where he studied with the innovator of nonobjective art, Hans Hoffmann. He brought back a highly intellectual scheme, at variance with the prevailing realist viewpoints. The figures depicted in Vytlacil's *Baseball Player* (1932) are featureless and impersonal, generating a strong visceral excitement without the ease of identification.

The diverse, highly individual styles of American modernism were based on personal insights as well as the determination to be independent of conformist values. The quality of John Marin's (1870–1953) drawing with its dynamic energy and staccato line reflected a continuing homage to urban New York and rural Maine. His vistas are encapsulated, engulfed in patterns and designs. Marin's vision remained constant for five decades. His pastel *Baseball* (1953) was completed the year he died. It depicts an elongated figure sliding desperately towards home plate. He is tagged unceremoniously in a flash of abstracted action. Perhaps he is safe; perhaps not. The outcome appears beside the point. It is the sheer audacity of the play that generates the excitement surrounding it.

The stock market disintegrated in 1929, bringing to a sudden, shuddering halt the growth and vitality of the much-heralded Industrial Age. Artists, in concert with many others, had been set adrift, left destitute, without recourse to their customary private patronage or useful employment. The government channeled its subsidies to them through relief agencies such as the Federal Arts Project of the Works Progress Administration. These projects attempted to make art a stronger, more recognizable factor in American daily life. Content and style were as diverse as the artists themselves, and as contradictory as the time. There were the realists, the social realists, the American Scene painters, and the abstract artists, all vying for public approval.

In the midst of economic disaster, baseball persisted, as much an escape valve as entertainment. The government built baseball parks as part of the public works projects and endowed them with the latest in modern technology. Baseball was the great leveler. From the bleachers to the boxes, fans, rooting for the home team, provided the unifying force. Artists understood that baseball represented American strength and determination, that it was a counteraction to the despair and inertia of the depression.

Morris Kantor's (1896–1974) work is clearly reflective of the regionalism of American Scene painting. The setting for *Baseball at Night* (1934) is a small town ballpark. The pitcher is the focus, his body distorted in the rhythmical contortion of the windup. The batter stands ready; the fielders are at attention. Seated on wooden benches, the audience appears relaxed and attentive. It is a study suspended in time. In contrast, Arnold Friedman's (1879–1946) *World Series* (undated, but privately acquired in 1938) is played in a wide, airy space with few specifics. The viewer is an active participant, placed amid the spectators in the crowded stands. Removed from the socioeconomic morass, it demonstrates the people's capacity for enjoyment even in the most difficult of times.

The social realists were the most politically involved, regarding the American scene painters' romantic visions with disdain. They were interested primarily in reaching a mass audience, influencing its thinking and effectuating change. Philip Evergood (1901–1973) epitomized their radical orientation. His work was an odd mixture of surrealism and narration. His simply outlined, detached figures populated a landscape heavy with detail. *The Early Youth of Babe Ruth* (1939) presents an allegorical interpretation of the American dream of success. The two cartoonlike images of the "Babe" in the foreground look back at a personal history, the lush farmland, the amusement areas of his native Baltimore, and the blue waters of Chesapeake Bay. The vista reflects his past; it is a narrative with definition.

Ben Shahn (1898–1969) had the rare ability to combine topical social issues with a sensitive humanism. His *Vacant Lot* (1939) portrays the loneliness of life in the poverty-ridden, impersonal city. A small boy swings a bat disconsolately as he walks slowly toward the corner of a rubble-strewn lot, confronted by the daunting presence of a seemingly endless brick wall. The joy of youthful play is paralyzed by the isolating environment.

Even within the confines of Social Realism, artists found ways of developing their own historical or personal perspectives. Jacob Lawrence (b.1917) depicted the black experience with compassion and understanding. His organized narrative paintings define the essence of living in the urban ghettos. *Strike* (1949) was painted two years after Jackie Robinson joined the Brooklyn Dodgers and one year after the Cleveland Indians put the legendary pitcher, Satchel Paige, on their roster. The batter, central to the action, has swung wide of the mark; only his single visible eye mirrors his frustration. The next man is up, kneeling in expectation. Vendors hawk their wares in the stands. The faces of the fans are featureless, their excitement generated by the intricacy and boldness of the pictorial arrangement.

The years of World War II were chaotic and disruptive, a time of extreme personal anxiety tempered by a universal dedication. Artists were pressed into service along with everyone else. They were foot soldiers and seamen, observer-illustrators and war correspondents. Artist-correspondent Edward Laning (1908–1981) worked for *Life* magazine, recording with meticulous detail the grinding battles for supremacy on Italy's difficult terrain. Actually, Laning had started his career as a modernist, but quickly became absorbed in the vibrant life around his mid-New York City studio, recreating the honky-tonk atmosphere, the teeming tenements, the day-into-night street life of his immediate neighborhood. His painting *Saturday Afternoon at Sportsman's Park* (1944) is a well learned lesson in reportage. The St. Louis Cardinals and the St. Louis Browns were battling for the first World Series championship to be played in its entirety west of the Mississippi River. Sportsman's Park was filled to the rafters with rapturous fans. Laning's painting expresses the intensity of their involvement. The wildly gesticulating fans have risen to their feet, their disproportionately large dark-toned figures almost obscuring the distant playing field. The painting is explicit, accurate in detail, but its expressive quality signifies a departure for the customarily detached Laning.

With the war over and the professionals returning to the field of play, baseball as big business became a reality. Franchises were developed. The south and west beckoned, wooing the business interests with seductive offers of giant stadiums and vast audiences.

The powerhouse Fifties were epitomized by the blockbuster Brooklyn Dodger team and the formidable New York Yankees. Brooklyn had always been a baseball town. In the mid-nineteenth century, the city of Brooklyn's rural character, its hospitable green and open terrain, contributed to its focal position in the development of the national game. It had spawned more than seventy teams by 1858. In 1913, Charlie Ebbets built a quintessential modern ballpark of concrete and steel. He situated it in a confluence of urban traffic patterns and made access easy for everyone.

The Brooklyn Dodgers were painted and drawn, illustrated, caricatured, and photographed. They symbolized the underdog overcoming great odds and achieving the farthest dream, the "Bums" making it after all. Their logo was Willard Mullin's (1902–1978) jaunty *Brooklyn Bum* (n.d.), down on his luck, with ragged clothing and half-shod feet, but, nevertheless, cheerfully swinging a bat and flicking a cigar ash as he strode along.

For many artists, portrayals of the players and the excitement they generated were drawn from memories of childhood or from history. Elaine de Kooning (1920–1989) did a quick study, probably on site, of *Campy at the Plate* (1953). The figures are spare and faceless, but the easy, open brushwork and splendid light enliven the image of a successful turn at bat. David Levine (b. 1926), on the other hand, remembers himself as one with the throng in the bleachers in his painting *Crowd at Ebbets Field* (c. 1960). He portrays an unusually dejected gathering of fans, signifying an expected Dodgers loss. The artist has identified these fans individually and with understanding while emphasizing their special quality: total empathy with the players on the field.

And then there are those who think of the history of an era as in Lance Richbourg's (b. 1938) *Jackie Robinson* (1988). Robinson's strong stance and the impending action provide the focus. The expertise and the excitement are with the player himself. Richbourg's shock of surrounding shades of red and the mottled paint surface enhance the gritty drama of the scene, lending it an immediacy that belies the fact that more than thirty years have passed.

Photo-realist Andy Jurinko (b. 1939) reproduced, in mammoth scale, an original photograph of the power lineup: Gil Hodges (first base), Roy Campanella (catcher), Duke Snider (center field), and Carl Furillo (right field), in his painting *Dodger Lumber '54* (1985). The players are relaxed as they smile benignly into the camera, caught in the time warp of the Fifties.

The unthinkable occurred in 1958. The Dodgers actually left Brooklyn for the smog-filled air of Los Angeles, and Walter O'Malley has never been forgotten or forgiven.

The Sixties was a decade of contrasts. Excess and availability were the bywords. Everything was larger than life-size. Cars, buildings, discotheques, and day-glo colors were everywhere. This was the atmosphere that provided the basis for an art movement that maintained a detached, uncritical view of the American environment. Named for populist attitudes, it was dubbed Pop Art. Everyday objects achieved a new monumentality: beer cans and hamburgers, lipstick holders and baseball bats. Narrative comic strips were reproduced intact. It was art out of mundane matter and it was inevitable that the images of the American national pastime would be worthy of inclusion.

Roy Lichtenstein's (b. 1923) images were derived from comic strip characters and newspaper photographs. As in many of his works, *Baseball Manager* (1963) may well have been screened directly onto the canvas, the Ben Day dots carefully overpainted. The brush strokes are bold and black with shadows establishing the outline and facial contours. The image is set flat on the canvas, totally depersonalized. The compositional elements give the picture weight, the recognition provides the pleasure.

The transition from Abstract Expressionism's diffusion of form and laid-on brush work to Pop Art's concrete images is overt in Robert Rauschenburg's (b. 1925) *Canto XXIX: Illustration for Dante's 'Inferno'*, (1959–60). The centered vision of purgatory is clearly delineated, but the umpire and the baseballs at the outer edges suggest an alternative plan of escape.

If the marketplace was the art palace of the Sixties, its entrepreneur was Andy Warhol (1928–1987). Warhol understood the public's passion for commonplace material objects and titillating images. He reproduced Brillo boxes and Campbell soup cans, pictures of celebrities and catastrophes. His work represents the narrative history of an age of excess. *Baseball* (1962), his first silkscreen print, repeats in series a grainy newspaper image of Roger Maris at bat. Each picture frame is forced into the next; the figures are whole or slightly cropped, projecting an action in progress.

Pop Art's appeal was national in scope. Wayne Thiebaud (b. 1920), a California artist, painted beautifully composed images of sustenance: nourishing staples and junk food, and pictures of pleasure: Mickey Mouse and marbles. His *Hats* (1988) depicts row after glittering row of baseball caps. Painted in bright primary colors, they are accorded an exceptional presence.

The English Pop Art movement was also characterized by the strength of its desire for material values. Juxtaposing multiple images, real everyday objects, and explanatory writing, the works were directed toward mass communication, a recapitulation of the known. Although an American, Richard Merkin (b. 1938) relates closely to the English penchant for providing a wealth of information in non-traditional spatial relationships, his huge mixed-media painting *Kirby Higbe (22–9), Whit Wyatt (22–10) and the Pitching Staff of the National League Champion Brooklyn Dodgers, 1941 Minus Tamulis* (1967) is evidence of the artist's desire to cover as completely as possible a comprehensive version of an event. He uses photographs, portraits, language and topical allusions to Brooklyn's Prospect Park and Flatbush Avenue, and to spring training amid the palm trees of baseball-crazy Cuba. It all makes sense and is certainly more entertaining than a newspaper box score.

An American studying in London, R. B. Kitaj (b. 1932) was influential in the development of English Pop Art. He moved, however, from the recognizable to the abstract, creating puzzles for the viewer to solve. *Upon Never Having Seen Koufax Pitch* (1967) is a color field painting, totally abstracted, with only a small square attached containing the words of the title. In contrast to Merkin, it is a minimal assemblage with the barest of facts; but the information it provides is inescapable. Sandy Koufax, the great Los Angeles Dodger pitcher, played his last season in 1966 and would not pitch again.

Contemporary artists have developed their own perimeters and critics have offered new stylistic definitions: construction, minimalism, neoexpressionism, pattern painting, naturalism. With the open exchange of creative concepts, the educational input of the artists themselves, and the availability and diversity of their works, a visual dynamic of remarkable intensity has been added to the public awareness. Artists have joined athletes in superstar status and acclaim.

Still-life painter Lisa Dinhofer (b. 1952) brings the implements of outdoor game playing indoors for her painting *Spring Street Hardball* (1988). The configurations of objects, set on antique lace and silk, communicate the enjoyment of leisure activity and the intrinsic beauty of the ordinary tools of the games, so often disregarded. Dinhofer moves back and forth in time harmoniously, creating different sequences and analogies. There are keepsakes and treasures, those welcome repositories of memories, and there are the vivid reflections of the future: baseballs, scuffed and brand-new, commemorative baseballs of silver and crystal, marbles, a tennis ball and a fortune teller's crystal ball, symbolic evocations of the past and the future. Seen in historical perspective, the lush viewpoint of nineteenth century still-life painting is evident; however, the hard edges and conceptual arrangements clearly relate to today's movement toward perceptual realism.

Granted the wide ranging styles, artists feel a freedom to explore areas other than those with which the major body of their work has been identified. Ralph Goings (b. 1928) is considered a photo-realist, a detached observer, utilizing the emotionless clarity of a camera lens to capture the very ordinary centers of everyday living. The expressive quality of his watercolor *Baseball* (1988) is a departure. Although a known instrument of lively play, the baseball is accorded a singular monumentality. It is isolated and out of context, but nevertheless retains its own character and sense of purpose.

The carefully crafted baseball, pedestrian as it may seem, is accorded an esthetic place in the iconography of the game. Ernest Trova (b. 1927) set a single brand new unscuffed ball off center on a dead black backdrop and let it hang in space for his painting, *Baseball* (c. 1960). Far from signifying isolation, it stands out as an object of force.

The relationship of industrial matter to the development of an image is the focus of Donald Sultan's (b. 1951) technical experiments and his tribute to this mechanistic age. Sultan glues linoleum tiles to wood, surfaces them with tar and uses industrial tools to create the figurative outlines. *Baseball and Bat* (1981) is set in an opaque ground. The bat is flattened against the heavy backdrop so that the lines where the tiles join appear as cross-hatchings on its face. A simple penciled arc signifies the place where ball and bat met, conceptually. The ball's slow movement is that of a floating moon across a black eternity.

In art as in baseball, illusion, myth and reality coexist in grand theatrical style and in personal introspection. Art and baseball remain the most exciting playgrounds of the American imagination.

Out of Left Field

Baseball and American Idiom

by Maggi E. Sokolik

I. Introduction

The genesis of baseball idiom in the U.S. has been documented as early as the first organized games in the 19th century. In fact, in the year 1913, there was a heated public discussion concerning the proper place of baseball "lingo." It seems a certain Professor McClintock of Chicago, now infamous for his interpretations of baseball, was calling for the total abolition of "baseball language" from American English. This call met with heated reaction. For example, from the Charleston *News and Courier:*

> The injury which is now proposed is the abolition of the language of baseball. This, as all the world knows, is a distinctive and peculiar tongue. It is not English. It is not precisely slang. It is a strange patois, full of idiomatic eccentricities, rich in catch phrases and technical terms, wonderfully expressive and in the highest degree flexible.

It finished on the note, "Long may the lingo live!" And from *The Washington Post:*

> [Professor McClintock] is quite off his base in knocking the use of slang. . . . The slang of today is the purest English tomorrow.

As we know now, not only did the baseball lingo not disappear, but much of it, as predicted by the *Washington Post* editorialist, has become an integral part of everyday American speech; metaphor that seems to have become a necessary part of our expressive powers, filling a gap in our language. Thus, many of us speak of *ballpark figures* in our business negotiations, take a *raincheck* for a missed dinner date, or, like the erstwhile Professor McClintock, have a few notions that are simply *off-base.*

In the discussion that follows, I will examine baseball idiom and the concept of metaphor and its relationship to American culture. In particular, I will discuss the primacy of baseball metaphor over that of other sports. In addition, I will look at how baseball metaphor has become a conventionalized, or standard, part of American idiom.[1] Finally, the discussion will turn to how this body of metaphor shapes and defines American life. As a sidebar, I will also take a very brief look at the language of baseball in three countries relatively new to the sport: Japan, Korea, and Italy, and at how baseball is affecting their languages.

II. Metaphor

The standard definition of the word metaphor is "a word or phrase applied to an object or concept that it does not literally denote in order to suggest comparison with another object or concept" (Ortony 1980:69). In other words, it is one image used to describe another. In order to understand metaphor, one must understand the elements being linked in it. Furthermore, one must comprehend the points of similarity between the two elements linked by metaphor. As pointed out by Quinn and Holland:

> Metaphors are extended, not willy-nilly from any domain to any other, but in closely structured ways. . . . The classes from which speakers select metaphors they consider to be appropriate are those that capture aspects of the simplified world and the prototypical events unfolding in this world, constituted by the cultural model. (Quinn & Holland, 1987:30)

The components of the basic metaphor have been variously named, but the most commonly used terms for these parts are the topic, vehicle, and ground. Take, for example, the following metaphor (from baseball, of course): "My sister Kate is a real screwball." The topic is the thing being described, that is, "my sister Kate"; the vehicle is the phrase used to describe the topic, here "a real screwball"; and the ground is the semantic basis for the metaphor, that is, the more literal sense of the phrase, here "my sister is quite eccentric."

Metaphor use can be classified into two basic types: *novel* and *conventionalized*. Novel metaphors are those created by the speaker for a particular use, either poetic or simply for more expressive power. These are metaphors in that they draw the requisite connection between vehicle and topic, but in a way not recognized as part of everyday idiom. For example, the recent quip "George Bush was born on third base, but thinks he hit a triple," is a novel use of baseball imagery to metaphorically portray a political opinion. The image created is clear, although there is no conventional metaphor "to be born on third base."

Conventional metaphors are defined as the types of metaphor that are "automatic, unconscious, and effortless" (Lakoff & Turner, 1989:112), and thus depend crucially on shared cultural knowledge. There are numerous examples of conventional baseball metaphors, many of which will be dealt with a little later in this chapter. But, for illustrative purposes, if I use the phrase, "My brother is a southpaw," you will understand that my brother is left-handed, without having to resort to knowledge about the orientation of baseball diamonds such that a pitcher's left arm pointed south, resulting in left-handed pitchers, and then left-handed people in general, being called southpaws. In fact, by virtue of having been conventionalized, it is unlikely that anyone besides the sports trivia buff would even have this knowledge to rely upon.

Thus, we see that metaphors can not only describe a topic in a new way, and convey the speaker's attitude or position in relation to it, but also express the more culturally determined attitudes in a conventionalized way. In addition, our conventional ways of talking about a subject may mask metaphors we are not even conscious of.

Conventionalization of metaphors may come about as a result of a cognitive tendency toward developing "image schemata" (Lakoff & Turner, 1989). An image schema is a knowledge structure that allows us to think about abstract ideas using the imagery of more concrete, visual entities. Thus, through metaphor, we can conceptualize the somewhat abstract notion of time in terms of innings, in the terms "to get one's innings in" or to "be in the final inning." As Lakoff and Turner point out, once a schema is learned, we do not have to relearn it (Lakoff & Turner, 1989:62); we can add to it, subtract from it, or reshape it in relevant ways, but the superstructure will still remain, shaping and organizing our perceptions of the world.

Metaphor, when conventionalized, or as part of an image schema, can thus be seen as a linguistic and cultural device used to describe, define, and limit the world we live in. That is, it represents a way to impute order to a world that may be chaotic without it (Quinn & Holland, 1987:3). In this sense, metaphor exists not merely in the words we use, but in our very conceptions of things (Lakoff & Johnson, 1980; Winner, 1988). This fact led Lakoff and Turner to state that "to study metaphor is to be confronted with hidden aspects of one's own mind and one's own culture" (Lakoff & Turner, 1989:214).

Metaphor, in its power to organize, gives meaning to properties of culture, both socially and psychologically. Cognitive models are acquired through our experience and through our culture. Thus, even the person who has never laid bat to ball, or rounded third base, can learn from American collective knowledge what it means to *strike out* or to *play hardball.*

We will address the following three questions with respect to baseball and metaphor: First, what aspects of baseball are highlighted by the metaphors used? Second, what aspects of baseball are not emphasized by metaphoric language? And, finally, how does our conceptualization of baseball help to organize or understand the larger, more abstract realm of interest, that is, American life itself? We thus turn from the general discussion of metaphor to the more specific treatment of baseball idiom and American culture.

III. Baseball Metaphor

"Baseball is America's language, even its glue" (Herron, 1989). And pity the American who dislikes baseball (and I can only surmise that such people exist, I cannot actually name any)—there is truly no escape. Seeking refuge in football, this person might be asked to make a *pitchout* (a short lateral pass behind the line of scrimmage); or if basketball were the preference, the center might transfer the ball to a teammate using a *baseball pass* or attempt to score with a *baseball shot;* and the golfer trained in the 1950s might continue to use the *baseball grip,* popular during that time. In fact, dozens of terms currently used in other popular sports were developed in baseball, and later adopted by other games. In fact, the sports pages were created in the 1890s primarily for baseball reporting, and only later were expanded to include other scores and stories.

Turning to other professions, the paratrooper might jump with a *baseball parachute* and a soldier might launch a *baseball grenade.* In gambling, you might place a *baseball bet* on the horses, find yourself playing a form of seven card stud called *baseball poker,* or playing *baseball dice.* Married to your ninth wife? Then she is your *baseball bride.*

However, beyond the borrowing of the terms and ideas of the baseball game itself, there is a set of common idioms in American English adopted from baseball that are used in describing events, activities, or people that have no relationship to baseball at all, or even to other sporting events. One notable thing about this fact is the relative lack of metaphor taken from other popular American sports.[2] From basketball, a rejected lover may be *on the rebound;* from football, when faced with making a decision, one might decide to *punt.* But, from soccer, polo, hockey, or a host of other popular sports, one is hard pressed to find much in the way of conventionalized metaphor, whereas in baseball, we have dozens, if not scores of examples. We will turn now to a more specific discussion of those examples.

The Baseball Image Schema

From the examples given above, we know that conventionalized baseball metaphor often fits a larger structure or structures into what has been called an "image schema." This image schema is a way of assisting the listener to visualize or better understand abstract ideas through concrete images.

In order to examine this idea of an image schema more fully, we will look at some possible interpretations of the use of baseball metaphor and the abstract items that they portray, such as "Time" mentioned earlier. The ten categorizations presented here by no means exhaust the possibilities of metaphors and their functions. As the categories develop, it becomes evident that there is some natural overlap between categories. These classifications will, however, provide a taste of how baseball terminology functions to color everyday life.

1. General Performance as Baseball Performance

Baseball terminology is frequently used to evaluate someone's performance in other domains such as work or school. If someone is performing well, it is said that he or she is *batting a thousand,* or has *hit a home run.* Even better than hitting a home run is hitting a *grand slam,* a phrase used in bridge which predates its use in baseball but has become nearly exclusively recognized as a baseball term. If someone is known to come through when things are difficult, he or she may be known as a *clutch hitter;* or someone who has a reputation for consistent top performance may be a *heavy hitter* or a *four hundred hitter.*

In a similar vein, with respect to particular tasks to be accomplished, if a job is a difficult one and success is doubtful, one might give it the *old college try;* conversely, if one finds a task simple, it may be described as a *breeze,* or that one *breezed through* the chore.

2. Cooperation as Teamwork

We know that the word baseball itself can be used as a metaphor. According to Dickson (1989:32), it is a general metaphor for any organized activity that relies on teamwork. In 1961, the Peace Corps was referred to as a baseball team by its then director R. Sargent Shriver, Jr. In fact, there are a number of such metaphors that indicate the teamwork aspect that is required in baseball. For example, to *play ball* is to negotiate or work together. Someone putting in a full effort is *in there pitching.* Anyone whose activities deny the self and sacrifice for the good of the team may be seen as a *sacrifice hitter, pinch hitter,* or *going to bat for* a teammate.

It is interesting to note the number of metaphors that arise out of the teamwork aspect of baseball, and how few arise from the competitive nature of the game. We can see, through this idealization of baseball, that we value self sacrifice, cooperation, and teamwork above individual accomplishment and stardom.

3. Status as Team Membership

In spite of what has just been said about the downplaying of individual accomplishment as evidenced in the baseball metaphors concerning teamwork, there is another aspect of baseball metaphor that emphasizes the importance of team membership and the status that it confers. The clear division between high status and low status is shown in the oppositions between *big league, major league,* versus *minor league* or *bush league,* so named because its teams play in towns that are considered to be nowhere—that is, in the bushes. Within the structure of the team itself, if you are among the best players, you are on the *A team,* which graciously loaned its name to a popular television program of the 1980s that had little to do with baseball. Similarly, contests of importance take on baseball's importance, such as the *World Series* of poker. During such events, an ill-prepared competitor may feel *out of his/her league,* that is, outclassed by the competition.

4. Personal Communication as Baseball Activity

The activity of baseball has lent itself quite well to the description of human communication and interrelations. The salesperson makes a sales *pitch,* a person being interviewed *fields* questions. In the course of the interview, one can be *thrown a curve,* that is, asked an unexpected question; or insist on *playing hardball,* that is, taking no nonsense from the interviewer.

In a less "competitive" communicative environment, as during the course of discussion, one may want to *touch all bases,* that is, cover all topics, even if only superficially; *touch base with* someone, that is, make initial contact; or *cover's one's bases,* protect oneself in some fashion. And, when speaking, we may decide we are not even in the same ballpark.

The relationship between baseball and acts of communication may not be as tenuously drawn as it might seem at first blush. If one looks at the activity on the diamond, the process of a game relies heavily on communication between players, communication being crucially related to the notion of teamwork.

5. Personal Relations as Baseball Activity

Beyond the mere communication aspect, however, baseball activity has supplied metaphors for the workings of closer personal relations as well. There is here, of course, the infamous *getting to first base*.

6. Quantifying Using Baseball Statistics

Statistics are paramount in the game of baseball, and this is reflected in the borrowing of baseball terms by other domains. The representation of a zero score is often referred to as a *goose egg*, first recorded in 1867, and having its origins in cricket, where to *break an egg* is to begin to score; thus, to fail to score is to *lay an egg* (Dickson, 1989:183). In financial negotiations, one can speak of *ballpark figures*, or one's performance can be described in terms of a *batting average*. In describing a stock that doubles in price as a *two-bagger*, Peter Lynch, mutual fund manager, used the terminology usually reserved for the *double*.

The importance of statistics to baseball is encapsulated in the phrase *inside baseball*, which refers to the small details and nuances that draw the attention of the experts, but few others. The *box scores* found in the sports pages originated in baseball, although now they are used by a number of different sports. The *box score* may be used in any kind of situation where a "score" is being kept to track performance in some domain, for example politics and government.

7. Intellect and Error Making as Baseball Ability

The reliance on scores and individual performances in baseball has given rise, quite naturally, to an important lexicon of terms for errors and stupidity. Conversely, it has a lexicon of such terms for intelligence as well. For example, a bright or well-prepared person is described as being *on the ball*. A beginner who shows incredible promise in any field may be called a *phenom*.

The language of error and stupidity is much richer, however. A mistake may be called a *boner,* which was probably committed by (and thus derived from) a *bonehead,* someone who probably does not have *much on the ball.* Ideas that are wrong are *off base,* but if you are *off your base,* you are completely crazy, a *screwball, out in/of left field.* Commit two errors of any type, and you will be said to have *two strikes against you;* three, of course, being lethal.

8. Time and Sequencing as Baseball Time

We have previously, but briefly, seen how baseball can serve as an image schema for the concept of time. The term *a whole new ball game* is used to indicate a new beginning in any event, while a *late inning* is its opposite, referring to lateness in any situation. Something that will be accomplished soon will be done *right off the bat,* and someone who is not yet *up* can be said to be *on deck,* that is, next in line. A succession of two events may be described as *back-to-back* or as a *double header,* and the postponement of any event, for reasons of rain or otherwise, calls for the issuance of a *rain check.* (In baseball, the first rain check was awarded in 1884 in St. Louis [Flexner, 1982:38].)

The concept of time as paralleling baseball time is a particularly interesting one. Unlike most other sports, bsseball time is indefinite, limitless, not confined by quarters or periods, whistles or buzzers. Thus, things are measured in terms of the sequence of events: who is up and who is on deck, as opposed to preordained timed limits. The parallel is appealing.

9. Spatial Locations as Baseball

Beyond the temporal relations expressed by baseball expressions, the spatial organization of the baseball field has led to the metaphoric meaning of some of its components. For example, you may be sent to the *dugout* or the *bench* if your performance is lagging. Many types of enclosures outside the field may be referred to as *bull pens,* although along with the word *fungo,* the origin of this word is one of the most debated in baseball lore.

To digress briefly, the subject of the bull pen requires a little more exposition. According to Dickson (1989), the earliest use of the term was found in 1915. Casey Stengel, in a 1967 *New York Times* article, explained that it was a place to keep players in order to warm them up. Otherwise, they would be apt to be sitting around "shooting the bull."

Another, more colorful and more commonly believed theory

comes from the fact that Bull Durham billboards were placed on the outfield fences near the enclosure where the pitchers warmed up. However, in spite of these two theories, the term bull pen was used long before it was brought into baseball, and in the most obvious way—as a cattle enclosure. Thus the discussion continues, but probably the truth lies somewhere in a combination of these theories.

The comments made earlier about baseball time are equally applicable to baseball space; that is, unlike the strict dimensions of the football field or basketball court, the limits of baseball are created only by the limits of the physical world—that is, by gravity, friction, wind, or other factors influencing the ball's trajectory (Voigt, 1976). Even some foul balls are playable, in sharp contrast to these other sports. Thus, the parallels of time and space, so easily carried to conventionalized use, may be possible because of the less artificial constraints placed on them—limited only by physics, rather than by prescribed rules.

10. Physiology in Baseball Terms

In addition to these image-schema metaphors, there is a set of metaphors which does not seem to render abstract ideas more visual or more imaginable. In fact, these metaphors merely describe other, possibly even more concrete, terms using a new set of concrete terms. At this point, it is important to make the distinction between the "reality structuring" types of metaphor discussed so far and a purely poetic use of metaphor. This set of metaphors contains, in particular, metaphors for parts of the body; that is, *bean* referring to the head, *paws* referring to hands, etc. Probably the most interesting of these poetic metaphors is the term *think tank*, which originated in baseball as early as 1903 as an alternative description for the head, but has now expanded in use to describe research institutes such as the Rand Corporation (Dickson, 1989:393).

It is also instructive to look at what sorts of baseball terminology have *not* passed into the common metaphor, although any baseball term could be used as novel metaphor and subsequently pass into popular parlance. Why, for example, in the realm of communication, have we not adopted the idea of *dummy signals?* Why has the *shortstop* position not been linguistically symbolized? What about the *batboy?* These questions are, of course, open for interpretation, and there is nothing preventing them from being adopted into common idiom, should a need arise.

IV. Baseball Language Abroad

As somewhat of an aside, I would like to comment briefly on the effect of baseball on the language of countries somewhat new to the game: South Korea, Japan, and Italy. In these cultures, many baseball terms have been adopted in their English forms, although in Japan, this did not happen until relatively recently, because of the constraints against the use of English during World War II. Although baseball is still called by its Japanese name, *yakyu*, literally "field ball," other terminology is in English, or Japanese-influenced English. For example, there is *gettsu* (gets two) for a double play; *sutoraikū* for strike; and *besu* for base. In Italian, baseball is called baseball, and the words *lineup*, *pitcher*, and *area di strike* (here meaning "home base"), among others, are used directly from English as well, although many of the positions are called by their Italian equivalents, such as the *interbase*, "shortstop," or the *esterno sinistro*, "left fielder" (Machetti & Masini, 1988).

Preliminary investigations into Japanese and Italian do not show any signs of metaphorization of baseball language into common parlance. In Korean, we have the single example of "Home run Start," the name of a morning radio program, broadcast in Korean, which has nothing in particular to do with baseball. Home run start merely means "a good beginning." And as often as we have observed baseball lingo having passed into American idiom, there is no reason to expect that its terminology will be similarly welcomed into the metaphor of either Japan or Italy. In fact, although the game itself is popular and passionately played, it may be that it is a unique expression of our own culture, insofar as the language and our conception of the universe are concerned. It will be interesting, as baseball spreads even farther beyond our borders, to Eastern Europe, South America and beyond, to see how far the influence of its language will go.

V. Conclusion

Baseball structures our time, space, interpersonal relationships, and standards of accomplishment in American culture. It is important to note that baseball metaphor is not just in the words we use—a convenient idiom, that is—but in our very ideas about baseball and its relationship to American life. In this way, we can see very clearly the place of baseball in American culture.

The understanding of life as a baseball game does not merely allow a simplified answer to the age-old question of the meaning of life, but rather it renders its meaning a richer and more expansive one; it serves to enhance our understanding of life, rather than to limit it. Baseball gives us another metric against which to measure the innings of our life, and, as metrics go, it could not be a more pleasing one.

Notes

1. Conventional metaphor is related in some sense to the "Dead Metaphor Theory" (cf., e.g., Fraser, 1979). However, the Dead Metaphor Theory contends that conventionalized metaphors are no longer metaphoric in meaning, but rather merely another standard definition for a word or term. In this, I side with Lakoff and Turner (1989), who claim that this misses an essential aspect of metaphoric and poetic language.

2. In some way, this may be related to the "(George) Plimpton Small Ball Theory":

> In brief, the theory holds that the smaller the ball the better the literature. There are almost no books on basketball that are of value. Only one or two on football. When you get to the smaller ones, baseball and tennis, the literature is wonderful. Then to golf it's even better. The greatest sports short story ever written, by Mark Twain, involved B-B shot. (George Plimpton, quoted in Claffey, 1989:48)

Bibliography

Broder, David S. "The Season Finally Arrives: Play Ball!" *The Boston Sunday Globe,* April 2, 1989, p. A31.

Claffey, C. E. (1989) "Baseball Books on a Hot Streak." *The Boston Globe,* Friday, May 12, p. 45.

Deford, F. (1989) "Of Billie Jean and 73-0." *Sports Illustrated,* Feb. 6, 1989, p. 70.

Dickson, P. (1989) *The Dickson Baseball Dictionary.* New York: Facts on File.

Flexner, S. B. (1982) *Listening to America.* New York: Simon and Schuster.

Frank, L. (1983) *Playing Hardball: The Dynamics of Baseball Folk Speech.* New York: Peter Lang.

Fraser, B. (1979) "The Interpretation of Novel Metaphors." In: Ortony, A. (ed.), *Metaphor & Thought,* pp. 172–184.

Herron, C. R. (1989) Review of *Diamonds Are Forever. New York Times Review of Books* (April 23, 1989).

Holland, D. and Quinn, N. (1987) *Cultural Models in Language and Thought.* Cambridge: Cambridge University Press.

Honeck, R. P., and Hoffman, R. R. (1980) *Cognition and Figurative Language.* Hillsdale, NJ: Lawrence Erlbaum.

Lakoff, G. and Johnson, M. (1980) *Metaphors We Live By*. Chicago: University of Chicago Press.

Lakoff, G. and Kövecses, Z. (1987). The cognitive model of anger inherent in American English. In: Holland & Quinn (eds.) *Cultural Models in Language and Thought*, pp. 195–221.

Lakoff, G. and Turner, M. (1989). *More Than Cool Reason*. Chicago: University of Chicago Press.

Lee, G. (1926) "In Sporting Parlance," *American Speech 1* (April 1926), pp. 369–370.

Literary Digest, The. (1913) "Peril of the Baseball Lingo," *The Literary Digest 47* (Sept. 6, 1913), pp. 379–380.

Machetti, C. and Masini, F. (1988). Ed ecco come si gioca. *Espresso*, August 1988, p. 28.

Nation, The (1913) "English and Baseball." *The Nation 97* (August 21, 1913), p. 161.

Ortony, A. (1979) *Metaphor and Thought*. Cambridge: Cambridge University Press.

Samuels, V. (1927) "Baseball Slang." *American Speech* (Feb. 1927), p. 256.

Thorn, J. (1985) *The Armchair Book of Baseball*. New York: Charles Scribner's Sons.

Voigt, D. Q. (1976) *America Through Baseball*. Chicago: Nelson-Hall.

Wallop, D. (1969) *Baseball: An Informal History*. New York: W. W. Norton & Co.

Whiteford, M. (1983) *How to Talk Baseball*. New York: Dembner Books.

Winner, E. (1988) *The Point of Words*. Cambridge, MA: Harvard University Press.

Appendix*

A team, any elite grouping
back-to-back, two consecutive events
bad call, any perceived misjudgment
balk, to recoil, to fail to deliver, such as a politician balking on tax reform
ball game, a coherent event, such as the movement of a bill through Congress
ballpark, a given realm, field of activity

---

*These terms are collected from Lee (1926), Dickson (1989), and my own knowledge of the subject.

ballpark figure, a rough estimate

baseball, a general metaphor for other organized activities relying on teamwork

batting a thousand, to be absolutely correct, to perform flawlessly

batting average, success or failure in other realms is often measured in terms of batting a thousand or batting zero

be in there pitching, to become active, to be part of the action

bean, the head, or to hit someone on the head

bench, figurative location of those who are not participating or have been taken out of participation

big league, the highest level of any given field

bonehead, stupid or foolish

boner, an error; hilarious classroom gaffe or howler

breaks, the, the breaks and the breaks of the game are common ways of connoting luck in many realms of modern life

breeze (through), popular term denoting ease of accomplishment

bush league, having to do with a group or class of things that is at best mediocre, but more likely inferior

clutch, a key situation in any endeavor

clutch hitter, anyone who can come through when it counts the most

cover one's bases, to protect yourself from attack

double play, two accomplishments made at the same time

doubleheader, two paired or consecutive events

dugout, realm of nonparticipation

farm out, to reassign

field, to answer, reply, or accept, as in a question

foul ball, a bad egg, an ignorant person

four hundred hitter, a heavy hitter

go to bat for, to take up someone else's cause or argument

goose egg, zero score in all sports

grand slam, anything extraordinary and or powerful

grandstand, to show off

grandstand play, a showy move or style that is usually both spectacular and ineffective

ground rules, a basic set of rules and procedures that is established in advance

hardball, a tough, relentless adversary or adversarial situation

have/get one's innings, to be afforded an opportunity or chance

heavy hitter, a person to be reckoned with

hit and run, an automobile accident where the driver leaves the scene

home run (1), big scoring plays in any sport

home run (2), any action that has been a clear success

home run (3), sexual intercourse
innings, opportunity or chances
inside baseball, details appreciated only by those expert in the field
jinx, bad luck
late inning, late
lineup, any listing of events or participants
major league, anything imposing and of the highest level
meal ticket, any person or object that brings success
minor league, anything not at the highest level
MVP, a key performer
new ball game, a new start
not much on the ball, not very bright
off base, to be wrong
off one's base, to be out of one's mind
old college try, a strenuous effort with little chance of success
on the ball, at one's best, alert
on deck, the next to have a turn
out in left field, disoriented, out of contact with reality
out of left field, rooted in the ridiculous, crackbrained, farfetched
out of one's league, to be outclassed
phenom, fast starter
pinch hitter, a substitute or understudy
pitch, to present, as in pitching a new product, as in sales pitch
pitcher, one who presents ideas and policy
play ball, to cooperate or participate
play the field, to date a variety of partners, or more generally, to sample
   a wide spectrum of items
play-by-play, any detailed verbal account
rain check, postponed or deferred acceptance
right in there pitching, putting forth one's best effort
right off the bat, from the start, immediately
sacrifice hitter, a term used for a political candidate who runs for the
   good of the party, but is likely to lose
screwball, an eccentric, zany or insane person
shut out, to prevent scoring
softball, an easy question
southpaw, a left-handed person
strike, a disadvantage or mistake
swing, to undertake some endeavor is to "take a swing at it"
switch-hitter, any person who radically alternates his or her orientation,
   especially bisexuals

think tank, originally meaning the brain, now a term for a policy
    research institute
throw a curve, to surprise
touch all bases, to cover a large variety of things
touch base with, make contact
up, taking or in a position to take one's turn
World Series, high-level contests in sports, games, and activities

I would like to thank Takanori Senoo and Nobuko Mizumoto for their information concerning the language of Japanese baseball. I would like to also thank, as always, Dr. Michael Smith, for his suggestions, comments, and criticisms. Special thanks go to the participants of the Symposium on Baseball and The American Culture for their insights and enthusiasm.

Sociocultural History of the Origin of Women's Baseball at the Eastern Women's Colleges During the Victorian Period

by Gai I. Berlage

Questions of whether Pam Postema should be allowed to be a major league umpire and whether women should be in baseball management or play on men's teams are topics of the 1980s. These issues seem new. Yet, it is hard to believe that these are issues today when one looks back at the early history of women in baseball. Women were playing baseball at many of the Eastern women's colleges in the late nineteenth and early twentieth centuries. In fact, one year after Vassar College opened in 1865, women were playing a form of baseball there. The teams were composed of eight, rather than nine, players. The June 1866 issue of *The Vassariana*, the Vassar College newspaper, mentions that there are two baseball clubs at Vassar. This is not too long after the first intercollegiate baseball game was played between Amherst and Williams Colleges in 1859 and three years before the first professional baseball club, the Cincinnati Red Stockings, was established in Cincinnati, Ohio.

Yet, most people are unaware of the fact that Victorian women played baseball. The image of women playing baseball seems an aberration, an impossibility. After all, most of us have learned our history well, and women of the Victorian period were frail, delicate ladies whom men placed on pedestals in order to protect them from the harsh realities of life. Immigrant women may have worked, but they were a coarser breed. Certainly, the frail constitution of upper-class women would never have permitted them to do strenuous exercise. But even if they could have, no fathers would have permitted their daughters to be so unladylike as to play baseball. The image of the swooning damsel with her smelling salts stands in stark contrast to the reality of healthy, robust, active upper-class women playing baseball at the women's colleges.

Maybe because of the long-lasting Victorian influence on American ideals of womanhood, this early history has been largely forgotten and ignored. If one reads books on the history of baseball, rarely is any mention made of women. If mention is made, it is usually about the first "Ladies Days" at the ballparks. Women are seen as fans or "groupies," not as players. Recently, some books have added a paragraph on the All American Girls' Baseball League of 1943 through 1954. But most books omit this. In fact, women are notably absent.

Even when one writes for information on women's baseball to the archive librarians and heads of the physical education departments of some of the early women's colleges where one has evidence of the existence of baseball clubs, the inquiries often come back stating that as far as they know women didn't play baseball at these colleges. Searching the archives on one's own will often produce conflicting dates as to the origin of women's baseball on these campuses. It is as if the existence of women in baseball is seen as such an anomaly that it has ceased to exist or has been lost from public view.

The early history of women in baseball is very important because it reflects the changing roles of women and the rise and fall of their early efforts to gain greater equality. Women's participation in baseball is very much a product of sociocultural factors and changes that were taking place in American society. This paper examines just one part of that history, the sociocultural factors that produced women's baseball clubs at the elite women's colleges during the Victorian period.

College education for women began in the second half of the nineteenth century. The elite eastern women's colleges, sometimes referred to as the "Seven Sisters," had their origin during this period. The earliest of these, Mount Holyoke, began as a seminary in 1837 and became a four-year college in 1861. Vassar College began in 1865; Smith and Wellesley, 1875; and Bryn Mawr, 1885. Radcliffe and Barnard, the other two of the "Seven Sisters," started as annexes to Harvard and Columbia and later became separate colleges. Radcliffe began as an annex in 1878 and became a separate women's college with its own charter in 1894. Barnard started as an annex in 1889 and became a separate institution in 1900. (Horowitz, 1984)

Ironically, the first women's colleges, notably the "Seven Sisters," had their origin at about the same time as professional baseball. The first professional baseball team was established in 1869, and by 1890 there were seventeen white professional leagues and two black professional leagues. (Vincent, 1981, p. 157)

The 1880s have been called the "Golden Era" of baseball. Americans of all backgrounds were enthralled with baseball and it was the most popular sport and the national game. It was the game of the decade both in terms of popular participation and in terms of spectatorship. This same baseball fever that affected the nation also caught the imagination of the young college women. They too wanted to have an active part and to play the game as did their brothers. Baseball to these girls was an exciting social and physical activity that surely offered a great deal more in terms of fun and competition than doing the physical exercises that were so much the vogue in the physical education classes at the women's colleges. However, it is somewhat amazing that the administrators and teachers at these schools, who were the guardians of "ladylike" conduct, permitted them to play. Certainly even in the early days of baseball when it was considered a gentlemanly sport and played at private upper-class men's clubs, women were not permitted to play. In fact, the wives of these men probably never even considered it. There was strict sex role segregation. Baseball was a social event. "Tea was served, the ladies were invited, gentlemanly conduct on the part of the contestants prevailed." (Coffin, 1971, p. 9) Gentlemen played and ladies cheered them on.

Baseball in the early days of its history fit into the upper-class image of what was considered appropriate sport. The game was played with decorum, and sportsmanship was of the utmost importance. Manners prevailed even in the rules of the game. Pitchers pitched the ball to where the batter asked for it. Form was more important than winning, and the emphasis was on how you played the game. For example, bunting was considered an inexcusable breach of taste. (Coffin, 1971, p. 10)

With the democratization of baseball and the popularity of baseball among all classes of people, the game became professionalized and it changed. It began to be seen by some as a game for ruffians of the lower classes.

From the beginning until the 1870s the *New York Times* adamantly opposed professional baseball. The *Times* considered the professional game not sport but a "purely business transaction." (Vincent, 1981, p. 104)

The *Times* characterized the professional player as "a shiftless member of the laboring class, prone to drink, having a loose moral code, and preferring to avoid an honest day's work by playing ball." (Vincent, 1981, p. 104)

Professional baseball players in the 1880s were seen as ruffians who lacked the Victorian social graces. There were "stories of players getting in trouble with managers for . . . eating with a knife, using spoons to eat pie, drinking the contents of finger bowls, and piling food scraps in soup bowls." (Vincent, 1981, p. 186)

Baseball was also considered a dangerous sport. According to statistics published in a *New York Times* editorial August 30, 1881, injuries were prevalent and serious. "It is estimated by an able statistician that the annual number of accidents caused by base-ball in the last ten years has been 37,518, of which 3 percent have been fatal; 25,611 fingers and 11,016 legs were broken during the decade in question, while 1,900 eyes were permanently put out and 1,648 ribs were fractured." (Leitner, 1971, p. 128)

Baseball in the late 1880s received mixed reviews. There were concerns about the drinking behavior of the crowds and the tendency to gamble, as well as opposition to playing games on Sunday. But there was also a widely accepted ideology that baseball was an American sport that typified all that was good about America. It was believed that baseball would teach children traditional American values. It would help to assimilate immigrants into the American culture, and participation in local clubs would provide a sense of community pride. (Riess, 1980, p. 7)

Mark Twain is quoted as saying "Baseball is the very symbol, the outward and visible expression of the drive and push and struggle of the raging, tearing, booming nineteenth century." (Somers, 1972, p. 115)

Baseball, to be allowed at the women's colleges, had to be seen as uniquely female and a very different game from that played by professional baseball players. A letter by Ruth Lusk, class of 1900 at Smith College, reflects this. She writes, "Someone remarked to President Seelye if he didn't think 'it was unladylike for us to be playing baseball just like men.' President Seelye asked the man if he had ever seen us play. The man said 'No'. Then President Seelye said, 'You wouldn't say they played like men.'"

The uniforms of the girls left little doubt that this was a female version of baseball. The girls wore long dresses with high necks and long sleeves. Although the uniform was a definite hindrance to running or sliding into bases, it did offer some unique advantages for trapping or stopping the ball. One such strategy was to catch or stop low balls with one's skirt. Gertrude Cooper, Smith class of 1906, created an illustrated booklet for her housemates to show them not only the proper methods of play, but also to encourage more girls to participate. She states that using one's skirt is the safest way to stop a low flying ball. However, she admits that there are pitfalls to this method, especially if the ball rolls under your skirt and petticoats. For higher balls, she recommends the more traditional method of using a baseball mitt. Certainly the uniforms and the catching methods were uniquely female. However, the rest of the equipment was standard. They used a regulation hardball, baseball gloves, and a face mask for the catcher.

It is important to remember that baseball in its early years had many different sets of rules and was a slower and less precise game. Even the rules officially established in 1846 by Cartwright to standardize the game were very different from the rules of today. Under Cartwright's rules, fielders were still allowed to let the ball bounce once on a fly before catching it for an out. However, players were no longer allowed to throw the ball at the runner for an out. (Frommer, 1988, pp. 3–4) Catchers stood a considerable distance behind the batter and caught the ball on the first bounce. (Leitner, 1972, p. 219) Players didn't wear gloves; in fact, gloves weren't generally accepted until the 1900s. Prior to that, players who wore gloves were thought of as "sissies." (Voigt, 1983, p. 74) However, this was the form of the game that was to be declared the "official game of baseball." The *Spirit of the Times* in a 1856 headline declared the nine-inning, nine-man team "The American National Game of Base Ball." (Frommer, 1988, p. 87)

On the whole, the women's colleges with independent and largely separate identities such as Vassar, Smith, Holyoke and Wellesley were to provide greater opportunities for women to participate in baseball than schools such as Barnard and Radcliffe that were annexes to men's colleges. Smith, Vassar and Holyoke with their separate campuses secluded from the view of outsiders offered a unique environment for women to develop in a world of their own.

Vassar had the earliest baseball teams, with baseball eights in 1866 and baseball nines in 1876. Smith had teams in 1879, four years after it opened; Mount Holyoke in 1891, and Wellesley in 1897. The other three were much later in fielding teams—Radcliffe 1915–1916; Barnard according to Ainsworth (1930) by 1925, although the archives librarian could find no reference; and Bryn Mawr by 1925. Other early women's colleges that had baseball teams were Wells College in Aurora, New York founded in 1868, Goucher College in Baltimore, Maryland founded in 1885, and Mills College in Oakland, California founded as a seminary in 1865 and as a college in 1885.

According to an address by Temple R. Hollcroft commemorating the seventy-fifth anniversary of Wells, "In the seventies and eighties the chief sports were boating and baseball."

Knipp's *History of Goucher College* written in 1938 makes this mention of baseball: ". . . baseball was introduced to Baltimore women through Goucher players. The 1920 season was much more satisfactory than previous ones because no attempt was made to combine baseball with Field Day. On the Maryland Avenue field, as well as indoors, are played interclass games, and there is a final game for the college championship. A contest between the champions and a faculty team is one of the most satisfying of sports events to the students looking on." (pp. 477–478)

An early history of the Mills College athletic association states that shortly after 1872 baseball became "the first outdoor sport at Mills—aside from walking, "quoits," and croquet. . . ." The 1914–1915 Mills yearbook, however, sets the origin of baseball at about 1894. "Baseball came in about '94, following upon our modern gymnastics suits, and took its place from the first as our most popular sport. At that early date games with outside teams, were recorded. . . ." However, in other references to baseball at Mills, careful mention is made that baseball was never an intercollegiate sport and was always an interclass activity. The discrepancy may be explained by the reference to the fact that when team sports didn't have regularly scheduled games with California and Stanford, it was the custom to have the winners of the upper and lower divisions represent the college in games with these colleges. So although officially there was no intercollegiate schedule, exhibition type games were played. There were also student faculty games. The eastern influence on Mills athletics was strong since Cyrus Mills was a Williams graduate and his wife, Susan Tolman Mills, was a graduate of Mount Holyoke Seminary. (Mills College Catalog, 1988–1989, p. 7)

It is ironic that the Victorian period marks both the beginning of college education for women and women's participation in baseball and other sports. Yet, the Victorian ideal of womanhood was probably the most restrictive in terms of women's roles in American history.

In some respects, the incongruities between the Victorian ideals of womanhood and the sports reality are a mirror image of the personage of Queen Victoria and the ideals that she espoused. Certainly Queen Victoria was anything but the "true woman" or the woman of the Victorian ideal. "Queen Victoria was strong willed and directly involved in the affairs of a powerful state. Yet women of the era—credited to Victorian mores—were expected to be passive, gentle, soft spoken, delicate, and unobtrusive." (Paul, 1981, p. 3)

The ideal woman was to devote her life totally to her husband and to motherhood. She was like a porcelain doll: frail, fragile and pure. Her domain was the home, in which she was to be protected.

The Victorian era encompasses the time from about 1876 to 1900. However, the reign of Queen Victoria of Britain, for whom the era was named, was from June 1837 to January 1901. (Powell, 1981, p. 4)

Gerber beautifully indicates why the Victorian ideal was antithetical to sports. "Sports require vigor; the ideal required delicacy. Sport takes one out of the home and into the tempting and defiling world. Sport places participants in positions where their flesh is exposed and their emotions are expressed; the ideal required modesty, propriety, and circumspectness. Furthermore, by exposing the face and reproductive organs to possible injury, sport endangers the ultimate Victorian goal: the twin functions of attracting a man and bearing a child." (Gerber, 1974, p. 12)

Several factors besides the Victorian ideal worked to limit women's physical activity. The dress fashions of the times severely restricted women's physical movement, and prevailing medical theories stressed not only that women were the weaker sex but that their whole existence revolved around their reproductive organs.

"By the mid-nineteenth century, the Victorian image of the 'true' woman as fragile, frail, weak, sickly, pale, and ruled by her hormones was an image antithetical to women's participation in any but the mildest pastimes." (Leonard, 1988, p. 265)

In the first half of the nineteenth century, a myth prevailed that if a girl read "exciting or dangerous" books, disaster could strike. It was believed that a young man might give a young girl exciting books to read in order to seduce her. "The man without honorable intentions always provides the innocent maiden with such books as a prelude to his assault on her virtue." (Welter, 1966, p. 166)

Medical opinion also supported and reinforced the image of women as weak and needing special care. Doctors believed that if women overexerted themselves all sorts of calamities could befall them, from nervous exhaustion to having defective offspring. One popular theory of the day was the idea of limited energy force, or that one was born with a finite amount of energy. Women, since they were the weaker sex, automatically had less energy than men and therefore had to be especially careful. If a woman used her energy on frivolous activities such as "reading, intellectual conversations, excessive sexual relations, and physical activity," she would not be able to adequately fulfill her role as mother. (Powell, 1981, pp. 12–13) Since it was believed that the uterus was connected to the nervous system, overexertion could produce nervous shocks that in turn could lead to the woman having degenerate offspring. (Twin, 1979, p. xviii)

The Victorian doctors even invented a new disease "neurasthenia" or nervous exhaustion to which the "better sort" of women—those of the middle and upper classes—were supposedly particularly vulnerable. The disease was brought on by a deficiency of nerve force. (Powell, 1981, p. 12) It is no wonder that by 1850, many women believed that ill health proved their femininity. (Twin, 1979, p. xviii)

An interesting contradiction was provided by the immigrant women, who worked long hours and continued to be robust. This contradiction would eventually lead many doctors to revise their opinions and promote limited exercise as necessary for good health.

For upper-class women, activities such as riding had always been acceptable. The upper-class men and women also shared some activities such as croquet. So there was a germ of hope for the development of some form of non-strenuous exercise program for women by the end of the Victorian period.

Fashions of the times also restricted women's activity and often produced medical problems. It was estimated that in the winter if a woman dressed in the height of fashion, her outfit would weigh thirty-seven pounds of which about nineteen hung from her waist. (Powell, 1981, p. 17) So even walking could be strenuous exercise. But it was not just the weight; women also wore corsets tied so tightly that their waists were reduced by three to fifteen inches. Pictures from the period show maids tugging mightily to lace the corset tight. Of course, this meant that the internal organs were pushed downward and upward. Breathing was also affected. It was estimated that the average lung capacity was approximately 134 cubic inches with corsets and 167 without. (Powell, 1981, p. 18) No wonder women fainted.

Two factors helped to change fashions. Some doctors were beginning to believe that restrictive dress, and especially corsets, led to some of the medical problems that they saw. They began to advise against tight corsets.

Also, the safety bicycle was introduced and became quite popular in the 1890s. Bicycling provided women with healthy outdoor exercise as well as the need for a new style of clothing. Shorter dresses, dresses without corsets, as well as blouse and skirt outfits became acceptable. The invention of the bicycle brought about a greater acceptance of modified dress or "bloomers," which Amelia Bloomer had unsuccessfully tried to introduce in the 1850s. (Swanson, 1974, pp. 44–45). Although there were opponents, an article appeared in the August

1895 issue of *Cosmopolitan* magazine which stated that bicycling would "bring delicate, fanciful women off their couches, and . . . rid them of vapors and nerves." (Mrozek, 1983, p. 150)

But it was the establishment of the first women's colleges that really led to changes in beliefs about appropriate roles for women, women's fashions, the importance of exercise for health, the acceptance of sports for women, and opportunities for women to play baseball. The early women's colleges were patterned after the men's. The founders were all pioneers in their time. They believed in giving women an education equal to that given to men, but they also believed that women's colleges would preserve femininity. In fact, that's why they advocated separate facilities. Women's needs were seen as very different from those of men. The view of Clark Seelye, the first president of Smith College, summarizes the early founders' philosophy of why one should obtain a liberal arts education. ". . . learning aimed only to develop mind and spirit. Just as a man might enter law, a woman might marry, but the college prepared neither: education opened to the student 'that all-perfect Mind, which is neither male nor female.' Woman, like man, aspired to perfection in imitation of God." (Horowitz, 1984, p. 73)

They also all believed that a healthy mind and body were entwined and that exercise was necessary to achieve health. Therefore, all the college programs required some form of exercise or physical education. These views were very progressive for their time and there were many opponents.

Some opponents believed that a college education would banish women's femininity and the "good wife." To Rayne and others, colleges would make the woman assertive and no longer passive. Rayne defined the duties of wife as to ". . . always think her husband wise, whether he is or not. She is a happy woman who can make her husband always a hero. She is happiest who is humblest, and who takes pleasure in looking up." (Rayne, 1893, p. 478)

Other authorities, basing their opinions on the current knowledge of women's physiology, stated that trying to educate women like men was pure folly. Medical evidence showed that "45% of women suffered from menstrual cramps, and another 20% suffered from assorted ills. Thus for physiological reasons, 65% of the women would require the college program to be adjusted for them. Also it was reported that overstudy would give the girls brain fever. They would be weak and unable to have children." (Spears, 1974, p. 27) The athletic, robust, healthy, competitive woman was the antithesis of the ideal and yet, by the 1890s, sports for women—and especially base-ball—were part of college life.

Founders of the women's colleges were alike in their passionate desire to establish women's colleges and to make women educational equals to men, but their motivations were very different. Mary Lyon was a very religious woman who, after the loss of her father, had worked hard to support and educate herself. She felt a spiritual need to develop a seminary that would educate women, especially poor farm women, for God's calling. It was her religious calling rather than a desire for modernizing women's roles that led her to seek an endowment to establish Mount Holyoke Seminary. (Horowitz, 1984, p. 19)

"Mount Holyoke's catalogue promised to make female education a 'handmaid to the Gospel and an efficient auxiliary in the great task of renovating the world.'" (Welter, 1966, p. 153)

In order to keep tuition costs low so that girls of modest means could attend the seminary, all domestic work was done by the students rather than by servants. Having worked on her brother's farm, Mary Lyon believed in fresh air and exercise as necessary for health. Therefore, she required all students to exercise by walking, doing calisthenics, and domestic work. In her Book of Duties she wrote, "The young ladies are required to walk one mile per day till the snow renders it desirable to specify time instead of distance, then three quarters of an hour. . . ." (McCurdy, 1909, p. 145) She believed that the development of mind, soul and body went hand in hand. Although these were very modern ideas for her time, Mary Lyon would not have seen herself as a feminist but rather as a person with a religious calling.

Matthew Vassar, a wealthy brewer, who founded Vassar College in 1861, had a very different motive. Vassar had no heirs and wanted to leave his money to a worthy cause and one that would bear his name. Founding a women's college met this need. He wrote to the trustees of his estate: "It occurred to me that woman, having received from her Creator the same intellectual constitution as man, has the same right as man to intellectual culture and development. . . . It is my hope to be the instrument, in the hands of Providence, of founding and perpetuating an institution which shall accomplish for young women what our colleges are accomplishing for young men." (Vassar, 1862, p. 55)

Vassar believed that a healthy mind as well as a healthy body were essential, and felt that Victorian women suffered from a lack of exercise. He spoke of the feminine image of the period as one in which "feminine beauty . . . too often blooms but palely for a languid or a suffering life, if not for an early tomb." (Spears, 1974, p. 27) To protect women against failing health, he wanted Vassar to have a gymnasium with the latest apparatus so that the girls could develop healthy bodies.

The importance of physical education for good health was also stressed by the trustees. "Good health is, in the first place, essential to success in study; and subsequently whatever attainments have been made at school or college, if the health has been sacrificed to secure them, will be valueless as a means of a useful or happy life." (Ballantine, *History of Physical Training at Vassar,* pp. 5–6)

The college program included light gymnastics patterned after those of Dr. Dio Lewis, swimming, skating, gardening and other feminine sports and games. All of these were to provide for good health as well as appeal to students. (Ballintine, p. 7)

The catalog states that every student was required to wear a light and easy-fitting dress for exercise, but that it was optional at other times. This suggested that this form of dress was appropriate for everyday wear. (Ballintine, p. 7)

Henry Fowle Durant, a trial lawyer who, after the death of his only son, devoted his life to the service of God, founded Wellesley College in 1875. He was a crusader for women's rights. He stipulated that the faculty of the college as well as the President should be women. (Davenport, 1976, p. 360) He believed that college education was the means for women to become more equal to men. "We revolt against the slavery in which women are held by the customs of society—the broken health, the aimless lives, the hopeless dependence, the dishonesties, and shams of so-called education." (Horowitz, 1984, p. 44) Durant too stressed the necessity of physical exercise so that women would be healthy and could develop to their fullest.

Sophia Smith, a wealthy spinster, founded Smith College in 1875 with the help of her solicitor John M. Greene. But it was two Amherst men who patterned the curriculum to mirror that of Amherst.

Byrn Mawr (1880) was founded by Joseph Wright Taylor to create a female Haverford for young Quaker women. (Horowitz, 1984, p. 6)

Radcliffe (1879) and Barnard (1889) had histories very different from the other women's colleges. They were not established distinctively as women's colleges, but rather as annexes to men's colleges. Radcliffe started under the auspices of "The Society for the Collegiate Instruction of Women" and became known as the Annex. The program for women was to be purely instructional. It was designed to give women an opportunity to be tutored by Harvard faculty. Elizabeth Agassiz, widow of the naturalist, Louis Agassiz, became the first president. She was adamantly opposed to establishing another women's college because she thought they were provincial. So it wasn't until 1893 that Radcliffe emerged as a separate women's college. (Horowitz, 1984, pp. 95–104)

Barnard had a history similar to that of Radcliffe. In 1899, the Columbia trustees established a female annex to Columbia. Columbia faculty taught women in a separate building. It wasn't until 1900 that Barnard became a separate college. (Horowitz, 1984, pp. 134–135) Consequently, in the early years, there were no athletic opportunities for women at either Radcliffe or Barnard.

The first women who attended women's colleges were pioneers. Their families, as well as the girls, were open to new ideas about the role of women. Sending a woman to college was a controversial issue. Those early women who went to the "Seven Sisters" felt a mission to prove that they were equal to men.

From the beginning, women at all these schools, with the exception of Radcliffe and Barnard prior to their becoming separate women's colleges, were encouraged to complement their studies with exercise and especially with outdoor activities. Boating in the spring, ice skating in the winter were activities that were encouraged. The physical and social aspects were encouraged rather than the competitive aspect, which was considered to be more a male component. Consequently, many activities that might be considered masculine were accepted for their health aspects. For example, at Mount Holyoke girls happily played ice hockey. Team sports were also accepted because they developed character, camaraderie, and discipline.

The women's college philosophy of encouraging women to play team sports is expressed by Lucille Eaton Hill, Director of Physical Training at Wellesley College at that time.

> College women are beginning to recognize the true relation of the body and mind and to value physical training as an aid to the best intellectual activity. . . . Women should also recognize the need for perfect organization in all parts calling for teams, crews and champions. The ethical value of athletics may be placed side by side with the physical value. The necessary submission to strict discipline, the unquestioning obedience demanded by the officers, the perfect control of the temper and sensitiveness under coaching, together with the fact that she must be absolutely unselfish in order to become a loyal and valued member of her organization, develops a young girl's character while she develops her muscles. (1903, p. 13)

In the 1890s, student athletic associations were formed primarily to govern competitive sports and other activities such as field day. The dates were: Bryn Mawr, 1891; Smith, 1893; Radcliffe, 1895; Vassar, 1895; Mount Holyoke, 1896; Wellesley, 1896; and Barnard, 1897. (Ainsworth, 1930, p. 79)

Baseball, because of its popularity nationally, was one of the first team sports to be played by college women. Vassar College lays claim to being the first college to have women's baseball teams. *The Vassariana*, June 1866, lists two baseball clubs: the Laurel Base Ball Club and the Abenakis Base Ball Club. However, these were teams of eight rather than nine.

A picture in the Vassar archives indicates that the first Vassar nine, the Resoluts, was formed in 1876. They wore caps, long-sleeved full floor-length dresses with a band around their waists with the team name.

Early yearbooks and the student newspaper make no other reference to the baseball clubs until 1876 when *The Vassar Miscellany*, October 1876, mentions that the baseball clubs have been consolidated and reorganized.

Sophia Foster Richardson, in recalling the so-called spontaneous introduction of baseball clubs in 1876 at Vassar, said she believed that the catalyst for their formation was the Vassar female physician, Dr. Webster, who was "wise beyond her generation." (Richardson, 1897, p. 1)

She explained: "The public, so far as it knew of our playing, was shocked, but in our retired grounds and protected observation . . . , we continued to play in spite of a censorious public. One day a student, while running between bases, fell, with an injured leg. We attended her at the infirmary, with the foreboding that this accident would end our play of baseball. Not so. Dr. Webster said that the public would doubtless condemn the game as too violent, but that if the student had hurt herself while dancing, the public would not condemn dancing to extinction." (Richardson, 1897, p. 2)

During the spring of 1877, baseball matches were played every Saturday afternoon. Somewhat later, matches between faculty and students were played on Founder's Day.

The *Daily Eagle*, November 11, 1895, reported on the first women's field day in the country, which was held at Vassar. The event was closed to outsiders. The various classes competed against each other in track and field events. The contestants wore gym suits while most of the spectators wore bicycle skirts. One of the annual field day events was the baseball throw, and records were kept over the years.

One article in the Vassar archives, probably written in the early 1900s and titled "The Vassar Girl in Athletics" (source and date unknown), brags about the superior accomplishments of the girls. "The year's annual field day at Vassar College, that home of the New Girl, proved that men can no longer pose as the superior being on the cinder track or in almost any athletic sports. For the girls performed feats of strength and agility that would make any man envious of their prowess, and while their records did not quite equal the best made by men, they came sufficiently near them to give a strong hint of what certainly will come to pass in a few years. . . . One girl actually threw a baseball the amazing distance of 195 feet 3 inches, effectively disposing the old fallacy that a woman cannot throw a ball at all."

The *New York Herald* magazine section, Sunday, June 18, 1911, had a feature article on Miss Dorothy Smith of New York, who broke two records on field day at Vassar and received her athletic letter. The headline read, "Vassar's Champion Athletic Girl." The reporter was especially impressed by Smith's establishment of a new baseball throw record of 204 feet 5 inches. "If a girl of eighteen can throw a baseball two hundred feet and turn Vassar College almost mad with joy by the accomplishment, then you reason that she must have thrown it just as a boy would. Girls are popularly believed not to know even how to throw a baseball. And as for throwing it straight and true, it isn't expected of them. So you put the question, knowing that it must turn out that the Vassar girl has learned the trick of throwing like a boy."

The reporter was not as impressed by Vassar's baseball teams. He writes, "Vassar, like several of the other girls' colleges, has its own baseball teams. The girls belonging to the college nines play regularly and practice hard. Yet it must be admitted that few are good at the game." However, Miss Smith explained to him the reason for their limited skills was that they lacked competition. Interscholastic sports were not allowed and so they could only play among themselves.

Vassar was not unique in its refusal to allow intercollegiate sports. The other "Seven Sisters" had similar policies. (Kenney, 1978, p. 111) In general, sports activities were acceptable as long as they were not too strenuous or too competitive.

In an article by Alice Fallows titled "Athletics for College Girls" (Vassar archives, source unknown), the virtues of sports are extolled. ". . . the average health throughout the women's college world is vastly better than it ever was in the days of nondescript, take-it-as-you-please exercise." (p. 65)

Further, participation in sports was seen as preventing nervous breakdowns. "Just here is the saving grace of athletics. . . . In the rush and whirl of some exercise that uses every muscle and requires each instant the judgment of an alert mind, there is no room for the little demon of worry . . . , the perplexing problem is forgotten; the player . . . takes up the next task with a fresher brain." (Fallows, p. 65)

But not everyone agreed. Mrs. M. L. Rayne, writing in 1893, attempted not only to discredit the schools and teachers who encouraged girls to exercise, but she told the mothers if they allowed their daughters to exercise they would become hopeless invalids. She said, ". . . we fear that certain fashionable schools have ruined the health of many a girl." For example, one teacher encouraged a student to exercise and now that "pupil thus advised lies to-day a hopeless invalid on her bed." She continued, "That teacher knew as much of pathology as she did of Hottentot." (p. 464) In general, the faculty and parents didn't take the girls' sports activities too seriously. Even baseball was seen as a relaxed, low key activity that got the girls out in the fresh air.

Smith College in 1879, four years after the college opened, also had intramural baseball teams. Eventually, there were interclass matches, interhouse matches, and even an annual faculty–student game.

A letter from Minnie Stephens, class of 1883, written to her classmates indicates how important baseball was in establishing sports at Smith. "Perhaps you have never really heard how Smith College happened to get the athletic field. . . . Way back in seventy-nine, I was more or less active and full of fun. It seemed to me that we ought to have some lively games in the way of wholesome exercise, so I got a few friends together and we organized a base ball club. We had no place to play except on the lawn in front of the Hubbard House. It was at that time quite extensive and although not an ideal field, it did very well for beginners."

A March 10, 1892, Boston *Herald* headline proclaims, "Smith Girls Play Ball." The freshmen beat the sophomores by a score of 29 to 9. However, interference led to some of the scoring against the sophomores. "In the first inning the sophs got in two runs, owing chiefly to the fact that the centre field caught in her dress skirt." There were also a few mishaps to dresses in the second inning, and the game was delayed and some pins applied.

There are other letters in the Smith archives written to parents or for the school archives which describe playing interhouse baseball. Two are especially informative.

One is from Ruth Lusk, class of 1900.

> The spring of 1898 and 1899—Dickinson House had a baseball team called White Squadron. Other houses had teams too, and we

played interhouse games. The ball our team used for practice was a regular hard ball and had been used in an Amherst–Williams game where Amherst was the Victor—4–0 I believe.

The second is a letter of April 20, 1908, from Margaret Towns-end, class of 1911, addressed to her parents urging them to send her a baseball glove: "Please ask Morgan [older brother] if he has a baseball mitt he can send me. We are practicing all the time now, and trying curves, and playing with a real baseball."

In November 1916, the three upper classes held a "Smith World Series." (Carson, 1951, p. 55) And by 1930, Smith College was touted as having the best outdoor athletic facilities which included a baseball field. (Rice, 1969, p. 300) In the 1930s or 1940s, there is mention of the custom of "traditional father–daughter baseball game during commencement week under the auspices of the Athletic Association." (Carson, 1951, p. 111)

Baseball became an organized sport rather than a club sport at Smith in 1916, and is listed as a major sport in the 1917 *Students' Handbook*. It is difficult to tell when baseball ceased to be played on the campus. The 1946–1947 *Student Handbook* lists softball rather than baseball. But equipment orders suggest that around 1940, softball equipment was being ordered. This would suggest that baseball was played for a considerable period at Smith, and yet no one in later years seemed to be aware of it.

The Mount Holyoke, Vol. 1, No. 1, June 1891, mentions the first official baseball club as of 1891. "Our first base ball club, organized during the spring term, has flavored the average conversation with 'strikes,' 'innings,' 'home runs,' etc. The diamond is in the quadrangle, and with the slope above fitted out for spectators, the Greeks would have thought it an ideal theater. Already the members have gone through most of the experiences naturally connected with the game, though disabling the umpire is a pleasure in store for the future. The organization was completed so late that they will not play in the intercollegiate league this year; but doubtless next season, they will compete on equal terms with nine other colleges." (p. 9) Although this is the first official record of baseball at Mount Holyoke, pictures in the archives show women playing baseball in the mid-1880s, unofficially.

Based on preliminary research, it appears that baseball was played at Wellesley in 1897, Radcliffe in 1915–16 and Barnard and Bryn Mawr by 1925. Baseball may have had its origin earlier on some of these campuses. Dorothy Ainsworth, writing in 1930, claims that by 1925 baseball was played at Vassar, Wells, Smith, Goucher, Wellesley, Bryn Mawr, Barnard, Rockford, Mount Holyoke, and Radcliffe. (p. 30)

Since baseball often was not part of the physical education program but rather an extracurricular activity often sponsored by houses or the athletic association, there are few official records. Letters, yearbooks, and student newspaper articles are the basis for much of the information. Consequently, one gathers a thread here and there, but an overall picture is difficult to obtain.

Ironically, although baseball was thought of as a man's game, it was not an issue on most women's campuses, probably because it was student-organized and remained to a large extent outside the physical education program. Most of the games were rather low key in terms of competition, and involved various houses on campus or clubs challenging each other. In general, anyone who wished to play could.

Basketball, which was introduced in 1892 at Smith College, became the catalyst for eliminating women's competitive sports on women's campuses. Basketball quickly became a popular and highly competitive game. Pressure from the students to make it an intercollegiate sport brought opposition from the physical education teachers. The female teachers, being products of the Victorian culture, worried about women's sports becoming too similar to men's sports. Lucille Eaton Hill, director of physical training at Wellesley College, summarized their concerns when she stated: ". . . fiercely competitive athletics have their dangers for men, but they develop manly strength. For women the dangers are greater, and the qualities they tend to develop are not womanly." (Gerber, 1974, p. 69)

In 1923, the Women's Division of the National Amateur Athletic Federation was formed. A platform of resolutions was established for governing female athletics. Basically, they called for programs of physical education that would stress universal participation rather than the participation of a select few. It was believed that individual records and the winning of championships should be discouraged and that the emphasis should be on physical fitness.

According to Dudley and Kellor, some of the reasons cited by physical educators for making women's sports less competitive were:

> Girls take things so seriously and the members of the defeated team cannot concentrate on studies for several days, especially where prizes are offered.

> Their behavior is generally demoralizing to the school; they try every means to meet in the library, halls and lavatory and talk games, of course.

> We have hundreds who would like to use the gymnasium but are unable to do so after school because the members of the team monopolize it. (1909, p. 151)

The platform proposed by the educators was adopted at the Conference on Athletics and Physical Recreation for Women and Girls, April 6–7, 1923. Most women's sports organizations accepted the platform. Its acceptance meant the elimination of intercollegiate athletics, so that 1923 marked the end of competitive sports for women on the college campuses. Baseball also faded from the scene. Sports activities were now geared to physical fitness rather than competition. On college campuses, women's participation in sports was severely curtailed. However, it was harder to stop the momentum of women competing in sports outside the schools.

For the society as a whole, it was the women's colleges that provided the image for the "new woman" in the late 1800s. Barney, in 1894, is quoted as writing: ". . . the girl who went fishing, climbed trees, and jumped fences was no longer inevitably looked upon as a tomboy or regarded with severe disapproval." (Quoted in Kenney, 1978, p. 108)

In the 1890s, sports participation became more acceptable for the masses because of the acceptance of sports for women at the eastern women's colleges and also because of upper-class women's participation in sport. Middle- and lower-class women emulated the roles of the upper class. Very often it was graduates from the women's colleges who were the physical education teachers in public and private schools. For example, 82.5% of graduates of Mount Holyoke from 1838 to 1850 taught school. Although most taught only until they married, which was usually less than five years, 26% taught for ten years or more. (Horowitz, 1984, p. 27) So the influence of the Seven Sisters was pervasive, both directly and indirectly.

Women's baseball in the late 1890s and 1900s was not unique to the upper-class women at the eastern women's colleges. In the society as a whole, some socially prominent women formed private baseball clubs and some women from humbler backgrounds played on professional women's teams.

Women's participation in baseball epitomized the changing role of women. The fact that this participation was relatively short-lived is also indicative of the changes that took place after women were granted the right to vote in 1920. The more the Suffrage Movement became acceptable, the greater the complacency and the greater the swing back to the Victorian ideal of full-time motherhood. As Gerber states: "The further in time from the end of organized feminism— defined as the movement for women's political and social rights which began in Seneca Falls and culminated in suffrage—the greater was the increase in women's return to domesticity and dependence." (Gerber, 1974, p. 21)

The 1890s and early 1900s were years that brought many opportunities for women. College education for women gained acceptance; the number of women who entered the professions increasd dramatically; women entered sports and were active in baseball; and the image of the "new woman" became accepted. But as the 1900s progressed and the battle for suffrage was won in 1920, complacency set in.

"Between 1890 and 1910," a Vassar professor recalled, women students "proudly . . . marched in militant processions and joyfully . . . accepted arrest and imprisonment for the sake of 'Votes for Women,' free speech, and to help a strike. By the 1920's, however, going to college had become an act of conformity rather than deviance, and the atmosphere of special purpose began to evaporate." (Chafe, 1972, p. 92)

Women's colleges dropped the sciences and "marriage" became the number one goal. Women's opportunities again declined and there was a return to the status quo. The era of women in baseball also came to an end.

References

Books and Articles

Ainsworth, Dorothy. *The History of Physical Education in Colleges for Women.* NY: A. S. Barnes & Co., 1930.

Ballintine, Harriet. "The Value of Athletics to College Girls." *American Physical Education Review,* 6 (June 1901):151–153.

Ballintine, Harriet. *History of Physical Training at Vassar.* Paper in Vassar archives.

Barney, E. C. "American Sportswoman." *Fortnightly Review,* Vol. LXII, Aug. 1894, 263–277.

Carson, Mary. *A History of Physical Education at Smith College.* Master's thesis, Smith College, 1951.

Chafe, William. *The American Woman: Her Changing Social, Economic, and Political Roles, 1920–1970.* NY: Oxford University Press, 1972.

Coffin, Tristram. *The Old Ball Game: Baseball in Folklore and Fiction.* NY: Herder and Herder, 1971.

Davenport, Joanna. "The Eastern Legacy—The Early History of Physical Education for Women." pp. 355–368 in Howell, Reet (ed.) *Her Story in Sport.* West Point, NY: Leisure Press, 1982.

Dudley, Gertrude and Frances Keller. *Athletic Games in the Education of Women.* NY: Henry Holt & Co., 1909.

Felshin, Jan, "Part 2: The Social View," pp. 179–279 in Gerber, Ellen, Jan Felshin, Pearl Berlin, and Waneen Wyrick. *The American Women in Sport.* Reading, MA: Addison-Wesley, 1974.

Frommer, Harvey. *Primitive Baseball: The First Quarter-Century of the National Pastime.* NY: Atheneum, 1988.

Gerber, Ellen, "Part 1: Chronicle of Participation", pp. 3–176 in Gerber, Ellen, Jan Felshin, Pearl Berlin, and Waneen Wyrick. *The American Women in Sport.* Reading, MA: Addison-Wesley, 1974.

Gerber, Ellen. "The Controlled Development of Collegiate Sport for Women, 1923–1936." pp. 432–459 in Howell, Reet (ed.) *Her Story in Sport.* West Point, NY: Leisure Press, 1982.

Gorden, Lynn. "Female Gothic: Writing the History of Women's Colleges." *American Quarterly,* 37 (Summer 1985): 299–304.

Haller, John, Jr. and Robin Haller. *The Physician and Sexuality in Victorian America.* Urbana: University of Illinois Press, 1974.

Hill, Lucile Eaton. *Athletic and Out-Door Sports for Women.* NY: Mac-Millan, 1903.

Horowitz, Helen. *Alma Mater: Designs and Experience in the Women's Colleges: From Their Nineteenth Century Beginnings to the 1930s.* Boston: Beacon Press, 1984.

Howell, Maxwell and Reet Howell. "Women in Sport and Physical Education 1900–1914," pp. 154–164 in Howell, Reet (ed.) *Her Story in Sport.* West Point, NY: Leisure Press, 1982.

Howell, Reet (ed.) *Her Story in Sport: A Historical Anthology of Women in Sports.* West Point, NY: Leisure Press, 1982.

Kenealy, Arabella, M.D. "Woman as an Athlete." 1899 article in *The Nineteenth Century Magazine* in Twin, Stephanie. *Out of the Bleachers: Writings on Women and Sport.* Old Westbury, NY: The Feminist Press, 1979, pp. 35–51.

Kenney, Karen. "The Realm of Sports and the Athletic Woman: 1850–1900," pp. 107–140 in Howell, Reet (ed.) *Her Story in Sport.* West Point, NY: Leisure Press, 1982.

Lee, Mabel. "The Case For and Against Intercollegiate Athletics for Women and the Situation Since 1923," *Research Quarterly,* 2 (May 1931):93–127.

Lee, Mabel. "Notable Events in Physical Education: 1830–1980." *Journal of Physical Education and Recreation,* 51 (Jan. 1980): 24–25.

Leitner, Irving. *Baseball: Diamond in the Rough.* NY: Criterion Books, 1972.

Leonard, Marcus, III. *A Sociological Perspective of Sport.* 3rd ed., NY: Macmillan Pub. Co., 1988.

Lucas, John and Ronald Smith. *Saga of American Sport.* Phila.: Lea & Febiger, 1978.

McCurdy, Persis. "The History of Physical Training at Mount Holyoke College." *American Physical Education*. XIV (March 1909): 138–150.

Mrozek, Donald. *Sport and American Mentality: 1880–1910*. Knoxville, TN: University of Tennessee Press, 1983.

O'Neill, William. *Everyone Was Brave: A History of Feminism in America*. NY: Quadrangle/The New York Times Book Co., 1971.

Park, Roberta. "The Rise and Development of Women's Concern for the Physical Education of American Women; 1776–1885: From Independence to the Foundation of the American Association of Physical Education," pp. 44–56 in Howell, Reet (ed.) *Her Story in Sport*. West Point, NY: Leisure Press, 1982.

Paul, Joan. "Conflicts Between the Victorian Pedestal and the Tomboy." Paper presented at the Southern District, American Alliance for Health, Physical Education, Recreation, and Dance, National Association for Girls' and Women's Sports, Orlando, Florida, Feb. 21, 1981.

Powell, Roberta. *Women and Sport in Victorian America*. The University of Utah, Ph.D. dissertation, 1981, University Microfilms International, Ann Arbor, MI.

Rayne, Mrs. M. L. *What Can a Woman Do?; Or, Her Position in the Business and Literary World*. Petersburgh, NY: Eagle Pub. Co., 1893.

Rice, Emmett and John Hutchinson. *A Brief History of Physical Education*. 3rd ed. NY: A. S. Barnes & Co., 1952.

Rice, Emmett, John Hutchinson, and Mable Lee. *A Brief History of Physical Education*. 5th ed. NY: The Ronald Press Co., 1969.

Richardson, S. F. "Tendencies in Athletics for Women in Colleges and Universities." *Popular Science*. (Feb. 1897):517–526.

Rickert, Edith. "What Has the College Done for Girls?" *Ladies' Home Journal,* Jan. 1912, pp. 11–12.

Riess, Steven. *Touching Base: Professional Baseball and American Culture in the Progressive Era*. Westport, CT: Greenwood Press, 1980.

Sargent, Dudley A., M.D. "Are Athletics Making Girls Masculine?: A Practical Answer to a Question Every Girl Asks." 1912 *Ladies' Home Journal* article in Twin, Stephanie. *Out of the Bleachers: Writings on Women and Sport*. Old Westbury, NY: The Feminist Press, 1979, pp. 52–62.

Sefton, Alice. *The Women's Division National Amateur Athletic Federation: Sixteen Years of Progress in Athletics for Girls and Women 1923–1939*. Stanford, CA: Stanford University Press, 1941.

Seymour, Harold. *Baseball: The Early Years*. NY: Oxford University Press, 1960.

Somers, Dale. *The Rise of Sports in New Orleans 1850–1900.* Baton Rouge, LA: Louisiana State U. Press, 1972.

Spalding, Albert. *America's National Game.* NY: American Sports Pub. Co., 1911.

Spears, Betty. "The Emergence of Sport as Physical Education" in *Coping with Controversy,* Wash., D.C.: The American Alliance for Health, Physical Education & Recreation, 1973.

Spears, Betty. "The Emergence of Women in Sport." pp. 26–42 in *Women's Athletics: Coping with Controversy.* ed. by Barbara J. Hoepner. Oakland, Calif.: DGWS Pub., 1974.

Spears, Betty. "Prologue: The Myth." in *Women and Sport.* Carole A. Oglesby. (ed.) Phila.: Lea & Febiger, 1978, pp. 3–15.

Squires, Mary-Lou. "Sport and the Cult of 'True Womanhood': a Paradox at the Turn of the Century." pp. 101–106 in Howell, Reet (ed.) *Her Story in Sport.* West Point, NY: Leisure Press, 1982.

Swanson, Richard. "From Glide to Stride: Significant Events in a Century of American Women's Sport." pp. 43–53 in *Women's Athletics: Coping with Controversy.* Barbara J. Hoepner (ed.) Oakland, Calif.: DGWS Pub., 1974.

Twin, Stephanie. *Out of the Bleachers: Writings on Women and Sports.* Old Westbury, NY: The Feminist Press, 1979.

Vassar, Matthew. "Matthew Vassar and the Vassar Female College." *American Journal of Education.* 7 (1862):52–56.

Vincent, Ted. *Mudville's Revenge: The Rise and Fall of American Sport.* NY: Seaview Books, 1981.

Voigt, David. *American Baseball, Vol. II: From the Commissioners to Continental Expansion.* Norman, Okl.: University of Oklahoma Press, 1970, pp. 279–306.

Voigt, David. *America Through Baseball.* Chicago: Nelson-Hall, 1976.

Wayman, A. R. *Education through Physical Education: Its Organization and Administration for Girls and Women.* 3rd ed. Phila.: Lea & Febiger, 1934.

Welter, Barbara. "The Cult of True Womanhood: 1820–1860." *American Quarterly.* 18 (Summer 1966):151–174.

Zeigler, E. F. (ed.) *History of Physical Education and Sport in the U.S. and Canada.* Champaign, IL: Stripes, 1975.

Newspapers

Boston Herald, March 10, 1892.
Daily Eagle, Nov. 11, 1895.
New York Herald, June 18, 1911.

Goucher College Archives

Knipp, *History of Goucher College*, 1938.

Mills College Archives

History of the Mills College Athletic Association 1899–1927.
White and Gold, 1 (Oct. 1894–June 1895).
Mills College Catalogs, 1909–1910; 1910–1911; 1913–1914; 1988–1989.

Mount Holyoke Archives

The Mount Holyoke, Vol. 1, No. 1, June 1891.

Smith College Archives

Students' Handbook 1917.
Students' Handbook 1946–1947.
Student letters.

Vassar College Archives

The Vassar Miscellany, Oct. 1876.
Vassariana, June 1866.

Wells College Archives

Holcroft, Temple R. Address Commemorating the 75th Anniversary of Wells College.

Blacks in Baseball

An Historical Perspective, 1867–1988

by Phil Mullen and Mark Clark

**Black Players and the Early Era of
Professional Baseball**

As one of America's more venerable institutions, baseball has proven to be an accurate reflection of this country's racial attitudes for more than a century. From its origins in Elysian Fields in June of 1846, baseball was popularized in the Civil War camps and successfully organized with the National League in 1876. With the formation of the American League in 1901, baseball became institutionalized as America's national pastime.

As baseball was popularized, blacks made their interest in baseball clear, and baseball made its attitude toward black involvement clear. In October, 1867, two organized black baseball clubs, the Excelsiors of Philadelphia and the Uniques of Brooklyn, played a contest "that was described by the press as the 'championship of colored clubs' " (Bruce, 5). The fact that the Excelsiors won this game at the Satellite Grounds in Brooklyn is of far less importance than the event that followed. In December of that year, the National Association of Baseball Players (NABBP) convened in Philadelphia. The black Python Club of Philadelphia sent a representative to the meeting. However, the nominating committee voted "unanimously . . . against the admission of any club that may be composed of one or more colored persons" (Bruce, 5). Citing political reasons and the desire to preserve the NABBP, the committee expressed sympathy to the Pythons.

With the passing of this motion, the NABBP drew a color line that persisted in organized professional baseball for nearly 80 years. "When the NABBP disbanded several years later, the written code of segregation perished with it" (Tygiel, 13). However, the organized leagues that succeeded it drew on this precedent and relied on unwritten "gentlemen's agreements" to exclude blacks.

Despite these continuing agreements, estimates conclude that more than 60 blacks (Bruce, 5) participated in the organized white leagues before the turn of the century. Baseball was becoming a highly competitive business with the potential for large financial profit. As a result, club owners competed, often unscrupulously, for the best players. Some of them were willing to sign blacks despite the unwritten "gentlemen's agreement." "Like the nation as a whole, baseball entered a period of experimentation regarding the role of black Americans" (Tygiel, 13).

The first known black professional player to play in the white leagues was Bud Fowler. Fowler had an extensive and distinguished minor league career, but was never permitted to play in the major leagues. Two other excellent black players excelled in the minor leagues during the 1880s. One was George Stovey, who won 34 games and lost 15 for Newark. Probably the best black player in organized baseball was Frank Grant, a second baseman who hit .366 for Buffalo of the International Association in 1887. Grant was favorably compared to the best white major league second basemen of his time.

Black players were often discriminated against by teammates and threatened with violence from white fans. Robert Higgins, a black pitcher, had compiled a 17–7 record for the Syracuse Stars of the International Association in 1888. Despite his success, Higgins encountered trouble with white teammates. Though he was accepted by the press and management, his teammates conspired to not support him in the field, hoping he would leave the team. "On June 9, 1888, the *Toronto Mail* reported that Douglas Crothers would not 'have his portrait taken with Higgins.' Crothers, also a pitcher, said that he would agree to have his 'heart cut out' before he would consent to being photographed with his black teammate" (Chalk, 31). In August, Higgins finally could take no more and left the team.

The players who went into the record books as the only two known black players in the major leagues before Jackie Robinson were Moses Fleetwood Walker and his brother, Weldy (Peterson, 22–24). Moses Walker was a catcher and played in organized ball for approximately six years. He played for Toledo in the American Association in 1884, then considered a major league. Moses was a good catcher and hit .263 in 42 games. His brother, Weldy, who also played in organized ball for several years, was signed to play left field when Toledo was plagued with injuries. He batted .222 in his five appearances with Toledo.

However, Weldy is best remembered for his passionate protest against the systematic discrimination that took place against blacks within organized ball during the 1887–1888 off season. By 1887, there were approximately 20 blacks playing in the professional leagues and the possibility of continued integration seemed promising (Tygiel, 14). In July of 1887, International League officials banned future contracts with black players. That summer, player discontent against blacks flared in other organized leagues. The Ohio State League followed suit by banning blacks. Weldy Walker, residing in Ohio, wrote a passionate protest to league president W. H. McDermitt.

> The law is a disgrace to the present age and reflects very much on the intelligence of your last meeting and casts derision at the laws of Ohio—the voice of the people—that say all men are equal . . . I ask the question again, 'Why was the law permitting colored men to sign repealed, etc.?' (Peterson, 32–33).

Weldy Walker's plea for equality and fairness was ignored by the baseball establishment.

> An article in the *Sporting News* in 1889 reported, "Race prejudice exists in professional baseball ranks to a marked degree, and the unfortunate son of Africa who makes his living as a member of a team of white professionals has a rocky road to travel" (Tygiel, 15).

By the close of the decade the color line had been firmly drawn; by 1895 there were no known blacks in organized baseball (Tygiel, 15).

Considered the best all-around player of his time, Adrian "Cap" Anson had a career that spanned 26 years. Playing largely with the Chicago White Stockings, Anson batted over .300 for 21 years, including two years over .400. He went on to manage the White Stockings.

Anson strongly shared the prevailing prejudice of the time against blacks. Sol White, player, manager, and the leading authority on 19th century black baseball, wrote of Anson:

> Just why Adrian C. Anson, manager and captain of the Chicago National League Club, was so strongly opposed to colored players on white teams cannot be explained. His repugnant feeling, shown at every opportunity, toward colored ball players, was a source of comment throughout every league in the country, and his opposition, with his great popularity and power in baseball circles, hastened the exclusion of the black man from white leagues (from White, cited in Peterson, 30).

During the time that racism was clearly establishing itself in organized baseball, it was just as clearly being reestablished in American society. The Civil War that had been fought ostensibly to free slaves, and had ironically helped popularize the game of baseball, was concluded 30 years prior to Sol White's exit from organized baseball in 1895. As historian C. Vann Woodward writes

> Just as the Negro gained his emancipation and new rights through a falling out between white men, he now stood to lose his rights through the reconciliation of white men (Woodward, 70).

Although history has singled out Cap Anson as the architect of baseball's color line, clearly if Anson had never existed the line still would have been sketched. Despite his strong hostility toward blacks, Anson alone could not be guilty of creating the prejudice of an entire society. However, his antipathy for black players resulted in nearly a one-man crusade to rid the game of black players. On several occasions he took his team off the field to protest the presence of blacks on the opposing team; he also attended numerous league meetings to campaign against the signing of blacks; and demanded firings of signed blacks (Tygiel, 14; Peterson, 29–30). His attitudes, coupled with the prevailing attitudes in society, exclusion of blacks from the professions, and a rising tide of court decisions enforcing the concept of Jim Crow, not only in the South but throughout the country, created an overwhelmingly hostile climate toward blacks attempting to play in organized baseball. Thanks to Anson, many of his fellow players, and the mores and direction of late 19th century America, the 20th century dawned with the national pastime as a Jim Crow enterprise.

In 1883, the United States Supreme Court reinforced this societal direction by virtually nullifying the Civil Rights Bill of 1875. In 1896, in the landmark *Plessy v. Ferguson,* the court stated legislation could not eliminate the racial instincts of a society. This case established the separate but equal doctrine that was to govern American society and baseball for the next half century (Woodward, 71). From this Jim Crow bleakness, black baseball unsteadily emerged.

Emergence of Black Teams

The genesis of professional black baseball occurred with the Cuban Giants. The Giants were formed in 1885 among waiters at the Argyle Hotel in Babylon, Long Island, and became the first salaried black baseball team (Peterson, 34). They were the prototype for black teams of the next 35 years, as they had no regular league affiliations but traveled around, or "barnstormed," playing both black and white teams.

By 1900 there were five black professional baseball teams (Peterson, 59) as it was becoming apparent that hopes for playing in the white leagues were futile. In 1902 the Philadelphia Giants were organized with the help of Sol White, while in 1905 the Royal Giants were organized by Brooklyn restaurant owner J. W. Connor. These two teams became the best teams of the first decade of the twentieth century.

During the second decade of the twentieth century, black professional teams multiplied but continued to lead a precarious existence. Many great teams, including the Chicago American Giants, Lincoln Giants of New York, Homestead Grays, and the Indianapolis ABC's, were founded. It was also during this time that the first two great black superstars—Joe Williams and John Henry Lloyd—appeared. Lloyd, a shortstop, was called the "Black Honus Wagner." Playing in Cuba in 1910, he outperformed the young Detroit Tiger star Ty Cobb (Chalk, 47). He is rated as the best shortstop in black baseball and often the best all-around player. Smokey Joe Williams pitched in obscurity for years in Texas before joining the LeLand Giants in 1910 at age 34. A hard-throwing right-hander, he often bested major and minor league all-star teams in exhibition competition. "A 1952 poll of black baseball figures voted Smokey Joe Williams the greatest black pitcher of all time, a single vote ahead of Satchel Paige" (Rogosin, 13).

Inception of the Black Leagues

Despite a proliferation of teams and some great players, black baseball continued to struggle as the 1920s approached. Several attempts at league organization had failed because of financial instability and a lack of effective leadership. In 1886, the Southern League of Colored Baseballists, a first attempt at a black league, broke up before a game was played (Bruce, 7). Several other short-lived attempts at organization were made before 1920, but none survived for more than a year.

However, during World War I, conditions for blacks in America saw some improvement. Despite the hardened racial attitudes and increased segregation laws of the first two decades of the twentieth century, World War I brought economic conditions that benefited blacks. Factory owners in the North, deprived of immigrant labor, began to hire blacks. This began a great migration of blacks to the North. Northern cities swelled with blacks, who, with their newfound prosperity, discovered they could support the institutions of their newly structured separate communities.

The economic climate was finally right for black leagues. All that was needed was a strong leader. That leadership emerged in the indomitable presence of Rube Foster.

Rube Foster stands alone as the dominant figure in the history of black baseball. As a pitcher he was considered one of the greatest of his time, gaining his nickname for defeating the great Rube Waddell in the early 1900s. Seeing him pitch in 1905, "Pittsburgh's great shortstop Honus Wagner reputedly called him 'the smoothest pitcher I've ever seen'" (Holway, 12). However, Foster's towering status in black baseball came not as a player, but as a manager, owner, and, most of all, as a league organizer.

By 1911 Foster became manager and co-owner of the newly formed Chicago American Giants. Due to Foster's managerial skill and business ability, the American Giants were the cream of black baseball through the decade. During this time, however, Foster became increasingly disenchanted with independent black baseball. "He was at the mercy of white booking agents and, in the increasingly hostile racial climate of post World War I Chicago, that reliance was inherently unsatisfactory" (Rogosin, 9). He envisioned a league modeled after the white major leagues, with black players playing for black owners and the money staying in the black community.

During the winter of 1919, Foster acted on his vision. He met with the owners of the best midwestern independent clubs in the Kansas City YMCA and proposed the formation of the National Negro League. The result of this historic meeting was an eight-team league. Additionally, Foster had hoped to organize a group of eastern clubs. However, hostility over player raids, ownership of eastern clubs by whites, and resistance to Walker as a czar made this impossible (Holway, 32). However, in 1923, with Foster's encouragement, the Eastern Colored League came into existence. In 1924, an uneasy truce was declared between the two leagues and the first Negro League World Series was played between the two leagues.

Unfortunately, Rube Foster did not live to see his final dream realized. He died in 1930 and his funeral was one of the largest Chicago had ever seen. As its founding father, he organized and gave black baseball respectability, and laid the groundwork for the successful integration of major league baseball.

In philosophy Foster was a disciple of the controversial black leader Booker T. Washington, who believed that the key to white acceptance lay in blacks "banding together and building counterparts to white institutions—whether cultural, welfare, religious, educational, economic or purely social . . ." (Meier, 138). Washington believed this strength would ultimately result in integration. Foster "wanted black baseball to develop so that when the white leagues were ready to integrate 'we would be ready'" (Holway, 21). Foster's vision proved correct as the Negro Leagues were ready to produce Jackie Robinson 25 years later when integration finally took place. They also produced a steady and ready supply of black athletes to play and excel on major league teams over the 15 years following integration.

The 28 years of Negro League baseball represent the pinnacle of black baseball. Despite financial problems, instability of ownership, poor traveling and accommodations, extensive barnstorming, and uneven training and coaching, black baseball was producing players and teams that black society could look to with pride. The Negro Leagues were accomplishing a sociological goal of the movement to build viable black institutions. They were also proving in concrete terms to the average black that blacks were at least equal to whites. They did this by winning "over sixty percent of their encounters with white major league opponents, though the records of these games are incomplete and difficult to evaluate" (Rogosin, 6). They did this as well by producing great stars like Oscar Charleston, Satchel Paige, Buck Leonard, and Josh Gibson, who proved themselves the equal of any players they performed against.

The Eastern Colored League and the Negro National League played their own World Series 1924–27. In 1928, the Negro eastern league, beset by financial instability, disbanded. Without Rube Foster's leadership (he was hospitalized in 1926 for a nervous breakdown), player wars resumed and the Negro Leagues appeared to be on the verge of total collapse. Rube Foster died in 1930 and "the *Kansas City Call*'s sportswriter concluded that 'when Foster died, Negro baseball as a league died'" (Bruce, 67). In 1931 the Negro National League existed on paper, but no final standings were published. As 1932 ended, the country was in the depths of depression, Rube Foster's National Negro League was finished, and black baseball was in disarray.

In 1933, W. A. (Gus) Greenlee, a Pittsburgh racketeer and owner–organizer of the Pittsburgh Crawfords, stepped forward to become the unlikely saviour of black baseball. Greenlee headed up the reorganization of the Negro National League. In 1937, the Negro American League was formed and the old two-league structure was returned. ". . . Greenlee had laid the foundation for a league that would survive, but with many changes until 1948" (Peterson, 93). During the late 1930s and early 1940s, these new black leagues achieved a degree of financial stability and became one of the largest black business enterprises in the country.

However, Greenlee made an even greater contribution to black baseball in 1933 when he organized the first East–West, or all-star, game played in Chicago's Comiskey Park. This game became the highlight of the Negro League season, surpassing the Negro World Series. For years it reigned as the dominant black sporting event in America. The all-star game drew attention to the high quality of play in the Negro Leagues and regularly drew crowds of 30,000–50,000 fans.

Despite the success of the Negro Leagues in the late 1930s and 1940s and the presence of star quality players, strong opposition to integration in baseball still existed. However, increasingly members of the white press and the white baseball establishment became outspoken in their support of integration. In the 1930s, sportswriters like Westbrook Pegler, Jimmy Powers, Heywood Broun, and Shirley Povich began to take up their pens in support of integration. For example,

> Dan Parker of the *New York Daily News* editorialized that "there is no good reason why in a country that calls itself a Democracy, intolerance should exist on the sportsfield, that most democratic of all meeting places" (Rogosin, 181).

Baseball people were slower coming to public support of integration.

> In 1938, Clark Grifith became the first member of baseball's official family to admit the possibility that Negroes might one day be in organized baseball (Peterson, 176).

Shortly thereafter, baseball managers and players began to be quoted by aggressive members of the press in support of integration. Leo Durocher, highly visible and outspoken manager of the Brooklyn Dodgers, asserted he "would hire colored players if they were not barred by the owners. I've seen a million good ones" (Rogosin, 182). Signs were beginning to appear that the "gentlemen's agreement" was once again in jeopardy.

However, this time the social context was much different from 60 years earlier. World War II, like World War I, had triggered a major population shift. Blacks, again drawn by the opportunity for employment in defense plants, migrated to the industrial north and now began to constitute a substantial proportion of the population of northern cities. Northern blacks, for the first time, became an appealing consumer market. While segregation and discrimination had continued to be potent forces after World War I, the racial climate began to change in the late 1930s. Economic power and voting power had a great deal of influence, but the major influence for change was World War II.

> Many historians view the war as a watershed in the struggle for civil rights. The conflict against Nazi racism exposed the contradictions of racial practice in the United States (Tygiel, 37).

All of these forces, combined with the increasing militancy of blacks and their supporters, translated into progress for integration during the 1940s.

> . . . while only ten bills favorable to civil rights were introduced in the 75th Congress (1937–38), the number of such bills increased in each succeeding Congress until in the Eighty-first Congress (1949–50) seventy-two were introduced (Woodward, 127).

It was in this political and social context that the erosion of the "gentlemen's agreement" took place.

In response to Leo Durocher's remarks, as well as mounting pressure regarding blacks, Baseball Commissioner Kennesaw Mountain Landis issued a formal statement in 1942 which stated in part:

> Negroes are not barred from organized baseball by the commissioner and never have been during the twenty-one years I have served. There is no rule in organized baseball prohibiting their participation and never has been to my knowledge. If Durocher or any other manager, or all of them, want to sign one, or twenty-five, Negro players, it is all right with me (Peterson, 178).

This statement is seen as an important moment since it was the first time the Commissioner issued a statement concerning the race issue, and it indicates the growing pressure for integration.

Although his biographer does not allude to the subject (Spink, 1947), a search of other literature reveals Commissioner Landis was never a friend to black baseball. A Federal Court judge selected as Commissioner in 1921 to restore baseball's image which had been severely damaged by the 1919 Black Sox Scandal, Landis had sought to oppose integration whenever possible without drawing public attention. Early in his tenure, Landis ordered that major leaguers not wear their uniforms when opposing blacks and that these games be labeled all-star contests. At times he even canceled integrated all-star contests, fearing his teams were being embarrassed by Negro League teams (Rogosin, 184).

When pressure for integration became more intense in the 1930s and 1940s, he used his office to suppress formal discussion of the race issue.

> During the mid-1930s, according to then National League President Ford Frick, Landis short-circuited a suggestion by several owners to debate the issue in closed session, ruling that the topic had not been properly placed on the agenda (Tygiel, 31).

In 1943, he allowed black leaders to appear at a major league meeting, but denied discussion of their proposals (Tygiel, 31). As was the case with Cap Anson, Landis could not have held the color line if the mores of the times had not still permitted.

In the fall of 1944, Landis died of heart failure. With Landis gone, proponents of integration took new hope. In April 1945, A. B. "Happy" Chandler, United States Senator from Kentucky, was chosen Commissioner. As a Southerner, Chandler's views on integration were initially suspect. However, Chandler's first public statements as Commissioner indicated support for integration. When queried regarding blacks in baseball, he responded:

> If they can fight and die in Okinawa, Guadacanal, in the South Pacific, they can play baseball in America. . . . And when I give my word you can count on it (Rogosin, 199).

With the new commissioner in office, events moved quickly. On October 28, 1945, Branch Rickey, owner of the Brooklyn Dodgers, signed a black baseball player named Jackie Robinson to play for the Dodgers' AAA team in Montreal. In 1947, Robinson starred for the Dodgers as they won the National League pennant. The opposition to Robinson and his subsequent success is well documented, and has become baseball legend. Robinson became the first black to play major league baseball in over 60 years. He broke the color line that required blacks to accept the same unequal status in baseball that they were forced to accept in society. Although baseball was slow to assimilate blacks, it became one of America's first institutions to undertake desegregation.

Desegregation—The Early Period

The breakthrough of the "color line" in 1947 has led to an influx of black players in current day major league baseball. While the acquisition of black major league baseball players has not equaled the proportions in professional football and basketball (see Table 1), nonetheless, they have exceeded black proportions in society as a whole.

Through the 1950s, the number of blacks increased steadily but slowly. Larry Doby, Willie Mays, and Hank Aaron starred, but in reality black participation was limited. By 1954, only 18 blacks (Coakley, 145) had made it into the major leagues, and it was 1959 when the last team (Boston Red Sox) finally desegregated. This pattern persisted through the 1960s, with 11% black participation in baseball, while black participation in professional football and basketball doubled and tripled. However, the impact of the black athlete in baseball was felt. As one reporter wrote, "Jackie's nimble, Jackie's quick, Jackie makes the turnstiles click" (from Lowenfish, cited in Coakley, 147).

Into the 1960s, the social phenomenon of the black athlete did not go unnoticed and several sociohistorical studies of this period attempted to shed light on the reality of circumstances (Grusky, 1963; Rosenblatt, 1967). The period is marked by an "opening of doors," but not necessarily an elimination of prejudice or the adoption of a positive attitude toward racial integration. As Coakley (149) succinctly states:

> Desegregation is marked simply by the opening of doors. The actual *elimination* of prejudice and the achievement of integration are marked by unqualified invitations to come through the doors and join *all* the activities going on inside regardless of where they are happening or who is involved. Jackie Robinson recognized these differences between desegregation and integration when he once remarked that some of his racist teammates on the Brooklyn Dodgers only tolerated him as a fellow athlete because he "could help fill their wallets." He knew those teammates never fully accepted him as a human being either on or off the field (especially off the field). The door to sport was opened for Robinson, but he knew there were no unqualified invitations to participate in everything going on inside or in the rest of the life outside of sport.

Race and Playing Position (1970–present)

As the United States moved into the 1970s, blacks and other social groups (e.g., women, the elderly) took a more intensive look at their own social circumstances. Protest came in many forms as these groups came to understand the negative aspects of their social realities. Athletics in general, and the black athlete in particular, were no exception to this concern and its concurrent self-study. It is at this point that the role of the black athlete becomes a highly visible social entity for study. How many blacks participate? What positions do they play? How do salary and performance of black athletes compare with white athletes? What is the relationship between black players and white (or black) coaches?

Studies which dealt with race and playing positions commonly referred to a phenomenon known as "stacking." Stacking was a coined term that meant bunching black players at specific positions and excluding them at other positions (Edwards, 1969; Edwards, 1973). In

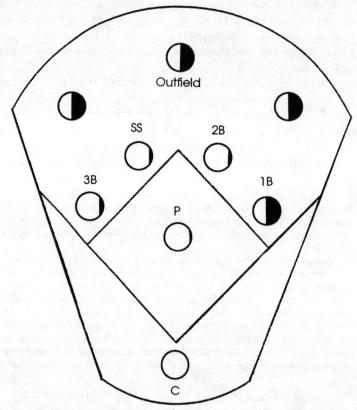

Figure 1—Blacks in Baseball by Playing Position
*   [This figure taken from Coakley, Sport in Society: Issues and Controversies, 1986]*

This Figure portrays the percentage of black players in each baseball position during the 1985 season, represented by the shaded areas. Blacks remain concentrated in the noncentral positions (outfield and first base) and underrepresented in the central positions, especially pitcher and catcher.

baseball, this translated to the outfield and first and third base. "Stacking" studies then led to studies dealing with "central" versus "non-central" playing positions (Loy and McElvogue, 1970).

The "centrality" studies evaluated player positions by race and function of the position. Those positions that touched the ball most, or that were critical to the movement of the ball (especially in football and basketball) were considered the most important and central to the team. In general, the studies found that whites occupied very high percentages of central positions and that blacks occupied very high percentages of non-central positions when related to the total number of blacks and whites in the sport as a whole. Investigators interpreted this finding to mean that whites occupied the leadership and thinking roles on teams, while blacks occupied positions based more on physical ability. This interpretation was then related to how Americans stereotypically viewed blacks and whites in society at large. The reality of this phenomenon in 1985 is depicted in Figure 1.

Table 1
Population Proportion Increase of Black Players in Baseball, Basketball and Football

Sport	*Year Black Player % Equaled General Population Proportion	1954	1962	1966	1970	1975	1980	1985
Baseball	1957	7%	12%	20%	22%	21%	22%	20%
Basketball	1958	5%	30%	51%	54%	60%	75%	75%
Football	1960	14% (1956)	16%	24%	34%	41%	49% (1982)	54%

*These figures taken from D. Stanley Eitzen and George Sage, *Sociology of American Sport*, page 239.

1975 percentages for all three sports taken from D. Stanley Eitzen and George Sage, *Sociology of American Sport*, page 239.

Baseball figures for years 1962, 1966 and 1970 taken from Gerald W. Scully, "Discrimination: The Case of Baseball," in *Government and the Sport Business*, ed. by Roger G. Noll (Washington, DC: The Brookings Institute, 1974).

Basketball figures for years 1962, 1966 and 1970 taken from Norman R. Yetman and D. Stanley Eitzen, "Black Americans in Sport: Unequal Opportunity for Equal Ability," in *Civil Rights Digest* (August 1972). 5(2):20–34.

Football figures for years 1962, 1966 and 1970 taken from Norman R. Yetman and D. Stanley Eitzen, "Immune from Racism? Blacks Still Suffer from Discrimination in Sports," in *Civil Rights Digest* (1977).

Baseball figures for years 1954, 1980 and 1985; football figures for years 1956, 1980 and 1985; basketball figures for 1954, 1980 and 1985 taken from Jay J. Coakley, *Sport in Society: Issues and Controversies* (1986).

Summary

Today, sport is in a state of flux, confusion, and uncertainty. Player strikes are with us, owner disagreements are continuous, "free agency" has changed some of the traditional owner/player relationships, people are no longer "flocking" to the stadiums and arenas unless a team "wins," and television viewing audiences were reported down in 1987 for the first time in years. With this in mind, the number of black players has continued to increase in football and basketball, while baseball notes a recent decline after years of increase (see Table 1).

Several answers have been suggested to explain this changing pattern. Some suggest that as blacks concentrate more heavily in inner cities, the "rural" flavor of baseball leads them into other types of sport activities. Others suggest that baseball-focused Central and South American countries represent a cheaper labor source than the United States for skilled players. Ongoing study should provide interesting outcomes in the future.

To the black community, black athletes are a source of "pride." Black athletes represent models of "brothers" who have made it in the American society at large. However, because black athletes continue to be one of the few "success" models for black youth, they help channel black youth into sports. This process in turn reinforces the process of directing black youth toward sports and away from other potential spheres of upward mobility. Thus large numbers of blacks in the sports world represent a detriment to the group's chance to be mobile across a wider spectrum of the American occupational structure.

The reality is that very few people (black or white) will have a chance to "make it" in professional sports. For example, in baseball, there are approximately 850 positions in the major leagues. Physical skill, luck, coaching, and other factors come into play as to who will "make it." The reality is that a person from the general population would have a better opportunity to become a lawyer, doctor, engineer, or business person rather than a professional athlete, given a similar amount of time spent to achieve occupational aspirations.

The authors have tried to present, in brief form, the rich history and contribution of black players to the American pastime of baseball. Additionally, we have tried to tie in social circumstances and key personalities of the presented era to add context and greater understanding of historical data. One can conclude that the attitudes exhibited toward blacks in baseball mirror societal attitudes.

References

Bruce, Janet. *The Kansas City Monarchs.* Lawrence KS: University Press of Kansas, 1985

Chalk, Ocania. *Pioneers of Black Sport.* New York: Dodd, Mead & Company, 1975

Coakley, Jay. *Sport in Society: Issues and Controversies.* (3rd ed.) St. Louis MO: C. V. Mosby, 1986

Edwards, Harry. *The Revolt of the Black Athlete.* New York: The Free Press, 1969

Edwards, Harry. *Sociology of Sport.* Homewood IL: The Dorsey Press, 1973

Eitzen, G., Stanley and George Sage. *Sociology of American Sport.* Dubuque IA: William C. Brown, 1978

Gursky, Oscar. "The Effects of Formal Structure on Managerial Recruitment: A Study of Baseball Organization." *Sociometry.* 26(1963): 345–353.

Holway, John. *Blackball Stars.* Westport CT: Meckler Books, 1988

Loy, John and Joseph McElvogue. "Racial Segregation in American Sport." *International Review of Sport Sociology.* 5(1970): 5–20.

Meier, August. *Negro Thought in America 1800–1915.* Ann Arbor MI: The University of Michigan Press, 1969

Peterson, Robert. *Only the Ball Was White.* Englewood Cliffs NJ: Prentice-Hall, Inc., 1970

Rogosin, Donn. *Invisible Men.* New York: Atheneum, 1985

Rosenblatt, A. "Negroes in Baseball: The Failure of Success." *Transaction.* 4(1967): 51–53.

Scully, Gerald. "Discrimination: The Case of Baseball." In *Government and the Sport Business* (R. Noll, ed.). Washington DC: The Brookings Institute, 1974

Spink, J. G. Taylor. *Judge Landis and Twenty-Five Years of Baseball.* New York: Thomas Y. Crowell Company, 1947

Tygiel, Jules. *Baseball's Great Experiment.* New York: Oxford University Press, 1983

Woodward, C. Vann. *The Strange Career of Jim Crow.* (2nd ed.). New York: Oxford University Press, 1966

Yetman, Norman and D. Stanley Eitzen. "Black Americans in Sport: Unequal Opportunity for Equal Ability." *Civil Rights Digest.* 5(1972): 20–34

Recent Baseball Fiction

An Intellectual Odyssey

by J. Michael Lillich

I've been a baseball fan all of my life, except for a few years in the late 1960s and early 1970s when I lost myself in a haze of rock and roll music, idealism, and highbrow intellectualism. I came back to the game in the mid-'70s, but in the last few years I've been obsessed with the Chicago Cubs. By this time, I should have left fanatical baseball fandom to the drunks in the bleachers, scaled down my interest to following the Cubs fatalistically on the radio at work and in the garden, and to making my annual pilgrimage to Wrigley Field with my ten-year-old son, Bret, the best pitcher in three deep Southern Illinois counties.

You see, I began my fifth decade of life and received a Ph.D. in English literature last year, and was expected finally to raise all of my life to a level of high seriousness. Graduation brought presents, though, and one of them was *Season Ticket: A Baseball Companion* by Roger Angell, baseball writer for *The New Yorker*. Angell writes about the great American pastime with an effortless grace and erudition that does justice to the elegance and nuance of baseball. He was the first living writer I'd read in four years, and I was hooked. I immediately went out and got his other books. In *Late Innings*, Angell writes about each game's "resonance and seriousness" (87) and of ". . . the humor and eloquence of the players and coaches (and fans and writers) . . . and the immense variety of their attachments to this complex game" (68).

I knew right away that the standard academic advancement mode of publishing the most promising chunks of the dissertation I'd spent the last year and a half writing would have to wait. Milton's project was to reconcile the ways of God to men. My project was no less serious: to reconcile (at least for myself) the ways of baseball to the Western literary tradition. Sportscasters try to level the sport/art disparity when they talk about the ballet of basketball, the warlike complexity and coordination of football, the concentration and physical power of boxing, the speed and grace of hockey. But to me it's all ultimately unconvincing. While I maintain a low-level addiction to other sports, it is only baseball that I think about with the kind of depth I usually reserve for literary analysis and theory. Or as Angell quotes the late Bill Veeck, the P. T. Barnum of baseball: " 'You can't *savor* a basketball game or a football game, can you?' " (75).

This is what I pondered as I took my seat on the third base side of the infield in the Terrace section of Wrigley Field last August for a contest between the Cubbies and the St. Louis Cardinals. I had arrived an hour before game time to experience baseball's great sounds, sights, and smells, the smack of a well-thrown ball into the glove, the vendors' squawks and hollers, that sharp crack of the bat, the cresting ebb and flow of the giant radio-static murmur of the crowd, the people of all ages and sizes, everyone equal as fans no matter what their status or position on Monday morning, the great American aroma of hot dogs, onions, and beer.

At this early stage in my investigation, I was also thinking that writing about sports was a strange marriage between the instinctive Zen concentration in the on-field reactions of athletes and the after-the-fact, conscious ruminations in words of writers. I looked down from the wide expanse of stands to the field and beyond to the bleachers, the classy, antique, manually-operated Wrigley Field scoreboard, to the pennants atop the walls denoting the day's standings in the National League East and West divisions, to the rooftops on Addison and Sheffield and beyond. Sitting there, I realized that baseball doesn't fit onto a TV screen. (Football, by contrast, was made for TV. It's no accident that pro football didn't really gain mass popularity until they put it on the tube.) Admittedly, at the ball game you don't see the replays or slo mos. If you turn your head, you've missed a play. No second chances. But at the park, the fans are part of the action. The involvement is more like reading than watching television.

At the game, you see and experience a thousand little dramas on the diamond: the game's centerpiece, the existential confrontation between pitcher and batter in which the difference between victory and defeat, life and death, is measured in fractions of inches and milliseconds; the pickup and toss by the shortstop, the double play pivot of the second baseman, leaping over the oncoming spikes of the base runner and throwing, all in one thrilling motion, to nip the runner at first; the arc of the fly ball hit to the right or left centerfield power alleys and the ensuing race between the ball's hitting the ground safely ("Come on, Gravity!") or the outfielder's plucking it off the top of the grass while running full speed toward the infield.

A ball game is an eternity. Baseball seen in person, it occurs to me, gives time and experience depth in the same way that great writing does. Depth because baseball reaches back in time to its origins in the nineteenth century with its formal, elegant human mechanics, conjuring up in the mind's eye yellowed photos of players dressed in their quaint, Victorian era high-stockinged uniforms. And depth because each game harkens back to its mythical archetype: the same nine stately innings, four balls, three strikes, three outs tie today's game to yesterday's, to Ruth's (real or apocryphal) called-shot homer at Wrigley Field in the 1932 World Series, to Bobby Thompson's "shot heard round the world" of 1951 that won the pennant in the last inning for the Giants against the crosstown, long-suffering, archrival Dodgers, to Don Larsen's perfect game in the 1956 World Series.

There is the undeniable poetry in Gabby Hartnett's ninth-inning home run that will be known forever as the "homer in the gloaming" as night descended on lightless Wrigley Field in the last week of the 1938 season. The mythic clout was an important home run, vaulting the Cubs over Pittsburgh and into the World Series. And what a sonorous, lyric turn of phrase, the "O" in gloaming picking up the sound of the "O" in homer, and the medieval "gloaming" suggesting a time of knights and heroic deeds towering over the forces of evil. That the powerhouse Yankees went on to annihilate the Cubs in four games takes nothing away from the poetry or the myth.

Baseball's literacy is underlined in the colorful nicknames of its greatest players. Babe Ruth's prowess as a player and a personality appropriately earned him two wonderful nicknames: "The Sultan of Swat" and "The Bambino." Ted Williams was "The Splendid Splinter" and "The Thumper," Joe DiMaggio "The Yankee Clipper," Willie Mays "The Say-Hey Kid," Pete Rose "Charlie Hustle," Ernie Banks "Mr. Cub," Stan Musial "The Man," Orlando Cepeda, "The Baby Bull," Phil Rizzuto, "Scooter." Sometimes, monikers are so apt that they obscure players' given names. None but the most fanatical fan can provide the given names of Babe Ruth, Pee Wee Reese, Yogi Berra, Moose Skowron, Duke Snyder, or Blue Moon Odom.

William (Sugar) Wallace in *The Ultimate Baseball Book* shows that baseball's nicknames can stand alone as poetry in their own right. Here are a few sample stanzas:

> Catfish, Mudcat, Ducky, Coot.
> The Babe, The Barber, The Blade, The Brat.
> Windy, Summy, Gabby, Hoot.
> Big Train, Big Six, Big Ed, Fat.
> The Georgia Peach, The Fordham Flash,
> The Flying Dutchman. Cot.

> The People's Cherce, The Blazer. Crash.
> The Staten Island Scot.
>   Skeeter, Scooter,
>   Pepper, Duster.
>   Ebba, Bama, Boomer, Buster.
> The Little Professor, The Iron Horse, Cap.
> Iron Man, Iron Mike, Iron Hands. Hutch.
> Jap, The Mad Russian, Irish, Swede. Nap.
> Germany, Frenchy, Big Serb, Dutch,
>   Turk. Tuck, Tug, Twig.
>   Spider, Birdie, Rabbit, Pig.
> Three-Finger, No-Neck, The Knuck, The Lip.
> Casey, Gavvy, Purmsie, Zim.
> Flit, Bad Henry, Fat Freddie, Flip.
> Jolly Cholly, Sunny Jim.
>   Shag, Schnozz,
>   King Kong, Klu.
>   Boog, Buzz,
>   Boots, Bump, Boo. (7)

You can read the history of this country in the nicknames in Wallace's poem, the rural beginnings, the irreverent creativity, the immigrant populations, the rough humor, the American slang, and joy in the game.

The art of nicknaming is waning, though, probably another casualty of television and commercialization, what Angell describes as "the continuing power of network television over common sense and good baseball" (61). Today's players, of necessity, have become serious businessmen equally at home in the executive suite as on the ballfield. A few players are still well-named. Dwight Gooden is known as "Dr. K," Andre Dawson "The Hawk," Will Clark "The Natural." Think about all this in terms of the oral poetic tradition in which the function of the poet was (and in many ways still is) that of namer.

Ruth, in his Yankee Stadium farewell address on June 13, 1948, called baseball "the only real game." Indeed. Major league baseball was a mature American adult before football and basketball were out of knickers. In the 1930s, the All-Star game was practically an undeclared national holiday. And you could, according to baseball lore, walk through the streets of Brooklyn in the 1950s and never miss a play in Dodgers' games because of the play-by-play emanating from the radios sitting in open windows in this pre-air-conditioned era. George V. Higgins in *The Ultimate Baseball Book* writes much the same thing about the Red Sox in New England:

> 'Boston' is bounded on the south by Long Island Sound and
> the New York–Connecticut border, on the west by the Buffalo city

limits, and to the north by Canada. One can take a two-hour ramble among the catwalks of the Nantucket Boat Basin, stopping to inspect yacht after yacht, without missing a single inning of the Red Sox game. When your car radio loses the signal from the station in Hartford (WTIC), you will have the choice of several more stations. One of them will be playing on the radio in the general store and gas station at which you make your pit stop in eastern Vermont . . . (331–32).

Note: In the 1989 Red Sox home opener when the fans cheered adulterer Wade Boggs and booed star pitcher Roger Clemens for disparaging the Fenway faithful, an AP story quoted an upper-deck patron: "You know what they say about Red Sox baseball. It's not life and death. It's more serious than that."

Given this kind of devotion, it's no surprise that baseball is the most written about sport. Throughout its history, grown (mostly) men have responded to this game with a sea of words, in newsprint, in novels, in essays, and lately in some fairly sophisticated films. All that has been written about other sports, I would venture, cannot compare in quantity or quality to the body of baseball's prose. What, I wondered, is behind this need to come to terms with the game on paper?

Angell writes of baseball's ability to make us see as children again, to view the world of the game in terms of good versus evil, the Charming Cubbies, with smiley little bears on their shirts, attempting to triumph against overwhelming odds as does a young dragon killer of old. Sparky Anderson, manager of the Detroit Tigers, recalls the legendary Yankee skipper Casey Stengel at age 73 telling him: "Never lose the kid in you, because if you do, you've lost it all." A lesson for life, that.

Baseball, more than any other sport, also returns us to childhood innocence culturally as the country boy's post-fieldwork pastime takes us back to a simpler, pastoral era before the technologies of war and mass media forever changed our view of human potential and the possibilities for its degradation. Listen to Thomas Boswell's eloquence on the subject:

> Born to an age where horror has become commonplace, where tragedy has, by its monotonous repetition, become a parody of sorrow, we need to fence off a few parks where humans try to be fair, where skill has some hope of reward, where absurdity has a harder time than usual getting a ticket (53).

The game accomplishes this by taking us back to a time when both the hopes and fears of one's individual and collective life were more nearly human-sized.

Baseball is still the most perfect of educational tools, the symbolic understanding of the complex relationship between individual and collective action. I must, at least subconsciously, have understood this when my son was born, because we started playing ball as soon as he could sit up. By the time Bret was three, he could switch hit and throw equally well with either hand. But then he revolted, flat out refused to hit or throw lefty. I accepted his decision stoically. But some of the early baseball training stuck because Bret has come to understand at an early age that he can pitch a shutout or get the game-winning clutch hit, but it's the team that wins. Nobody wins unless we all win. And nobody wins every day. Here are essential lessons of interpersonal relationships, of being a member of a family, an organization, and a society.

For the adult fan, all this enters the realm of the sublime, the pure, and the mythic, away from the world of compromise and tones of real life, the adult world of moral and ethical grays. How can we love the Cubbies, the Bums, and the Bosox in all their tragedy, their valor, and their ineptitude? Angell provides a clue when he writes:

> Serious fans forgive bad baseball in the end, for they know how hard this game really is, and a shocking error or a poor game or series only whets the appetite for our appreciation of the opposite: the clutch play, the big hit—courage and triumph in the unfair presence of danger (62).

Ironically, by the time we can appreciate at this level, with all its intricacies, symbolisms, and traditions, we are adults, older than the heroes on the field. Son Bret carefully used to keep in his head a (short) list of major league players older than I am. But when he and I watch a game together, we're the same age. Angell writes: "Nobody can know all about this game—not even Yaz" (58). And: "In baseball, Yogi Berra once said, 'you don't know nothing'" (100).

The Literature of Baseball

The visible, commercial writings about baseball are largely self-serving: books ostensibly written by the stars of the game "with" (in small print) a professional writer. Rick Talley, formerly a sportswriter for the *Chicago Tribune,* and the *Los Angeles Daily News* whose book, *The Cubs of '69,* came out in 1989 to generally good reviews, performed the "with" function in Jay Johnstone's 1985 best-seller, *Temporary Insanity.* His description of the *modus operandi* is instructive. Talley began, he says, by taping hours of conversation with the game's self-proclaimed flakiest flake. Talley then had the tapes transcribed, categorized the material into chapters, and wrote the manuscript in the first person. The published result became a best-seller largely because its sale was banned at Dodger Stadium (showing incredible lack of awareness by the front office types on how the modern media machine works, namely, that no ink is bad ink). Be that as it may, Dodger brass deemed *Temporary Insanity* unbecoming to the national pastime and a corrupting influence on the youth of the nation. This, because it contained a verbatim rendition of former Cubs' manager Lee Elia's legendary x-rated blasting of Wrigley's supposed diehards. The attention accorded the banning brought publicity, sales, and a sequel, *Over the Edge.* It was not as successful as the first book. "I couldn't figure out a way to get it banned," said Talley sardonically. When it was all over, Talley was none too enamored of the whole process. "The players all have agents, and everybody wants a piece of the action while you do all the work."

From the serious baseball reader's point of view, the problem is different. What's produced in the "with" books today is generally disappointing, surpassing in length but not in depth the post-game television interview. Even worse, these superficial, commercial, and hurried productions tend to trash all baseball literature by association. Suffice it to say that not many of my buddies over in the English department are reading baseball fiction.

While you can list some impressive literary figures who have written about baseball here or there (William Kennedy, John Updike, Philip Roth, Garrison Keillor, Ernest Hemingway, and Marianne Moore come immediately to mind), what's surprising is that there hasn't been much more high-quality baseball fiction. Earl R. Wasserman, writing about Bernard Malamud's *The Natural,* puts the paucity of baseball fiction into its proper perspective.

> The wonder is that we do not have a whole library of significant baseball fiction since so much of the American spirit has been seriously poured into the game and its codes until it has a life of its own and affects the national temperament (47).

I've given the relatively small number of good fictional treatments about the national pastime a fair amount of thought, and the problem, it seems to me, is that baseball is too big to be a metaphor for anything else, that the essence of metaphor for a writer is to zero in on the elemental and the essential in the midst of human and social complexity. Baseball won't reduce to elemental metaphor because of its own complexity, nuance, characters, and mythology. The result is that even fiction writers tend to write essays, and not fiction, about baseball.

There can be no question how deeply embedded is baseball in the core of the American experience. Angell quotes from Chicago novelist James T. Farrell that " 'change in baseball runs parallel with other changes in American life' " (75). Wasserman, in his Malamud article, refers to Virginia Woolf's statement that baseball provided the means for Ring Lardner to come to grips with

> . . . one of the most difficult problems of the American writer; it has given him a clue, a centre, a meeting place for the divers activities of people whom a vast continent isolates, whom no tradition controls. Games give him what society gives his English brother (63).

This is not only extraordinarily on the mark but also an incredible insight on the part of Woolf, the modernist English novelist and one of the last people on earth one would expect to appreciate baseball or even appreciate the appreciation of baseball.

Clearly, baseball hasn't had its Melville or Tolstoy, but there are more than a few novels about baseball that are successful esthetically, manage to do the game justice, and add to its appreciation. Mark Harris, for example, wrote in 1953 a wonderful novel, *The Southpaw*, in which we see the growth and development of a young, left-handed pitcher, Henry Wiggen, from childhood through his first season with the fictional New York Mammoths. We also see an awkward boy become a somewhat less awkward young man.

I came upon *The Southpaw* not completely by accident. Harris was an English professor I knew slightly at Purdue University when I went to grad school there in the early 1970s. So I was familiar with his name and picked up the book to complete an armload I was checking out of the library in pursuit of serious baseball fiction.

I found it in the story of Henry Wiggen through his halting and, by his own admission, not quite literate words. (Harris wrote the book while in graduate school and commented later in an interview that he was out to see what he could accomplish artistically using plain language. He refers to his baseball fiction as "in the Henry Wiggen manner.") *The Southpaw* is your classic *Bildungsroman*. As Henry tries to make sense of the world, his development as a baseball player outruns his maturity as a man. Besides the social symbolism of baseball, the game also functions here as an index of personal development.

The Southpaw kept knocking around in the back of my head, as good art always does, and I thought about giving Harris a call and maybe even sitting down over a beer with him the next time I visited my parents. And then I thought, he wrote the book almost 40 years ago. Was he even at Purdue any more? Could he even talk about the book if he wanted to? I got my answer to the second question when I went back to the library and found a 1979 book by Harris, *It Looked Like Forever*. Harris, through a distinguished career as a novelist and a teacher, never forgot Henry Wiggen. Almost three decades after the publication of *The Southpaw*, Harris gives us a fortyish Henry cut by his team and passed over as manager, using wiles as tricky as a backdoor curveball to catch on with a team for one more chance. Financially secure through insurance sales and investments, Henry still can't seem to face the world without his comfortable, understandable medium of baseball.

Certainly, Henry is more sophisticated after his 17-year career in Harris' fictional big show. His problem (and ours as a culture, perhaps) is that as his understanding has increased, the world hasn't stood still. The simple, pure time of daytime baseball has succumbed in fact and fiction to the demands of big money, television, and the World Series played at night in October under domes. The lost days of baseball and the world that surrounded it are what Henry really seeks. In his more contemporary present, he has a bright, troubled daughter, and a whole host of other women in his life whom he doesn't quite understand. No wonder he wants to stay on the pitcher's rubber above the modern tide of unresolvable complexities where he can be in control, where the lines between male and female, right and wrong, winning and losing, success and failure are more clearly drawn. Finally, both baseball and Henry are every bit as removed from their pastoral beginnings as the supermarket from the self-sufficient homestead.

Among many literate baseball enthusiasts, at the top of baseball's fictional heap is Robert L. Coover's *The Universal Baseball Association, Inc., J. Henry Waugh, Prop.*, a novel about another Henry, a middle-aged accountant not a player, a man who makes up his own complex chart and dice game based on baseball—a whole league, in fact. (Think about Oscar Wilde, life's imitating art, and the rotisserie baseball craze here.) As Henry gets more involved in his baseball creation, he gets more removed from his "real" life. He finally quits his job and dedicates himself to running his imaginary league. The initial crisis of the novel is a decision about whether he will alter the probabilities he has created to save the life of Damon Rutherford, the league's star rookie pitcher and Henry's sentimental favorite. He doesn't, choosing the product of his imagination over the world's agreed-upon definition of reality's limits. Later, he does alter the dice to kill Jock Casey, the beanball killer (perhaps premeditated murderer) of his young star. More and more, though, the characters and inner dynamics of Henry's imaginary baseball association occupy center stage in the novel as the made-up characters take on lives and individuality much more interesting than Henry's real-life human acquaintances and experiences. Henry, for example, goes to the neighborhood bar after the death of Damon, and he is surrounded by Universal Baseball Association players, veterans, and officials in a scene as wild, bawdy, and surrealistic as any you've ever read.

Since *The Universal Baseball Association,* Coover has gone on to a very successful writing career. But, he said in 1988, from Brown University where he teaches creative writing, *The Universal Baseball Association* remains special to him. It has remained in print continuously since its publication in 1968. And in 1988, Coover celebrated a 56th birthday, the same age as his protagonist, Henry Waugh. "That sounded terribly old to me when I wrote the book," he laughed.

The impetus for writing *The Universal Baseball Association* came, Coover explained, "in a box of old rubbish" his parents had hauled around for years after Coover was grown and on his own. When they finally pressed the box on him, he found old scorecards of an imaginary baseball board game he and a friend of his had made up when they were kids in Iowa. When Coover's family relocated to Southern Illinois, Coover and his friend played for awhile by mail.

Looking through the old scorecards, Coover realized that he could remember his imaginary players—even what they looked like in his mind's eye—as well as the St. Louis Cardinals whose games he listened to Harry Carey and Gabby Street broadcast from Western Union ticker tape from which they supplied their own made-up, colorful details. "It was pure invention, great fiction in its own right," Coover remembered.

So Coover, the serious adult artist, set out to make great fiction of his own out of this kid's game. Baseball was not, he stressed, a mechanical device pressed into the service of some larger truth, but rather something that came out of his own imaginative childhood experience. The writing began as a short story, but soon blossomed into *The Universal Baseball Association.* For Coover, baseball, then, was not a metaphor. Boswell describes baseball rather as a "source" of metaphor.

The game, which remains one of our broadest sources of metaphor, changes with our angle of vision, our mood; there seems to be no end to our succession of lucky discoveries (57).

And in his 1989 *The Heart of the Order:*

Baseball is an apolitical, open-ended source of metaphor; the story of Babe Ruth's life doesn't belong to any party or ideology. In sports, as in few other corners of our world, we agree to settle for the disconnected, inclusive insights rather than insisting on correct and final canons (125).

Coover, I think, would concur. His description of writing *The Universal Baseball Association* testifies to the natural way the game flowed into the writing: "As a writing experience, it was very pleasant," he remembered. "I was living in Spain, and I wrote it in five weeks, five short weeks, actually. I revised it between academic terms." Other novels have taken him years to complete.

So, has this winner of some of the nation's most prestigious writing awards become a self-conscious *artiste* and forsaken the national pastime? No indeed. Living in New England, Coover has joined the fans closest to those of the Chicago Cubs in terms of endurance of loss and self-imposed frustration. I am speaking, of course, of none other than the Boston Red Sox, raising the hopes of their long-suffering fans once again in 1988 by making it to the play-offs only to be mangled by the Oakland A's.

So here we have Coover, a well-respected writer—and one who has been exploring the limits of state-of-the-art literary esthetics (Take my word for it or read, for example, *Pricksongs and Descants.*), and he not only hasn't gotten beyond baseball but still lives and dies with the Bosox. So for him and his reader, there's clearly more involved here than child's play in the choice of baseball, as Lois Gordon's commentary in *Robert Coover: The Universal Fictionmaking Process* illustrates:

. . . baseball is not only an American religion; it is the American way, representative of activities and a unique psychology worshipped by Americans. In its dogged competition of men set against one another, it represents the American capitalist system (with jargon like 'trading,' 'property,' and even 'stealing'); it exemplifies the Horatio Alger myth, in that anyone, regardless of heritage, can achieve fame and wealth through application and achievement. In its stylized version of men combating other men, it satisfies a nation's lust for (and guilt toward) war and power, but it also fulfills a primitive power lust, and its teams often have animal names or generic names of the hunt or conquest (Tigers, Giants, Pirates,

Braves). Baseball also reflects the eternal rivalry between the generations, the cyclical transcendence of the young and vital over the old and worn. With time still the enemy and success dependent upon good or bad form, baseball reinforces a prominent distinction in American culture between the old and young. A few, elite aged are always honored as advisers to the now young in their prime, while the rest are put out to pasture (43).

Obviously serious stuff, cultural and baseball literary criticism, if you will. It is, however, mostly wrong, snorts one serious St. Louis baseball maven: "What about the Cubs, the Cardinals, the Orioles in the hunt thing? And baseball is a game where time doesn't count. Obviously, she doesn't know a damn thing about baseball." Warming to his task, he continues: "Football, not baseball, is the game that symbolizes American war, power, and domination. When do they play football? In winter, in the season of death. When do they play baseball? In the spring when life begins and in the summer, the season of growth." But, despite the (perhaps sexist?) sniping here, there's a lot to what Gordon says. In many ways, of course, games can be seen as places where a culture symbolically acts out its deepest realities. Let's not deconstruct baseball, though.

On one level, the daily athletic grist from the mill into which newspaper sportswriting has devolved is male soap opera, the chance to follow a player's career from high school, college, or the minor leagues, through the majors, into retirement, and even to join the immortals in Cooperstown. Clearly, though, newspaper baseball writing isn't what it used to be in the pre-television days that Roger Kahn wonderfully describes in the early chapters of *The Boys of Summer*. An old hand sends him out to cover his first assignment with this vivid example of baseball writing ringing in his head:

> 'Barney pitched as though the plate were high and outside.'
> That's the way I want to see you write baseball. You can do it.
> 'Barney pitched as though the plate were high and outside' (87).

Later, Dick Young explains to the fledgling writer that the real fan already knows the score and what happened. He wants something else in his written accounts. There are three rules of baseball writing, Young goes on to explain, after ordering another drink. " 'Tell 'em fucking why or make them laugh.' " And: " 'Don't be so fucking sure' " (103). These are rules that work for just about any kind of writing, by the way. If the profanity offends, Kahn, a few pages later in response to his father's statement that " 'profanity is superfluous to English,' " thinks, " 'But you have inverted reality, Father. English is superfluous to baseball profanity' " (115).

It's ironic that baseball journalism is generally so weak and pallid now due to complex social reasons that are often beyond the writer's control. It's also sad because baseball and newspapers came of age together. But with the proliferation of games on television, and the fans not only knowing what has happened but probably having seen it, too, Young's realistic fan-based rules of writing become more, and not less, relevant today. Baseball journalism, like its haughtier counterparts—"hard" news and editorials—presents doses of reality or interpretations of reality on a daily basis during the season, not once a week as in football or twice a week as in basketball. But the proliferation of baseball books suggests a desire to understand the success and failure of an imaginative Other in mythic, timeless terms. Again, Gordon, writing about Henry Waugh's Universal Baseball Association, hits upon the eternal fascination of the imaginative and emotional apprehension of the game for the fan:

> . . . it reflects and indeed defines Henry's personal life. Designed to keep him from the brink of loneliness and boredom and to distract him from the full realization of his own limitations and limited possibilities, Henry's baseball satisfies his deepest needs. A game of tremendous excitement, it pits control against chance; each and every move offers its players potential great accomplishment, public adulation, and even immortality (40).

Certainly, the distraction from individual limitations part of the commentary is true, as is the importance of the element of chance. In baseball, as in life, the bad hop grounder and the bloop hit can foil brilliant strategy and precise execution. On the other hand, again demonstrating she needs to take a seat not in the stacks but in the grandstand, Gordon fails to realize that baseball demands above all that we come to terms with failure. For baseball is more about failure than success. Three base hits in 10 at bats is the measure of a superior hitter. This means that seven times out of 10, the batter fails. A pitcher who gets credit for winning six games in 10 over the course of a career in which he pitches with skill, courage, and artistry has a shot at the Hall of Fame. Boswell understands all this:

> If you do everything right every day, you'll still lose 40 percent of your games—but you'll also end up in the World Series (56).

Kahn, too, understands that failure lurks at the heart of baseball, responding to Duke Snider's statement that the Dodgers were a better team even though the Yankees had just won the 1953 World Series:

"That's the hell of it. That's the rottenest thing in this life, isn't it? The best team doesn't always get to win" (185–86). Finally, listen to Clem Labine talking to Kahn almost two decades after giving up the winning hit in the 1953 World Series to Billy Martin:

> . . . I broke down a little, but I learned. After that, when I lost a big one, I asked myself two questions: Did I do my best? Hell, yes. Do I want sympathy? Hell, no. Looking back, it was good that I learned about losing (213).

So what the game is really about is responding to failure and loss, of picking oneself up out of the dirt and attempting once again to triumph against all odds.

As I continued to think about baseball and baseball writing, I began to think that the complexity of this kid's game makes baseball more akin to apprehending great literature than other sport. But can you really cast into the intellectual trash heap the highbrow/lowbrow distinction between art and sport? As I thought about these potentially weighty matters, fate intervened like a wind-blown double when my daily *Chicago Tribune* carried an article about the film *Field of Dreams*, the movie adaptation of W. P. Kinsella's 1982 novel, *Shoeless Joe*.

This seemed to be my answer. I read the novel in two sittings. The baseball/literary fantasy (that incidentally sold 500,000 copies) in which the main character (named Kinsella by author Kinsella) follows the behest of voices ("the ballpark announcer," character Kinsella calls him) telling him to do outrageous things: to build a baseball field in his Iowa cornfield so his father's hero, "Shoeless" Joe Jackson, disgraced and thrown out of the game after the infamous 1919 "Black Sox" scandal, will have a place to play; to kidnap J. D. Salinger, recluse author of *Catcher in the Rye*, and take him to a Red Sox game at Fenway Park to "ease his pain" (incidentally, Salinger's lawyers wrote Kinsella that he was "outraged and offended to be portrayed in the book"); to go in search of and find in Minnesota a former player, Moonlight Graham, twenty years dead, who played in one major league ball game during his career but never had an official major league at bat.

The culmination of the novel is a Chicago baseball fan's dream game, a spectral confrontation between the 1919 Black Sox and the Chicago Cubs with the legendary Tinker-to-Evers-to-Chance double play combination.

Clearly, Kinsella plays with time here. Players—including character Kinsella's father—rise from the dead to play ball in Iowa. (How much of baseball is about fathers and sons?) Kinsella demonstrates that as there are no time limits in baseball, there are no imaginative limits either, which moves the game into the realm of the timeless—like literature, that is, with a palpable tradition and integrity that other sports can only hope to achieve. Baseball, in fact, has been an American institution for as long as literature has been studied at the university level in this country. Great books and great writers, great games and great players don't exist in the dead past, but rather eternally in the imaginative present of succeeding generations. It works. The figures of Cy Young, Babe Ruth, Shoeless Joe Jackson, and Ty Cobb tower over the American consciousness (at least in its male incarnations) as clearly as do Huck Finn, Captain Ahab, Jay Gatsby, and Nick Adams. This is what Harris, Coover, and Kinsella underline in their imaginative tales spun out of the strong sinews of a country boy's game that grew up with America.

References

Angell, Roger. *Late Innings*. New York: Simon and Schuster, 1982.

Boswell, Thomas. *The Heart of the Order*. New York: Doubleday, 1989.

Coover, Robert. *The Universal Baseball Association, Inc., J. Henry Waugh, Prop.* New York: Random House, 1968.

———. Unpublished personal interview. 7 Oct. 1988.

Einstein, Charles, ed. *The Fireside Book of Baseball*. Fourth Edition. New York: Simon and Schuster, 1987.

Gordon, Lois. *Robert Coover: The Universal Fictionmaking Process*. Carbondale: Southern Illinois University Press, 1983.

Harris, Mark. *The Southpaw*. Indianapolis: Bobbs-Merrill, 1953.

———. *It Looked Like Forever*. New York: McGraw-Hill, 1979.

Kahn, Roger. *The Boys of Summer*. New York: Harper & Row, 1971.

Kinsella, W. P. *Shoeless Joe*. Boston: Houghton Mifflin, 1982.

Okrent, Daniel, and Harris Lewine, eds. *The Ultimate Book of Baseball*. Boston: Houghton Mifflin, 1979.

Talley, Warren D. (Rick). Unpublished personal interview. 10 Nov. 1987.

Wasserman, Earl R. "*The Natural:* Malamud's World Ceres." *Bernard Malamud*. Harold Bloom, ed. New York: Chelsea House, 1986.

Putting Yourself in Your Place
or
The Decline of Local Beers, Metropolitan Newspapers, and Passenger Trains, and the Resurgence of Minor League Baseball

by Paul L. Gaston

We may pick a year, not too long ago. For instance, 1954. An afternoon in the late summer—July, August.

In Hammond, Louisiana, a small strawberry-farming town about 60 miles from New Orleans, a man and his son stand on a station platform, a little after three o'clock in the afternoon. They await "The Louisiane," Illinois Central Train No. 3, not the fastest or most luxurious train on the IC, but a reliable means of local transportation among towns and cities between Chicago and New Orleans.

When the train pulls in at 3:24, father and son will board for the hour's ride to the Carrollton Avenue station in New Orleans. The station stands adjacent to Pelican Stadium, the home of the New Orleans member of the AA Southern Association. Because they will be an hour or so early for batting practice, they will stop by a neighborhood cafe. There the father will drink a cold Regal Beer while his son reads the afternoon *Item* for news of the Pelicans and the Nashville Vols. They will have an exciting evening at the stadium, watching George and Gene Freese and other Pelicans play for Danny Murtaugh's Pirates farm team.

Now, we move forward by a decade. What remains? Not Regal Beer. Not the "Louisiane." Not the New Orleans *Item*. Not the Pelicans.

Instead of Regal, Budweiser. Instead of the "Louisiane," a crowded Interstate 55. Instead of the *Item*, a newspaper monopoly operated by the *Times-Picayune*. Instead of Pelican Stadium, a motel. And instead of the New Orleans Pelicans, televised games from inside the Houston Astrodome.

The unwieldy title of this chapter was chosen with care for, with one recent and significant exception—minor league baseball—every reference in it points to an institution fallen into steep decline recently within our lifetimes.

Local breweries have closed as their industry has become largely the province of a very few large corporations. In 1880, there were more than 2,000 breweries in the United States. Every city and many towns had at least one brewery they could call their own. Following Prohibition, only 750 remained, and many of these were in precarious financial condition as a result of the Great Experiment. Today, despite a misleading proliferation of labels and brands, there are fewer than 50 mass market brewers.

The story is the same with regard to metropolitan newspapers. In the early 1900s, there were nearly 2,000 daily newspapers in the United States. Among these, more than half were major metropolitan dailies. As late as 1960, New York City alone had eight, including the *Times,* the *Herald-Tribune,* the World-Telegram and Sun, the *Journal-American,* the *Post,* the *Daily News,* and the *Daily Mirror.* Now, despite enormous growth in potential readership, the number of major metropolitan newspapers continues to dwindle.

New York may be fortunate that three of its dailies have survived, for nearly all major cities now depend on newspaper monopolies. Even more disturbing is the fact that many of these monopolies are themselves controlled by a few large corporations.

As for trains, no admirer of passenger rail travel should speak ill of Amtrak, which in 1971 rescued a transportation system on the brink of total collapse. Following the 1960s, when the Interstate Commerce Commission granted railroads the right to discontinue more than 1,000 passenger trains (Stover, 192), Amtrak did well to salvage a vestigial route system and to maintain reasonably reliable service.

Yet the fact remains that the latter half of the century has witnessed the end of the passenger train as a realistic travel option in the United States for most people for most trips. Relatively few cities enjoy passenger rail service. (You cannot catch a train in Chattanooga, for instance; the Chattanooga Choo-Choo is now a Holiday Inn!) And the low frequency of remaining services would preclude convenient connections, even if those connections were still serving the towns which trains once linked so efficiently to major cities—and they are not.

Indeed, many small cities and towns no longer have access to any form of long-distance public transportation. Throughout the United

States, a lengthy automobile ride to a heavily subsidized, poorly patronized regional airport has replaced a five-minute ride to the local train station.

These phenomena may at first appear to have little in common beyond their capacity to evoke an earlier era which was in some ways more charming than the present, in some ways, less. Taken together, however, they illuminate a compelling paradox: a strong sense of place, once regarded as a singular characteristic of the American consciousness, has grown progressively weaker among Americans, as local institutions, tastes, accents, entertainments, and urban environments have given way before broad appeals to sameness.

In Pittsburgh and Montgomery, the same hotels and motels roll out the same welcome mats. In Fort Lauderdale and Wichita, identical cantinas pour identical margaritas during afternoon happy hours. In Atlanta and Chicago, trendy restaurants with the same offbeat Irish name and the same raffish memorabilia on the walls serve from the same eclectic menu the same entrees. And on the downtown corners of Des Moines and Baton Rouge and Phoenix and Salt Lake City, outside glass-and-aluminum boxes named One Main Place or Republic Centre or Mercantile Square, you will find vending machines selling—what else?—*USA Today*.

Most American cities, large and small, now remind one of the comment regarding Oakland which was attributed to Gertrude Stein: "When you get there, there is no there, there."

But if our sense of place has grown weaker, have we, at least, gained as compensation a more generous acceptance of regional and cultural differences? Has our increasingly homogeneous environment encouraged a more tolerant and generous society?

There is good reason to conclude otherwise. Indeed, a sense of social cohesion and continuity, which once supported bonds between neighborhood and town, between town and city, and between different cities, appears to have eroded as well. St. Louis provides an instructive example. Within the metropolitan St. Louis area, St. Louis "city" and St. Louis "county" remain locked in bitter rivalry, with different school systems, different governments, and different priorities. St. Louis lost its professional football team in part because both city and county wanted to build a new football stadium, and neither would support the efforts of the other. It almost has lost its rapid transit funding for the same reason.

And if this rivalry were not problematical enough, Missouri's citizens living outside its metropolitan areas periodically express through the ballot box disapproval of their city cousins. No new taxes for zoos and symphony orchestras and museums in St. Louis and Kansas City!

For other examples, we might consider the deep social and political divisions which divide Washington, D.C., from its Maryland and Virginia suburbs. Or the fierce insularity of Highland Park and University Park, towns which resist identification with Dallas, the city in which they are, literally, embedded. Or the suspicions that separate North Atlanta from South Atlanta. Or San Francisco's contempt for Oakland. Or Memphis and West Memphis. Or St. Louis and East St. Louis.

Though there are exceptions to the pattern, by and large, for the last 35 years, both anonymity and insularity have risen together in painful paradox as opposed but linked coordinates on a graph tracing the increasingly troubled American spirit. That is, as our cities and towns have grown more and more alike, those who dwell within them have grown more and more detached from one another.

Twenty-five years ago, Susanne Langer, in her essay "The Ultimate Unit," defined the process of which these phenomena are symptomatic as one of "individuation." In contrast with "involvement," the basis for human society, "individuation" leads to a repudiation of those ties—ancestral, civic, regional, religious, patriotic—which inform and define society. "Most people today, and especially the thoughtful and serious ones," Langer says, "feel that they are not bound by any commitment they have not made themselves" (121).

Lewis Mumford is another who read the early evidence regarding the effect of "individuation" on the modern metropolitan area. Holding in view both inner-city decay and anonymous suburban spread, Mumford in 1961 described a typical metropolitan dweller as one who works in the city, lives in the suburbs, and "renounces the obligations of citizenship at both ends" (502).

At the end of the 1960s, Asa Briggs drew similar conclusions: "It is clear that the sense of the city as a particular 'place' means little to large numbers of alienated people" (96).

It is also clear that those unable to share a sense of place in the city have gained little (and perhaps lost much) from their flight to the suburbs. Again Lewis Mumford:

> This movement from the center carries no hope or promise of life at a higher level. Just as our expanding technological universe pushes our daily existence ever farther from its human center, so the expanding urban universe carries its separate fragments ever

farther from the city, leaving the individual more dissociated, lonely, and helpless than he probably ever was before (503).

Local beers, metropolitan newspapers, and passenger trains— their declines are of course symptoms of, not causes for, the increasing isolation and alienation of the individual American in an increasingly homogeneous society. However, because they are symptoms which together point to a profound weakening in our sense of place, they deserve careful and detailed consideration.

Distinctive local beers, owned by the notables of one's city, brewed with the city's water, and sold by one's neighbors in neighborhood taverns, now offer little competition to the thin brews marketed to the millions by anonymous corporations. We buy beer in the supermarkets, not the corner tavern. Our companion as we drink our beer probably will be not a neighbor, but the television set. A closed cycle: television tells people what beer to buy and keeps them company while they drink it.

Local beers once confirmed our sense of place in another way as well. Many beers bore on their labels some local landmark or natural feature—Mount Rainier, a statue of Andrew Jackson, the headwters of the Tum, a city skyline, or an engraving of the brewery itself.

Others took their name from their places of origin, as a few survivors will attest: Falls City, Lone Star, Dixie, Grain Belt, Chippewa Falls, Iron City, Steel Valley, Reading, Valley Forge, Utica Club, Duquesne. But whatever the label, whatever the name, there was a strong sense of regional pride evident in brewing and in drinking the local beer.

Now, the few local beers that remain must struggle to hold a respectable market share in their own backyard. In New Orleans, for instance, Dixie cannot compete in advertising or in distribution resources with the Miller Brewing Company and Anheuser-Busch. As a result, when you visit New Orleans, you will find Miller and Bud far more easily than you will find Dixie.

Consider again metropolitan newspapers, which in the days of competition contributed distinctive, idiosyncratic perspectives to local debates. Attached to time and place, they contrasted with one another in their makeups, in their editorial opinions, and in their respective journalistic styles. They created healthy differences of opinion among neighbors. In large cities, commuters might well be able to stake out a position on a local issue by buying one paper instead of another.

Competition encouraged energetic journalism. But if there is only one newspaper in town, will a reporter work as diligently? Every story becomes an "exclusive." Will the city editor risk taking chances with the goodwill of powerful advertisers if the resourcefulness of the paper's reporting has little bearing on its circulation? And what incentive is there to invest in international or even national reporting if there is no competitor around to show up a paper relying too heavily on the wire services?

The decline in competition among newspapers may represent at least part of the explanation for the decline in influence of those that remain. How many, home from work, still pick up an afternoon newspaper to read what their neighbors have written, thereby learning about the people who live in the place where they live? Instead, television—network, local, and cable—dominates the delivery of news in the afternoon and evening.

The decline of the passenger train also illustrates the two tendencies pursued here—one, away from a sense of place in a society grown increasingly homogenous, the other, towards the isolation of the individual from that society.

It is helpful to recall that trains, however lengthy their runs, carried with them a strong sense of place. Like local beers, in fact, they often bore names associated with the places they served: The City of Miami (Illinois Central), The Grand Canyon (Santa Fe), The Hell Gate (New Haven), The Gulf Wind (L&N), The Piedmont Limited (Southern), The Broadway Limited (Pennsylvania), or The Empire State Express (New York Central).

Moreover, just as the passenger train provided frequent, reliable links between town and city, it offered its passengers for the duration of their trips the society of other travelers. At mealtime, in fact, dining car practice required total strangers to share their tables and, inevitably, their conversations—conversations which might well continue after dinner over cigars and highballs in the lounge.

By contrast, both inefficient automobiles and crowded airplanes serve effectively to isolate the traveler, both from place and person. Both discourage the traveler from forming new acquaintances, either with features in the landscape or with other travelers.

But these are the forms of travel in which we have invested our public funding. Both the airlines and the Interstate Highway System thrive on massive public subsidies, while Amtrak must make its case in Congress annually for the continuance of modest federal support.

For those seeking to understand the ills besetting the nation's spirit, these are worrisome symptoms indeed. As they read the same newspapers, drink the same beers, and earn their frequent flyer points on the same few airlines, Americans seem to have lost touch with the places where they live and with one another. And they seem, many of them, at least, neither to notice nor to care.

But there may be some good news!

Minor league baseball, another institution with its roots in a more sociable and coherent society, appears to be emerging as an important—and heartening—exception to a continuing trend towards uniformity and isolation. Once an apparent victim of this trend, its newfound promise now offers evidence of a countertrend: from isolation to camaraderie, from network entertainment to local fun, from detachment to engagement.

In 1988, minor league baseball drew 22 million fans, an increase of 4 million in just two years. And with new or beautifully restored parks in cities like Albuquerque, Chattanooga, Richmond, Louisville, and Buffalo, the 160 minor league teams may still be approaching their era of real prosperity. "Catch minor-league fever," writes David Brill in a magazine published in spring 1989 for free distribution in college bookstores. "Join the fans flocking to see baseball's rising stars take a shot at the big leagues."

There may be good news in such omens. Like the local newspaper, a minor league baseball team encourages and exposes idiosyncratic personalities, carries on local traditions, and arouses indigenous enthusiasms. Like local beer, minor league baseball can thrive on the justifiable pride of a local economy; having one's own professional baseball team playing on the dirt and grass of one's own backyard can become far more compelling than the opportunity to watch a situation comedy manufactured in Hollywood. And, finally, like the passenger train, minor league baseball on the one hand offers an opportunity for neighbors to enjoy one another's company. On the other hand, again like the train, minor league baseball provides towns and small cities with tangible links to other towns and cities along the line. "He's on his way to Louisville," a fan in Little Rock may say after watching a good pitching performance. Or, conversely, "He'll soon be back in Springfield if he doesn't raise his batting average."

If minor league baseball should continue to grow more popular with an American public increasingly disenchanted with the bland and uniform distractions available through its more expensive entertainments, its return to favor may one day appear to have been a harbinger for a more proud and more spirited society.

That rosy view may find additional justification in a few other signs as well. Some venerable local beers, such as Anchor Steam in San Francisco, Rolling Rock in Latrobe, Pennsylvania, and the aforenamed Dixie, are once again thriving. And some innovative new brews, such as Boston's Samuel Adams, southeast Louisiana's Abita, and Vermont's Catamount, are winning loyal regional followings.

Amtrak's ridership continues to grow, and cities without rail passenger service are refurbishing decaying stations in hopes of one day being included. It worked for Indianapolis!

Big city newspapers continue to fail—St. Louis and Miami are recent examples—though there may be some promise in the increasing prosperity of daily newspapers in smaller cities.

Yet, for all these promising signs, the growth of minor league baseball may signify more. If, as Tom Boswell has said, "time begins on opening day," it just may be the case that the first rays of new promise for American society have dawned within the Stadiums, the Fields, and the Parks of Eugene, Toledo, Phoenix, Erie, Nashville, Columbus, Orlando, Jackson, Boise, Memphis, and Indianapolis. In just such places as these, Americans may be coming home again. For it is singularly in the playing fields of minor league baseball that we can put ourselves in our places.

For those who follow and enjoy minor league baseball, such a ringing assertion of its potential value for society might well be sufficient argument. Nevertheless, this optimistic view of minor league baseball's growth (still, by most standards, a modest phenomenon) may raise more questions than it answers.

Why speak of minor league rather than major league baseball? Or, why not find equal comfort in the large crowds that attend high school football or basketball games?

It is true, for instance, that major league baseball has grown even more dramatically than minor league baseball—in attendance, in profits, in franchise value. So why not celebrate major league baseball instead?

Indeed, we may well celebrate major league baseball, which, except for rare occasions, offers the secure pleasures of consistently superb performance. There remains an unparalleled pleasure in sharing an engrossing major league pennant race and joining 50,000 other fans in a large stadium to cheer home a winner.

Even those most devoted to minor league baseball should continue to make periodic pilgrimages to major league parks, if only to recalibrate the fan's judgment according to major league standards. Those who go for very long without seeing Ozzie Smith play shortstop may begin to celebrate mere competence at that difficult position!

But however admirable major league baseball may be, the reinvigoration of the minor leagues appears a more significant social phenomenon than the explosive growth of the majors.

First, a minor league baseball team depends for its support not on an amorphous "market area," served by radio and television networks and by advertising promotions, but on its place, the particular community which is its home. Even more than a major league club, a minor league team depends on the regular, repeated attendance of its fans. And the lower prices it charges—not only for tickets, but for everything else as well—make frequent attendance affordable.

Second, most minor league teams operate as small businesses in close touch with their communities. Living far from the ethereal regions of today's corporate aristocracies, the minor league general manager is more likely to belong to the Kiwanis than to the Century Club, more likely to eat a plate lunch than a power breakfast.

Third, and most important, a minor league team offers the baseball fan the opportunity to train and to exercise his or her critical faculties. Major league teams, like wine lists in exceptional restaurants, offer for our pleasure the results of refined and expert evaluation. But watching a minor league team, like visiting a large wine store, requires some degree of connoisseurship. While it is always great fun to cheer for the home team, the special pleasure reserved for the fan of minor league baseball is the opportunity to recognize emerging talent and to observe its development over the course of the season.

In sum, minor league baseball, unlike the major leagues, offers the people of a community the opportunity to share in an enterprise that operates within the community—even if it is an enterprise which may send reverberations down the line. (If the catcher in Louisville puts together a hitting streak, the *Post-Dispatch* in St. Louis is likely to follow it. When the Chattanooga right fielder steals home in the 11th to win an important game, Cincinnati should pay attention.)

A second question arises: Why should one not find equal cause for optimism in the large crowds in attendance at high school football and basketball games? Certainly, such games offer the opportunity to express civic pride, to join neighbors in a common cause, and to assess emerging athletic talent.

The important difference, at least in simple anthropological terms, appears to be one between raising a family and recruiting an army. High school athletics elicit familial and communal pride in the emerging prowess of the young. The celebration of school athletics represents an avowal of confidence in the future. In watching the local high school team defeat its cross-county rival, the elders enjoy the assurance that the young men and women whom they have nurtured and protected are growing in strength and agility and cunning, and thus will become in their turn the protectors of the community.

But in minor league baseball (as in local soccer throughout the rest of the world), support for the local team arises from deliberate partisanship, not from genealogy. The young men in minor league uniforms are not our sons, but—again in anthropological terms—chosen standard-bearers in competition against invading foes. The game they play as our representatives, wearing the name of our city on their chests, is profoundly more serious than the skirmishes among our children. These professional athletes "profess" our interests and take the field for us in return for our feeding and clothing them.

The very language of baseball, which speaks of the quest to reach "home" "safely" before being "put out," takes on a certain gravity in this context. From time to time, one player may even "sacrifice" himself for another. At the stadium, we inhabit the elemental ground of existence, divided between the "fair" and the "foul."

As Dennis Porter has observed, "The fact that home is simply represented by a geometrical shape on the ground and the good sought is counted in the wholly symbolic form of runs does not prevent the fan from understanding the latent import of a game." Hence, an RBI "may signify the survival of a tribe" (146).

Now, even if we were willing at this point to grant minor league baseball privileged status among the sports, a more difficult question may be whether any sport should be taken seriously as a point of departure for a consideration of society's ills. If our concern is with the building of a stronger sense of community, why not look instead at the civic pride expressed through local symphony orchestras? Through art museums? Through churches? Through United Way campaigns?

Why ground a hopeful prognosis for society on—of all things—minor league baseball?

While we may share the hope that all of society may one day be brought into a closer relationship with the fine arts, the fact remains that the appeal of sports currently spans the divisions in society far more effectively than high culture or denominational religion. It is in the ballpark—not the symphony hall, or the museum gallery, or, alas, the church sanctuary—where we are most likely to find ourselves among neighbors from a wide range of ages, cultures, and socioeconomic strata.

Moreover, while we may believe in and support civic altruism and private philanthropy, the contemporary interest in achieving a "kinder, gentler" America largely through the charitable instincts of individuals reflects for the most part a particular political inclination. An alternate inclination holds that society as a whole must seek to allocate opportunity more evenly and to support all its members more generously.

It seems unlikely, in short, that fund-raising efforts, as commendable as they may be, will go very far toward healing the divisions in society. In fact, such efforts may in some cases exacerbate these divisions.

Finally, it may be worth observing that minor league baseball is a curiously unalloyed pleasure. Neither a cultural nor a social obligation, it draws only those who genuinely seek and enjoy its appeals. A leisurely doubleheader is not for those tied to cellular telephones or to electronic beepers. Rude concertgoers who bolt for the symphony hall doors before the final notes of the fourth movement die away have no place in a minor league park. Those unwilling to measure their time in innings should stay at home and watch Australian rugby on ESPN.

The problems of American society are complex and disturbing, impossible to ignore and difficult to address. Yeats's highly charged vision—

> Things fall apart; the centre cannot hold;
> Mere anarchy is loosed upon the world. . . .

has more than once been quoted as a prophecy for our own society, where wealthy, self-righteous suburbs spin off ever further from urban centers abandoned after five o'clock each afternoon to the homeless, the mercenary, and the addicted.

But for all the suggestions advanced here, minor league baseball, perhaps more than other institutions, can offer not so much an escape from a highly problematical society, as an opportunity to embrace and celebrate an alternative.

For a few hours, we join our neighbors from throughout our community. We eat hot dogs. We drink out of paper cups. We record the exploits of the city's team in our scorebooks. We stroll around between innings. We smile indulgently as local characters perform.

We have not spent a day's salary in order to watch the game. No one need leave early to beat a traffic jam on the freeways.

And when the local second baseman times a hanging curveball just right and lifts it over the left field fence, we rise as a community, young and old, black and white, laborers and lawyers, embracing a shared commitment, a shared joy, and we spill our beer, and we yell, "All right!"

References

Briggs, Asa. "The Sense of Place." *The Fitness of Man's Environment.* Washington, D.C.: Smithsonian, 1968. 77–97.

Langer, Susanne K. "The Ultimate Unit." *Philosophical Sketches.* 1962. New York: Mentor, 1964. 107–122.

Mumford, Lewis. *The City in History.* New York: Harcourt, 1961.

Porter, Dennis. "The Perilous Quest: Baseball as Folk Drama." *Critical Inquiry.* 4:1 (Autumn 1977) 143–157.

Stover, John F. *The Life and Decline of the American Railroad.* New York: Oxford, 1970.

The Geography of Major League Baseball Player Production, 1876–1988

by Carl F. Ojala and Michael T. Gadwood

Though some individual players, and even entire teams, were paid in years prior to 1876, major league professional baseball as we know it originated in that year with the founding of the National League. Eight franchises were established by club owners who invested $100 each for the right to field teams representing Boston, Chicago, Cincinnati, Hartford, Louisville, New York, Philadelphia, and St. Louis. The geography of the sport was very unstable during the early years of the league's existence. Some franchises appeared and disappeared from one year to the next, while others had more success and stability. Most large cities in the northeast supported teams at one time or another in those days. Some smaller ones such as Worcester, Providence, and Troy even had short-lived "major league" status before the turn of the century.

In 1900, the American League was formed, seeking recognition as another major professional baseball league. By 1901 the National and American leagues were in competition for players and recognition by the country's fans. Each league crowned a champion that year. By 1902 separate National and American league structures had been established. The geography of big league baseball that was organized then remained essentially unchanged until 1953, when the Boston Braves moved to Milwaukee. Despite westward migration of the country's population during the first half of this century, sixteen major league baseball teams remained concentrated in ten northeastern cities. The south and the west had no representation.

However, in recent years several more teams have shifted locations, and 10 new franchises have been established. Twenty-six teams represent 22 urban areas today. The geography of major league baseball is more representative of the nation's population distribution than at any time in history.

All these new teams represent opportunity for more players to make it to the "big time." But where do the players who do succeed originate? What states, regions, or countries produce major league talent? Where did they come from in earlier times? The purpose of this chapter is to determine the source or production regions of major league baseball talent, from the origin of the National League in 1876 to the present time.

Production regions can be determined through an examination of the geographic origin, or birthplace, of every player who has participated throughout the history of the game. For purposes of this study, it is assumed that these players, in most cases, learned at least the fundamentals of baseball in or near their hometown. For this analysis, the most recent issue of the *Baseball Encyclopedia* was used to determine the birthplaces of all major leaguers who have ever appeared in a big league game.

The state or country of birth of all players was entered into a computer by the decade in which that player participated. Exactly 12,919 entries were made. If a player's career spans two or even three decades, he appears in the computations for each decade in which he played. Hence, adding participation statistics for all decades totals more than the 12,919 players who actually played throughout the history of the game. However, it was felt that production regions for each decade were of paramount importance, so multi-decade players are included in as many decades as they appear. Care was exercised to insure that such double-counting did not affect the composite total in any way.

There are two principal ways in which player production may be measured in a study such as this. The first would involve a simple statement of numbers of players produced in each state in the nation. In such case, obviously, the more populous states would be most likely to appear as major producers every time.

However, it seems that more meaningful results would be obtained if, in order to eliminate this population bias, data were reduced to a per capita basis. Then, states without large numbers of potential major leaguers, but with relatively high production, would appear more significant in spite of their smaller populations.

Therefore, after total production per decade was determined, a method for eliminating the population bias was devised. Utilizing data from the United States Census of Population for each decade since 1870, this was accomplished by developing ratios to measure production (number of players) relative to the number of males in the 20–39 age group in each state. This group, generally the age of major leaguers, was used in calculating each ratio. For example, in the decade of the 1980s, the national norm for big league player production was one player per 19,334 males in the 20–39 age category.

California produced one major leaguer for each 8,827 males in that group, so its ratio is 2.19, more than twice the nation's productivity (or more than twice what the state would be expected to produce based on its population). Maryland, on the other hand, produced one major leaguer for each 36,211 males in the age group. Its per capita ratio in the 1980s is 0.53, about half of what it should be producing based on its population.

Findings by Decades

1876–1879 (Figures 1 and 1a)

During these early years immediately after the National League was organized, most of the players came from northeastern states. New York (58), Pennsylvania (46), and Massachusetts (22) led in player production. Washington, D.C. had the highest per capita production at more than six times the national norm. Southern New England and the Middle Atlantic states were producing at more than twice the norm. Missouri (12) and Iowa (3) provided the only players from west of the Mississippi, and Missouri and Ohio were the only states west of Pennsylvania to exceed the national average on a per capita basis. Of the 13 foreign-born players in the major league at this time, one was Canadian and 12 were from the British Isles.

1880–1889 (Figures 2 and 2a)

The decade of the 1880s witnessed substantial westward movement in the production pattern. Ohio and Illinois produced 85 and 67 players, respectively. Missouri's output jumped to 49, and even California produced 23. But the dominance of the northeast continued with Pennsylvania (190), New York (141) and Massachusetts (112). Washington, D.C. continued its per capita lead along with southern New England and Pennsylvania. Thirty-four Canadians played in the 1880s; the British Isles and Germany were the main source of overseas players.

1890–1899 (Figures 3 and 3a)

The pattern changed very little during the 1890s with high production, both absolute and relative, almost entirely confined to the northeastern quarter of the country. Although Ohio, with 133 players produced, moved into second place behind Pennsylvania (202). Kentucky (51) began to emerge as a baseball state. Nineteen Canadians played during the decade, while Europe remained the other primary source of foreign-born major leaguers. Ireland was most important.

1900–1909 (Figures 4 and 4a)

By the turn of the century, when the American League began competing for baseball talent, players were coming from almost all states. However, Pennsylvania (220), Ohio (169), and New York (117) continued to lead. Only Washington, D.C., Ohio, and Delaware had per capita production greater than two. For the first time, California's ratio exceeded the national norm. Foreign-born players continued to come mainly from Canada and Europe.

1910–1919 (Figures 5 and 5a)

The second decade of this century was characterized by the emergence of Illinois (191), Indiana (82), Texas (79), and California (74). Pennsylvania (236) and Ohio (193) remained leaders in production, and the south generally remained a small source region for major leaguers. With the exceptions of New York and New Jersey (whose rising populations caused low ratios), per capita production remained high in a ribbon of states from New England westward to Kansas. However, none were producing at twice the national norm as had occurred in previous years. Twenty-seven players came from a variety of European sources, and 16 were from Canada. Latin American production began in this decade, with 12 players coming from Cuba.

1920–1929 (Figures 6 and 6a)

The "roaring twenties" witnessed the continued growth of Texas (110) and California (93) baseball. Missouri (85), North Carolina (58), and Tennessee (51) also produced important numbers of major leaguers in this decade. The dominance of Pennsylvania (157) and Ohio (94), which had occurred since the 1890s, had begun to diminish, though Pennsylvania was still the leader. Again, on a per capita basis, no state was developing major leaguers at twice the national norm. Of the foreign-born players, 10 were from a variety of European countries, 10 were from Cuba, and Canada's share dropped to nine.

1930–1939 (Figures 7 and 7a)

California (133) became the leading producer of major league baseball players during the 1930s, followed closely by Illinois (121),

① BIRTHPLACE OF MAJOR LEAGUE BASEBALL PLAYERS
1876-1879

More than 200
150-200
100-149
50-99
Less than 50

Ireland   7
England   4
Scotland   1

(R.L.Ferrett)

①a BIRTHPLACE OF MAJOR LEAGUE BASEBALL PLAYERS:
PER CAPITA RATIOS
1876-1879

>1.25
0.75-1.25
<0.75

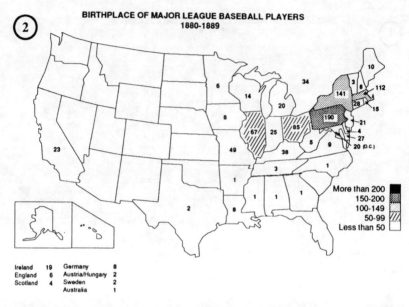

BIRTHPLACE OF MAJOR LEAGUE BASEBALL PLAYERS
1880-1889

More than 200	
150-200	
100-149	
50-99	
Less than 50	

Ireland	19	Germany	8
England	6	Austria/Hungary	2
Scotland	4	Sweden	2
		Australia	1

(R.L.Ferrett)

BIRTHPLACE OF MAJOR LEAGUE BASEBALL PLAYERS:
PER CAPITA RATIOS
1880-1889

>1.25	
0.75-1.25	
<0.75	

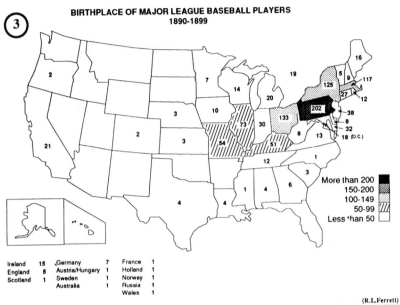

BIRTHPLACE OF MAJOR LEAGUE BASEBALL PLAYERS
1890-1899

Ireland	15	Germany	7	France	1
England	5	Austria/Hungary	1	Holland	1
Scotland	1	Sweden	1	Norway	1
		Australia	1	Russia	1
				Wales	1

(R.L.Ferrett)

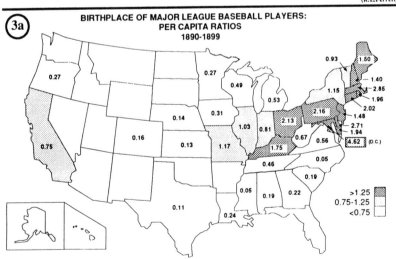

BIRTHPLACE OF MAJOR LEAGUE BASEBALL PLAYERS:
PER CAPITA RATIOS
1890-1899

(R.L.Ferrett)

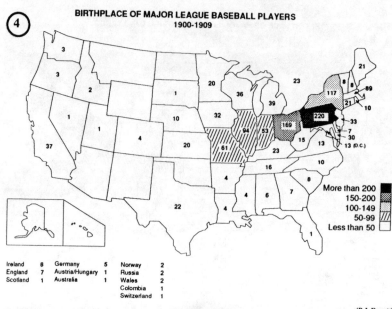

BIRTHPLACE OF MAJOR LEAGUE BASEBALL PLAYERS
1900-1909

Ireland	8	Germany	5	Norway	2
England	7	Austria/Hungary	1	Russia	2
Scotland	1	Australia	1	Wales	2
				Colombia	1
				Switzerland	1

(R.I. Ferrett)

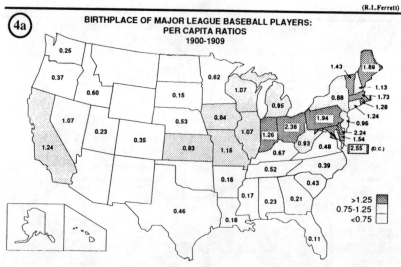

BIRTHPLACE OF MAJOR LEAGUE BASEBALL PLAYERS:
PER CAPITA RATIOS
1900-1909

(R.I. Ferrett)

Pennsylvania (116), and Texas (100). This was the decade that saw most southern states exceed the national per capita index for the first time in history. In fact, North Carolina was the only state in the nation with an index greater than two. Most of the northeastern region, the old bastion of player production, continued to slide in both absolute and relative terms. Of only 21 players with foreign heritage in the decade, eight each were from Latin America and Canada, while five were European.

1940–1949 (Figures 8 and 8a)

There was a reemergence of the northeast as a player source, and a relative decline in the south in this decade. Pennsylvania (165) had regained the overall lead from California (158). By the 1940s, major league baseball player production had become a national phenomenon, with only Nevada not supplying at least one athlete. Only North Carolina was producing at more than twice the national norm. Of the foreign-born, Cuba provided 23 and Canada 21, while other European and Latin sources produced a few.

1950–1959 (Figures 9 and 9a)

During this decade, California (161) once more became the primary source region for major leaguers, a position it has retained to the present. Pennsylvania (124), New York (115), and Illinois (103) continued their usual high productivity. Missouri was the only state with a per capita ratio greater than two. On a per capita basis, several southern states became highly important sources of players. By the 1950s, Latin America had begun to dominate as a source of foreign-bred major leaguers. Cuba (40), Puerto Rico (15), and Mexico (10) were most important, but others also produced. Canada provided 16, while European sources had declined significantly.

1960–1969 (Figures 10 and 10a)

Almost a mirror image of the 1950s, the same four states led the country in the same order; California (240), Pennsylvania (108), New York (107), and Illinois (95). No state had a per capita ratio greater than two. Arkansas was the per capita leader at 1.89, followed closely by several other states in that south-central part of the country. Again, Latin countries such as Cuba (51), Puerto Rico (33), and the Dominican Republic (24) dominated foreign production. Canada supplied 22 players during the decade, while European sources provided five.

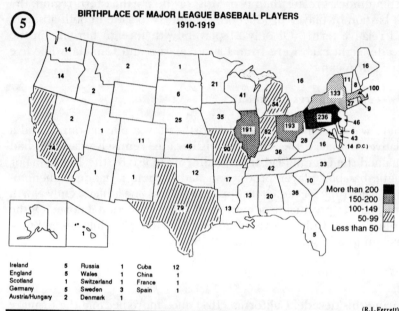

BIRTHPLACE OF MAJOR LEAGUE BASEBALL PLAYERS
1910-1919

More than 200
150-200
100-149
50-99
Less than 50

Ireland	5	Russia	1	Cuba	12
England	5	Wales	1	China	1
Scotland	1	Switzerland	1	France	1
Germany	5	Sweden	3	Spain	1
Austria/Hungary	2	Denmark	1		

(R.L.Ferrett)

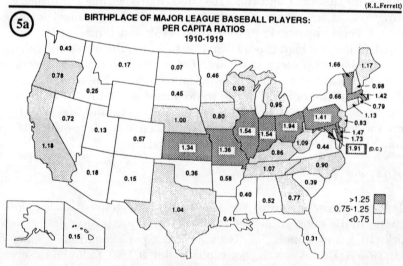

BIRTHPLACE OF MAJOR LEAGUE BASEBALL PLAYERS:
PER CAPITA RATIOS
1910-1919

>1.25
0.75-1.25
<0.75

(R.L.Ferrett)

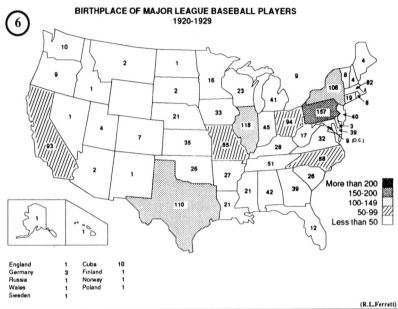

BIRTHPLACE OF MAJOR LEAGUE BASEBALL PLAYERS
1920-1929

		More than 200
		150-200
		100-149
		50-99
		Less than 50

England	1	Cuba	10
Germany	3	Finland	1
Russia	1	Norway	1
Wales	1	Poland	1
Sweden	1		

(R.L.Ferrett)

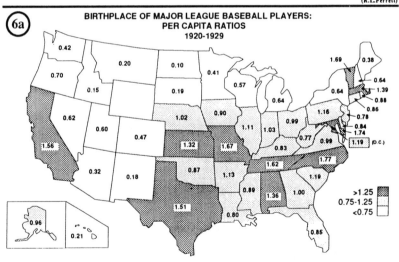

BIRTHPLACE OF MAJOR LEAGUE BASEBALL PLAYERS:
PER CAPITA RATIOS
1920-1929

>1.25	
0.75-1.25	
<0.75	

(R.L.Ferrett)

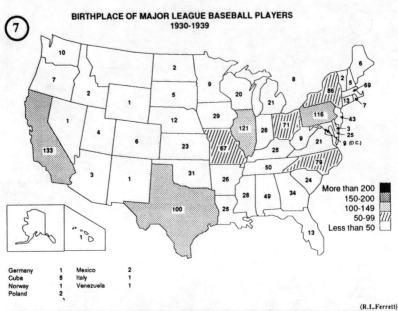

BIRTHPLACE OF MAJOR LEAGUE BASEBALL PLAYERS
1930-1939

Germany	1	Mexico	2
Cuba	5	Italy	1
Norway	1	Venezuela	1
Poland	2		

(R.I. Ferrett)

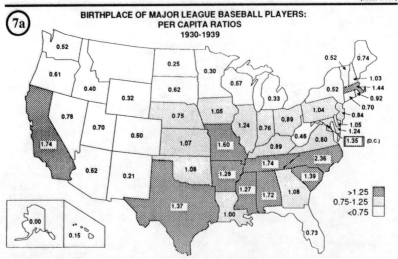

BIRTHPLACE OF MAJOR LEAGUE BASEBALL PLAYERS:
PER CAPITA RATIOS
1930-1939

(R.I. Ferrett)

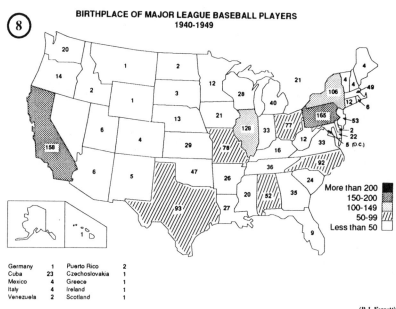

BIRTHPLACE OF MAJOR LEAGUE BASEBALL PLAYERS
1940-1949

Germany	1	Puerto Rico	2
Cuba	23	Czechoslovakia	1
Mexico	4	Greece	1
Italy	4	Ireland	1
Venezuela	2	Scotland	1

(R.L.Ferrett)

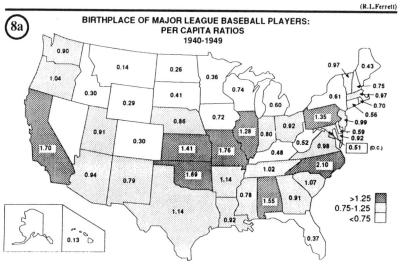

BIRTHPLACE OF MAJOR LEAGUE BASEBALL PLAYERS:
PER CAPITA RATIOS
1940-1949

(R.I.Ferrett)

BIRTHPLACE OF MAJOR LEAGUE BASEBALL PLAYERS
1950-1959

More than 200
150-200
100-149
50-99
Less than 50

Cuba	40	Czechoslovakia	2
Mexico	10	Scotland	1
Italy	2	Virgin Islands	1
Venezuela	4	Poland	1
Puerto Rico	15	France	1

Panama	5
Dominican Rep.	2
Austria	1
Bahamas	1

(R.L.Ferrett)

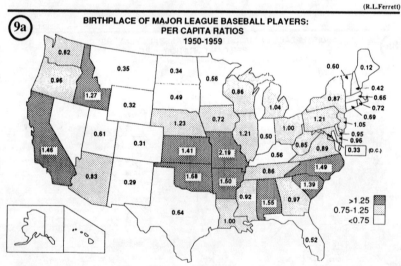

BIRTHPLACE OF MAJOR LEAGUE BASEBALL PLAYERS:
PER CAPITA RATIOS
1950-1959

>1.25
0.75-1.25
<0.75

(R.L.Ferrett)

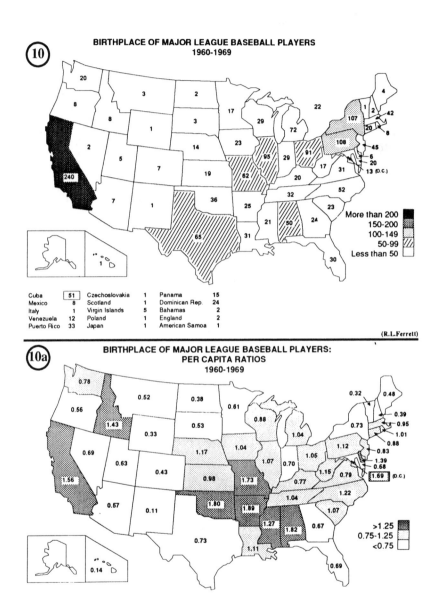

BIRTHPLACE OF MAJOR LEAGUE BASEBALL PLAYERS
1960-1969

Cuba	51	Czechoslovakia	1	Panama	15
Mexico	8	Scotland	1	Dominican Rep.	24
Italy	1	Virgin Islands	5	Bahamas	2
Venezuela	12	Poland	1	England	2
Puerto Rico	33	Japan	1	American Samoa	1

(R.L.Ferrett)

BIRTHPLACE OF MAJOR LEAGUE BASEBALL PLAYERS:
PER CAPITA RATIOS
1960-1969

(R.L.Ferrett)

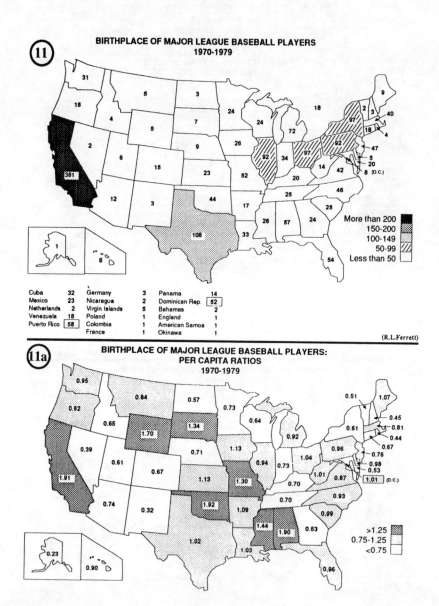

BIRTHPLACE OF MAJOR LEAGUE BASEBALL PLAYERS
1970-1979

More than 200
150-200
100-149
50-99
Less than 50

Cuba	32	Germany	3	Panama	14
Mexico	23	Nicaragua	2	Dominican Rep.	52
Netherlands	2	Virgin Islands	5	Bahamas	2
Venezuela	18	Poland	1	England	1
Puerto Rico	58	Colombia	1	American Samoa	1
		France	1	Okinawa	1

(R.L.Ferrett)

BIRTHPLACE OF MAJOR LEAGUE BASEBALL PLAYERS:
PER CAPITA RATIOS
1970-1979

>1.25
0.75-1.25
<0.75

1970–1979 (Figures 11 and 11a)

During the 1970s only two states, California (381) and Texas (108) produced at least 100 major leaguers, though several old producers such as New York, Pennsylvania, Ohio, and Illinois were close. Once more, no state's per capita ratio exceeded two, but Oklahoma, California, and Alabama all had ratios only slightly lower than that figure. By this decade, Latin America had evolved into a primary source region for major league baseball. Cuba (32) was declining in number, but Puerto Rico (58) and the Dominican Republic (52) were increasing sharply. Other Latin countries provided a total of 67 more players. Canada supplied 18, and a few still came from European sources.

1980–1988 (Figures 12 and 12a)

In this decade, California (468) became established, by far, as the predominant source of major league baseball players in the nation, a position it began to nurture several decades ago. No other state can approach its productivity since the 1950s. What Pennsylvania was to the major leagues from the 1880s to the 1920s, California has become, even more so, in modern decades.

In fact, since major league baseball began more than 100 years ago, California's production of 1,257 players has exceeded every other state as of 1988 (Figure 13). Interestingly enough, California took the composite total lead from Pennsylvania (1,255) only as recently as last year. As of 1987, the composite total was in favor of Pennsylvania (1,250 to 1,233). But in 1988, California out-produced Pennsylvania 24 to 5 to take the all-time lead. In fact, during the 1970s and 1980s California's production of major leaguers progressed at a phenomenal rate, vaulting the state into a position it appears it will not relinquish again. Given its huge population, its per capita ratio of 2.19 to 1988 was amazing in itself.

Besides California during the 1980s, only Texas (126) and New York (106) produced more than 100 players. Florida's output (86) has risen rapidly in recent years as has that of the Dominican Republic (79) and several other Latin countries.

In fact, one of the most significant geographic developments in the production of major league baseball players in the last two decades has been the rise of Latin America as a source region. It should be noted that, by the 1970s, Puerto Rico and the Dominican Republic were among the top twelve producers of big leaguers for the decade, and by the 1980s Venezuela had joined them among the top twenty.

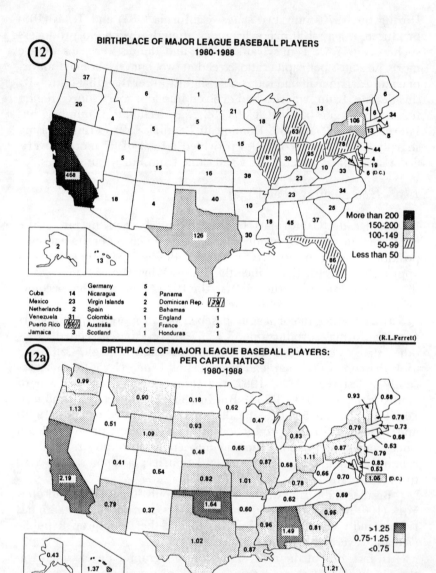

⑫ BIRTHPLACE OF MAJOR LEAGUE BASEBALL PLAYERS
1980-1988

More than 200
150-200
100-149
50-99
Less than 50

		Germany	5		
Cuba	14	Nicaragua	4	Panama	7
Mexico	23	Virgin Islands	2	Dominican Rep.	79
Netherlands	2	Spain	2	Bahamas	1
Venezuela	31	Colombia	1	England	1
Puerto Rico	55	Australia	1	France	3
Jamaica	3	Scotland	1	Honduras	1

(R.L.Ferrett)

⑫a BIRTHPLACE OF MAJOR LEAGUE BASEBALL PLAYERS:
PER CAPITA RATIOS
1980-1988

>1.25
0.75-1.25
<0.75

BIRTHPLACE OF MAJOR LEAGUE BASEBALL PLAYERS
Composite: 1876-1988

Legend:
More than 1200
900-1200
600-899
300-599
Less than 300

Puerto Rico	126	England	26	Sweden	6
Cuba	125	Panama	25	Bahamas	5
Dominican Rep.	118	Scotland	8	Italy	5
Venezuela	50	Virgin Islands	8	Nicaragua	5
Mexico	49	Austria/Hungary	6	Russia	5
Ireland	36	France	6	Poland	4
Germany	32				

Three or less

Colombia	Australia	Greece
Czechoslovakia	Wales	Honduras
Holland	Am. Samoa	Japan
Jamaica	China	Okinawa
Norway	Denmark	Switzerland
Spain	Finland	Netherlands

BIRTHPLACE OF MAJOR LEAGUE BASEBALL PLAYERS:
PER CAPITA RATIOS BY REGION
1876-1988

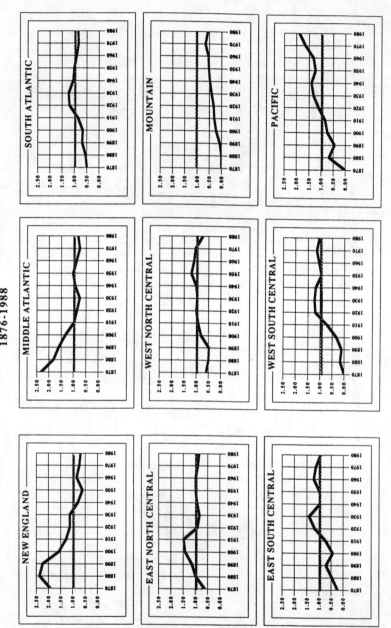

When player production is analyzed on a per capita basis by United States census regions*, the trends over time are clearly displayed (Figure 14). New England and the Middle Atlantic regions were the primary sources in the earliest years of professional baseball. The East North Central region was most significant just prior to and after the turn of the century. The three census regions in the South became important only after the 1920s, and then never really have dominated production as regions, though individual states such as Alabama, Texas, and Oklahoma have been important. The West North Central region was significant during the period from the 1940s to the 1970s, while the Mountain region never reached the national norm at any time. Finally, the Pacific region, spearheaded by California, has been above the national norm since the 1920s, and the nation's leading region since the 1940s.

With 26 teams offering more playing opportunities, the geography of professional baseball player production is more representative of the national population distribution than at any time before. Today, essentially every corner of the nation is a source of major leaguers. It is obvious that baseball has evolved into a truly national game from the geographic standpoint. It is also evident that, in terms of sources of players, it has, in fact, evolved into an international game.

---

*The census regions are composed as follows:
New England: ME, NH, VT, MA, CT, RI
Middle Atlantic: NY, NJ, PA
East North Central: MI, OH, IN, IL, WI
West North Central: MN, IA, MO, ND, SD, NE, KS
South Atlantic: DE, MD, DC, VA, WV, NC, SC, GA, FL
East South Central: KY, TN, MS, AL
West South Central: AR, LA, OK, TX
Mountain: MT, WY, ID, NV, CO, UT, AZ, NM
Pacific: WA, OR, CA, AK, HA

Farmers, Orphans, and Cultists

Pastoral Characters and Themes in Baseball Fiction

by Richard Gaughran

Christopher Lehmann-Haupt reports that his father regarded baseball as a " 'silly game they play in little boys' knickers, with the man on the hill who acts like a dog at a hydrant' " (17). However, various essayists have demonstrated that the sport is more than "a silly boy's game," and they have consistently referred to certain features: the game's peculiar relationship to nature, its bucolic associations; the nostalgic qualities of baseball and the game's profound implications regarding time and timelessness; and the game's clarity and articulation, which make it appear ritualistic. Roger Angell, Donald Hall, Murray Ross, George Grella, and others have noted that such features provide the game's mythic foundation. In short, baseball is a pastoral sport. Frederick Karl has noted that the sport, in turn, has given rise to a body of fiction that is pastoral, and he refers to a few examples (64).

The reader who has read only one or two baseball novels may not realize, however, how pervasive pastoral themes are in baseball fiction. In particular, there is a remarkable resemblance and correspondence between baseball fiction's characters and the Jeffersonian ideal of the farmer/gardener. Also, many of baseball fiction's characters attempt to defeat time, to turn back the clock. And there is a tendency among various characters, driven by baseball's precise arithmetic and geometry, to see a baseball game as a religious ritual.

It is no secret that the American ethos includes the belief that the New World is, or can become, a garden and that the highest calling is one that puts man in his proper place as a tender and shaper of nature. There are many examples of the nation's founders' expressing such beliefs. Here, for one, is Thomas Jefferson in 1811, on the desirability of life in a garden:

> I have often thought that if heaven had given me choice of my position and calling, it should have been on a rich spot of earth, well watered, and near a good market for the productions of the

garden. No occupation is so delightful to me as the culture of the earth, and no culture comparable to that of the garden. (Marx, 138)[1]

Ralph Waldo Emerson expresses similar views, perhaps more unabashedly than Jefferson. The following is from a 1844 lecture, "The Young American":

> The land is the appointed remedy for whatever is false and fantastic in our culture. The continent we inhabit is to be physic and food for our mind, as well as our body. The land, with its tranquilizing, sanative influences, is to repair the errors of a scholastic and traditional education, and bring us into just relations with men and things. (Marx, 236–237)

Emerson, in the same lecture, decries urban values and encourages renunciation of commercial concerns: "How much better when the whole land is a garden, and the people have grown up in the bowers of a paradise" (Marx, 239).

Rarely, if ever, do baseball fans consciously connect their sport to the ideals of Jefferson and Emerson, but ardent followers of the sport often believe, or are exposed to the belief, that baseball displays man in his proper relationship with nature. The late commissioner A. Bartlett Giamatti has spoken of the game as " 'not paradise . . . but . . . as close as you're going to get to it in America' " (Siebert, 48). And he explains what he means by "paradise," in effect updating Jefferson's ideas:

> "The word 'paradise' is originally an old Persian word meaning an enclosed park or green. Anything that's closed is fundamentally artificial. Nature doesn't enclose things perfectly. You fly over a great city at night and you look down and you see lit up this green in the middle of the city and you realize that the reason they're in the middle of the cities is that there is in us a fundamental, vestigial memory of an enclosed green space as the place of freedom or play. . . ." (Siebert, 36)

There is a correspondence, then, between playing on a baseball field and tending the soil—with all that that implies in terms of supposed virtue and harmony with the world. It is no coincidence that Cooperstown, N.Y., the site of the Baseball Hall of Fame and Museum, is also the home of the Farmers' Museum, which, like the Hall of Fame, was originally funded by the Clark family.[2]

The association of baseball with farming provides part of the foundation of baseball fiction. In fact, there is often a simple substitution of a baseball player for the tender of the land. This transferral accounts in part for the portrayal of players as "country bumpkins" or "rubes," the most notable examples being Ring Lardner's Jack Keefe in *You Know Me Al* (1914) and Danny Warner in *Lose With a Smile* (1933), Bernard Malamud's Roy Hobbs in *The Natural* (1952), and Harry Stein's Joe Jackson in *Hoopla!* (1982).

Often baseball literature makes the connection clear by overt references to farming or gardening. Again, there is a close association between farming and baseball; the two are often presented as interchangeable. In Bernard Malamud's *The Natural*, for example, Herman Youngberry, the pitcher who strikes out Roy Hobbs at the end of the novel, nurses agrarian dreams: "He didn't say so but he had it in mind to earn enough money to buy a three hundred acre farm and then quit baseball forever. Sometimes when he pitched, he saw fields of golden wheat gleaming in the sun" (212).

Also, Malamud's Pop Fisher, the manager of the New York Knights, on a day when the ineptitude of his players has become particularly trying, comically wonders why he did not follow his impulse to farm:

> "I shoulda been a farmer. . . . I shoulda farmed since the day I was born. I like cows, sheep, and those hornless goats—I am partial to nanny goats, my daddy wore a beard—I like to feed animals and milk 'em. I like fixing things, weeding poison oak out of the pasture, and seeing to the watering of the crops. I like to be by myself on a farm. I like to stand out in the fields, tending the vegetables, the corn, the winter wheat—greenest looking stuff you ever saw. When Ma was alive she kept urging me to leave baseball and take up farming, and I always meant to but after she died I had no heart for it. . . . I have that green thumb . . . , and I shoulda farmed instead of playing wet nurse to a last place, dead-to-the-neck ball team." (37)

The narrator of W. P. Kinsella's *Shoeless Joe* (1982) lives in an Iowa farmhouse, fifty yards from a corn field that he converts into a baseball field. He came to Iowa to study but, after marrying Annie, decides not to leave:

> I chose willingly, lovingly, to stay in Iowa. Eventually I rented this farm, then bought it, operating it one inch from bankruptcy. I don't seem meant to farm, but I want to be close to this precious land, for Annie and me to be able to say, "This is ours." (5)

It is noteworthy that in both this passage and Pop Fisher's soliloquy, the speaker implies that farming is somehow passé or unapproachable because of changing times or personal temperament. The baseball field suits these would-be farmers more than the actual corn field does. (Pop Fisher does not mean what he is saying, of course.) There is an implication that the Jeffersonian ideal of the farmer is no longer realizable, that because this is the twentieth century, the values imputed to farming must be transferred to another activity, baseball. And so Kinsella's narrator, whose name is Ray Kinsella, speaks of the careful husbandry and meticulous observation of others that he brings to his landscaping efforts:

> My intuition told me that it was the grass that was most important. It took three seasons to hone that grass to its proper texture, to its proper color. I made trips to Minneapolis and one or two other cities where the stadiums still have natural-grass infields and outfields. I would arrive hours before a game and watch the groundskeepers groom the field like a prize animal, then stay after the game when in the cool of the night the same groundsmen appeared with hoses, hoes, and rakes, and patched the grasses like medics attending to wounded soldiers. (7)

In Kinsella's second baseball novel, *The Iowa Baseball Confederacy* (1986), the magic of Gideon Clarke's baseball dreams is associated with the magic of cultivation. On several occasions flowers sing to him. And his friend Stan, who travels through time to participate in a forgotten, magical baseball game in 1908, assumes a suggestive name when he enters the playing field: The Left-handed Farmhand (114). The narrator also celebrates the accomplishments of the groundskeeper, Frank Hall, who somehow manages to keep the field playable in spite of forty consecutive days of rain (199).

The assumed wholesomeness of farming and its association with baseball are obvious in Donald Hays's *The Dixie Association* (1984). The man who manages the Arkansas Reds, Lefty Marks, also runs a cooperative farm, sells vegetables to baseball fans in the parking lot of the ballpark, and helps people buy their own farms. He says that he prefers " 'mules to tractors, farms to factories, talk to television, singing to listening to the stereo . . .' " (375–376).

Hog Durham, the narrator of Hays's novel, is an ex-convict who robbed liquor stores and a bank, but he was raised on a farm and evidently returns to this calling when his homerun-hitting, first-base-playing days are over. To be sure, he knows that farming is not easy and remembers the restlessness that drove him from farming when he was younger. Nevertheless, he gradually moves back toward his origins, considering that farming, after baseball, is the only pursuit that can keep him out of jail: "I did begin to think that farming was the only decent choice I had left" (233). Later he sounds surer about his pastoral calling: " '[A] man's a fool not to play while he can. Ball game in the sunshine, good woman at night, maybe a little garden spot and a collie dog. Shit, they can have the rest of it' " (371).

Other characters in Hays's novel reinforce the bond between baseball and farming. For example, Ernesto Guerrero, one of the Cubans who comes to play for the Arkansas Reds, mentions life in Cuba during the time of sugar cane harvests: " 'When we did not play ball, we worked in the fields' " (371). Guerrero is not fond of sugar cane, but he expresses a personal preference, not a rejection of pastoralism. He says, " 'My family grew coffee and fruit in the mountains. . . . My heart was there and in pitching baseball' " (371).

Baseball, then, is pastoral in the way it evokes a particular relationship with nature. Baseball literature, in turn, draws upon this basic pastoral value.

Baseball's unique relationship to the passage of time is also decidedly pastoral. Unlike other team sports, it is not governed by a clock. The linear progress of a game is measured by outs, not by minutes. And because games do not end in ties, extra innings are sometimes required. If no team breaks the tie, or if each team scores the same number of runs in the same extra innings, a game can, theoretically, last forever. Or, if one team does not make three outs in a given inning, if it keeps getting men on base and scoring runs, the game cannot end. As Roger Angell says, "[A]ll you have to do is succeed utterly; keep hitting, keep the rally alive, and you have defeated time. You remain forever young" (303). Furthermore, when a baseball team succeeds by getting men on base and scoring runs, its members proceed around the bases *counterclockwise,* figuratively turning back the hands of a clock.

Besides having a structure that suggests the attempt to overcome time, baseball has a slow, bucolic pace that renounces the bustle of twentieth-century urban life. In "baseball-time" Donald Hall says, "we have left the clock behind us. Nothing is *over,* nothing is *ongoing.* By entering baseball-time, we have walked into the great day where successiveness is canceled. Now is always; now is forever; now is Wrigley Field and Yankee Stadium" (224).

The desire for eternal youth; the wish to stop the clock; the belief that one can cancel successiveness; the insistence on living the moment, the eternal *now,* without reference to temporal moorings— these are familiar themes in American thought and literature. In 1782, J. Hector St. John de Crèvecoeur described the settlers of this country as attempting to recreate themselves, to start over, to negate their pasts:

> Urged by a variety of motives, here they came. Everything has tended to regenerate them: new laws, a new mode of living, a new social system; here they are become men: in Europe they were as so many useless plants, wanting vegetative mould and refreshing showers; they withered, and were mowed down by want, hunger, and war; but now, by the power of transplantation, like all other plants they have taken root and flourished! (68–69)

Americans are regenerated, Crèvecoeur maintains. They start fresh; they are born again. The European who comes to this land "begins to feel the effects of a sort of resurrection" (82). Earlier I noted the common home of the Baseball Hall of Fame and the Farmers' Museum. Above the entrance to the Farmers' Museum in Cooperstown, N.Y., are words that express Crèvecoeur's ideas, words that emphasize early settlers' attempts to start anew through the pastoral act of shaping nature:

> Through these doors you will experience a rural life museum that shows how men, women, and children created a new society from a wilderness, and laid foundation for their dreams.

Henry David Thoreau also expresses the American urge to defeat time. In *Walden,* he speaks of his days in the woods, spent "rapt in a revery, amidst the pines and . . . sumachs, in undisturbed solitude and stillness." Unlike his Concord days, these are not "minced into hours and fretted by the ticking of a clock" (Marx, 249). To be sure, the clock is the great enemy of pastoral values.

Not surprisingly, this American belief that one can defeat time, which the sport of baseball seems to express, informs baseball fiction. Sometimes the reference to the defeat of time is overt. In *The Natural,* for example, Roy Hobbs hits a dramatic home run that smashes the stadium clock: "The clock spattered minutes all over the place, and after that the Dodgers never knew what time it was" (162).

Malamud's novel makes it clear that Hobbs's desire is to regain his youth, to remain forever young. Hobbs wishes that "he could have lived longer in his boyhood" (105), and he hopes that his prowess in baseball will keep him from death, grant him a kind of immortality: "'[I]f you leave all those records that nobody else can beat—they'll always remember you. You sorta never die'" (142). He is vague concerning his past—"'My past life is nobody's business'" (108)— believing that he can recreate himself through baseball.

The motif of the orphan, which runs through much baseball fiction, further expresses the attempt to escape time. An orphan is a person without normal connections to the past. Therefore, he is figuratively one without a past, a person who arrives from a place outside of time. Unlike characters with known parentage, he is not bound by the past. He can create himself as he wishes. Roy Hobbs is one such character. Another is Donald Hays's Hog Durham in *The Dixie Association*, who at age three was abandoned by his parents. Trying to escape the past and not believing in the future, he sees baseball as a timeless paradise: "'The game takes over. It's outside of time'" (54). Elsewhere he tells Pansy Puckett, "'You know what, love? The simple, shameful, God's truth of it is that all I want to do is hit .400 forever'" (161). Another "orphan" is Eversole, who was raised in the San Antonio Methodist Home for Boys. At forty-six he is the best pitcher on Hog Durham's team, and in the entire league.

Because of the unusualness of Robert Coover's *The Universal Baseball Association, Inc.* (1968), the presentation of the orphan-player reaches the point of absurdity in this novel. The players have no material existence. They abide in the mind of J. Henry Waugh and are represented by pieces of paper on a kitchen table. In the novel's final chapter, the point of view shifts so that we no longer see and hear these "players" through the filter of Henry's consciousness. The narrator here presents them as having consciousness apart from Henry. They speculate philosophically about many things, including their lack of parentage. One "player" says, "'We have no mothers. . . . The ripening of their wombs is nothing more than a ceremonious parable. We are mere ideas, hatched whole and helpless, here to enact old rituals of resistance and rot.'" The narrator then sums up their condition, calling the "players" "reluctant participants in a classic plot, too wise to fable a fortune, too distressed ever to invent their childhoods, left with nothing but the spiky imprint of their cleats upon the turf and the passage from envelope to maddening envelope of inscrutable space" (230).

But the orphan motif is particularly emphasized in Jerome Charyn's *The Seventh Babe* (1979). Babe "Rags" Ragland is not really an orphan, and his real name is Cedric Tannehill, the son of a man who made millions from copper mines. Recreating himself according to the pastoral myth, Rags emphatically forsakes his past and all its associations:

> He was leather, air, and horsehide on a ball. He was knickers and dirty brown grass, the first twist of a double play. He couldn't live apart from a baseball diamond. He was married to a fifty-cent glove.
> Copper wasn't his birthright. *No.* He hadn't slept in any cradle in his father's house. He was born in a pile of mud near the pitcher's box. A baseball baby. Orphan Rags. (219–220)

Rags embellishes the story of his invented past, which is to say no past at all, with the appropriate details. When Miz Marylou remarks on the oddity of having "Babe" as a Christian name and then apologizes for being impolite, he tells her of his, and Babe Ruth's, orphanage:

> "You don't have to be sorry. The brothers at St. Mary's always said 'Babe' to me. 'Come here, Babe.' 'Go to sleep, Babe.' Things like that. Maybe there's a different name on my birth certificate. But it's hard to tell. Because nobody knows where that certificate is. I'm a foundling, ma'am. The brothers picked me right off the front step. I was two and a half." (47–48)

And naturally, others within baseball collude with him in this fabrication. During the game that occurs just after the newspapers break the story about his actual past, the stadium crowd becomes defiant:

> A peculiar bedlam broke out in "Duffy's Cliff." You could see the snaky rhythm of six thousand shoulders, as the men and women on that hill began to scream like demented cats. "We got an orphan here." The whole stadium picked it up.
> "Orphan, orphan, we got an orphan here." (112)

All of the Yankees, playing Rags's Red Sox during this game, try to upset the "orphan" by taunting him with information from the papers—all of them, that is, except Babe Ruth, who, standing on third after hitting a triple, comforts his rival: " 'Kid, . . . Fuck the newspapers. They're out to get orphans like us' " (112).

The characters of Charyn's novel use baseball, aided by voodoo, to escape the passage of time. Babe Ragland gets outside of time to such an extent, in fact, that while playing for the Cincinnati Colored Giants he needs constant reminders of what year it is. About thirty years pass without his noticing:

> [B]aseball took Rags out of any specific order of time. Seasons didn't count. Winter and summer meant the same thing: baseball diamonds in the hinterland, Carl and his hawkers scrambling for games. February looked no different from July. The Cincinnatis searched out warm, leafy spots, away from sheriffs' offices, and near a village or two. . . . It was 1929. Or did he have the wrong year? (253–254)

Elsewhere the narrator says, "[N]o amount of magic could thrust a calendar into the kid's head" (289), and on several occasions Rags is referred to as Rip Van Winkle (255; 318–319). Toward the end of the novel, a seventy-nine-year-old Garland James, a teammate of Ragland's from more than fifty years earlier, meets Rags and Miz Iva and wonders, "Shouldn't the girl have had some gray specks in her hair? She had to be seventy, or sixty-nine? Did you kick old age in the pants when you traveled with the Giants?" (343).

The attempt to defeat time is central to the baseball fiction of W. P. Kinsella. In *The Thrill of the Grass* (1984), for example, the narrator of the story "The Night Manny Mota Tied the Record" is offered a chance to undo Thurman Munson's death. The mysterious Mr. Revere, an emissary from beyond time, says, " 'Death . . . need not be as final as many of us are used to believing' " (94). Approaching the suggestion that the narrator might want to change places with Munson, he says, " 'What would you say . . . if I told you that it might just be possible to move time back, like a newsreel being played in reverse, and undo what has been done?' " (94–95).

In Kinsella's *Shoeless Joe,* players of the past travel to the present to play a baseball game. These include the title character, who, as one of eight players banned from baseball for life as a result of the 1919 "Black Sox Scandal," is, in fiction, given a second chance; he is "born again" in the pages of a baseball novel. In the same novel, the fictional J. D. Salinger describes baseball's backward-looking nature and constancy: " 'I don't have to tell you that the one constant through all the years has been baseball. . . . It constantly reminds us of what once was, like an Indian-head penny in a handful of new coins' " (213).

In Kinsella's *The Iowa Baseball Confederacy,* characters travel to the past to participate in what seems to be a never-ending game. Gideon Clarke, the narrator of the later novel, marvels at his seeming good fortune: "I am adrift in the past, roughly thirty-five years before I will be born. And I can be anybody I want to be" (132). Later he seriously contemplates the impossible, saying, "Perhaps there does not have to be any more death. Perhaps time can be defeated" (275).

Besides its central plotting device of time travel, *The Iowa Baseball Confederacy* has innumerable minor references to the pastoral wish to conquer time. A few examples will suffice. There is the "Backwards Plague," an odd ailment said to have afflicted many in the early 1900s, whereby fully grown men and women regressed mentally and physically until they hit their birth weight, when they started to grow again (64–66). There is the "Twelve-Hour Church of Time Immemorial," the name itself suggesting, albeit confusingly, an altered view of time. And the Church's favorite hymn, "I Shall Not be Moved," further testifies to the belief that time's passage can be halted. Moreover, the flood that destroys Big Inning, Iowa, resulting from a forty-day rain, obviously refers to the Genesis Flood, the destruction said to be necessary so that a second creation could take place. After the floods, the one in Genesis and the one in the novel, the past no longer counts; life starts over again. In Kinsella's novel, the antediluvian world is forgotten, as Big Inning becomes Onamata. Of the town's residents the narrator says, "'They think Onamata just appeared there in 1909, that it was dropped from heaven, that there was never a flood, never another town—'" (83).

Besides its pastoral presentations of space and time, baseball has an accompanying characteristic, which Roland Garrett calls its clarity and articulation, that makes its mark in baseball literature. Stated simply, baseball's space and time are meticulously measured. The distance from the pitcher's rubber to home plate is sixty feet, six inches; the distance between bases is ninety feet; and so on. And baseball measures its progress in units of threes: three strikes; three outs; nine innings (three times three); nine batters in a lineup.

Baseball is also statistically precise and complete, further providing a realm of intelligibility and clarity (Garrett, 661). Even casual fans can recite lists of records and statistics. Seemingly everything in baseball is recorded. Besides the familiar batting averages, runs scored, runs batted in, home runs, etc., listed in *The Baseball Encyclopedia* (and, for the current season, regularly updated in newspapers), baseball statisticians, calling themselves sabermetricians, have devised many new categories. Many of these sound esoteric. Bill James, perhaps the guru of sabermetricians, refers to defensive efficiency records, range factors, runs created, the Brock2 system, etc. Thomas Boswell refers to Total Average (137–144), and the Elias Sports Bureau breaks down each player's performance in minute detail. A fan can learn how his favorite player does on grass compared to how he fares on artificial turf, how well he hits at night compared to how well in daylight; he can see how a given player performs in a certain month, in a particular ballpark, after a particular inning, against certain batters or pitchers, and so on.

Although mathematics may seem to be antithetical to pastoralism, the desire for order, the pastoral wish, undoubtedly nourishes this obsession with numbers. Life cannot be measured so precisely, as much as we might wish otherwise. However, baseball creates the pastoral illusion that everything is contained and accounted for, that there is no threatening chaos, no disturbing disorder of any kind.

The attraction to the clarity and articulation of baseball's rules, records, and other statistics finds its way into baseball literature, further defining the genre. J. Henry Waugh, the protagonist of Robert Coover's *The Universal Baseball Association, Inc.,* is obsessed by the richness of baseball's arithmetic:

> American baseball, by luck, trial and error, and since the famous playing rules council of 1889, had struck on an almost perfect balance between offense and defense, and it was that balance, in fact, that and the accountability—the beauty of the records system which found a place to keep forever each least action—that had led Henry to baseball as his final great project. (19)

Henry invents his own baseball game, played on his kitchen table with dice and charts of statistics, forsaking not only real life but also real baseball, so that he can accentuate this aspect of the game:

> Nothing like it really. Not the actual game so much—to tell the truth, real baseball bored him—but rather the records, the statistics, the peculiar balances between individual and team, offense and defense, strategy and luck, accident and pattern, power and intelligence. And no other activity in the world had so precise and comprehensive a history, so specific an ethic, and at the same time, strange as it seemed, so much ultimate mystery. (45)

In Eric Rolfe Greenberg's *The Celebrant* (1983), the narrator's father-in-law, Mr. Sonnheim, engages New York Giants pitcher Christy Mathewson in a conversation about the nature of baseball. They emphasize the game's mathematical precision. Sonnheim refers to Alexander Cartwright, one of the reputed founders of the game: "'He once defined his endeavor as an attempt to balance the arithmetic of the game against its geometry. That was his phrase: to balance the arithmetic against the geometry'" (84). The fictional Mathewson continues the theme: "'All those balances—so exact, so demanding and tantalizing. Nothing in the game is easy, yet nothing is impossible. It's a game of intricate simplicity'" (84). When the narrator alludes to the belief that baseball is like life, Mathewson disagrees, again emphasizing the game's orderliness:

> In truth, nothing appealed to me as much as [baseball's] unreality. Baseball is all clean lines and clear decisions. Wouldn't life be far easier if it consisted of a series of definitive calls: safe or out, fair or foul, strike or ball. Oh, for a life like that, where every day produces a clear winner and an equally clear loser, and back to it the next day with the slate wiped clean and the teams starting out equal. (86–87)

Aware of the precision and clarity of the game, some baseball enthusiasts debate the question of the sport's origins, looking for that one genius to praise, whether he be Alexander Cartwright or Abner Doubleday. Kinsella dismisses the question in *The Iowa Baseball Confederacy* by bringing to life Leonardo Da Vinci, who owns up: " 'It took me years of calculations to get the dimensions just right. I'm pleased that it works in practical application as well as on paper' " (240). Drifting Away, the mystical American Indian of Kinsella's novel, remarks, " 'Baseball is the one single thing the white man has done right,' " and the Indian emphasizes not the game's straight lines but its circularity: " 'Think of the circles instead of the lines—the ball, the circumference of the bat, the outfield running to the horizon, the batter running around the bases. Baseball is as close to the circle of perfection as white men are allowed to approach' " (166–167).

Because of this sense that baseball is perfectly articulated, whether in its lines or its circles, in much literature the game becomes a sacred ritual, often displacing religion. Those "touched" by the game's sacredness are regenerated spiritually and sometimes healed physically. In Charyn's *The Seventh Babe,* the symbiotic interaction of voodoo and the magic of baseball enables players to perform magnificently, even into their old age. A Roy Hobbs home run miraculously heals a boy in Malamud's *The Natural* (134). The sacred power of a baseball game delivers a man and a woman from death and injury in Nancy Willard's *Things Invisible to See* (1985), a novel bulging with allegorical religious references.

No doubt the most exuberant example of evangelical fervor in baseball fiction is the speech delivered by Eddie Scissons in Kinsella's *Shoeless Joe.* He works up his audience, those seated in the bleachers, by having them chant the word "baseball," then launches into a sermon full of New Testament allusions and the cadences of a Bible-belt revivalist:

> "Can you imagine walking around with the very word of baseball enshrined inside you? Because the word of salvation is baseball. It gets inside you. Inside me. And the words that I speak are spirit, and *are* baseball. . . .
> "We have to have the word within us. I say you must get the word of baseball within you, and let it dwell within you richly. So that when you walk out in the world and meet a man or woman, you can speak the word of baseball, not because you've heard someone else speak it but because it is alive within you." (192)

Baseball fiction, then, in its presentation of bucolic space, of timeless existence, and of precise order, conveys American pastoral ideals. Leo Marx summarizes the American pastoral myth:

> In its simplest, archetypal form, the myth affirms that Europeans experience a regeneration in the New World. They become new, better, happier men—they are reborn. In most versions the regenerative power is located in the natural terrain: access to undefiled, bountiful, sublime Nature is what accounts for the virtue and special good fortune of Americans. It enables them to design a community in the image of a garden, an ideal fusion of nature with art. The landscape thus becomes the symbolic repository of value of all kinds—economic, political, aesthetic, religious. (228)

However, though baseball fiction draws upon and is defined by the pastoral myth, its best examples do not simply affirm these pastoral values. If they did, we would be right to dismiss them as sentimental and escapist. Careful readings of most examples of baseball fiction reveal that these works often express skepticism regarding the values they ostensibly advocate. At the very least, the expression of pastoralism becomes ambiguous. The fiction frequently seeks a middle ground between utter rejection of pastoral values and unrealistic, sentimental embrace of them.

Complete repudiation of pastoral beliefs may be as foolish and simplistic as uncritical acceptance of them. Sometimes, certainly, a protagonist who attempts to live outside of time, which is to say outside of life itself, must reject his idealism if he is to live; he must awaken from his dreams. However, much baseball fiction seems to suggest that the dreamer does not necessarily renounce his dream. The dream is an expression of beauty and an experience of pleasure. Rather, the dreamer must call his dream a dream, distinguishing between it and the world of time.

A review of Leo Marx's distinction between sentimental and complex pastoralism is helpful. "Complex pastoralism," he says, "acknowledges the reality of history. . . . In the characteristic pattern of complex pastoralism, the fantasy of pleasure is checked by the facts of history." Sentimental pastoralism, on the other hand, allows "faith [to] oust fact" (363). It is not possible to review or even mention every example of baseball fiction that expresses complex pastoralism. I will review just one example in order to demonstrate the tendency and then briefly suggest the ways that certain other examples of baseball fiction present a tension between simplistic acceptance of pastoralism and utter rejection of it.

Because W. P. Kinsella's short story "The Thrill of the Grass" (in a collection of the same name, 1984) may seem to be a nostalgic and sentimental work of fiction, I use it as an example of the kinds of tension that appear in baseball literature. It is not an ironic story.

Indeed, it ostensibly moves away from complex awareness toward a simplistic embrace of sentimental pastoralism. However, even "The Thrill of the Grass" does not ignore historical realities, nor is sentimentalism at its center.

The narrative is simple: during the baseball players' strike of 1981, the narrator, a locksmith, organizes a group of baseball fans who, at night, enter the local baseball stadium, temporarily empty and unused, in order to replace the artificial turf with sods of real grass. The fans, after a few nights, have completely returned their ballpark to its natural, idyllic state, evidently reversing the intrusions on baseball's pastoral purity represented by the artificial playing surface.

Although the story's movement seems to be toward simplicity, it begins and ends in tension. The narrator presents certain facts at the outset, none of which is changed by his actions. First, players are striking. Baseball in 1981 does not evoke images of a timeless garden; it is a business. Second, the narrator, we learn, is "a failed shortstop" who once saw himself making spectacular fielding plays, "like a cat leaping for butterflies," and leading the American League in hitting. Instead, he had had to accept the reality that he hit .217 in his last year of high school while making 1.3 errors per game (188). Third, the narrator speaks of the game and the stadium in some decidedly antipastoral ways. Besides the strike and the artificial turf, he describes the debris in the parking lot: "Faded bottle caps, rusted bits of chrome, an occasional paper clip, recede into the earth" (188). And he refers to the traffic on the freeway that passes the stadium.

Tugging on these realities are the narrator's dreams. He is disturbed by the strike because even compromised baseball is meaningful to him: "Summer without baseball: a disruption to the psyche" (187). Although he cannot participate in the sport physically, as a player, he does so mentally, as a fan. And with the disturbing images of the city and its debris, he mixes pastoral descriptions. He is aware that "outside the city the corn rustles and ripens in the sun" (187). He also describes the parking lot as it appears to him before games. He sees a community in relative harmony: "I like to watch young families beside their campers, the mothers in shorts, grilling hamburgers, their men drinking beer. I enjoy seeing little boys dressed in the home team uniform, barely toddling, clutching hot dogs in upraised hands" (187).

The narrator is not the only pastoral visionary. When he asks a fellow fan what he thinks of artificial turf, the man answers, " 'That's what the strike should be about. Baseball is meant to be played on summer evenings and Sunday afternoons, on grass just cut by a horse-

drawn mower'" (190). These two, along with their sod-carrying re-
cruits, attempt to turn back the clock by their actions. But they recognize that they are dreamers (190–191), and all their outlaw gardening
occurs at night, the time of dreaming. When the work is completed,
the narrator anticipates the surprise of the players and others when
the nighttime activities appear in the light of day, saying, "I feel like a
magician who has gestured hypnotically and produced an elephant
from thin air" (195).

It is significant that the story ends before anyone except the
pastoral conspirators sees this handiwork. Because we do not see the
reactions of those who attend the first game after the strike, we, like
the narrator, must imagine them. The pastoral vision, therefore,
though it has been materialized in this removal and replacement of
artificial turf, remains a dream—something imagined, not something
realized. The narrator, moreover, imagines that the grass will activate
the memories of the older players: "[A]s they dress, they'll recall
sprawling in the lush outfields of childhood, the grass as cool as a
mother's hand on a forehead" (196). In other words, they will not
experience the grass of the stadium as itself and for its own sake; they
will think instead of other grass. Pastoralism remains a vision or a
memory, not a reality. Youth is not restored or relived in this story. It is
remembered. The pastoral practical joke does not defeat time. Instead it, like the story itself, spurs imagination and memory.

Much baseball fiction similarly presents a tension between simplistic acceptance of pastoralism and complete rejection of it. *The
Natural*'s Roy Hobbs fails to defeat time; instead, he himself is defeated but learns a valuable lesson: that suffering, a result of time's
passage, is a necessary part of the human condition. Pastoral values
can be realized only for a time. Jerome Charyn's Babe Ragland removes himself from time, but *The Seventh Babe* is not soft on baseball.
The organized game in the novel is brutal, corrupt, racist. Eric Rolfe
Greenberg's narrator in *The Celebrant* must struggle to attain a dual
awareness: he must suffer disillusionment but avoid cynicism. W. P.
Kinsella's magic realism in *Shoeless Joe* and *The Iowa Baseball Confederacy* toys with the possibilities of achieving baseball perfection, but
this perfection is always imaginative, not concrete. Harry Stein's
Hoopla! employs two narrators. One, journalist Luther Pond, is cynical
and self-serving; the other, the banned player Buck Weaver, is be-
wildered but still in love with baseball, especially the game he remembers, the game of his imagination.

There is a consistent theme, then, in baseball fiction: pastoral
values can be realized only in the imagination, never for very long in

the real world. This theme gives birth to a considerable body of baseball fiction that is metafictional, or self-apparent, that is, about the writing of fiction or the operations of language rather than about the actual game. Robert Coover's *The Universal Baseball Association, Inc.* (1968), Philip Roth's *The Great American Novel* (1973), and Jerome Klinkowitz's *Short Season* (1988) fit this category. The works draw upon baseball's pastoralism, but they do not end in simple pastoralism but in complex examinations of language and literature.

Baseball fiction, therefore, is a rich genre. It derives from a boy's game, perhaps, but one that is profoundly evocative. Recent examples of the genre avoid sentimentality at the same time that they give expression to qualified American pastoral values.

Notes

1. I am indebted to Leo Marx's *The Machine and the Garden* for my understanding of American pastoralism and, as noted in the text, for some of these quotations from early American writers.
2. My thanks to Professor Paul Lilly of SUNY–Oneonta for drawing my attention to the proximity and common origins of the two museums.

References

Angell, Roger. *The Summer Game.* New York: Viking, 1972.

Boswell, Thomas. *How Life Imitates the World Series.* New York: Penguin, 1982.

Charyn, Jerome. *The Seventh Babe.* New York: Arbor, 1979.

Coover, Robert. *The Universal Baseball Association, Inc.* New York: Random, 1968.

Crèvecoeur, J. Hector St. John de. *Letters from an American Farmer and Sketches of Eighteenth-Century America.* 1782. New York: Penguin, 1987.

Garrett, Roland. "The Metaphysics of Baseball." Rpt. in *Sport Inside Out.* Eds. David L. Vanderwerken and Spencer K. Wertz. Fort Worth: Texas Christian UP, 1985. 643–663.

Greenberg, Eric Rolfe. *The Celebrant.* 1983. New York: Penguin, 1986.

Hall, Donald. "Baseball-Time." *Southern Humanities Review* 20 (1986): 223–225.

Hays, Donald. *The Dixie Association.* New York: Warner Books, 1984.

James, Bill. *The Bill James Historical Baseball Abstract.* New York: Villard, 1986.

Karl, Frederick. *American Fictions: 1940–1980.* New York: Harper, 1983.

Kinsella, W. P. *The Iowa Baseball Confederacy*. New York: Ballantine, 1986.

—————. *Shoeless Joe*. New York: Ballantine, 1982.

—————. *The Thrill of the Grass*. New York: Penguin, 1984.

Klinkowitz, Jerry. *Short Season and Other Stories*. Baltimore: Johns Hopkins UP, 1988.

Lardner, Ring. *Lose With a Smile*. New York: Scribner's, 1933.

—————. *You Know Me Al: A Busher's Letters*. 1914. New York: Scribner's, 1960.

Lehmann-Haupt, Christopher. *Me and DiMaggio*. New York: Dell, 1986.

Malamud, Bernard. *The Natural*. 1952. New York: Avon, 1980.

Marx, Leo. *The Machine in the Garden: Technology and the Pastoral Ideal in America*. New York: Oxford UP, 1964.

Roth, Philip. *The Great American Novel*. New York: Holt, 1973.

Siebert, Charles. "Baseball's Renaissance Man." *The New York Times Magazine* 4 Sept. 1988: 36–38 +.

Stein, Harry. *Hoopla!* New York: St. Martin's, 1983.

Willard, Nancy. *Things Invisible to See*. New York: Bantam, 1985.

From Dreams to Diamonds to Dictionaries

Baseball as Acculturating Force

by Linda A. Kittell

Many oriental children entered Moscow (Idaho) Junior High School to register for the coming Babe Ruth Baseball season. They came, usually with their mothers, chattering away in different languages then stepped up to the registration table to conduct the exchange and to fill out the necessary forms in English—position: pitcher, first base, outfield, shortstop. As they left the school, the boys returned to their first language.
(Field notes: June 1–3, 1983)

In *Touching Base: Professional Baseball and the American Culture in the Progressive Era*, Steven Reiss writes:

> Two of the principal functions ascribed to baseball were that it would teach children traditional American values and that it would help newcomers assimilate into the dominant WASP culture through their participation in the sport's ritual.[1]

As the United States continues to socialize the various race or ethnic groups along with welcoming immigrants, baseball still retains the two functions that Reiss cites. Organized baseball at any level—Little League to Major League—is a socializing force; it provides both the American youngster and the newcomer a way of learning our cultural traits and social constructs. Through an association with baseball, the "newcomer" will come to understand some very important American values or "culturally prescribed criteria by which individuals evaluate persons, behavior, objects, and ideas as to their relative morality, desirability, merit or correctness."[2]

While baseball teaches the newcomer some American values, it can also provide the non-American English speaker with information about and understanding of many words and idioms of American English which without some, even minimal, exposure to baseball would be unintelligible.

This chapter, then, is divided into two parts. In the first section, ways in which baseball exemplifies our American values will be presented. The second section will deal with the influence of baseball on

American English—how exposure to baseball will deepen the new-comer's understanding and appreciation of our language.

From Dreams to Diamonds

A larger number of cultural anthropologists, sociologists, physical educators, historians and philosophers agree that sports mirror or reflect the cultures in which they are found (e.g., Boyle, 1963; Voight, 1966, 1970; Loy and Kenyon , 1969; Haerle, 1973; Real, 1975; Lipsky, 1978; Sage, 1980; Reiss, 1980). Because of baseball's uniquely American origin, it is traditionally seen as our National Pastime as well as the sport which best serves as a mirror of our culture. So it is through baseball that the foreigner will be able to make important distinctions between what Americans say is true and what Americans actually do. Like a mirror that points up a pimple or a double chin, baseball shows, with honesty, the disparities between our beliefs—what we say is true—and our values—what we see as good.

The first generation of immigrants—like the mothers walking their sons to Babe Ruth registration—come to the United States full of hope, believing the promise of streets paved in gold, of equality among people, of the prevalence of religious freedom. It is the second generation of immigrants—the sons who register—who, in order to survive in the United States, must learn the culturally prescribed values of this nation. Through participation in or observation of organized baseball the immigrant will discover some of these important values.

*White Rather than (Black)**

---

*According the M. M. Tumin in *Social Stratification*, Americans assess people on thirteen points. Tumin says: "in American society one is generally considered better, superior, or more worthy if one is:
    White rather than (Black)
    Male rather than Female
    Protestant rather than Catholic or Jew
    Educated rather than Uneducated
    Rich rather than Poor
    White Collar rather than Blue Collar
    Of Good Family Origin rather than Undistinguished Family Origin
    Young rather than Old
    Urban or Suburban rather than Rural Dwelling
    Of Angle-Saxon National Origin rather than Any Other
    Native Born rather than of Foreign Descent
    Employed rather than Unemployed
    Married rather than Divorced[4]
I have chosen to borrow some of Tumin's categories for section headings.

Before Jackie Robinson was admitted to the major leagues in 1947, he spent three hours in the office of Branch Rickey, the general manager of the Brooklyn Dodgers. During that conference, Robinson answered questions and was told how he should conduct himself in the white world of organized ball.

> Rickey insisted on a "cloak of humility" as a part of his strategy to have Robinson accepted by the baseball world. Robinson asked if he wanted a ball player afraid to fight back, to which Rickey replied, "I want a ball player with guts enough not to fight back! You've got to do this job with base hits and stolen bases and fielding ground balls, Jackie. Nothing else!"[3]

Today, along with their major league uniforms, black players are still issued the "cloak of humility" Rickey spoke of over forty years ago. Presently, there are two black major league managers—Frank Robinson of the Baltimore Orioles and Cito Gaston of the Toronto Blue Jays. This lack of black managers may be related to a study in *Racial Segregation in American Sport*. In this article, Loy and McElvogue assert that racial segregation is related to centrality, that non-whites play positions that are isolated (outfield) and that do not require much integration with white players. According to their 1967 study (which featured all players who played at least fifty games during the 1967 season, not including pitchers), 36 of a total of 55 blacks played outfield positions. Since a high percentage of managers come from infield positions (see table), the odds are overwhelmingly against a

Former Playing Positions of Managers, as of Opening Day, 1983 (see Appendix for Opening Day, 1989)

Amer. League	Manager	Position	Nat'l. League	Manager	Position
East:					
New York	Martin	2B	St. Louis	Herzog	OF
Milwaukee	Khuen	SS, 3B, 1B, OF	Montreal	Virdon	OF
Boston	Houk	C	Philadelphia	Corrales	C
Toronto	Cox	3B	Pittsburgh	Tanner	OF
Detroit	Anderson	2B	Chicago	Elia	SS
Cleveland	Ferraro	3B	New York	Bamberger	P
Baltimore	Altobelli	1B			
West:					
California	McNamara	C	Atlanta	Torre	C, 1B, 3B
Chicago	LaRussa	2B	Los Angeles	Lasorda	P
Texas	Rader	3B	San Diego	Williams	OF, 3B, 1B, 2B
Seattle	Lachman	C	San Francisco	Robinson	OF
Minnesota	Gardener	2B	Cincinnati	Nixon	C
Kansas City	Howser	SS	Houston	Lillis	SS
Oakland	Boros	3B			

black player becoming a manager of a major league team. This is not because blacks are inferior as ball players. A 1977 study in *Sport and Social Systems* shows that not only blacks, but also Latins have significantly higher batting averages than white players. However, since infield positions are more complicated, requiring more obscure knowledge than outfield positions, more managers come from infield positions.

Bob Gibson, a pitcher for the St. Louis Cardinals from 1959–1975, who posted a lifetime E.R.A. of 2.91 with a total of 3,117 strikeouts, is the subject of a chapter in Roger Angell's *Late Innings*. About Gibson, a black pitcher and an exception for that reason, Angell writes:

> But a little later he mentioned the many times he had been harassed by semiofficial white people—hotel clerks and traffic cops and the like—who later fawned on him when they learned he was *the* Bob Gibson, the famous pitcher. "It's nice to get attention and favors," he said, "but I can never forget the fact that if I were an ordinary black person I'd be in the shithouse, like millions of others."[5]

Though we may have moved farther away from segregated restaurants and buses, our treatment of blacks in baseball reflects our value of white rather than black.

Male Rather than Female

Conversation between Kellie Johnson, age seven, a young Moscow Blue Devil fan and the Blue Devil American Legion Baseball team assistant coach, Moscow, Idaho:

Kellie Johnson: *He* (pointing to young fan) says girls aren't good enough to play baseball.
Young Fan: Look how many play in the major leagues.
Kellie Johnson: (To coach) Why don't girls play there?
Coach: Because of some stupid rules.
                              (Field notes, June 19, 1983)

The observation of the young fan is correct; no women have played ball at the major league level—in the American, National or Federal Leagues. Baseball has not only omitted women from the fields of play, but also from the locker rooms and thereby from the field of sports reporting. Only a small minority of male reporters and players welcome the female reporter. In "Sharing the Beat," Roger Angell writes about the humiliations imposed on the female reporter trying to do her job. In Angell's interview with Diane K. Shah, associate editor of *Newsweek*, she says:

> . . . Finally I got my pass to go out on the field, but when I went out during batting practice I found that none of the players would talk to me, they simply wouldn't answer when I asked them questions. Then I discovered that there had been a team meeting, where they'd been told I was coming and to watch their language . . .
>
> Before the game, Dick Bresiani, the assistant public relations man, took me up on the roof where the press box and pressroom are. I could see he was terribly uncomfortable about something, and when we got there he explained that I could come into the press box but that the pressroom was a social place, for eating and drinking, and no women were allowed there. I saw that they'd set up a little ice cream table outside the pressroom, with one chair and one place setting, and there was a little folder on it with 'Ladies' Pavilion' written across it.[6]

After the 1982 All-Star game in Montreal, I watched as a sports reporter was made to wait outside the American League locker room because she was a woman and was not allowed in because of her sex. Instead of getting direct quotes from players, she had to ask rather reluctant colleagues for their quotations.

Baseball only welcomes women on the periphery—as anxious writers outside the locker room door or as aerobic instructors at spring training, or as an umpire stuck in the minor leagues. The "newcomer" can see, from baseball, that American society does not welcome women unless they come bearing sandwiches and cookies.

Work (or Play) before Religion

In a country that offers religious freedom, our national pastime shows that we value religion less than we value our work. Administrators in organized baseball demand that players forego religion of any sort rather than let the diamond's demands supersede the sabbath.

The Boise Buckskins, a Class A team out of Idaho, folded after one year partly because of bad management (should it be mentioned that the general manager was a woman?) and partly because of bad press over the religious preferences of the team. General manager Lanny Moss was a born-again Christian as was her field manager, Gerry Craft. With JESUS painted in twelve-foot red-and-white letters on a right field billboard and a picture of Christ Himself in left field, the religious orientation of some team players and organizers was difficult for the press to pass over.

Among Buckskin team members was Dan Thomas. Of superstar

potential, Thomas played two seasons for the Milwaukee Brewers before he was forced to choose between his religion—World Wide Church of God—which required a twenty-four-hour layoff from Friday night to Saturday night for *Bible* study, and baseball. Thomas's religious convictions and organized ball's belief in baseball before God, work before religion, met head on and Thomas was released from the Brewers in 1977.

With the Buckskins, Thomas was allowed his religion. He left the ball park slightly before Friday's sunset and arrived mid-game after Saturday's sunset. The Bucks in management put religion before work, but then religion, in part, caused the downfall of the Buckskin organization. Because Danny Thomas was such an outstanding player, he was given advantage over less phenomenal players; organized ball was patient with his quirks for a time, but not too long a time. To have strong religious convictions that may take away from the work week is impossible in baseball, just as the mixture of church and state is frowned on in American society.

Organized ball is not the only form of institutional baseball that discourages religious interruptions from the play. An American Legion-age player whose religion may require a Sunday layoff is subtly discouraged from spending any of his summer on the field. Because so many games are scheduled for Sundays and because missing any games is regarded with disfavor, the player with strong religious orientation would, most generally, be removed from the roster.

A newcomer to the U.S. may notice that we value our work (and our play) over our religious orientation.

Educated Rather than Uneducated

The playing of a sport of any kind is particularly admired in the United States. Outside of the admiration of peers gained from field heroics, it seems that an involvement with sport encourages attainment of education. The student is socialized, often not too subtly, to see that the reward for study is sports participation. (Many high schools require a minimum of a "C" average in order for the student to participate in a sport.)

Four successive studies "Bend (1968), Rehberg and Schafer (1968), Spreitzer and Pugh (1973), and Otto and Alwin (1977) found that a greater proportion of high school male athletes than nonathletes expected to enroll in a four year college program."[7] It may well be that these athletes are going to college mainly to play sports, but sport is the driving force behind education, the carrot. Athletes are often encouraged toward higher education with scholarship offers, and high school coaches generally take special interest in seeing a star athlete choose the right college. If we did not see education as important and valuable, the reward for education would not, most likely, be participation in one of our most valued activities.

$omething Worth A$piring To[8]

The 1981 All-Star Money Team	Yearly Salary
1B: Eddie Murray (Orioles)	$1,000,000
2B: Rennie Stennett (Giants)	600,000
3B: George Brett (Royals)	1,300,000
SS: Rick Burleson (Angels)	767,000
C: Ted Simmons (Brewers)	820,000
OF: Dave Winfield (Yankees)	1,500,000
OF: Fred Lynn (Angels)	1,300,000
OF: Dave Parker (Pirates)	1,000,000
Andre Dawson (Expos)	1,000,000
DH or Utility:	
Rod Carew (Angels)	900,000
Pete Rose (Phillies)	800,000
Garry Maddox (Phillies)	800,000
Gary Matthews (Phillies)	800,000
George Foster (Reds)	700,000
P: Nolan Ryan (Astros)	1,170,000
J.R. Richard (Astros)	1,000,000
Phil Neikro (Astros)	900,000
Don Sutton (Astros)	900,000
Bruce Sutter (Cardinals)	800,000

As one prominent baseball writer says:

> I have carefully reminded myself that the irony of our laying out hundreds of thousands of dollars in salary for a fireballing young relief pitcher or an indomitable veteran switchhitter but only a small fraction of such sums for a first-class teacher or a promising poet or pathologist says a good deal about our society but can't quite be blamed on baseball itself.[9]

What these salaries may indicate to a newcomer is that Americans admire baseball players and that being a baseball player is something worth aspiring to. Not only do we value our sportsmen greatly, but we value our own leisure enough to pay our entertainers, our ball players in this case, great quantities of money for their performances. We are willing to pay our baseball players more than our statesmen, our scientists, our writers, and our teachers.

Young Rather than Old

> July 1973: Willie Mays, who is now, at forty-two, the oldest
> player in the National League has so far resisted the clear evidence
> that he should retire. He plays sporadically, whenever he is well and
> rested, and gives his best, but his batting reflexes are gone, and so is
> his arm . . . but his failings are so cruel to watch that I am relieved
> when he is not part of the lineup. It is hard enough for the rest of us
> to fall quite apart on our own; heroes should depart.[10]

As a relatively young country which broke away from a much
older order, we pride ourselves in youngness and newness. "Youth is
valued because it represents achievement, competition, power, and
success, whereas old age is devalued because it does not reflect the
attributes of achievement, independence, and productivity."[11] We are
a fast-paced society that has little room for the slower, the older. We
relegate our old people to "homes" and ask that our baseball players
retire no later than age forty. The Willie Mayses, the Gaylord Perrys,
and Carl Yastrzemskis make us uncomfortable. They are past their
prime; they are hangers-on. Just as we read and wondered about the
age versus competency factor of our last president, we are sure that
the over-forty ball player has nothing to offer us. In 1979, the Northwest League, a Class A system, adopted a rule favoring younger
players and making it nearly impossible for someone 26 or older to be
placed on a roster. Give the younger fellows a chance; retire at 65.
Baseball reflects our fears of old age and our value on the young.

Rewriting the Pitch

Call him Roy Hobbs or Mickey Mantle, Satchel Paige, Connie Mack
(an Americanized form of Cornelius McGillicuddy) or Fernando Val-
enzuela. The stories are similar. Out in Oklahoma or South Carolina
or near the Mexican border, he was throwing apples at the barn. His
mother worried about feeding the large family; his father said the
crops were worse than usual. Then, just as the boy was gathering
another handful of apples, he noticed a trail of dust rising off the
road and a shiny black car rolled into the yard. Out popped a city
dude who handed Roy or Fernando a ball and a glove. Then the dude
slipped on a catcher's mitt and squatted himself in the dirt, saying:
"Just fire it here, son." So Mickey did and the other guy shook his
catching hand with pain and pulled out a check with the other. Then
Satchel went inside to pack his cardboard suitcase.
    David Voigt calls this Alger–American Dream story[12] a myth and

Tristram Coffin calls it legend or folklore, but the stories of ball players in fact or in fiction are a basis for explaining some of America's cultural values. Baseball teaches the younger American and the foreigner something about the ways in which Americans evaluate people and things. Like the 14th century morality plays, the stories around baseball reflect the struggle of good over evil, climaxing in the hero's choice of what is valued as good in that culture.[13] Tristram Coffin claims that baseball rarely serves a purpose after the second generaton of an ethnic group because the game has already served its purpose by acculturating the group. Once comfortable in the American culture, able to better understand our cultural values, the newcomers, too, "are tossing aside old peasant ways, feeling embarrassment over their backgrounds; learning to act and speak like the people who make up the bourgeois flow of American, urban life. It is the old American phenomenon of the immigrant boy or country boy making good in the city, learning that his background is best discarded or modified,"[14] speaking only American English to his son on their way to the Babe Ruth Baseball registration.

From Diamonds to Dictionaries

In an article entitled "Sportuguese," in *Sport, Culture and Society,* authors Noah and Tannenbaum assert that:

> It is a fairly common assumption among linguists and anthropologists that the more frequent an event in a given linguistic culture—or, at least the more important that event is within that culture—the greater number and diversity of words associated with that event. The notion here is simply that language vocabulary mirrors the interests of the people who speak that language.[15]

Since we have seen that baseball mirrors our societal values and may help the American child or the foreigner to become socialized to those values, it would be expected that American English would reflect the importance of our national pastime, "mirroring the interests of the people who speak" American English.

Edward Nichols submitted his dissertation, "An Historical Dictionary of Baseball Terminology," in February of 1939. In the 116 pages of his dissertation, Nichols traces 2,500 words and expressions that originated on the baseball diamond and their entrance into American English. "This pioneer work served to convince academicians of the value of studying a 'frivolous' institution like baseball for insights into the American character."[16]

Nichols' work covers terms added mainly between 1920 and 1937, but also includes terms from the late 1800s when baseball was first gaining popularity. Even so, 2,500 words is a phenomenal addition to American English for one sport and for such a short time;* the addition of so many words would support Noah and Tannenbaum's contention.

It should be noted that there are two main sources for baseball jargon or cant. First and most obvious are the players themselves, second, the news media. At the time Nichols was doing his research, he limited himself to baseball terms for which he could find a printed record. So in Nichols' dictionary, the baseball jargon of sportswriters predominates.

In an effort to make their stories fresh and lively, Nichols tells us, sportswriters were continually coming up with new verbs. He says:

> [the verb] category is illustrative of the free imagination which characterizes the baseball language and American slang in general. When a batter swings at and misses a ball thrown to him he 'beats the breeze.' 'fans the ozone.' 'saws the air.' or 'swishes the atmosphere.'[17]

Nichols also points out changes in word usages, instances of metonomy (ash for bat), alliteration (Bronx Bombers), conversion—changes in parts of speech (e.g., noun to verb as in to *bench* a player), back formations (to pinch hit from pinch hitter) that appeared on

---

*Even though baseball evolved from the English game of cricket, the "new" game, the new variation, caught on rapidly in the United States. At first considered a "gentlemen's" game with tea served after matches, once baseball went professional (circa 1876) people from the lower classes were invited (or hired) to play for professional teams. The game then became a way for the lower classes to climb out of poverty through personal achievements on the field. (Tristram Coffin points out many instances where baseball has served to acculturate the ethnic groups who generally make up and have made up our lower classes.) The phenomenal addition of words to the American English vocabulary through baseball may have been encouraged because baseball allowed for rapid social mobility of the lower classes. Unlike the situation in Britain after the Norman conquest when few people were exposed to French and almost no people from the lower classes were exposed to French, baseball cut across the class structure with its popularity. Baseball language is, and was, a part of the language of the commoner, of the masses, the lower classes. Baseball terms could easily filter into the common language, making rapid progress from American diamond to American dictionary.

sports pages. He cites examples of proper nouns becoming common nouns: Fred Merkle becomes merkle—a boner, a mistake. (As a ball player, Fred Merkle is legendary for his error-riddled performance on the field.) Nichols also provides a list of baseball idioms such as 'cup of coffee'—"A tryout with a major league club, named for the board this (sic) is furnished."[18]

Because Nichols restricted his study to only printed baseball terms, even a borderline baseball fan would be able to add terms like "rhubarb" and idioms such as "come dab" and "seeing eye hit" that have since appeared in print. The borderline fan would also notice words in Nichols' dictionary that have undergone meaning and sound shifts. For example, "bingle"—a base hit got a single—has shifted to "bingo" both for ease of pronunciation in ballpark chatter and for meaning, reinforcing the key hit situation by shouting "bingo." Another example of change is "clothesline"—a parallel to the ground hit or throw—now called a "rope." The metaphoric extension between clothesline and rope seems clear; both are made of the same or similar materials. Many of Nichols' terms have been dropped and replaced by new terms—"Stu Miller" for "freight delivery," "rain delay" for "Old Pluvy," and "a pilfer" for a "second story act."

A reader of Nichols' dictionary will also notice the large number of baseball words that have become commonplace. At the time Nichols was researching his project, he noted the progress on the new *Dictionary of American English*. Under the letters *A, B*. and part of *C* were 62 terms of diamond origin.

In his chapter "Baseball Talk," Tristram Coffin writes:

> This [baseball] cant, when used exclusively, is nearly unintelligible to an outsider. However, much of it has entered slang and colloquial speech, a good bit has become acceptable in the most conservative standard speech, and a little in formal American English. The overall contribution of this cant is truly amazing. No other sport has contributed even a fraction of the phrases and words baseball has. There is some truth in the statement that a foreigner wishing to learn our language might as well start in the ballpark.[19]

Coffin and Nichols agree that many baseball words and phrases have become integral to American speech, so much so that we no longer connect the word with its diamond origins. An example of such a phrase would be "Charley horse," a phrase that first appeared in 1891 in the June 16th edition of the *Chicago Herald,* meaning "the muscular soreness of a baseball player's leg."[20] The phrase "charley horse" is now so deeply embedded in our language that most people would have trouble describing the ailment if the phrase were taken from them. In fact, the *Journal of the American Medical Association* printed an article as long ago as November 30, 1946, entitled "Treatment of the Charly Horse," rather than "Treatment of Injury to the Quadriceps Femoris." Such a usage indicated the phrase to have been part of even the most formal American English for a quarter of a century.[21]

Coffin also lists words and phrases which he suggests even the "most inattentive Americans know well the meaning of," words like bleachers, southpaw, pinch hitter, raincheck, and benchwarmer. He also reminds the reader of the teenage slang of "getting to first base," i.e., kissing a girl, and so on around the diamond.

In *Language of Sport*, a dictionary of sport terms, researchers list 57 terms as words commonly used in situations far away from the diamond—ace, ballpark figure, hit and run, lineup, meal ticket, muff, raincheck, flakey, razzberry (raspberry), shag, whitewash, and shut out. Though we may use many of these words without being conscious of their ballpark origins, to understand some of these terms and the terms Coffin lists, the speaker/hearer would be helped by a familiarity with baseball in some, if only a vague, form.

A non-American English speaker, a foreigner or a young child, upon first hearing some of these terms and never having been exposed to baseball, would naturally be confused. What do American English speakers mean by a "raincheck"? Since we have been exposed to baseball, we know that baseball is usually played out-of-doors. We also know that a heavy downpour or a constant drizzle makes it impossible to complete a baseball game. After waiting out a "rain delay," until the umpires call the game, ticket holders would be (and still are) given a "raincheck" to come back the next day to see the game to its completion. When we are given a "raincheck" in a store, most American English speakers are able to understand the transfer of meaning from ballpark to K-mart. We know that the store is out of the product we want and, therefore, unable to complete our order on a particular day. We should come back, instead, on the next day when the product we requested should be on hand.

Just like "raincheck," other baseball terms have similar diamond to dictionary transfers and shifts. A "doubleheader"—a metaphoric transfer from the original meaning of a two-engined train—means two games by the same two teams on the same day. This meaning has widened to mean any two things following one after another. ("I had to go to two weddings on Saturday—a doubleheader.") "Batting a thousand," originally meaning a perfect batsman, has come to represent any person who is doing a perfect job, so that phrase has also widened in meaning. ("We got all the yard work done; we're really batting a thousand today.") We read about "hit and run" drivers daily in the newspaper and don't stop to consider the meaning or diamond origin of the phrase. Down the hall, a co-worker says: "I like Harry. He's always on the ball." We have transferred the meaning from the ballpark to the office; we certainly aren't talking about Harry's pitching ability.

In a couple of hours of casual listening, reading, and observing, one can find many baseball references used in non-baseball situations (especially in warmer months) and dependent on some degree of awareness of baseball:

—A June 22nd, noon newscast with Paul Harvey: Reporting about the orbiting spacecraft, Harvey described the crew's day, including the testing of a mechanical arm. With this arm, the crew played 'pitch and catch spaceball.'

—From a situation comedy "Give Me a Break" on June 23rd: A main character is given a speech to read and told that the reason for using this speech is that it "touches all the bases."

—An Arby's Restaurant advertisement shows a sports glass giveaway. None of the glasses to be given away represents baseball; they are all cartoons of individual sports. "Here's Arby's *lineup* of great glasses."

—An article in *Guideposts Magazine,* a spiritual guide that offers suggestions on how faith can help a person overcome the odds, talks about the conflict between a smalltown hamburger joint and a MacDonald's moving in next door. '"Everybody's sure fired up about MacDonald's moving to town," said Wilma. "It's as if Sapulpa has suddenly *hit the big leagues.*"[22]

In all of these instances, the speakers or writers used baseball terms to get their points across readily and in a few words. As speakers of American English, we are able to transfer these ballpark idioms to other fields. But without some exposure to baseball, these commonplace ideas might be lost.

A knowledge of baseball not only helps us to understand some of our everyday language, but also deepens our understanding and appreciation of American English. A foreigner, a non-American English speaker, and a young child can come to understand baseball and begin to appreciate smalltown store names like "Shortstop," a double entendre on the baseball position and on the speed of the patron's visit. A restaurant called "Home Plate" directly across from the softball fields will come to mean more than a place where you eat off dishes like you have at home.

Baseball has added significantly to the vocabulary of American English as well as adding colorful and descriptive terms to our language. Because American English reflects the importance of our national pastime, it is important for the non-native American English speaker or young child to become somewhat familiar with baseball in order to understand much of commonplace American English and some of formal American English. By doing so, the learner of American English can really be a *hit* and move from the *bushes* to the *big leagues* in language acquisition. The *rookie* American English speaker really should start at the ballpark *right off the bat* to learn the American English language.

Appendix

Former Playing Positions of Managers, As of Opening Day, 1989

American League	Manager	Position	National League	Manager	Position
East:					
New York	Green	P	St. Louis	Herzog	OF
Milwaukee	Trebelhorn	3B, C, 1B	Montreal	Rodgers	C
Boston	Morgan	2B, SS	Philadelphia	Leyva	3B, SS
Toronto	Williams	SS, 2B	Pittsburgh	Leyland	C, 3B, SS
Detroit	Anderson	2B	Chicago	Zimmer	3B, 2B
Cleveland	Edwards	C	New York	Johnson	2B
Baltimore	Robinson	OF			
West:					
California	Radar	3B	Atlanta	Nixon	C
Chicago	Torborg	C	Los Angeles	Lasorda	P
Texas	Valentine	OF	San Diego	McKeon	C
Seattle	Lafebvre	2B	San Francisco	Craig	P
Minnesota	Kelly	OF, 1B	Cincinnati	Rose	OF, 2B, 3B
Kansas City	Wathan	C	Houston	Howe	2B, 3B
Oakland	LaRussa	SS, 2B			

Notes

1. Steven Reiss, *Touching Base: Professional Baseball and American Culture in the Progressive Era* (Westport, Conn.: Greenwood Press, 1980), p. 7.

2. George H. Sage, ed., *Sport and American Society* (Reading, MA.: Addison-Wesley Publishing Company, 1980), p. 113.

3. John T. Talamini and Charles H. Page, *Sport and Society: An Anthology* (Boston: Little, Brown and Company, 1973), p. 237.

4. Melvin M. Tumin, *Social Stratification: The Forms and Functions of Inequality* (Englewood Cliffs, N.J.: Prentice-Hall, Inc. 1967), p. 27.

5. Roger Angell, *Late Innings: A Baseball Companion* (New York: Simon and Schuster, 1982), p. 289.

6. Ibid., pp. 142–143.

7. John W. Loy, Barry D. McPherson, and Gerald Kenyon, *Sport and Social Systems: A Guide to the Analysis, Problems, and Literature* (Reading, MA,: Addison-Wesley Publishing Company, 1978), p. 231.

8. Roger Angell, *Late Innings: A Baseball Companion* (New York: Simon and Schuster, 1982), pp. 327–328.

9. Ibid., p. 327.

10. Roger Angell, *Five Seasons: A Baseball Companion* (New York: Popular Library, 1978), p. 90.

11. John W. Loy, Barry D. McPherson, and Gerald Kenyon, *Sport and Social Systems* (Reading, MA.: Addison-Wesley Publishing Company, 1978), p. 397.

12. This idea is gleaned from the work of Richard D. Keller in his article "Kids and Sports Books," North American Society for Sport History. *Proceedings of the Eighth NASSH Convention* (Banff, Alberta, May, 1980), p. 36.

13. Ibid.

14. Tristram Potter Coffin, *The Illustrated Book of Baseball Folklore* (New York: The Seabury Press, 1975), p. 26.

15. John H. Loy, "Sportuguese: A Study in Sports Page Communication," in *Sport, Culture and Society,* ed. by John Loy and Gerald Kenyon, (London: The MacMillan Company, 1969), p. 333.

16. David Quentin Voigt, *American Baseball: From Commissioners to Continental Expansion, Vol. II* (Norman: University of Oklahoma Press, 1970), p. 240.

17. Edward J. Nichols, "An Historical Dictionary of Baseball Terminology" (unpublished Ph.D. dissertation, Pennsylvania State College, 1939), p. VI.

18. Ibid., p. VIII.

19. Tristram Potter Coffin, *The Illustrated Book of Baseball Folklore* (New York: The Seabury Press, 1975), pp. 46–47.

20. Edward J. Nichols, "An Historical Dictionary of Baseball Terminology" (unpublished Ph.D. dissertation, Pennsylvania State College, 1939), p. 13.

21. Tristram Potter Coffin, *The Illustrated Book of Baseball Folklore* (New York: The Seabury Press, 1975), p. 52.

22. Jim Summers, "Little Me and Big Mac," *Guideposts,* August, 1983, p. 34.

Bibliography

Angell, Roger. *Five Seasons: A Baseball Companion.* New York: Popular Library, 1978.

——————. *Late Innings: A Baseball Companion.* New York: Simon and Schuster, 1982.

——————. *The Summer Game*. New York: Popular Library, 1972.

Boyle, R. *Sport: Mirror of American Life*. Boston: Little, Brown, 1963.

Boswell, Thomas. *How Life Imitates the World Series*. Garden City, New York: Doubleday and Company, Inc., 1982.

Bouton, Jim. *Ball Four*. New York: Dell Publishing Co., Inc., 1970.

Crepeau, Richard C. *Baseball 1919–1941: America's Diamond Mind*. Orlando: University Presses of Florida, 1980.

Coffin, Tristram Potter. *The Illustrated Book of Baseball Folklore*. New York: The Seabury Press, 1975.

Harris, Janet C. and Roberta J. Park, eds. *Play, Games, and Sports in Cultural Contexts*. Champaign, Illinois: Human Kinetics Publishers, Inc., 1983.

Hart, Marie and Susan Birrell, eds. *Sport in the Sociocultural Process*. Dubuque: William C. Brown Company Publishers, 1981.

Holway, John. *Voices from the Great Black Leagues*. New York: Dodd, Mead, and Company, 1975.

Guttman, Allen. *From Ritual to Record: The Nature of Modern Sports*. New York: Columbia University Press, 1978.

Jordan, Pat. *The Suitors of Spring*. New York: Warner Paperback Library, 1974.

Kahn, Roger. *The Boys of Summer*. Signet Books. New York: New American Library, 1973.

——————. *A Season in the Sun*. New York: Berkley Medallion Books, 1978.

Lieb, Fred. *Baseball as I Have Known It*. A Tempo Star Book. New York: Ace Books, 1977.

Lipsky, R. *How We Play the Game: Why Sports Dominate American Life*. Boston: Beacon, 1981.

Loy, John and Gerald Kenyon, eds. *Sport, Culture, and Society: Reader on the Sociology of Sport*. London: The MacMillan Company, 1969.

Loy, John, Barry McPherson, and Gerald Kenyon, eds. *Sport and Social Systems: A Guide to the Analysis, Problems, and Literature*. Reading, MA.: Addison-Wesley Publishing Company, 1978.

Rappaport, Ken. *Diamonds in the Rough*, Tempo Books. New York: Grosset and Dunlap, 1979.

Reiss, Steven A. *Touching Base: Professional Baseball and American Culture in the Progressive Era*. Westport, CT: Greenwood Press, 1980.

Reichler, Joseph L., ed. *The Baseball Encyclopedia*. New York: Macmillan Publishing Company, Inc., 1979.

Ritter, Lawrence S. *The Glory of Their Times*. Collier Books. New York: Macmillan Publishing Co., Inc., 1966.

——————— and Donald Honig. *The Image of Their Greatness: An Illustrated History of Baseball from 1900 to the Present.* New York: Crown Publishers, Inc., 1979.

Sage, George H., ed. *Sport and American Society: Selected Readings.* Reading, MA.: Addison-Wesley Publishing Company, 1980.

Senzel, Howard. *Baseball and the Cold War.* New York: Harcourt Brace Jovanovich, 1977.

Smith, Leverett T., Jr. *The American Dream and the National Game.* Bowling Green: Bowling Green University Popular Press, 1975.

Talamini, John T., and Charles H. Page, eds. *Sport and Society: An Anthology.* Boston: Little, Brown and Company, 1973.

Tumin, Melvin M. *Social Stratification: The Forms and Functions of Inequality.* Englewood Cliffs, N.J.: Prentice-Hall, Inc., 1967.

Voigt, David Quentin. *American Baseball: From Gentlemen's Sport to the Commissioner System, Vol. I.* Norman: University of Oklahoma Press, 1966.

———————. *American Baseball: From the Commissioner System to Continental Expansion. Vol. II.* Norman: University of Oklahoma Press, 1970.

Periodicals:

Haerle, Rudolf. "Heroes, Success Themes, and Basic Cultural Values in Baseball Autobiography, 1900–1970." Paper at the Third National Meeting of Popular Culture Association. Indiana, 1973.

Angell, Roger. "Easy Lessons," *The New Yorker,* May 2, 1983, pp. 43–65.

North American Society of Sport History. *Proceedings of the Eighth NASSH Convention.* Banff, Alberta, May, 1980.

———————. *Proceedings of the Ninth NASSH Convention.* Hamilton, Ontario, May, 1981.

International Review of Sport Sociology. A Yearbook Edited by the Committee for Sociology of the International Council of Sport and Physical Education and the International Sociological Association. Vol. 7. Warsaw: Polish Scientific Publishers, 1972.

———————. Volume 3–4 (15.) Warsaw, 1980.

Unpublished Materials:

Nichols, Edward J. "An Historical Dictionary of Baseball Terminology." Unpublished Ph.D. dissertation, Pennsylvania State College, 1939.

An Examination of Professional Baseball Players as Heroes and Role Models

by Monty E. Nielsen and George W. Schubert

Introduction

An examination of professional baseball players as heroes and role models in this century requires understanding the dynamics and variables which have influenced and shaped baseball during periods of growth and change in America. The purpose of this examination is to gain an increased understanding of 1) selected individuals who have graced and circled the diamond and, 2) the American character and its values, which are deeply ingrained in the timber of the game and those who play it.

This chapter is divided into four major sections: 1) Introduction (questions and statements regarding the importance and significance of baseball in the American culture); 2) Professional Baseball Players as Heroes (an analysis of heroic characteristics and qualities of selected players); 3) Professional Baseball Players as Role Models (an analysis of those characteristics and qualities perceived as desirable in role models for young people); and 4) Synthesis (summary and conclusion concerning professional baseball players as heroes and positive role models for young people).

Significance of Baseball in the American Culture

What makes baseball significant in the American culture? Congressman Robert L. Livingston of Louisiana (1989) said:

> To me, baseball has become America's symbol because it so perfectly echoes our society. It is a team sport, but one that demands each player's initiative. The successful baseball player requires quickness, tempo and stamina. He must make split-second decisions and bear full consequences for the result. . . . It's a great spectator sport, and for the players, the demands of teamwork and personal achievement are illustrative of America's initiative.

Baseball is tightly interwoven in the fabric of the American culture. It is younger than the nation itself, but in degree of importance as an American institution, it has been ordained "the National Pastime of America, the democratic game. It was a game of the people, played by and for them . . . it could be played in a sandlot, pasture, or street. It was . . . within the reach of all men, satisfying to both spectator and player" (Crepeau, 1980). The symbolic significance of baseball in America was patriotically framed by Warren C. Giles (cited by Lee Allen, 1965), then president of the National League, when he said, "At war and in peace, good times and bad, our people have never failed to find time for baseball. It is as much a part of America as the freedoms we cherish and the liberties we defend." To place baseball on the same plane as "life, liberty, and the pursuit of happiness" perhaps is an overstatement; but baseball, simple by nature, is a game underscored by hyperbole. The overstatement is derived from the competitive spirit of the game and the classic confrontation between pitcher and hitter, which ultimately determines the outcome as each game reaches its precisely measured destiny. It is from this daily drama that heroes and, one hopes, positive role models are born.

Governor Mario M. Cuomo of New York (1989) described what he thinks significantly sets baseball apart from other professional sports:

> Baseball, more than any other sport, is a uniquely American tradition that binds generation to generation, unlike any other ritual in society. It's a Little Leaguers' game that major leaguers play extraordinarily well, a game that excites us throughout adulthood. The crack of the bat and the scent of horsehide on leather bring back our own memories that have been washed away with the sweat and tears of summers long gone . . . even as the setting sun pushes the shadows past home plate.

Crepeau (1980) discusses America's early interest in football at the college and professional levels during the 1920s. Some believed that football might replace baseball as the "national game." Baseball advocates disagreed. Crepeau (1980) cited *The Sporting News,* which claimed football's popularity was due primarily to Red Grange's popularity. Grange's departure would reduce football to minor status. It was argued also that football had weak roots: half of football's attendance was a result of the tradition of the colleges competing. Very few people understood football. Its claim to being amateur was attacked because wealthy alumni were paying college players. Football was a game supported by the rich. It was also very physical and rough. None of these statements characterized baseball.

Baseball's most redeeming value was its common union with democracy (Crepeau, 1980). Consider, for example, the system of checks and balances that governs each day's play. The players on the field could be considered as the legislative body representative of their constituents, the fans, who pay their salaries while viewing and critiquing their performance. The manager and the coaches on the field could be looked upon as the executive branch responsible for direction, leadership, motivation, stragegy, etc. The umpires on the field could be viewed as the judiciary responsible for maintaining a system of fair play and justice consistent with the laws that govern and protect the game. This democratic characterization of baseball appeared to be the predominant basis for its claim to be the "national game." Commissioner A. Bartlett Giamatti quoted by Frank Deford in *Sports Illustrated* (April, 1989) accented the preeminent significance of baseball in contrast to football and basketball. He responded, not so democratically, to National Basketball Association (NBA) commissioner David Stern's statement that ". . . baseball is America's pastime, but football is America's passion, and basketball is America's game," by stating, "I can live with that, . . . as long as you understand that I have historical priority, and therefore I run the country."

Early Media Influence

The infusion of professional baseball into the American culture became pronounced in the 1920s due partly to the advent of radio as a major medium, which then complemented only newspaper coverage. Newspaper coverage, however, was not limited to the daily and weekly tabloids of big city and small town America, but also included the "bible" of baseball—*The Sporting News*—which, until well into the second half of the 20th century, was devoted entirely to baseball. According to Wayne Towers (1979), "The poetic praises of 1920s baseball poured forth from two main sources: the press and the radio." To explain this partnership, Towers stated ". . . radio provided an immediate but not necessarily coherent description of the game, while newspapers provided a delayed, but concise, summary of the festivities." In the years that followed, numerous publications such as *SPORT* magazine evolved, which chronicled the successes and failures of numerous baseball heroes. In addition, the expansion of the baseball card industry resulted in Americans of all ages, but particularly youth and adolescents, having cardboard images of their heroes that contained concise, positive pieces of information and vital statistics, which typically became etched in the memory of the young admirer.

Heroic Parallels

The game of baseball, and deductively, professional baseball players, possess characteristics and qualities that in some respects give them the same status as the military hero, statesperson, inventor, artist, and others who live out the American personality. A modern day comparison was made by Louisiana Congressman Livingston (1989) who wrote: "From the quiet dignity of Jackie Robinson and'Lou Gehrig to the down-home amiability of Yogi Berra and Bob Uecker, baseball has provided America with some of our most beloved heroes. We revere them with a spirit usually reserved for military commanders and elder statesmen." The immortal Christy Mathewson was once described by Jack Sher in *SPORT* magazine (1949) as being to baseball what Washington and Lincoln were to the country. Another parallel might be to diplomats or ambassadors of good will, as players portray the character and civility of the institution of baseball both at home and away.

The comparability of professional baseball players to military heroes has some basis in the acknowledgment of Abner Doubleday as the father of our national game. According to Crepeau (1980), this was ". . . attractive for several reasons . . . it connects the National Pastime with a military figure who became a general in the war (between the states) to preserve the Union, thus establishing the patriotic link." During the 20th century, particularly during both world wars and the Korean conflict, many professional baseball players served in the armed forces, forging patriotic links between baseball and democracy, and providing an opportunity for baseball heroes to sometimes be military heroes as well.

The presence of baseball as a theme in literature, both poetry and prose, demonstrates the esthetic characteristics of the game (e.g., the natural, pastoral setting in which baseball is sometimes played, as well as the balance, beauty, and rhythm of the sometimes balletlike movements performed on the field), in addition to the real-life drama being acted out on the field during each game, and in the off-the-field lives of the "heroes" who play the game.

Characteristics of the Game

Some characteristics of the American culture best depicted by professional baseball are identified by Crepeau (1980):

> Morality, truth, justice, opportunity, the self-made man;
> Horatio Algerism, competition, individualism and team play, initiative, hard work, relentless effort, and hustle;
> Instant and automatic action, self-independence, never-give-up-the-ship, and the passion for victory for victory's sake;
> Respect to proper authority, self-confidence, fairmindedness, quick judgment and self-control;
> It is all important that the game be clean; and
> Good sportsmanship.

Giamatti (1986) concurs that "Individual merit and self-reliance are the bedrock of baseball, . . . (and) part of the appeal of baseball is that it focuses on the individual with such clarity in such ambiguous circumstances," Giamatti (1986) speaks directly to the interrelatedness of baseball and the American culture when he states:

> The ambiguities surrounding being on offense or defense, surrounding what it means to stand where you stand, endlessly re-create the American pageant of individual and group, citizen and country. In baseball and daily life, Americans do not take sides so much as they change sides, in ways checked and balanced. Finally, in baseball and daily life, regardless of which side you are on and where you stand, shared principles are supposed to govern.

Paul J. Zingg (1986) quotes Albert G. Spalding, who declared that baseball is "the exponent of American Courage, Confidence, Combatism; American Dash, Discipline, Determination; American Energy, Eagerness, Enthusiasm; American Pluck, Persistence, Performance; American Spirit, Sagacity, Success; American Vim, Vigor, Virility."

What these characteristics tell us about ourselves as Americans is that in part we are unique; that we are a democratic people who place the highest premium on both the individual and the team or the masses; and that each person can excel while neither the individual nor the team is independent of the other. A dual spirit of competition and cooperation exists: an essential ingredient of American culture. This dual spirit provides a unique force that moves the American culture forward. By competition, we challenge one another and ourselves to put forth our best effort; and by cooperation, we combine those best efforts which result in the common good. Success in America and in baseball is the effort of the individual along with the combined effort of the team. The driving forces in America and baseball are the people. To understand better the place of baseball in the American culture is to understand those who are its heroes, some of its positive role models.

Baseball and Heroes

Baseball was baptized as the national game; it was marketed and promoted from its infancy as the national game; and although constantly challenged by other competitive "American" sports, in principle and perception, it has remained the "national game." Because of the status of baseball as an American institution and the democratic principles it embodies, it is logical that heroes should be as much a part of the culture of professional baseball as the cultures of the military, government, industry, and the arts, that together weave the overall fabric of the American culture.

Accepting the premise that professional baseball players are legitimate heroes in American culture, next it is helpful to examine selected players who have been labeled as heroes; to identify the characteristics and qualities that made them heroes; and to parallel, where possible, their characteristics and qualities to the period in which they played. This examination should provide insight as to whether the player reflects only the game, or the American culture as well.

Professional Baseball Players as Heroes

Definition

Baseball, as an American institution, has been a rich and abundant source for the evolution of heroic figures. Webster defines a hero as "a man of great courage, nobility, etc., or one admired for his exploits." To apply this definition to professional baseball players requires understanding the context in which the definition is used. Courage is defined as "the quality of being brave." Few would dispute this quality as applicable to baseball players considering, for example, the potential for injury resulting from the impact of a pitched, batted, or thrown baseball, all traveling at high speeds, as well as the various injuries that players sustain and endure while playing the game. Many hitters, such as Tony Conigliaro, have been struck by pitched balls, resulting in serious injury that has shortened or ended a playing career. Herb Score, who was struck by a batted ball, bravely attempted to regain the masterful form he had displayed before his misfortune; he was never able to do so, but was still considered heroic because of his attempt to "come back." Professional baseball players typically are not thought of as being noble. However, according to Barnhart and Barnhart (1982), noble can mean "high and great in character; excellent; fine; splendid; magnificent"—all of these being characteristics or qualities achievable, and certainly desirable, in professional baseball players.

Exploits that require skills in pitching, hitting, running, fielding, and throwing have been admired by players and nonplayers since the inception of the game. It is useful, in defining baseball players as heroes, to examine the times in which they played. Lucas and Smith (1978) defined an "American hero," at the beginning of the 20th century, as:

> a doer, not necessarily a thinker—he was a practical person, not an intellectual . . . the hero was the man of action who appeared larger than life . . . Americans glorified the self-reliant, industrious and financially successful person . . . this type of hero remained in society and in sport in the early 1900s. . . .

By comparison, who and what do Americans glorify today? In an article entitled "What Are Our Real Values?" Nicols Fox (1989) states, "Look who our heroes are. . . . Mainly they are the rich and the famous and the successful and the beautiful, the film and sports stars, the Wall Street barons. . . . Look at what we read. Look at what we choose to do with our spare time. That's what we value." A 1981 study (Smith, Patterson, Williams, and Hogg) pertaining to "hero worship among committed sports fans" noted the following qualities as those most admired: player's skill in the sport, dedication, leadership ability, sportsmanship, modesty, and community involvement. These are positive qualities. Would one find similar characteristics and qualities in professional baseball players? What are the characteristics and qualities most commonly found in professional baseball heroes during this century?

Early Twentieth Century Heroes

The beginning of the 20th century produced such immortals as Christy Mathewson, Honus Wagner, Ty Cobb, Walter Johnson, and Babe Ruth. Because these five were the first players elected to the National Baseball Hall of Fame in Cooperstown, New York, their heroic status would seem to be without question, especially in relation to their baseball skills and abilities. But what other heroic qualities did these men possess, and were these qualities reflective of the American culture?

Jack Sher in *SPORT* magazine (1949) labeled Christy Mathewson "the game's first national hero." Sher stated, "Only one other ball player, George Herman Ruth, ever attained such worldwide fame, adoration, and respect as this magnificent man and pitcher, Christy Mathewson." Sher (1949) describes the heroic qualities of Christy Mathewson:

> As a player and a man, he was to our national game what Washington and Lincoln were to our country. . . . He established what is the "great tradition" in baseball, the principles of courage, honor, patience, modesty, and selflessness. . . . He acted the way he looked, always completely a gentleman, soft-spoken, well-mannered, somewhat shy.

Sher, citing Grantland Rice, credited Christy Mathewson with providing "the game a certain touch of class, an indefinable lift in culture, brains, personality. . . ." Sher, citing W. O. McGeehan, said Mathewson's "greatest asset was his calm courage." Sher continued, citing from an unidentified source, that "before anything else, he was a gentleman." Sher further described Mathewson's heroic qualities from the perspective of the fans: "They respected his shy dignity. They seemed content to worship from a distance. They seemed to know, instinctively, that here was a fine, gentle, decent man." Sher summarized Christy Mathewson's greatness when he said, "In the (darkest) days of baseball, Christy Mathewson was the big ray of hope as to what sort of standards and men the game would eventually develop." What were the qualities of others during this era? Did they possess the qualities of Christy Mathewson, or are there other heroic qualities that can be found in men such as Honus Wagner, Ty Cobb, Walter Johnson, and Babe Ruth?

In 1950, Grantland Rice authored an article for *SPORT* magazine entitled "Who Is Baseball's All-Time Greatest?" He attempted to answer the question by surveying twelve knowledgeable baseball men, plus himself. The twelve included Ed Barrow, Fred Clarke, O. J. Elder, Billy Evans, Clark Griffith, John Kieran, Al Lang, Connie Mack, Bill McKechnie, Branch Rickey, H. G. Salsinger, and Ed Wray. The answer resulting from this survey was Honus Wagner, who received six votes, while Ty Cobb received five and Babe Ruth, two. Rice quoted Elder as saying that Wagner "excelled in every detail of his position . . . was an outstanding hitter . . . (and) an outstanding base runner. . . ." In terms of his heroic qualities, Rice again cited Elder, who said, "Wagner was always a gentleman, both on the field and off; and his exploits on the field of play could not have failed to furnish inspired leadership to every man on his team . . . he is the greatest ball player of all time."

Also included among Wagner's attributes (Rice, quoting Bill McKechnie) was his unselfishness: "he was a team ball player. . . . He was the young ball player's dream and those who did not have the opportunity to see him perform have missed their baseball education." Wagner was further described by Fred Clarke (once his manager) (Rice, 1950) as competitive, without meanness, fair, and congenial with team members.

Rice's summary of those who selected Cobb focused on his baseball abilities and competitive spirit, while those who voted for Ruth focused on his greatness as both hitter and pitcher. Neither Cobb nor Ruth, however, was described with the personal characteristics or off-the-field qualities attributed to Wagner and Mathewson.

Shirley Povich in *SPORT* (1950) characterized Walter Johnson as gentlemanly and modest, putting him in like company with Christy Mathewson and Honus Wagner. The heroic qualities which described Mathewson, Wagner, and Johnson were characteristic of early 20th century America. Their combination of superior baseball skills and abilities, along with a competitive spirit plus gentlemanlike qualities, made them classic heroes and reflective of that era of American culture.

As 20th century America reached young adulthood in the 1920s, a new set of characteristics and qualities began to emerge that were reflected in a new type of baseball hero, fully personified in George Herman Ruth. What heroic traits did Ruth possess that made him not only baseball's preeminent hero, but also possibly America's most prominent hero at that time?

Babe Ruth, during his era, hit more home runs than anyone else ever had, in an even larger way than anyone might have imagined—in distance and in quantity. The fact that he had been a successful major league pitcher prior to his conversion to a full-time slugger further demonstrated the breadth and depth of his overall baseball skills. He was large physically, with a large appetite for many of life's pleasures. Babe Ruth became a dominant, major force in baseball at a time when confidence in the credibility of the game had been shaken, in particular by the questionable outcome of the 1919 World Series. Despite any character flaws Babe Ruth may have had, or been perceived to have had, his physical presence, in addition to his home run prowess, made him a larger-than-life hero for the Yankees, in the news media capital of a nation that was experiencing unprecedented confidence and growth. America, in the 1920s, had passed through a period of innocence and into a period that was more open, exciting, and daring. Babe Ruth, through his on- and off-the-field exploits, symbolized this new excitement in America.

Part of Babe Ruth's appeal as a hero was clearly portrayed in his relationship with children. Claire (Mrs. Babe) Ruth, in a 19-chapter newspaper series printed in 1959 *(The Omaha World Herald)*, said, "Kids understood Babe. Babe understood kids. Babe was bluff and blunt, but he could reduce the shyest of kids to the status of a bosom companion in three minutes or less." She also said, "The Babe went to see more sick kids than any man who ever lived. And every visit tore him to pieces. . . . Whenever the Babe made a hospital visit, he would find the kids in awe of their hero. He would sit on a bed and in a couple of minutes the kids would climb all over him, kiss him and hug him."

Earle F. Zeigler (1987) in "Babe Ruth and Lou Gehrig: A United States Dilemma," epitomized Ruth's heroic influence on American culture in the 1920s. He cites Crepeau (1977): "Ruth is the essence of the rugged individual playing the national game of the cow pasture in an urban stadium before the cheering masses of the machine age." Zeigler (1987) also cites Smelser (1975) who asked, "What did the man Ruth do, what did he have, to merit this?" Smelser answered by stating, "He is our Hercules, our Samson, Beowulf, Siegfried. No other person outside of public life so stirred our imagination or so captured our affection."

This mythic quality of Ruth's was vividly conceived and conveyed by Graham McNamee over the air and Grantland Rice in print in the 1920s (cited by Towers, 1979). Each was describing Babe Ruth, the hitter, during World Series play. McNamee's over-the-air description included:

> If the roar had been deafening before, it would have been drowned out, could it have been matched with the one that now followed, as a thick set figure swinging a bat advanced to the plate. If ever the stage was set for a hero's entrance, it was then. For here was the most advertised athlete in the game, one whose name appears in headlines more often than the President's, Babe Ruth at bat—with the bases full. One little crack—just a solid connection between ash and leather, and the Series would be over. The chance that was immortal Casey's was now the Babe's. He had the World Series in the hollow of his hand.

Rice's written imagery was similar:

> The one Yankee who might have saved the day once more was only given one chance in five times up to show his stuff. The big Babe had his mighty howitzer trained on the right field stands, but Haines and Alexander kept it spiked with a flock of passes. The impotent Babe pawed the muddy ground with his feet and waved his big mace back and forth, but through most of the afternoon he had to look upon wide balls thrown beyond his reach. . . .

Babe Ruth was an American hero, and ultimately a legend, whose abilities and skills became magnified and even sacrosanct, as Roger Maris learned later when he mounted his assault on Ruth's single-season home run record of sixty. It can be safely stated that Babe Ruth was more than a part of the American culture; he, in part, influenced and shaped the American culture of his time. He was seen by many as a "culture hero."

Zeigler (1987), however, finds inconsistency between the definition of "culture hero" and the bestowing of that honor by society in post-World War I America upon Babe Ruth, rather than upon his Yankee teammate, Lou Gehrig. To make the case that baseball's "Iron Horse" was the best qualified as "culture hero," Zeigler advanced the following argument on behalf of Gehrig:

> He (too) . . . started out as a poor boy, that he demonstrated conclusively all of the finest character and personality traits, that he was picked by professional observers as the backbone of his club for a number of years, that he was undoubtedly a "professional's professional" in the best sense of the term, that he was respected and loved by all who knew him during that period, and that he went to a tragic death with dignity.

Zeigler, like sportswriters of an earlier time, cites the value of Gehrig's virtues, i.e., being gentlemanly and sportsmanlike, as qualifying him for a higher level of hero status than he received. Zeigler, in referring to Babe Ruth's character flaws, is also, and more importantly, referring to the character flaws of America. He poses critical questions:

> Is it possible that we condone certain actions in sport and athletics at any level at any time, and then turn right around and condemn similar behavior in every day life? . . . If we really want the United States to be the finest of nations in all regards . . . what role has sport to play? If youngsters and people of all ages tend to look up to outstanding athletes at a time when the number of heroes is few, what qualities should these models possess?

These questions are larger than the pure identification of heroic characteristics and qualities, because what Zeigler is suggesting, in his comparison of Ruth's heroic qualities to Gehrig's, is that a person can be elevated to heroic status without a full complement of heroic qualities. Yet, another person with well-defined heroic qualities can be denied the heroic distinction and recognition that is unquestionably deserved. Zeigler continues, summarizing his argument by proposing "that we give the highest acclaim and pay the most reverence to those who demonstrate through sport both a high degree of athletic ability and the finest of personality and character traits."

Lou Gehrig's playing career extended beyond Babe Ruth's, through the period of the "Great Depression," and overlapped briefly with that of another Yankee great who was also to become a "culture hero" in America during the post-Depression World War II, and post-World War II era—the "Yankee Clipper," Joe DiMaggio.

Mid-Twentieth Century Heroes

Why was Joe DiMaggio an American hero? What heroic characteristics did he possess? Grantland Rice (1949), in the forward to a book written by Joe DiMaggio entitled *Lucky to Be a Yankee*, described the great slugger's trademarks: "Joe DiMaggio possesses that magic gift of perfection in his swing at the plate. If ever an athlete was meant for a sport, DiMaggio was meant for baseball. I know of no athlete who gives you quite the same sense of effortless ease that DiMaggio does in the performance of his baseball tasks." These two characteristics, perfection and effortless ease, along with his extraordinary baseball skills and abilities, were symbolic of his heroics. Red Smith (1947, cited in 1983) summed up Joe DiMaggio's heroic qualities:

> If he were not such a matchless craftsman, he might be a more spectacular player. And so, perhaps, more colorful. And so, more highly rewarded.
>
> But you don't rate a great ball player according to his separate, special talents. You must rank him off the sum total of his component parts, and on this basis, there has not been, during Joe's big league existence, a rival close to him. None other in his time has combined such savvy and fielding and hitting and throwing. . . .

Joe DiMaggio was the next link in the chain of Yankee immortals whose career was to overlap briefly with his heir apparent, Mickey Mantle. Although DiMaggio's career ran concurrently with that of three other professional baseball players who achieved hero status in the American culture—Ted Williams, Stan Musial, and Jackie Robinson—it was DiMaggio who was asked by Simon and Garfunkel in 1968 (Levine, 1981), "Where have you gone. . . ? A nation turns its lonely eyes to you, . . .," which was nearly two full decades after Joe DiMaggio had retired as a player from professional baseball. In addition to his skills, perfection, and effortless ease, he was respectful and complimentary of teammates and opposing players, and was a reserved, nonarrogant personality in his interactions with the fans, the press, and others. This gave him a degree of class that was admirable, and characteristic of earlier heroes such as Gehrig, Wagner, and Mathewson.

Beginning of Player Desegregation

As DiMaggio's era was drawing to a close, and before the era of his heir apparent began, another new type of American hero in professional baseball was coming into being. In 1947, it had been four score and two years since the end of the War Between the States which had freed the slaves and supposedly had provided them with the same freedoms and rights guaranteed all Americans. It wasn't until 1947, however, that the first black American was given the opportunity to play major league baseball. Jackie Robinson was that black American, and he was a hero of a new dimension. The substance of his heroic character was instantly observable. Milton Gross (1951) in *SPORT* magazine wrote:

> Jack Roosevelt Robinson of the Brooklyn Dodgers made his precedent-shattering invasion of organized baseball wearing an armor of humility. . . . Hiding his true combativeness behind the armor carefully selected for him by Branch Rickey, allowed to vent his boundless competitive instincts only with his bat, glove and flying feet, Jackie was the unresponsive target for barbs of humiliation that no man but Robinson could fully appreciate. . . . There was reserve in Jackie, far more reserve than any white ball player had ever shown . . . he managed to restrain his emotions when it had to be done to assure his success. . . . It is a noteworthy milestone in the history of baseball that Robinson is today (1951), at long last, his own man.

In attempting to understand the restraints imposed on Jackie Robinson, consider the following account offered by Gross (1951), using the nomenclature of the day:

A complete code of conduct was foreordained for Robinson before he ever stepped on a field. Wherever he was due to appear as America's pioneering Negro, Rickey sent his advance man and advance plans to control the natural—and some times bestial—forces. . . . This conduct on and off the field was to be decided for him and supervised from day to day. . . . He could not endorse breakfast foods or lend his name to magazine articles or newspaper stories, which go to swell a player's income and reputation. He came to the ballpark secretly and left the same way. Adulation had to be avoided as much as criticism from the stands and fans. It was feared Jackie would represent a symbol more than a ball player attempting to look good.

Jackie Robinson played on a team that possessed several heroes, but according to Gross (1951):

There is an ecstasy that borders on religious relief as the crowd sees Jackie and crushes itself into an immobile mass on either side of him.

They call his name in a way no other player's name is called. They plead to shake his hand or ask for his autograph. They touch his clothes as he walks by, unhurrying, pleasant, friendly, cooperative, because Jackie has never lost sight of what the game has meant to him and what he has meant, means now, and will always mean to his people.

Because of segregation in baseball, and Jackie Robinson's role in desegregating the game, his characteristics and qualities unquestionably were heroic. However, all of baseball did not become integrated with the admission of Jackie Robinson in 1947. In April, 1962, the editors of *SPORT* discussed the issue of "Spring Training Unsegregated—Almost." They identified the teams and described the steps each were taking "to break down the antique caste system." Using the nomenclature of 1962, the *SPORT* editors stated: "The Negro ball player in Florida still must choose carefully his eating places and where he takes his recreation, just as he has to in the North. And in some Florida ballparks, Negro fans must still all sit together."

Steve Gelman writing for *SPORT* magazine (July, 1964) interviewed St. Louis Cardinals' first baseman, Bill White, an influential black player and now president of the National League. Gelman provided the following account of Bill White, the baseball player, as hero:

Keane, White and others cannot recall any heroics of singular significance in his (White's) career. He never won a pennant, say, with a home run as Bobby Thomson did; he never starred, nor even played (at that time), in a World Series game. A biographer searching for a dramatic baseball scene in the life of Bill White ends up frustrated. In 1961, White tied a 49-year-old major league record held by Cobb by making 14 hits in consecutive doubleheaders, and that record typifies White's way of baseball heroism. His base hits and his fine fielding plays come in consistent bunches.

White, quoted by Gelman (1964), provides his own definition of heroic qualities: "The real great ball players are quiet. They lead by example and by doing little things on the ball field. Guys like Dick Groat. You don't hear him yelling all the time. He talks up only at the right and rare time." According to Gelman, "White is such a leader."

Bill White's own leadership skills extended beyond the base lines and warning tracks of the playing field, and into an area of human concern for him: the role and status of blacks in major league baseball. Gelman's (1964) article on White was entitled "A Man Must Say What He Thinks Is Right." That theme is echoed in the following quote from White (Gelman, 1964):

> As far as I'm concerned . . . baseball owners have treated Negroes without discrimination; . . . But we do not seem to be able to get what we should in added income from the outside. There's an answer to this. Ball players, not only Negroes, should form a corporation to represent them and to make contacts for them after they retire. They should do it for themselves . . . Many of us Negroes have the ability to play superior ball, and we should get what we deserve in pay. Too many times you think only of yourself. We've become part of the one percent of American Negroes who have done well. When you're part of the one percent, there is a tendency to forget the 99 percent.

Gelman (1964) summarizes White's humane concern about baseball's inequities as he states:

> . . . There are few Negro benchwarmers in the big leagues. He implies that a quota system of sorts is observed in the major leagues. . . . He is disturbed, too, because there are few jobs, as coaches or managers or television commentators, or front office men, for Negroes. "Surely," he says, "there must be some place in baseball for people like Jackie Robinson and Monte Irvin." "And the Negroes in baseball themselves," White says, "could do more for the Negroes of the United States at large. I think we could use someone to lead us."

Today, a quarter of a century later, Bill White again has the opportunity to exercise his leadership skills and his sincere concern for the well-being of his people: this time as president of the National League.

Increased Media Influence

The era of the 1950s, like that of the 1920s, was also considered the "Golden Age" of baseball. The 1920s introduced the full complement of professional baseball heroes to the listening public through the medium of radio. Obviously, this presentation of baseball personalities and their heroic characteristics and qualities had its limitations, since the listening fan heard only what the announcer allowed the audience to hear. Television made its first appearance in 1939, and the first TV sportscast was a baseball game between Princeton and Columbia (*Grand Forks Herald*, 1989). The television revolution began to escalate in the 1950s as it introduced the newest baseball heroes to emerge on the major league diamonds of America, as well as to re-introduce veteran heroes who were widely known and respected. Apart from attendance at a limited number of major league ballparks located predominantly in the northern and eastern United States, the average American fan could now follow the careers and heroics of professional baseball players through daily box scores and newspaper coverage, supplementary publications such as *The Sporting News*, *SPORT*, and *Sports Illustrated*, daily radio, and weekly broadcasts on television of the "Game of the Week," including pre-game and post-game interviews that gave additional insight to the character and qualities of the baseball hero. Baseball fans, through television, were now able to electronically view the skills, abilities and other heroics of such veterans as Bob Feller, Stan Musial, Duke Snider, Warren Spahn, and Ted Williams as well as the promising rookies of the day, which included such heroes-to-be as Henry Aaron, Roberto Clemente, Don Drysdale, Al Kaline, Sandy Koufax, Mickey Mantle, and Willie Mays, to name only a few.

Despite the changes that came about in baseball in the 1950s as a result of television, the heroic characteristics and qualities that best exemplified professional baseball players were similar to those exemplified in the players of an earlier day. For example, in 1950, the editors of *SPORT* selected New York Yankees Tommy Henrich as their Athlete of the Year, and described his heroic characteristics and qualities:

> He loves competition for its own sake. . . . He is a throwback to the rugged, adventurous early days of baseball in that he shrugs off injuries philosophically and, with no fuss of any kind, quietly goes out on the field. . . . He is, at the same time, the finest example of the modern ball player—quick-thinking, alert, well-spoken, intelligent, moderate in his habits, personally likable, and keenly aware of the importance of his position as a major league athlete.

The decade of the 1950s is looked upon with much nostalgia by those who followed the game and its heroes. The influence of television was in its infancy, and even though Joe DiMaggio had become the first $100,000-per-year player, the astronomical salaries that have since become commonplace were not a part of the reward system for the heroics performed. The heroes of the 1950s were located primarily in New York, playing either for the Dodgers, Giants, or Yankees. Among the more prominent and publicized was the young Mickey Mantle.

Mickey Mantle, who had been groomed to replace the irreplaceable Joe DiMaggio, was next in the line of great Yankee sluggers—Ruth, Gehrig, and DiMaggio. As such, he helped maintain the tradition of Yankee greatness in skills and abilities that produced a disproportionate amount of Yankee pennants, World Series championships, and mammoth home runs. Like Babe Ruth, Mickey Mantle, while hitting from both sides of the plate, produced home runs in large quantities and of great distance. He possessed very good defensive skills and base-running abilities to complement his long-ball prowess. Frequent strikeouts also were a part of Mantle's heroic qualities since, more than anything else, they represented his effort to hit home runs. In addition, Mantle's career was plagued by injuries that placed limitations on what he might have accomplished if he had been completely healthy, and this, too, added to his heroic character. Mickey Mantle was willingly responsive to the press, which is beneficial to the creation and maintenance of a baseball player's heroic image. Although he hit fewer home runs than the all-time home run leader Henry Aaron, and fewer than cross-town rival Willie Mays, whose overall career statistics exceed Mantle's, "The Mick," because he was a part of the direct lineage of Ruth, Gehrig, and DiMaggio, and because he was the last in the chain of greats, was never replaced in the lineup the way he replaced DiMaggio, and in the way DiMaggio replaced Gehrig, and Gehrig replaced Ruth. Mickey Mantle represented the end of a heroic era, perhaps one that will never be duplicated. Mickey Mantle's heroics are perhaps best exemplified today in the appreciation value, monetarily and nostalgically, in his Topps baseball cards from 1952 to 1969.

Perhaps the highest compliment paid to the baseball skills and abilities of Willie Mays, Mantle's all-star rival, came from Ray Sadecki in 1973 (Red Smith, 1982) when he said, "This game was invented for Willie Mays a hundred years ago." Red Smith (1974, cited in 1982), in his column, identified Henry Aaron's heroic characteristics and qualities when he described his (Aaron's) "Finest Hour." Among them were "his accomplishments as a player and his acts of graciousness, generosity and loyalty as a person . . ." In addition, Smith (1974, cited in 1982) described Aaron as a "courteous, modest man." These heroic characteristics paralleled those of past greats. Mays and Aaron both were players of outstanding skills and abilities, yet in general, were not elevated to the same heroic status as players whose baseball accomplishments were less than those of Mays or Aaron. Perhaps this was a reflection of their personalities, or perhaps it was a reflection of their minority status. Regardless of the perceived level of heroic status, or lack thereof, held by these men, their characteristics, qualities, and contributions are exceptional.

In 1961, as part of the 15th anniversary of *SPORT*, the magazine selected its top performers of that 15-year period (1946–1961). In baseball, the choice was Stan Musial. His selection, in part, was based on heroic characteristics and qualities. The author, Al Silverman (1961), quoted Ty Cobb as having said, "Stan Musial . . . is the closest to being perfect in the game today." Silverman (1961) added the following assessment of Musial's heroic character: ". . . Stan Musial is also an uncommon human being. He has never made an enemy, and everybody has been his friend. He has played the game with a joy and richness and a flavor all his own that can be summed up in one word, inspirational. He, of them all, has set an unexcelled example." In the same issue of *SPORT* (1961), Ed Linn profiled Stan Musial who described the heroic quality within himself, and one that is befitting of others as well: "When I go . . . I'll know that I always did my best. If a man gives his best for as long as he can give it, why should he have any regrets?"

During Stan Musial's era, he was rivaled and paralleled on the field primarily by Ted Williams. Ted Williams' heroics were highlighted by his .406 batting average in 1941 (the last major league hitter to achieve a regular season .400 average), as well as hitting a home run in his last major league at bat. Williams' heroics centered on his exceptional hitting ability, but also extended from the playing field to the battle field. Like many players of his era and earlier, he served in the armed forces during World War II and in the Korean conflict. He distinguished himself as a fighter pilot, and as a result of his time spent in the service away from professional baseball, the number of his baseball accomplishments was reduced. Obviously, his willingness to serve and to take the risks attendant to being a fighter pilot were characteristic of Williams' personal skills and courage.

Changing Times—New Frontiers

Throughout the three decades since the end of the 1950s (1960–90), professional baseball players have continued to emerge as heroes, but in different ways with different characteristics. The players and their values are changing. The plethora of television exposure of the game during the regular and post seasons, throughout the week, day and night, as well as weekends; television's in-depth analyses of the players, as a result of a more aggressive and investigative style of journalism; and now television's impact, as a result of large profit-centered contracts, on the financial health of major league teams, have all had a dramatic influence on the heroic characteristics and qualities that are viewed and perceived by the average American fan. Some selected players, who reflected the subtle changes in perceived heroic characteristics and qualities, include men such as Roger Maris, the only player to break Babe Ruth's single-season home run record, and selected for consecutive Most Valuable Player (MVP) awards in 1960 and 1961, but who repeatedly fell short of election to the Hall of Fame through his period of eligibility; Curt Flood, an above-average player, but remembered more for his challenge of baseball's reserve clause rather than any of baseball's hitting or fielding milestones; Denny McLain, the last pitcher to win 30 games in a season, but later convicted of criminal activities; Catfish Hunter, a Hall of Fame pitcher, but also one of baseball's first millionaire free agents; Pete Rose, the only player to break Ty Cobb's all-time base hits total, but currently under suspension from baseball for gambling activities (Joe Jackson was "permanently" banned from professional baseball for his alleged association with gamblers in 1919, and Mickey Mantle and Willie Mays were "temporarily" banned from baseball for their association with gambling casinos, but later reinstated); Wade Boggs, an above-average hitter and potential challenger to Rose's hit record, but tainted as a result of an extramarital affair; Steve Garvey, a prototype player and person, tainted also as a result of affairs off the diamond; and Jose Canseco, the first player to hit more than 40 home runs and steal more than 40 bases in the same season, cited also for traffic and firearms violations. The list could continue; the point, however, is that America and the changing decades since the end of the 1950s reflect a more comprehensive view that does not exclude shattering or tarnishing yesterday's and today's heroes.

Momentary Heroes

In addition to the obvious, everyday professional baseball hero, there are other categories of heroes. There are the momentary heroes such as Bobby Thomson, whose dramatic home run gave the Giants the pennant over the Dodgers in 1951; Don Larsen, whose perfect game in the 1956 World Series was the only perfect game ever pitched in World Series play; Bill Mazeroski, whose dramatic home run in the last inning of the seventh game won the 1960 World Series for the Pittsburgh Pirates. The list could continue. These men experienced the ultimate, on-the-field heroic that was not routine for them.

Unsung Heroes

There is a group that wears the label "unsung heroes." They are the performers whose steady play and quiet leadership game in and game out, season after season, provide the consistency and stability that are vital to team attitude and performance. These "unsung heroes" typically are not the ones who will be elected to the Baseball Hall of Fame. Instead, they are regulars, role, and utility players who, if they are not the core or heart of the team, are critical to its foundation. Players such as Richie Ashburn, Ken Boyer, Larry Doby, Nellie Fox, Dick Groat, Elston Howard, and Tony Oliva fit into this category (this list could also continue). Their contributions to their teams were invaluable. Their heroics, though not rewarded in the same way as those of superstar status, are as essential and important to the attitude and performance of a team as are the heroics of the superstar. The Brooklyn Dodgers of the 1950s, in particular, were a team with many heroic characteristics and qualities, but only one world championship as a reward for those heroics. It was their character, not the number of championships, that best exemplified their heroics.

Monetary Influence

What effect do salaries have on the premise of professional baseball players as heroes? If the formula of increased heroics (meaning here production) equals increased salary, then is the converse true, i.e., does increased salary equal increased heroics (production)? Is salary (base, incentives, multi-year contracts, etc.) a primary motivation for heroics? Is it true that, as some players say, they would still play professional baseball even if they weren't being paid to do so, and if that is not true, then to what extent is salary a motivation for heroics, or is it a work ethic or a pure love for the game and what it represents that motivates their heroics? There are no right or wrong answers to these questions. They are posed only to provide insight into the understanding of heroic characteristics and qualities.

Professional baseball is a livelihood. Like other occupations and professions, it requires a specific set of abilities, skills, and specialties that are mastered only by a select few, although those numbers are increasing due to expansion, facilities, physical conditioning and training, and population shifts. Professional baseball is also a form of entertainment that is appealing to people of all ages, economic and educational backgrounds. As long as fans come to the ballparks in record numbers; as long as television networks pay astronomical amounts for the contract rights to regular and post-season play; as long as team owners share their profits with the players in the form of multimillion dollar contracts, and as long as baseball remains a democratic game in a materialistic, open market culture, then the effect of salaries on the heroic characteristics and qualities of professional baseball players will be paramount and possibly pejorative.

Heroic Influence and the American Culture

It appears that those characteristics and qualities that are most heroic in past and present professional baseball players are those that are or have been valued by the country, whether it be at peace or at war; characteristics that include exceptional skill and ability, courage, democracy, fairness, leadership, humility and pride, individual and team play, and dedication to a high level of performance, to cite some of the more common.

The extent to which a culture is influenced by professional baseball players as heroes varies to the extent to which the individual allows oneself to be influenced. As a society, we recognize that children, youth, and adolescents have professional baseball players as heroes, and these young people are influenced in terms of values, by these heroes. Denise Fortino (1984) writes, in an article entitled "Why Kids Need Heroes," that "the heroes themselves have changed, but not the need to admire, identify with, and emulate them, to turn to them as sources of inspiration and direction, especially at a time when we are most confused and vulnerable—during childhood." Fortino stated that in the middle years of childhood "adults who are at a distance become the heroes." However, Fortino notes a general decline in the quality of heroes and asks, "Where have all the 'heroic' heroes gone?" She cites "One mother who suggests that heroes of the old-fashioned variety are on the wane because adults in public life have toppled from their pedestals." Fortino contends this is due in large part to the media. Referencing *Psychology Today,* Fortino states, "There is no lack of potential leaders, but rather an overabundance of information about them. . . . By exposing too much of everyone, it is leveling a death blow to old-time heroism."

Heroes as Role Models

Given the impact of the media and other forces (including character flaws and human failings) on the status of professional baseball players as heroes, what then are the role and responsibility of the professional baseball player to the youth and adolescents of America who still view the baseball player as one with heroic characteristics and qualities? Who are America's role models? What characteristics do they possess? Where do we find them? Why do we need them? Why are they important? How do we select them? Are professional baseball players role models as well as heroes? If so, are they role models only during the course of the game, or in their off-the-field activities and behaviors as well? Have baseball's best role models also been baseball's everyday heroes, momentary heroes, unsung heroes, or only yesterday's heroes? What are our expectations of professional baseball players as role models, and by what standards do we expect them to live?

These and other questions will be examined further to determine if professional baseball players are role models both on and off the field, and to identify those characteristics that are sought in positive role models, especially by youth and adolescents growing up and maturing in late 20th century America.

Professional Baseball Players as Role Models

> Let's hope positive heroes can and will continue, but it will be harder under the glare of TV and the new investigative journalism that sells more papers by ripping perceived heroes apart or, at the very least, showing their warts and pimples. I am sure that some (former players) . . . may well have suffered under today's scrutiny.—Joe Kearney, Commissioner of the Western Athletic Conference and former athletic director at the University of Washington and Michigan State University (1989)

Although the American culture continues to change, former and current professional baseball players are still portrayed and admired as American heroes. But under the microscopic eye of the American media, today's American hero is frequently suspect. If being a hero once meant that only positive things were reported about an individual, then present-day journalism has ended that era! Any unacceptable actions and behaviors on the part of these heroes are magnified by the media. This leads to concern and confusion on the part of youth and adolescents who emulate these heroes. It is clear that there is a need in today's culture for positive role models as well as heroes.

Accepting the premise that professional baseball players are heroes and also serve as role models for youth and adolescents, the next
step is to determine whether professional baseball players are positive
role models. To gain a current, qualitative perspective on this premise, a brief questionnaire was developed and mailed to a selected
sample of professional baseball players (retired and active) and to a
selected sample of identified leaders, primarily in education, government, and journalism. Before reviewing and analyzing the responses
to the questionnaires, it is appropriate to discuss a framework for
examining role models. To construct this framework, definitions are
provided; selected examples of role models in American culture are
presented; questions are raised inquiring into the need for role models, while an attempt is made to identify role models that are positive;
and a review of nonstereotype baseball role models is presented.

Definitions

Barnhart and Barnhart (1982) define "role model" as: "A person
whose behavior, especially that exhibited in a particular capacity,
serves as a role model or standard for another person to follow: I am
unclear what a role model is, but those who used the term seemed to
be saying that teachers are people children tend to emulate (Russell
Baker)." Teaching, as a profession, is a fundamental source of role
models. In *Education Week* (March, 1989), James A. Gross' book *Teachers on Trial: Values, Standards, and Equity in Judging Conduct and Competence* is reviewed. The review contains an analysis of teachers as role
models:

> Generalizations about teachers as role models presume a cer-
> tain "Mr. Chips" teaching style, personality, and environment for
> teaching that simply does not apply to all or even most teachers and
> teaching situations. . . . (It) is mainly the students' perceptions that
> determine not only whether role modeling takes place but also what
> being pulled down from a pedestal will actually mean—simply
> rejecting the teacher as a role model, or possibly rejecting the
> teacher as a teacher, or possibly, as inferred in most role-model-
> based decisions, being dragged down themselves by compulsively
> emulating their role model's lying, stealing, drug dealing, alco-
> holism, sexual abuse, or other offenses.

The analysis above can be paralleled to professional baseball
players as role models for youth and adolescents. First, a person does
not need to be an educator by profession to teach. Adults who interact
with and/or are observed by young people are teaching by their

actions and behaviors. Professional baseball players interact with and constantly are observed by young people; in a comprehensive definition, professional baseball players are "teachers." Second, like teachers, professional baseball players, as a result of their actions and behaviors, are prone to "being pulled down from a pedestal" and being rejected as role models and/or teachers; and, even more destructively, having unacceptable, criminal, or negative behaviors emulated.

Whether professional baseball players acknowledge or deny being examples for young people to emulate, much like members of other occupations and professions in American society, they are indeed such examples. Barnhart and Barnhart (1982) further define the word "example" as "a person or thing to be imitated; model; pattern." Barnhart and Barnhart then label "a person or thing worth imitating; good model or pattern" as an "exemplar."

Athletes as Role Models

Janet Harris, in her 1986 study "Athletic Exemplars in Context: General Exemplar Selection Patterns in Relation to Sex, Race, and Age," found:

- Approximately two-thirds of exemplars chosen are public figures;
- Generally athletic exemplars are public, star performers;
- Youths are more oriented toward athletes and entertainers ("The ultimate purpose of playing the game of baseball is to bring pleasure to the American people." A. Bartlett Giamatti, quoted by Frank Deford in *Sports Illustrated,* April, 1989);
- Famous athletes appear to be a special focus of youths, and black athletes appear to be particularly salient; and
- Outstanding athletes appear to be prominent exemplars.

Tom Barnidge, editor of *The Sporting News* (1989), states:

. . . Sports heroes are role models, with or without their consent, and they might as well be receptive to the idea.

It is the unwritten part of the job description. It defies logic and ignores reason. But the practice persists, and a chosen few athletes who are able to shoulder the burden can sometimes counterbalance the negative image fostered by so many of their contemporaries. . . .

A baseball player is no better prepared to be society's role model than is a cab driver, a hog farmer or a circus clown. But he is far more visible. And his feats are more glamorous. That, apparently, is reason enough for a society that values image over substance to expect him to be a person worth emulating.

Are we, as Barnidge suggests, a society that values image over substance, or are we as Governor Cuomo of New York (1989) suggests:

> a nation (s)triving to reach one's potential(?) Baseball stars and professional athletes have a profound impact on our young people as role models because they provide standards of excellence to which our children can aspire. . . . They were larger-than-life figures who, on most occasions, were able to meet our greatest expectations. They were, I suppose, expectations we really held for ourselves . . . even if we weren't aware we held them at the age of 9 or 19.

Again, in support of the premise that professional baseball players are role models in the American culture, National Collegiate Athletic Association (NCAA) Executive Director Dick Schultz (1989) states:

> . . . All athletes, especially those in highly visible sports, such as professional baseball, have a responsibility to be good role models, not only for young people, but for adults as well.

> . . . In most instances, I think the vast majority of athletes are typical role models, and are what we all hope they would be. However, because of the visibility of competitive athletics in America, the actions of a few can blemish thousands. Because of this, there needs to be renewed emphasis on all athletes to assume their responsibility as major public figures. Athletes and coaches today have to be perfect people in an imperfect world. If they are not, their deeds will be written about and the impact on society can be quite severe.

Cordell Wynn, president of Stillman College, in *Black Issues in Higher Education* (1989), states:

> The pressing need to develop and maintain positive black role models with whom young blacks can identify is, indeed, an ever-pressing obligation of the local community as well as communities across the nation. . . . People influence much of our behavior. For black youth, the influence often comes from role models both within and outside the immediate environment, from blacks who have "made it" in spite of barriers.

From Wynn's comments, several responses emerge to the question "What kind of role models should professional baseball players be?" He identifies black youths in need of positive role models "who have 'made it' in spite of barriers." This need could be generalized to the population at large to include all young people and adolescents who may be confronted with barriers such as race, creed, ethnic origin, gender, physical ailments or handicaps, economic disadvantages, or educational disadvantages.

Many professional baseball players have "made it" in spite of barriers. This characteristic is considered desirable in positive role models, and, as with heroes, there are numerous examples.

Role Models in Spite of Barriers

Ethnic origin may be a significant factor in the selection of heroes and role models. Lee Iacocca (a descendant of Italian immigrants), in his autobiography (1984), wrote: ". . . Joe DiMaggio, Tony Lazzeri, and Frankie Crosetti—all Italian—were my real heroes. Like most boys, I dreamed of playing in the major leagues. . . ."

Jackie Robinson, as a black American, made it possible for other males of his race to realize their goal of becoming major league baseball players. His emergence into major league baseball brought into focus other black Americans who had the skills, abilities, and personal characteristics and qualities necessary to be major league baseball players, but who had been denied the opportunity because of the color of their skin. Jackie Robinson's first major league at bat was 44 years ago; racial barriers have diminished for players, but as Bill White said back in 1964, barriers still exist for managers, television commentators, and front office personnel. This is a barrier with which blacks, and other minorities, have to contend.

There have been professional baseball players who played while suffering from physical ailments, some severe enough to have led to the player's death. A prominent example is Lou Gehrig, whose career and life were terminated by amyotrophic lateral sclerosis (A.L.S.), a rare disease, commonly referred to as "Lou Gehrig's disease." Jerry Kindall, former major league player and now head baseball coach at the University of Arizona, indicated (1989) that as he was growing up Lou Gehrig was one of his role models, particularly because Kindall's mother had multiple sclerosis (M.S.).

Dick Howser, former major league player and then manager of the Kansas City Royals, died of brain cancer in 1987. Joe Donnely (writing for *Newsday*, cited from the *Hastings Tribune*, June, 1987) stated, "What he (Howser) lacked in size was more than compensated for by the internal qualities of the man. . . . The lasting impression of Howser, . . . is that he was an honest man. It is what those who played for him usually alluded to first."

Death without forewarning has claimed many professional baseball players such as Ken Hubbs, Roberto Clemente, Lyman Bostock, Thurman Munson, and Norman Cash, to cite only a few. Clemente is immortalized as a positive role model because of the generous and genuine act of charity and compassion (airlifting food and supplies to disaster-stricken Nicaragua) he was performing at the time of his death. Hubbs, Bostock, Munson, and Cash are noteworthy because, like Clemente, their untimely deaths remind each of us, youth, adolescents, and adults, of life's uncertainties and our own mortality.

Nonstereotype Role Models in Baseball

There are numerous examples of baseball players who have played with physical ailments or handicaps that permitted them to display their heroic characteristics and qualities, and, more importantly, to present themselves as positive role models who were successful despite barriers. A few examples include:

- Mordecai Brown, a Hall of Fame pitcher in the early 1900s, who had only three fingers on his pitching hand, yet led the National League in wins (27) in 1909;
- Pete Gray, a one-armed outfielder who played for the St. Louis Browns in 1945;
- Monty Stratton, a pitcher who lost a leg in a hunting accident, and had it replaced with an artificial limb, then later won 18 games in a season for the Chicago White Sox;
- Roy Campanella, a Hall of Fame catcher with the Brooklyn Dodgers, who was paralyzed and confined to a wheelchair following an automobile accident in 1958 (this ended his playing career, but his portrayal as a positive role model continues today);
- Ron Santo, a former major league infielder with the Chicago Cubs, who played his entire career while keeping his diabetes under control;
- Bob Gibson, a Hall of Fame pitcher with the St. Louis Cardinals, who battled asthma as well as opposing hitters during his illustrious career;

- Harvey Kuenn, who, with an artificial limb, managed the Milwaukee Brewers to an American League pennant in 1982;
- Mike Gallego, current infielder for the Oakland Athletics, who underwent cancer surgery and has resumed playing on a regular basis;
- Greg Walker, former first baseman for the Chicago White Sox, who suffered an epileptic seizure during the 1988 season, but recovered and resumed playing while keeping his condition under control; and
- Jim Abbott, a one-handed pitcher currently with the California Angels, who was also a stand-out player on the U.S. Olympic team, as well as in college and high school.

The number of professional baseball players who have attended or completed college is increasing. Those who have not attended college generally have completed high school. Hall of Fame pitcher Dizzy Dean, however, was not in either of these categories. Fran Kentling (writing in the *Wichita Beacon-Eagle,* summer, 1988) stated that, according to Dizzy "He never really finished second grade." Following his retirement from baseball in 1941, he became a baseball announcer on radio. Moving from the position of baseball hero to baseball announcer placed Dizzy in the position of being a vocal role model for the youth and adolescents of the American culture. Dizzy's limited education was apparent in his vocabulary. Kentling noted that in the summer of 1946, a group of Missouri schoolteachers complained to the Federal Communications Commission that Dean's broadcasts were "replete with errors in grammar and syntax" and were having "a bad effect on the pupils." Things like:

> Come on, Tommy, hit that patata.
> This boy looks mighty hitterish to me.
> Boy, they was really scrummin' that ball over today, wasn't they?
> (and)
> He karmed one off the wall and slud into second with a two-bagger.

Despite the negative vocal role model effect Dizzy's grammar may have had on young people at the time, there were those who were supportive of his broadcasting skills, abilities, and personality, and ultimately he was able to continue his broadcasting career. His deficiencies in the use of the English language were a result of his limited education, rather than a deliberate abuse of a moral code or ethic as has been seen in other individuals who serve as negative role models.

Part of Dizzy's attractiveness, like that of Will Rogers, was Dizzy's colorful, down-home, lighthearted, simplistic view of baseball and the American culture.

The Chronicle of Higher Education (March, 1989) profiled a role model not yet seen in major league baseball, but appearing at the collegiate level—a female collegiate baseball player: Julie Croteau. Charles J. Hartley (1989) wrote:

> Although no one is positive, most people believe that her (Julie Croteau's) spot on the team (St. Mary's College of Maryland), which competes at the Division III level of the National Collegiate Athletic Association, makes her the first woman ever to play intercollegiate baseball. The N.C.A.A. has no rules that bar women from men's sports teams. "People here don't seem to care whether I'm a girl or a boy," she said. "People are open-minded here. They have an enlightened attitude. They just treat me as a player, and that's all I've ever wanted!
>
> "I don't consider myself on a mission," she said. "I like baseball. It may be easier for other girls to play baseball in college because of what I have done, but I play simply because I like the game!"
>
> Mr. (Hal) Willard (her college coach) says he has noticed how much she enjoys playing the sport: "Julie is not playing to make a name for herself or to make a big deal out it," he says. "She's doing it for the sheer enjoyment of playing the game. She loves baseball."

Whether or not Julie Croteau, or any other female baseball player ever becomes a major league baseball player is irrelevant. What is important is that she, like her male counterparts, is a positive role model for youth, adolescents, and adults, female and male, because she too overcame a barrier with civility, determination, and a love for what she wanted to do—play baseball.

Youth can also look to their peers as role models. A recent example is Jon Peters, a pitcher for the Brenham (Texas) High School Cubs, who pitched a record 51st consecutive win. With this accomplishment, he has established himself as a role model for his peers. He is not without his own hero and role model, however. Rick Reilly, in *Sports Illustrated* (May, 1989) writes:

> But most of all, he (Peters) has a bull-backed will, like that of his role model and idol, all-time major league strikeout leader Nolan Ryan. Didn't Ryan too come from a small town in Texas (Alvin)? And hadn't Ryan pitched right here in Brenham once (1965)? Like Ryan, Peters is nothing if not stubborn. In the four-year life of the streak, he has won in the rain, won with the flu, won with his best stuff and won with his worst. . . .

These characteristics, descriptive primarily of Peters' baseball talents, also portray a positive role model for other youth and adolescents.

Survey Responses from Player and Non-Player Samples

To gain insight beyond the literature regarding professional baseball players as role models, a survey was developed and mailed to 100 former and current professional baseball players. Included in this survey were living members of the Baseball Hall of Fame, as well as everyday heroes, momentary heroes, and unsung heroes from the 1950s to the present. In addition, 100 non-players who had an affiliation with baseball or athletics and who were or are in leadership positions predominantly in education, government, or journalism, were surveyed. The survey questions were the same for both samples. The latter group was given the option of completing the survey or providing a letter expressing their thoughts on professional baseball players as heroes and role models. After the original correspondence, follow-up requests were not made to either group.

From the player sample, a total of 17 returned the survey and, in addition, James "Cool Papa" Bell, because of failing eyesight, sent a newspaper clipping about his career. Two of the 17 chose not to comment on any of the questions. From the non-player sample, a total of 29 returned the survey or wrote a letter. Five of the 29 provided a letter stating they were declining participation, or that they were unable to participate in the survey. Some of the 71 who did not respond in writing called either to decline or to indicate they would respond at a later date.

Due to the limited response from both samples, the information presented from these responses is treated in a qualitative manner rather than a quantitative manner. A review of selected responses follows.

QUESTION 1: Generally, do you think that present day professional baseball players serve as positive role models for young people?

Selected players from different eras who responded affirmatively commented:

> "Yes, because they are public figures on display more than just about anyone else. More than any other sportsman, movie star, etc. Whether (you) want to or not, you do serve as a role model. People will always put more faith in baseball players than anyone else."
> —Brooks Robinson

"Generally speaking, today's players can be an example of what hard work, dedication and perseverance can do to make a person successful."—Steve Garvey

"Most players now I think do a good job. I have coached up until the eighties and there are a lot of fine young men. Just a very few who spoil it at times."—Bob Doerr

"Perhaps; also, other major sports' more successful players as well."—Bob Feller

"Baseball has its problems, note the drug situations, . . . But for the most part, players are excellent role models."—Rich Ashburn

"The positive effect is generally offset by the negative effect of the press and media."—Ralph Kiner

"Occasional, well publicized mistakes—should highlight great majority who set fine examples."—Tony LaRussa

Three who responded negatively, commented:

"(No) I believe most young people still use their parents as the role model or their brothers or sisters."—Gil McDougald (Bob Feller [1948], in a book he authored entitled *Strikeout Story*, was asked, "Who was the greatest figure in your baseball career?" Feller responded, "My father.")

"Not as much now as before because of drugs and scandals. Not just baseball, but all sports."—Tom Kelley

"Salaries (are) too high."—Walter F. "Buck" Leonard

Two who responded yes and no stated:

"Some do—some don't. There are some players that are still very cooperative and only do good deeds. Others are looked upon as greedy, selfish and non-talented. The Pete Rose story has been devastating to their (young people's) faith so far."—Monte Irvin

"Too much drugs. Some do. Others do not."—Enos Slaughter

Selected non-players who responded affirmatively commented:

"In every instance there are exceptions, but overwhelmingly there is a positive role model for younger people."—Gerald Ford, former President of the United States.

"The majority of players are people who can be looked up to. Unfortuantely, the minority spoil it. Young people tend to pay more attention to the ones who receive the most publicity."—Bob Wolf, *Los Angeles Times*

"Obviously it is more difficult for youngsters to view today's athletes as positive role models than it was several decades ago because of the manner in which the media today focuses on the negative aspects of an athlete's life style compared to the free ride all athletes were given in the past. Nevertheless, I believe that there are still any number of professional athletes, including baseball players, who serve as positive role models, e.g., Dale Murphy of the Atlanta Braves."—Albert M. Witte, University of Arkansas, Law School

"You only hear of the small percentage who get involved with drugs, alcohol, etc. Many, like Kirby Puckett and Kent Hrbek of the Minnesota Twins, are excellent role models."—Paul Giel, former player (All-American in both baseball and football) and former Athletic Director, University of Minnesota.

"In spite of the moral failure of some of our 'stars,' still kids admire ball players and try to emulate them."—Jerry Kindall, former player and head baseball coach, University of Arizona

"That's a tough call with all the drugs and greed and ego problems. Generally, though, I think pro baseball players are positive role models. They are not murderers. They could do things much worse than they do."—Charles J. Hartley, *The Chronicle of Higher Education*

"Most are shown putting forth an all out effort. Doing their best, striving to be the best they can be. I also think it's positive to see racial balance on teams and the players interacting positively (mostly) with each other."—Joel Medd, North Dakota District Judge

"They are role models certainly. Are they 'positive' role models? In a sense, yes. They compete, they persevere, they excel. Some prove to have human foibles—feet of clay. But in a broad sense, they are positive role models."—Bruce Keidan, Sports Editor, *Pittsburgh Post-Gazette*

"For the most part, I believe that they do. Media emphasis on negative events distorts the overall image."—Robert C. Khayat, Executive Director of the NCAA Foundation

"(Yes) However, there are growing tendencies for baseball players to charge for autograph sessions, not give autographs, behave poorly in public, show lack of loyalty to their organization. This concerns me if it continues to get worse."—Noel W. Olson, Commissioner of the North Central Intercollegiate Athletic Conference

Some non-players who responded negatively, commented:

"Young people look up to professional and college athletes because they represent what youngsters hope to achieve. Unfortuantely, the athletes should be role models, but too many are not. I firmly believe the athletes, professional and college, have a responsibility to be positive role models."—Jerry A. Miles, Executive Director, American Baseball Coaches Association.

". . . Some players are positive role models, however, the way the media enlarges the few negative role models, the net result is negative."—Thurston Banks, Tennessee Tech University, NCAA Division I Council Member

"Today's players are too focused on money and their own pleasures."—Dick Leslie, *Chicago Tribune*

". . . I believe a combination of factors exists which result in types of people in professional baseball that are less than positive role models. These factors include lack of education beyond the high school level, immaturity, inflated salary levels, too much free time in cities and locations that are not 'home,' pressures of being a professional performer, etc. . ."—Donald Wermers, University of Wisconsin-Madison

"A few of them are good models; most are not. They are greedy, childish, and self-centered. Most are greatly overpaid and thus become too egotistic."—Francis W. Bonner, Furman University, NCAA Executive Committee

"They are models only for superior athletic performance on the field. In my off-field contacts with professional ball players of all ages, I have found them by and large to be in a state of arrested adolescence."—C. W. Gusewelle, *The Kansas City Star*

Some of the non-players who had neutral opinions commented:

"Like all human beings, professional baseball players have their ups and downs. Moreover, while many of them can be terrific role models for youth (Kirby Puckett), others with publicized problems involving alcohol, drugs, and/or sex can be terrible role models. The recent trends have been negative largely because of the pervasive influence of drugs in professional sports."—Nicholas J. Spaeth, Attorney General, North Dakota

"Sometimes, but often not. Those who do are the ones who demonstrated some grace, responsibility and discipline off the field, and who reflect an understanding that baseball is a game and there are more important interests: drug rehabilitation, charitable activity, etc."—Charles Haga, *Minneapolis Star-Tribune*

"Some do, some don't. Same ratio as any other public field, probably. That ball players are expected to be role models is at least partially a business claim by clubs, sponsors, TV, etc. Who said they should be?"—George Vecsey, *New York Times*

QUESTION 2: As you were growing up, which professional baseball players served as role models for you?

In both player and non-player samples, several players were named at least once. Among the players' sample, those named more than once included Lou Gehrig, Babe Ruth, Stan Musial, and Walter

Johnson. Among the non-players' sample, those named more than once included Joe DiMaggio, Ted Williams, Lou Gehrig, Jackie Robinson, Babe Ruth, Mickey Cochrane, Stan Musial, Mickey Mantle, Roger Maris, Yogi Berra, Roy Campanella, and Brooks Robinson.

QUESTION 3: What characteristics do you think best exemplify professional baseball players as role models for young people in American society?

The responses from both samples produced lengthy lists of positive characteristics, as well as some negative characteristics. The selected, most comprehensive and representative responses from the players' sample were:

> "They should be honest, and respected, by everyone. (He) should share his kindness with his fellow man. Some of the players live in a shell by themselves. (Be) useful as the baseball career is short lived."—Joe Sewell

> "Talent, dedication, and ability. It's important not to appear selfish. Super stars should give back to the community some of the tax money that the government is going to get anyway."—Monte Irvin

> "Hard work, dedication, sportsmanship, communication with the (fans) and the press. A statement of 'faith' when given the opportunity and a shared feeling of being proud to be an 'American.'"
> —Steve Garvey

> "Clean liv(ing). They should live clean, free of drugs."—Walter F. "Buck" Leonard

> "Competitive; hard working; get what earn; handle pressures, stress, public exposure; improved eating/drinking habits."—Tony LaRussa

> "Success—hard work. Came from small towns—and were from poor or low income famil(ies)."—Bob Feller

The selected responses from the non-player sample, which were the most comprehensive and representative of the others, were:

> "Performance excellence."—Gerald R. Ford

> "Competitive excellence, determination, willingness to sacrifice individual goals for group goals."—Bruce Keidan

> "Skill and devotion to the game, basic morals, unselfishness."
> —Francis W. Bonner

> "1. Behavior patterns in public that are worthy of their positions.
> 2. Friendly manner.
> 3. Hard work and hustle as a player.

   4. Loyalty to fans, team, and total organization.
   5. Play whenever needed—play through injuries and prob-
      lems."—Noel W. Olson

   "1. Overcoming failure.
   2. Strength and speed.
   3. Showing their human and compassionate side; would there
      were more players willing to do that."—Jerry Kindall

"Guys that act like professionals, who know how to lose with class
and win with humility. Guys who come ready to play every day.
Guys who are HONEST. *Greedy* players are among the most dis-
tasteful."—Charles J. Hartley

"Willingness to accept their roles as models for youth, to give
autographs, visit the sick and donate to charitable causes. Refusal to
be carried away by their own importance."—Bob Wolf

"Americans tend to admire high achievers. Professional baseball
players are high achievers and, because of the nature of the business, they get a lot of publicity. I also think that their presence in the
limelight enables them to say or do things which make people like
them, whether it's working for charitable causes or speaking out on
issues of concern. Thus, the position of center stage that professional baseball players have enables them to serve as role models."
—Nicholas J. Spaeth

One survey respondent saw only negative characteristics being exemplified:

   "Avarice, petulance, indiscipline, disloyalty to the organizations
by which they are employed."—C. W. Gusewelle

   QUESTION 4: What influence do you think the present day
salary structure has on professional baseball players as role models?
   Within the players' sample, those who saw the present day salary
structure as a positive influence commented:

"None!! (Salaries) make them an even more high profile and visible.
Players are paid to entertain the fans, to do things that the fan has
always dreamed about."—Brooks Robinson

"I assume it is very important to anyone that has any athletic
ability."—Charles L. Gehringer

"I really don't think salar(ies) are thought about that much by
kids—they still seem to be interested in what they (the players) do
on the field."—Tom Kelley

"Their ability to donate money to worthwhile causes."—Ralph Kiner

Those players who saw the present day salary structure as a negative influence commented:

"Negative effect for many."—Tony LaRussa

"Each person is reaching for a higher salary."—Walter F. "Buck" Leonard

"It is all out of line with most of the players as they cannot handle the prosperity that goes with the salaries. If they have someone to handle it for them that would be fine."—Joe Sewell

"It's inflationary—divisive and apparently obscene for some players with ordinary talent to make so much money."—Monte Irvin

"Too much money, not enough heart into the game and to the fans."—Enos Slaughter

"There is a tendency for financially secure people to not put forth the effort to do the little things that separate the hero from the average player—or person for that matter."—Steve Garvey

"To a small degree I feel the salary structure has stifled motivation in some players."—Rich Ashburn

"Very little. It may in some cases cause overconfidence of the players."—Bob Feller

"It may hurt in a way that if they do anything wrong, the kids feel they can, too."—Bob Doerr

Two player respondents stated:

"None."—Gil McDougald

"No comment."—Joe Adcock

Among the non-players' sample, none who responded saw the present day salary structure as a positive influence. Within this group, those who saw the present day salary structure as a negative influence commented:

"Catastrophically negative."—C. W. Gusewelle

"A very negative influence. Some of the highest paid players are fine people. Rick Sutcliffe of the Cubs is a prime example. He has a foundation for the needy and both donates and raises hundreds of thousands of dollars annually. However, he is in the minority."—Bob Wolf

"Very negative. Levels are unrealistically high and players devote most of their energies to pushing them higher."—Dick Leslie

"Very detrimental! Most of them are highly overpaid. Management is to be blamed, but the players are obviously greedy."—Francis W. Bonner

"A sorry influence. Ball players are vastly over paid and because of this, have lost their identity with the public."—Jerry Kindall

"Negative influence. It distances the athletes from the public. Creates a nouveau riche class of jocks who are out of touch with middle class America."—Bruce Keidan

"Obviously it's had some negative impact because in the minds of many, baseball players are seen as greedy. In fact, the reality is much more complex than that, but I suspect that many young people and even a lot of older fans resent what's happened in the modern salary structure."—Nicholas J. Spaeth

"The present day salary structure, combined with level of education, level of responsibility, degree of maturity, amount of free time, traveling life style, etc., all have a generally negative influence on players as positive role models. . . ."—Donald Wermers

"The salary structure fosters greed and egomaniacs. It puts a strain on everyone to play better to make more money, which goes against the philosophy that players should play well simply to play well."—Charles J. Hartley

"There is some evidence that the present salary structure in baseball makes some players less dedicated to their profession and less interested in the appearance they present to the public."—Albert M. Witte

"It makes it much easier for them to be their true selves. They don't have to worry about being 'nice guys' to appease management."—George Vecsey

"It makes them take themselves too seriously, and it makes them often surly. It preoccupies them with money."—Charles Haga

"Even though I understand 'what the market brings' type philosophy, and though I know their careers are short—it has gotten out of hand. I believe it promotes an attitude of inflated values regarding material things."—Noel W. Olson

"Present salary structure is certainly an incentive but our youngsters may get a distorted view of monetary rewards throughout our society."—Gerald R. Ford

"It makes them more superstarish. In our society money is stature—it makes becoming a professional athlete more of a lure."—Joel Medd

"With young athletes, it has made them even bigger model roles. With older fans, the big salaries has made them much more critical of the players. Many resent the money athletes are being paid."—Jerry A. Miles

One respondent was neutral regarding the influence of the present day salary structure and commented:

> "I don't think it has any more effect today than 20 years ago. Salaries are all relative in regards to your question."—Paul Giel

QUESTION 5: Do you think that baseball will be as significant a part of the American culture in the 21st century as it has been in the 20th?

Among the respondents in the player sample, three had no comment, others responded positively:

"Yes."—Walter F. "Buck" Leonard

"Definitely and the big reason is that baseball is a great game. The fact that baseball is still so popular despite what some owners and players have tried to do to it, is amazing. Baseball has survived and will thrive."—Rich Ashburn

"It's the best game invented and greedy owners and selfish players can't ruin or spoil it. It's our national pastime and always will be. It's as American as apple pie."—Monte Irvin

"The game I think keeps getting better."—Bob Doerr

"It should be better if the powers in control will control it and not let it get out of line. (They) will have to keep a close watch on it and keep the right men in control."—Joe Sewell

"It will always be one of the top games in the U.S.A. and may be even more so in some foreign countries."—Joe Adcock

"Yes—the history of baseball parallels in many ways the last 120 years of Americana. The sport continues to increase in popularity and should clearly be America's #1 sport in the 21st century."—Steve Garvey

"(Yes) Deserves its place in essential pace of American life year in and out."—Tony LaRussa

"I believe baseball will always play a part in American culture because of the tremendous exposure given to it by all media."—Gil McDougald

"(Yes) Due to the increased exposure of the players thru TV."—Ralph Kiner

More so—sports are a part of our society that will be growing even more."—Brooks Robinson

"I see all sports (colleges included) continuing to grow in the foreseeable future."—Bob Feller

"Since more and more cities are trying to have sports teams come to

their city than ever before, I cannot see the sports fields dwindle."
—Charles L. Gehringer

"I feel that baseball will always be popular but—all the scandals and drugs are hurting. The amount of money being paid may also hurt because people cannot relate. In fact I can't either."—Tom Kelley

Among the respondents in the non-player sample, a limited number thought that baseball will not be as significant in the 21st century; one respondent did not know; and the others thought that baseball will be as significant. The comments were:

"It has, indeed, become less significant in the last two decades, in my view."—C. W. Gusewelle

"I feel that sports are continually changing. New and modified sports will assume the places of those of the 19th and 20th centuries."—Thurston Banks

"If the trend continues—higher and higher salaries, etc.—people will tend to become 'fed up.' And other sports are reducing the popularity of baseball."—Francis W. Bonner

"Football is becoming more dominant. Baseball can be very slow moving."—Joel Medd

"I tend to think probably not because of the emergence of other sports which will compete for fans' attention. Soccer is one sport that I think will continue to grow in popularity and will be a dominant sport in America in the twenty-first century. There are other sports that will also grow and I think baseball will no longer be as important. Indeed, it is clear that baseball is less important to America now than it was fifty years ago."—Nicholas J. Spaeth

"People have too many other interests, too many other heroes."
—Charles Haga

"Don't know."—Bruce Keidan

"Yes."—Robert C. Khayat

"Why not?"—Albert M. Witte

"I see no reason why it should change."—Gerald R. Ford

"If anything, baseball is becoming more important than ever in the life of the average American."—Bob Wolf

"It's a great game played at a great time of the year."—Dick Leslie

"Baseball is so much a part of America that it will continue to maintain an important role in our society."—Jerry A. Miles

"More than ever—even with horrors like domed stadiums and artificial turf, baseball will have a tireless, traditional structure that will appeal to future oil-slicked, nuclearized, television-benumbed, illiterate generations."—George Vecsey

"For whatever reason the sport seems to be getting better all the time. Apparently the wealth of management and ownership allows the inflated costs to continue and not hurt an organization."—Noel W. Olson

"I see no reason the game cannot continue to successfully compete in the entertainment market for its share of the entertainment dollar . . ."—Donald Wermers

"The last four years under Peter Ueberroth have shown a tremendous increase in attendance at baseball games and it will continue to increase."—Paul Giel

"Baseball makes people feel good. We enjoy it, and it is legal. People like to do things that feel good. Watching baseball and playing baseball feels good. It will not change in the 21st century."—Charles J. Hartley

"Baseball has an eternal quality about it that carries from generation to generation. If we (baseball) can avoid scandal and loss of public confidence, it will remain, perhaps even increase, (as) an important part of our culture."—Jerry Kindall

The opinions stated in the survey by the player and non-player respondents contained both favorable and unfavorable comments. The majority of respondents in each sample viewed present day professional baseball players as positive role models for young people. Those players who were identified as role models by the respondents consisted of a variety of well-known and not so well-known professional baseball players. The characteristics which the respondents thought best exemplified professional baseball players as role models for young people were extensive and overwhelmingly positive. The influence of the present day salary structure on professional baseball players as role models received both positive and negative responses from the player sample, and somewhat to very negative responses from the non-player survey sample. The responses from the player and non-player samples suggest, with some exceptions, that baseball will be as significant in the American culture of the 21st century as it has been in the 20th.

The opinions expressed by the players and non-players involved in the survey are not definitive, but provide insight into the question of whether professional baseball players are positive role models for young people in the American culture. This question, plus others raised by the respondents, merit further examination.

Synthesis

Summary

John Papanek, in a *Sports Illustrated* article (1987), posed the question "Athletes or Role Models?" He asks:

> Isn't it time we stopped turning every successful athlete into a role model. . . ? We shouldn't pattern our lives after someone simply because of his talent or smile. Many athletes are worth emulating for the way they conduct themselves, others are surely not. If children are not being taught that athletes are human, just like their parents and neighbors, we had better start getting real.
>
> . . . Today we can't be certain that our athletes won't turn out to be drug abusers. Nor can we be certain that our children, husbands, wives, teachers and best friends won't. We have to learn to help them. . . . Athletes are no worse and no better than the rest of us.

Dan Shaugnessy (writing for the *Boston Globe,* cited from the *Grand Forks Herald,* March, 1989) contends, "Ballplayers are human, too." He substantiates this argument:

> Professional athletes. They are what they do. . . .
>
> The spring of 1989 is the season of the witch for baseball's role models. Sex and gambling this spring have rocked the sport as drugs rocked it in past seasons. . . .
>
> Investigative sports journalism isn't going to go away. . . . The thing to keep in mind is that if we don't think of the athletes as role models, we won't be so disappointed when they fail off the field. . . .
>
> In a perfect world, our youths' role models would be their parents, teachers, and coaches. These are the people who interact with our children.
>
> What about professional athletes with whom the average fan has no personal contact? Watch them. Enjoy them. They are what they do. Nothing more.

The opinions expressed by Papanek and Shaugnessy are sympathetic to the character flaws and human failings possessed by professional baseball players. However, these arguments tend to mask the problem rather than solve it. It is agreed that, as a society, people must learn to help each other, and it is also agreed that athletes, like doctors, lawyers, business people, farmers, educators, and others, are no worse and no better than other individuals. But to relieve professional baseball players of the ethical and moral responsibility that individuals have, as coaches, parents, and teachers, neither eliminates nor resolves the disappointment that our young people have when their "role models" stumble or fall. Because professional baseball players are highly skilled, when they perform athletic skills especially well they are viewed as "super" humans. Youth and adolescents admire physical skill and ability on the playing field, and they may expect the standards established off the field to parallel those standards set on the field. Is that an unreasonable demand to make of any person? Youth and adolescents want to be reassured that their "role models" represent quality, if not ideal, behavior.

Crawford and Stoneburner (1987), in an article entitled "The Sports Hero as Villain: An American Perspective," summarized the dilemma of sports hero as role model, and suggested some future directions:

> . . . It can be persuasively argued that the gross commercialization of sport has spawned this phenomenon (sports hero as villain) and thus the professional sport bodies have a duty to regulate and monitor the sorts of public and private antics that bring the sport into disrepute. Significant numbers of children make their athletic idols role models. . . . With primary and secondary school physical education programs the teacher and coach should consciously set out to present, as equally palatable, both aesthetic and heroic values. Is it possible to draw up counseling procedures to assist celebrity professionals (as well as famous amateur athletes) to cope with public pressure? What leads to the decline and destruction of certain folk heroes. . . ? Are not champion athletes morally bound to project a good, wholesome and pleasant personality? Is it time to subject the mass media to some form of a 'code of ethics' to protect the stellar sportsperson. . . ?

It is without question that youth and adolescents, in the past, today, and in the future, need positive role models. Because of the significance of baseball in the American culture, professional baseball players are heroes, and, more importantly, they are role models. Because of the need for positive role models in the American culture, it is critical that professional baseball players take this responsibility seriously. Objectivity and responsibility on the part of the media that transmit, project, and magnify the on- and off-the-field lives of professional baseball players are also critical. It is incumbent upon the many teachers of youth and adolescents to point out that professional baseball players can and should be positive role models, but should not be deified. Characteristics and qualities that are positive and worthy of emulation should be identified and encouraged; those that are negative and destructive should be identified also, but discouraged because of the harmful effects associated with them.

Conclusion

America's future has always been, and will continue to be, dependent on its young people. If youth and adolescents in America are going to be able to emulate positive characteristics and qualities in professional baseball players, it is obvious that professional baseball players should demonstrate, on and off the field, the sorts of behaviors that are exemplary. These are behaviors that parents should model to their children, teachers to their students, and coaches to their players. According to Barnidge (1989):

> . . . A role model must reflect an assortment of values, few of which have anything to do with hitting or fielding a baseball.
>
> But right or wrong, players are often expected to serve in this capacity simply because of their visibility in the limelight and their success in athletic endeavors.
> So fairness matters not at all. What matters is inevitability. . . .

Understanding and accepting this maxim can: 1) help prepare professional baseball players for the dual role they play in baseball and the American culture and 2) help prepare youth and adolescents who look to professional baseball players as heroes and role models to emulate their positive behaviors, but understand that baseball players are vulnerable to temptations and failure. The ability of professional baseball players to retain characteristics and qualities that are admirable and exemplary, while overcoming failure rather than being overcome by failure, is critical to positive role modeling and becoming a "real" hero.

Governor Cuomo of New York (1989) captures the essence and spirit of professional baseball players as heroes and role models in the American culture as he writes: "The extent that today's ballplayers continue to keep our young dreams alive is the degree to which baseball will continue its magical and ineffable hold on the American psyche. That is, it seems to me, sufficient reason to celebrate the game's arrival every spring."

References

Adcock, Joe. Personal Correspondence Response to Baseball Survey, Spring, 1989.

Ashburn, Rich. Personal Correspondence Response to Baseball Survey, Spring, 1989.

Banks, Thurston. Personal Correspondence Response to Baseball Survey, Spring, 1989.

Barnhart, Clarence L. and Robert K. Barnhart. *The World Book Dictionary*, rev. ed. 1982.

Barnidge, Tom. Personal Correspondence Response to Baseball Survey, Spring, 1989.

Bonner, Francis W. Personal Correspondence Response to Baseball Survey, Spring, 1989.

Crawford, Scott A.G.M., and Gary H. Stoneburner. "The Sports Hero as Villain: An American Perspective." *Momentum,* Spring, 1987, pp. 41–60.

Crepeau, Richard C. *Baseball: America's Diamond Mind, 1919–1941.* Orlando: University Presses of Florida, 1980.

Crepeau, Richard C. "Tensions of the Twenties: Lindbergh, Ford, and Ruth." In *Proceedings of the North American Society for Sport History,* 1977, p. 51.

Cuomo, Mario M. Personal Correspondence Response to Baseball Survey, Spring, 1989.

Deford, Frank. "A Gentleman and a Scholar." *Sports Illustrated,* April, 1989, pp. 88–99.

Doerr, Bob. Personal Correspondence Response to Baseball Survey, Spring, 1989.

Donnelly, Joe. "Howser Remembered as Winner." *Hastings Tribune,* June, 1987.

Feller, Bob. Personal Correspondence Response to Baseball Survey, Spring, 1989.

Feller, Bob. *Strikeout Story.* New York: Bantam Books, 1948.

Ford, Gerald. Personal Correspondence Response to Baseball Survey, Spring, 1989.

Fortino, Denise. "Why Kids Need Heroes." *Parents,* November, 1984, pp. 214–229.

Fox, Nicols. "What Are Our Real Values?" *Newsweek,* February, 1989, p. 8.

Garvey, Steve. Personal Correspondence Response to Baseball Survey, Spring, 1989.

Gehringer, Charles. Personal Correspondence Response to Baseball Survey, Spring, 1989.

Gelman, Steve. "Bill White: 'A Man Must Say What He Thinks Is Right.'" *Sport*, July, 1964, pp. 52–59.

Giamatti, A. Bartlett. "Baseball and the American Character." *Harper's,* October, 1986, pp. 27, 30.

Giel, Paul. Personal Correspondence Response to Baseball Survey, Spring, 1989.

Giles, Warren C. Forward to *The National League Story,* by Lee Allen. New York: Hill and Wang, 1965, p. ii.

Gross, James A. "Teachers as Role Models: Ethics and Evaluations." *Education Week,* March, 1989, p. 27.

Gross, Milton. "The Emancipation of Jackie Robinson." *SPORT,* October, 1951, pp. 12–15, 80–85.

Gusewelle, C. W. Personal Correspondence Response to Baseball Survey, Spring, 1989.

Haga, Charles. Personal Correspondence Response to Baseball Survey, Spring, 1989.

Harris, Jean C. "Athletic Exemplars in Context: General Exemplar Selection Patterns in Relation to Sex, Race, and Age." *Quest,* August, 1986, pp. 95–111.

Hartley, Charles J. "A Freshman Who 'Just Wanted to Play Baseball' Gets Her Chance in College." *The Chronicle of Higher Education,* March, 1989, pp. A35–36.

Hartley, Charles J. Personal Correspondence Response to Baseball Survey, Spring, 1989.

Heyn, Ernest V., Grantland Rice, Albert Perkins, John Winkin and Griffith Foxley, eds. "Sports Athlete of the Year." *SPORT,* February, 1950, p. 16.

Iacocca, Lee. *Iacocca: An Autobiography.* New York: Bantam Books, 1984.

Irvin, Monte. Personal Correspondence Response to Baseball Survey, Spring, 1989.

Kearney, Joe. Personal Correspondence Response to Baseball Survey, Spring, 1989.

Keidan, Bruce. Personal Correspondence Response to Baseball Survey, Spring, 1989.

Kelley, Tom. Personal Correspondence Response to Baseball Survey, Spring, 1989.

Kentling, Fran. "Ain't Got Enough Spart . . ." *Wichita Beacon-Eagle,* Summer, 1988.

Khayat, Robert C. Personal Correspondence Response to Baseball Survey, Spring, 1989.

Kindall, Jerry. Personal Correspondence Response to Baseball Survey, Spring, 1989.

Kiner, Ralph. Personal Correspondence Response to Baseball Survey, Spring, 1989.

LaRussa, Tony. Personal Correspondence Response to Baseball Survey, Spring, 1989.

Leonard, Walter F. "Buck." Personal Correspondence Response to Baseball Survey, Spring, 1989.

Leslie, Dick. Personal Correspondence Response to Baseball Survey, Spring, 1989.

Levine, Arthur. *When Dreams and Heroes Died*. Washington: Jossey-Bass Publishers, 1981.

Linn, Ed. "Stan Musial—Man of the 15 Years." *SPORT*, September, 1961. pp. 34–35, 86–88.

Livingston, Robert L. Personal Correspondence Response to Baseball Survey, Spring, 1989.

Lucas, John A., and Ronald A. Smith. *Saga of American Sport*. Philadelphia: Lea and Febiger, 1978.

McDougald, Gil. Personal Correspondence Response to Baseball Survey, Spring, 1989.

Medd, Joel. Personal Correspondence Response to Baseball Survey, Spring, 1989.

Miles, Jerry A. Personal Correspondence Response to Baseball Survey, Spring, 1989.

Olson, Noel W. Personal Correspondence Response to Baseball Survey, Spring, 1989.

Papanek, John. "Athletes or Role Models?" *Sports Illustrated*, June, 1987, p. 84.

Povich, Shirley. "Walter Johnson: The Big Train." *SPORT*, January, 1950, pp. 49–58.

Reilly, Rick. "An American Classic." *Sports Illustrated*, May, 1989, pp. 18–21.

Rice, Grantland. "Who Is Baseball's All-Time Greatest?" *SPORT*, November, 1950, pp. 50–53, 89.

Rice, Grantland. Forward to *Lucky to Be a Yankee*, by Joe DiMaggio. New York: Bantam Books, 1949.

Robinson, Brooks. Personal Correspondence Response to Baseball Survey, Spring, 1989.

Ruth, Claire. "The Babe and I: Chapter 11." Reprinted in *The Omaha World Herald,* 1959.

Schultz, Dick. Personal Correspondence Response to Baseball Survey, Spring, 1989.

Sewell, Joe. Personal Correspondence Response to Baseball Survey, Spring, 1989.

Shaugnessy, Dan. "Ballplayers Are Human, Too." *Grand Forks Herald,* March, 1989.

Sher, Jack. "The Immortal 'Big Six.' " *SPORT,* October, 1949, pp. 57–66.

Silverman, Al. "The Top Performers of the Past 15 Years." *SPORT,* September, 1961, pp. 28–33, 80.

Silverman, Al, Steve Gelman, Joe Donnelly, Berry Stainback, Fred Katz, eds. "Spring Training Unsegregated Almost." *SPORT,* April, 1962, p. 96.

Slaughter, Enos. Personal Correspondence Response to Baseball Survey, Spring, 1989.

Smelser, M. *The Life that Ruth Built.* NY: Quadrangle/The New York Times, 1975.

Smith, Garry J., Brent Patterson, Trevor Williams, and John Hogg. "A Profile of the Deeply Committed Sports Fan." *Arena Review,* September, 1981, pp. 26–42.

Smith, Red. *The Red Smith Reader.* Edited by Dave Anderson. New York: Vintage Books, 1982.

Spaeth, Nicholas J. Personal Correspondence Response to Baseball Survey, Spring, 1989.

Towers, Wayne M. " 'Gee Whiz!' and 'Aw Nuts!': Radio and Newspaper Coverage of Baseball in the 1920s." Paper presented at the 62nd meeting of the Association for Education in Journalism, Houston, Texas, August 5–8, 1979.

Vecsey, George. Personal Correspondence Response to Baseball Survey, Spring, 1989.

Wermers, Donald. Personal Correspondence Response to Baseball Survey, Spring, 1989.

Witte, Albert M. Personal Correspondence Response to Baseball Survey, Spring, 1989.

Wolf, Bob. Personal Correspondence Response to Baseball Survey, Spring, 1989.

Wynn, Cordell. "Developing Positive Black Role Models for Black Youths: An Ever-Pressing Need." *Black Issues in Higher Education,* March, 1989, p. 25.

Zeigler, Earle F. "Babe Ruth and Lou Gehrig: A United States Dilemma." *The Physical Educator,* Spring, 1987, pp. 325–329.

Zingg, Paul J. "Diamond in the Rough: Baseball and the Study of American Sports History." *The History Teacher,* May, 1986, pp. 385–397.

Time for Heroes

A Dramatistic Analysis of Baseball Novels in the 1970s and 1980s

by Sally A. Canapa

Four summers ago, on a long night in June, I sat at County Stadium in my customary box seat just to the first base side of home plate. The Brewers were playing the Kansas City Royals, and had been for hours. The game moved so slowly that at times it seemed almost to stop. I was sleepy, but the night air was warm, and the game was tied. So I stayed.

The batter, a strong, square switch-hitter with a reputation for intelligence, stepped into the box. It was the bottom of the ninth, the score was still tied, and there were two men out. The bases were as empty as the upper decks. He peered into the darkness beyond the outfield, examined his bat for invisible flaws, and stared into the mind of the pitcher. After taking several balls and strikes, he pulled one into the open area between the left field grandstand and the bleachers. I looked at the clock on the scoreboard, as those remaining in the stadium cheered. 11:59 p.m. Blink. Midnight. Yesterday's home run had won the game.

Baseball is a game of moments and years, of leagues and individuals. Each game is a text, and each text is different, etched out as we watch it and then framed in our memories. Roger Angell describes the nature of the game:

> Form is the imposition of a regular pattern upon varying and unpredictable circumstances, but the patterns of baseball, for all the game's tautness and neatness, are never regular. Who can predict the winner and shape of today's game? Will it be a brisk, neat two-hour shutout? A languid, error-filled 12–3 laugher? A riveting three-hour, fourteen-inning deadlock? (286)

And like a literary text, each game text features at least one hero, along with, necessarily, at least one goat. Some *one* will hit the game-winning RBI; some *one* will make an impossible catch in the outfield; some *one* will pitch the ball that was hit for the RBI, or caught for the out. It is in the nature of the game to spotlight individual players. The pitcher stands alone, elevated slightly on a circular dirt mound. The batter faces him alone. The outfielders are scattered across a wide green expanse, where they tense and wait with each pitch. The catcher squats behind the plate, the only defensive player who faces the diamond and outfield.

Perhaps it is the dramatic nature of baseball that makes it such a fit topic for fiction. In his introduction to *The Armchair Book of Baseball,* John Thorn calls it "the writer's game" because it "plays upon the heart and mind so subtly" and because "thinking about baseball provides a pleasure quite different from that had by watching it" (xi). Quite different, yes; but this pleasure Thorn speaks of is bonded to the nature of the game itself and our enjoyment of it. This unique interrelationship between the game and the writing is what interests me here, and because of the keen, dramatic edge that somehow defines baseball, Kenneth Burke's dramatistic theory seems an appropriate method of analysis.

The baseball novel belongs to a genre that dates back to the turn of the century, beginning with dime novels and children's series. Ralph S. Graber analyzes the history of the baseball novel in his 1967 *English Journal* article, "Baseball in American Fiction," and identifies four subgenres that have appeared since World War II. While the pre-World War II baseball novel typically dealt with "realistic, tough situations free from . . . idealization, banter, and horseplay . . ." (1112), post-war fiction falls into these categories:

> . . . the stories of farce and fantasy, the hardboiled realistic novel that is chiefly only a good story, those which use a baseball game as a framework or include a leading character connected with the game, and those books about the game that are far more than baseball novels, but are concerned with the problems of existence (1112).

Graber lists and briefly describes novels representative of each category. He concludes that baseball fiction has developed qualitatively over the years, and now is good enough to "attract the intellectual to examine the game in literature for the light it sheds on American life and the paradoxes of modern existence" (1114).

This final sentence of Graber's is intriguing. Does baseball fiction provide its reader with some sort of Burkean "equipment for living"? Since this is in part a question of popular culture, I turned to the *Journal of Popular Culture* to see if any scholars since Graber have found answers. In the eighteen existing volumes of the *JPC* there are sixteen essays explicitly concerning baseball. Only one of these, "The All-American Boys: A Study of Boys' Sports Fiction," by Walter Evans (Volume 6, #1, pages 104–121), deals with the baseball novel.

Melvin Palmer's 1982 article, "The Heyday of the Football Novel," however, claims that baseball novels "died out" in the sixties and were replaced by basketball and football fiction. He speculates that "In 1968 in America the old verities were fast disappearing and new rituals were being created. Because baseball could no longer carry the burden of the time, America needed a new sports myth; and just as baseball lost its number one position in mass popularity (gate receipts and so forth), the old baseball novel gave way to football" (49). Apparently, Palmer believes, baseball novels simply did not successfully provide equipment for living in the late sixties and beyond. In fact, he takes his analysis one step further, and states that

> . . . the conditions of American culture are at the root of the transition of emphasis from baseball to football. As America lost its innocence in the jungles of Vietnam and the riot- and assassination-torn streets back home, the great American game of baseball, with all its nostalgic associations, was simply inadequate structurally, if not too sacred, to reflect America of the sixties (52).

Since I could find nothing more recent than Graber's 1967 article on baseball novels, and since I knew from my own reading that quite a number of such novels were written in the seventies and eighties, I decided to follow up, in a sense, on both Graber's and Palmer's findings. If it is true that baseball books did not suit the sixties, what has happened since, to them and to us? What kind of novel do we see now, and why? How can Burkean dramatism help us answer these questions? Before I begin the analysis, however, a brief summary of the four novels I have selected will be helpful.

The Great American Novel by Philip Roth (1973) is the story of the fictional Patriot League and its demise, as told by a garrulous old sportswriter named Word Smith ("Call me Smitty"). Challenged by Ernest Hemingway himself to write a great book, and desperate to prove the existence of a third league now expunged from all the record books, Smitty tells his tale in the form of a novel—and so *The Great American Novel* becomes fiction within fiction.

The story follows the Patriot League Ruppert Mundys on their 1943 season, which they spend entirely on the road, since the Mundy brothers, who own the team, have rented the home stadium to armed services as an embarkation camp. Able-bodied athletes, of course, are all off to war, and thus the Mundys' personnel are necessarily motley—there is a catcher with a wooden leg, a 52-year-old pitcher, a one-armed right fielder. The Mundys lose every game until they play in exhibition against the residents of an insane asylum—and win. After that they lose some more, until, through a tangled skein of events, an unnamed foreign substance is introduced into their morning Wheaties, and they go on a tear.

But a homeless team is not meant to be successful. Midway through the 1944 season, a Communist plot to demoralize America by destroying its national game is violently revealed, and the teams of the Patriot League go down like a row of dominoes, until they no longer exist, not even in the ghostly columns of statistics in the record books. Only Smitty, imprisoned in the Valhalla Home for the Aged, remains to try and prevent the rewriting of history in the name of patriotism.

John Alexander Graham's 1973 novel, *Babe Ruth Caught in a Snowstorm*, has two narrators: Petashne, a player, and Slezak, an owner, alternate chapters. Again the action of the book involves a fictional baseball team—the Wichita Wraiths of Braintree, Massachusetts. Slezak, a son of wealth, tires of squandering his money on meaningless projects and decides to do something worthwhile—so he organizes and manages a semiprofessional baseball team. Instead of recruiting players on the basis of talent, he advertises in the newspaper: "Baseball Players Wanted For Professional Team. Must Love The Game. Ability Not Necessary—Only Desire Counts" (12). The resulting team is rag tag but enthusiastic, and after a winning first season, the Wichita Wraiths are enfranchised by the expanding National League.

But Slezak, who barely knew how to manage a small-potatoes ball club playing in mismatched uniforms on a back lot ball field, hasn't a clue as to how to run a major league team. The merchandising parasites arrive, and Slezak promptly sells out. He puts in artificial turf. He sells the roof of the big new stadium—"airspace"—to a contractor for low income housing. He sells the land beneath the playing field—"earthspace"—to a garbage disposal company. He sells the boiler room to a mysterious company that conducts secret "hardware research."

After an explosion in the adjacent locker room which kills the Yak, the Wraiths' good-natured right fielder, the team stops play and demands explanations. To appease them, poor beleaguered Slezak arranges a benefit game, players versus management. If the players win, he promises to leave. If management wins, the players must promise to return to the field and finish the season.

But Slezak cheats and loads his bench with all-star players from other major league teams, dressed in costumes instead of uniforms—Leo Tolstoy, Giuseppi Verdi, Rutherford B. Hayes, Thomas Aquinas. . . . The game ends in a riot. The Wraiths disband, and "before the year was out the team had disappeared entirely from the national media" (279).

Shoeless Joe, by W. P. Kinsella (1982), is about baseball, dreams, and eternity. Ray, the narrator, carves an outfield from his Iowa corn field, and, as promised to him by a disembodied, prophetic sports announcer who lives in his head ("If you build it, he will come"), Shoeless Joe Jackson arrives one warm summer evening. The more of the field Ray completes, the more of the 1919 Black Sox arrive, until his team is nearly complete.

The prophetic announcer speaks to Ray again: "Ease his pain." Ray promptly leaves his farm and family and travels to New Hampshire, where he kidnaps J. D. Salinger and brings him back to Iowa. On the way back they pick up Moonlight Graham, who played one inning of one game for the New York Giants in 1905, and Eddie Scissons, the "oldest living Chicago Cub." When they return, they find Ray's father, a long-dead, class B catcher, working out with the phantom Black Sox. And so the game begins.

Kinsella's 1986 novel, *The Iowa Baseball Confederacy*, is the story of how the narrator and main character, Gideon Clarke, sets out to prove that the world champion Chicago Cubs traveled to Onamata, Iowa, in the summer of 1908, to play an exhibition game against allstars from the amateur league known as the Iowa Baseball Confederacy. Somehow this information has been lost; no one living at the time remembers the event, and no newspapers carry any account of it. It's as if it never happened.

But Gideon *knows* it happened. He slips through a "crack in time," taking only his trumpet and his friend, Stan Rogalski, and journeys to Big Inning, Iowa, where he takes part as a mascot in an apocalyptic, 2000-plus inning, forty-day game that ends in a flood, washing the town away. The game itself is a surreal manifestation of the old baseball maxim, "It's never over until it's over," and before it's over involves not only Gideon and Stan, but the spirit of an Arapaho Indian named Drifting Away, a holy tree, the Twelve-Hour Church of Time Immemorial, Leonardo da Vinci, and a granite Black Angel from the village's cemetery who ends up playing right field when one of the Confederacy's players is struck by lightning.

What can these four novels tell us about baseball and baseball fiction in the last two decades? Each novel is actually a text about a text; each book features the complicated interplay of agent, act, and scene. In *Kenneth Burke's Dramatism and Popular Culture,* C. Ronald Kimberling summarizes the possible critical uses of the dramatistic method. There are

> three major concepts which can be used in dissecting the formal aspects of any type of art. First is the Pentad, which allows us to examine both authorial intention and audience response. Secondly, we have the concepts of identification and patterns of experience, which provide the links between the incidents in a fictional story and the Scenic backdrop of everyday life. Finally, we have the specific types of form as outlined in the "Lexicon Rhetoricae." Added together, these methodological tools allow us to better penetrate the mysteries of form in the popular arts (54).

(I find Kimberling's phrase "the mysteries of form" especially fitting in this application, because it is the form of the game of baseball—the configuration of the diamond and the field, the precise distances measured between pitcher and batter (sixty feet, six inches), between base and base (ninety feet)—that seem to give it its aura of stability and familiarity. Even though that form was determined over a hundred years ago, it still measures the absolute strength and speed of pitcher, batter, and runner.)

The Pentad

Kimberling tells us that use of the Pentad allows critics to examine "both authorial intention and audience response" (54). Although it is usually impossible to be certain about what an author *intends* to do in a particular work, it seems clear that in the four novels I've chosen, the authors wish to depict the primacy of what is called the Agent in Burkean terms. Each novel has its hero or heroes, and in each novel the Acts of this hero-Agent determine the outcome.

The narrator/author of *The Great American Novel,* Smitty, has devoted his few remaining years of life to getting the Patriot League back into the record books. He wants to restore to the heroes of his youth—especially the ill-fated Luke Gofannon of the Ruppert Mundys—the glory he feels their play deserves. This is something he believes he must *do*—and action (as opposed to mere motion) is central to the Burkean model.

The team itself is filled with fallen or broken heroes. Yet each retains his peculiar dignity. Each, at one time or another in the novel, has a moment in which he is frozen in glory: we see Mike "The Ghost" Rama crashing mindlessly into the outfield wall, but holding onto the ball, or one-armed Bud Parusha hitting "the first and only home run he or any other one-armed man would ever hit in the majors" (209).

In *Babe Ruth Caught in a Snowstorm*, the makeshift team is composed of individuals who couldn't possibly "make it" playing baseball in the real world because they just don't have the ability. In Slezak's unfallen world, however, they all make it—and only because of desire. Each one is a hero.

The heroes in Kinsella's books come from both past and present. Shoeless Joe and the rest of the Black Sox are resurrected to play on a sweet green field in Iowa—and one gets the feeling they are thus somehow redeemed. Ray, the narrator, the builder of the corn field ballpark, the fetcher of J. D. Salinger and Moonshine Graham and the oldest living Chicago Cub, is directly responsible, through his brave, crazy deeds, for the initiation and progression of the action.

In *The Iowa Baseball Confederacy*, Gideon Clarke performs an analogous role. Because of his determination to prove the existence of the Confederacy and the occurrence of the exhibition game against the Cubs, he finds a way to travel back into time, where he becomes an integral part of the game itself. Because he is an albino, he is made a mascot by the Iowa ball players, who enthrone him on their bench and run their muddy hands through his white hair for luck. When he comes to bat in the 2204th inning, the Cubs have taken the lead, and are one out from victory. He faces Three Finger Brown, no less, whom he knows could strike him easily, and taunts him until Brown finally throws a beanball. Gideon as Agent takes one for the team. "The game isn't lost yet, I think as I fall toward the earth and unconsciousness" (277).

The primacy of the Agent is not something baseball novelists have applied to their subject matter, the way one would apply fertilizer to the outfield grass. The notion comes from the game itself. Stephen Jay Gould, a noted paleontologist who is also a student of the game, remarks that "In baseball, each essential action is a contest between two individuals—batter and pitcher, or batter and fielder—thus creating an arena of truly individual achievement within a team sport" (Thorn, 145). Since none of these Acts could be accomplished without their respective Agents, the latter become primary, ancestral. Or, as Commissioner Peter Ueberroth would say—"But mainly, baseball is about heroes" (Thorn, x).

Identification

Perhaps one of the most apparent similarities between these four novels is their whimsical mixing of fact and fiction. Real, historical players and teams compete against fictional players and teams, often with other historical or mythical figures looking on. A Burkean analysis would examine the reasons for this recurring phenomenon. Kimberling points out that "Aspects of the ordinary world are most often presented in popular art because they facilitate 'audience identification' with the patterns of experience symbolized by the work" (82). These "patterns of experience" form "links between the incidents in a fictional story and the Scenic backdrop of everyday life" (70).

The "scenic backdrop" of the 1970s and 1980s has included plenty of "deadly disorder and paradox" (Brummett, 259). In the 1970s, Vietnam worsened and finally ended, slowly and painfully, leaving us with over 50,000 American dead, uncounted missing, and "peace with honor." Few believed that. Richard Nixon hit his zenith (visits to China) and his nadir (Watergate), and public disgust became as real as a bad smell. The 1980s have seen no open war on the scale of Vietnam, but plenty of plain old horror, faithfully documented every evening on the news. Terrorism, nuclear weaponry, starvation, AIDS, Star Wars. Yuppies labor to forget; politicians struggle to remember.

Baseball—or at least its trappings—has changed during these decades as well. "These years brought significant new events—divisional plays, artificial turf, the designated hitter, free agency; new luminaries—Rose, Seaver, Jackson, Schmidt, Steinbrenner, and new trends—statistical analysis, revisionist history, tell-all memoirs" (Thorn, xii). It isn't yet clear how many of these changes are good for the game or the fan.

The decades during which Roth, Graham, and Kinsella wrote their books have been characterized by the ordinary man's lack of control. We sat, helpless, before our television sets as Vietnam, Watergate, Khomeini, Qaddafi, Chernobyl, Ethiopia and Rock Hudson flickered before us. Even baseball seemed caught in the flux—strikes, plastic grass, Steinbrenner and Martin, huge salaries, cocaine, lights at Wrigley Field.

We see these chaotic, threatening "patterns of experience" in the baseball novels. In *The Great American Novel,* the fear of communist infiltration leads to the destruction and disappearance of an entire league (domino theory). A player is inadvertently shot by a crazed umpire looking for revenge (random violence). History is rewritten to conform to the aims of those in power *(1984).*

The villain in *Babe Ruth Caught in a Snowstorm* is rampant commercialism; the owner's pursuit of profit destroys an otherwise good team whose only desire is to play baseball. Burke himself recognized the impact on our lives of this particular aspect of society: "In contemporary America the distinguishing emergent factor is obviously mechanization, industrialization, as it affects our political institutions, as it alters our way of living . . ." (107).

In *Shoeless Joe* and *The Iowa Baseball Confederacy,* the chaos of the scenic backdrop is matched by the equally chaotic actions of the narrators, both of whom simply assume that objective reality isn't all there is. Ray doesn't allow the fear of losing his farm to keep him from pursuing his dream; Gideon leaves his home and even his time in an effort to find the truth.

What sort of identification occurs between these novels ánd their readers and baseball people in general? Critics like Graber and Palmer would have it that art reflects society, but Burkean dramatism goes beyond this one-way explanation: "The Burkean model . . . provides a tentative answer to the frequently posed question as to whether art reflects or engenders social values and mores. Dramatism would suggest that it does both" (Kimberling, 84). The readers and the writers of these books are engaged, in other words, in a sort of conversation about baseball and about life. "Look, see how absurd this situation is." "Yes, I see that. What would be better?" Perhaps it is this dialogue that gives healing powers to the novels. Somehow the books recognize that while chaos and change are inevitable and perfection is impossible, life and magic and especially baseball continue. Complete identification between two humans is not possible either (Burke, 179); however, successful communication accomplishes whatever it can as a result of reaching for that perfection. "The aim of the poetic dialectic . . . is to strive toward perfection through the vicarious sharing of experience made possible through art" (Kimberling, 29). Baseball novels achieve their peace and their power through this dialectic.

Form

"I need to think something lasts forever . . ." (A. Bartlett Giamatti, "The Green Fields of the Mind," in Thorn, 143).

Form is the web that connects the four novels to each other and to the worlds they represent. Kimberling, following Burke, describes form as a "set of analogs to inner states of being" (122). The subject matter of these novels is the game of baseball. How does the game, then, manifest itself in the form of the novel—and how is it analogous to the "inner states of being" of the reader?

The experiences of going to a baseball game and reading a novel (any novel) are similar in one important way. In each case, time is suspended. We can usually read for pleasure at our own pace; we can experience a particular text as we choose to experience it. There is no limit to the amount of time we can take to finish reading a book. Neither is baseball subject to the clock. A game text isn't officially over until some *one* makes the last out (until the Fat Lady sings). And even then, in both cases, the text continues. We all can remember reading a particular novel and then having it follow us about in our minds for days or weeks or years thereafter. In the same way, moments and plays in a particular baseball game can remain with us, clear in every detail, for the rest of our lives.

In the four novels analyzed here, this "timelessness" takes on special contextual forms. In *The Great American Novel,* the "time" of the patriot League Ruppert Mundys is erased from the record books. *Babe Ruth Caught in a Snowstorm* begins with a vivid flashback, moves into the "present," and then travels back into time and "re-lives" the events leading up to the opening scene. The book also ends with the scene in the opening flashback, of course. In Kinsella's novels, time becomes almost another character. Ray's ghostly team can only come together because of time's generosity and grace, and even so, there is a sort of price to be paid:

> The process is all so slow, as dreams are slow, as dreams suspend time like a balloon hung in midair. I want it all to happen now. I want that catcher to appear. I want whatever miracle I am party to, to prosper and grow; I want the dimensions of time that have been loosened from their foundations to entwine like a basketful of bright embroidery threads. But it seems that even for dreams, I have to work and wait. It hardly seems fair (23).

In *The Iowa Baseball Confederacy,* Gideon slips through a "crack in time" into the past. He encounters a religious denomination that calls itself the "Twelve-Hour Church of Time Immemorial" and lives twelves hours ahead (or behind) everyone else (so that when it's "day" for them, it's "night" for the rest of humanity). He communicates with an immortal Arapaho Indian named Drifting Away, who "tampers with reality of Johnson County, Iowa" (177) and eventually wins the game for the Confederacy with a pinch hit home run on the fortieth rainy day of play. Through all of this, time remains fluid, mutable, magical.

It is also possible to talk about the form of these novels in terms of Burke's five aspects: syllogistic progression, qualitative progression, repetitive form, conventional form, and minor or incidental forms (Burke, 124–126). For example, in syllogistic progression, "The arrows of our desires are turned in a certain direction, and *the plot* follows the direction of the arrows" (emphasis mine) (124). This aspect of form does not seem to dominate either the game of baseball or the novels written about it; just as we cannot predict with any certainty at the beginning of a baseball game what the eventual tenor of that particular game will be, we cannot predict at the beginning of any of these four novels the twists and turns of plot and character we will encounter. "The arrows of our desires" in both cases are not pointed in any particular direction at all. We simply await the angle of their flight.

Qualitative progression is "subtler" than syllogistic progression, and means only that "the presence of one quality prepares us for the introduction of another" (125). Early in each of the four novels, the reader encounters surprising, even bizarre characters and events and is thus "prepared," in some sense, for the subsequent surreal action.

"The consistent maintaining of a principle under new guises," Burke's "repetitive form," appears in these novels as the Big Game. At some point in the convoluted plot of each book, there is a game that is in some way or ways decisive. In *The Great American Novel,* the final game of the second season, in which the center fielder is accidentally shot to death by umpire Mike the Mouth, triggers a series of events in which a communist plot is revealed and the Patriot League disbanded. The wild game that frames *Babe Ruth Caught in a Snowstorm* is similarly a climactic event that signals the end of the short-lived Wichita Wraiths. The game in *Shoeless Joe* is the culmination of Ray's faithful efforts, and allows fallen heroes to regain their joy and integrity. The Black Sox are symbolically redeemed, Ray is reunited with his father, Moonlight Graham gets to play more than one inning, and Eddie Scissons, the oldest living Chicago Cub, gets a dying man's last request—he is buried in center field. Finally, of course, *The Iowa Baseball Confederacy is* the game. The plot becomes so impossibly tangled that after a while all we are aware of is the unrelenting nature of the game itself. Even impending apocalypse will not end it until the last out or the last score is made.

All four books are rich in minor or incidental forms, as all good fiction should be. Smitty's novel-within-a-novel boasts attributes of everything from *Moby Dick* to *Tom Jones,* as well as stylistic excesses typical of enthusiastic, homely sportswriting. Analyzing Kinsella's use of myth and symbol would be a task worthy of a dozen dissertations (probably to his considerable amusement).

But it is the conventional aspect of the form of these books that is most interesting. In what sense can we say that the form of baseball novels today appeals "as form"? What expectations do consumers of such fiction have prior to reading (Burke, 126)? If we accept Burke's notion of the reciprocity of social values and art, then we can see how lovers of the game would turn to baseball fiction for equipment for living. According to Burke, "A form is a way of experiencing; and such a form is made available in art when, by the use of specific subject-matter, it enables us to experience in this way" (143). Most people who read baseball novels will never play major league baseball; they love something that is, for them, unattainable. The experiences of reading books like those written by Roth and Graham and Kinsella helps them to identify with this otherwise impossible dream.

But the books do more than that. Because they emphasize the primacy of the Agent and the fluid timelessness of the Scene, they are books of hope and power, rays of optimism in a darkened, confused world. Of course, many novels accomplish that these days; what's so special about baseball? Gideon Clarke's father Matthew has an answer to that:

> "Why not baseball?" my father would say. "Name me a more perfect game! Name me a game with more possibilities for magic, wizardry, voodoo, hoodoo, enchantment, obsession, possession. There's always time for daydreaming, time to create your own illusions at the ballpark. I bet there isn't a magician anywhere who doesn't love baseball. Take the layout. No mere mortal could have dreamed up the dimensions of a baseball field. No man could be that perfect. . . .
>
> "And the field runs to infinity. . . . You ever think of that, Gid? There's no limit to how far a man might possibly hit a ball, and there's no limit to how far a fleet outfielder might run to retrieve it. The foul lines run on forever, forever diverging. There's no place in America that's not part of a major-league ball field; the meanest ghetto, the highest point of land, the Great Lakes, the Colorado River. Hell, there's no place in the *world* that's not part of a baseball field.
>
> "Every other sport is held in by boundaries, some of absolute set size, some not: football, hockey, tennis, basketball, golf. But there's no limit to the size of a baseball field. What other sport can claim that? And there's no more enigmatic game; I don't have to tell you that" (Kinsella, *Iowa*, 44–45).

Perhaps we need enigma to help us deal with enigma. In any case, there is a peculiar relationship between baseball, language, and people that I find especially suited to Burkean dramatistic analysis. The novels here embrace the protean nature of human beings and blend it with the patterns of baseball in such a way as to help us understand ourselves and our world a bit better. There is something about this game that helps us "make sense" of the chaos around us. Donald Hall writes, in an article appropriately titled "Baseball and the Meaning of Life," ". . . baseball sets off the meaning of life precisely because it is pure of meaning. . . . The diamonds and rituals of baseball create an elegant, trivial, enchanted grid on which our suffering, shapeless, sinful day leans for the momentary grace of order" (1034). Any art form, written or pitched, that contributes to this grace of order deserves our critical attention. Play ball.

References

Angell, Roger. *The Summer Game*. New York: Ballantine Books, 1972.

Brummett, Barry. "Electric Literature as Equipment for Living: Haunted House Films." *Critical Studies in Mass Communication* 2 (1985), 247–261.

Burke, Kenneth. *Counter-Statement*. Berkeley: University of California Press, 1968.

Graber, Ralph S. "Baseball in American Fiction." *English Journal* 56 (November 1967), 1107–1114.

Graham, John Alexander. *Babe Ruth Caught in a Snowstorm*. Boston: Houghton Mifflin Company, 1973.

Hall, Donald. "Baseball and the Meaning of Life." *National Review* 33 (4 September 1981), 1033–1034.

Kimberling, C. Ronald. *Kenneth Burke's Dramatism and Popular Arts*. Bowling Green, Ohio: Bowling Green State University Popular Press, 1982.

Kinsella, W. P. *The Iowa Baseball Confederacy*. Boston: Houghton Mifflin Company, 1986.

————*Shoeless Joe*. New York: Ballantine Books, 1982.

Palmer, Melvin D. "The Heyday of the Football Novel." *Journal of Popular Culture* 16 (Summer 1982), 48–54.

Roth, Philip. *The Great American Novel*. New York: Farrar, Straus and Giroux, 1973.

Thorn, John, ed. *The Armchair Book of Baseball*. New York: Charles Scribner's Sons, 1985.

Baseball and the Reconstitution of American Masculinity, 1880–1920[1]

by Michael S. Kimmel

All boys love baseball. If they don't
they're not real boys.
—Zane Grey

Baseball is sport as American pastoral: more, perhaps, than any other sport, baseball evokes that nostalgic longing, those warm recollections of boyhood innocence, the balmy warmth of country air, the continuity of generations. More than this, baseball is a metaphor for America, "the very symbol, the outward and visible expression of the drive and push and rush and struggle of the raging, tearing, booming 19th century," as Mark Twain wrote in 1889 (cited in Barth, 1980: 182).

Baseball expresses the contradictions that lie at the heart of American culture. The ballpark itself is a bucolic patch of green nestled in a burgeoning urban landscape. The relaxation of an afternoon spent languidly in the bleacher sun is a sharp counterpoint to the excruciating tension that hangs on every pitch. Carefully calculated strategies (like hit and run, the double steal) executed with drill-like precision contrast with the spontaneous enthusiasm of the great catch. The players' cold professionalism at the bargaining table is antithetical to their boyish exuberance on the field.

And baseball is about remaining a boy and becoming a man. Like other sports, baseball fuses work and play, transforming play into work and work into play, thus smoothing the transition from boyhood to manhood. Play as work generates adult responsibility and discipline; work as play allows one to enjoy the economic necessity of working. Some studies suggest that men who were successful as boyhood athletes become more successful in business; contemporary high-tech corporations have introduced team sports among managers on the premise that such teamwork will increase productivity.

But unlike other sports, baseball inspires a literary eloquence that is unmatched, perhaps because it is so delicately poised between boyhood and manhood. No other sport has produced a Roger Angell or a Donald Hall; interestingly, each explores the link between baseball and family memory. Angell writes that, for him, "going through baseball record books and picture books is like opening a family album stuffed with old letters, wedding invitations, tattered newspaper clippings, graduation programs, and curled up darkening snapshots," so that, for writer and fan, baseball players "seem like members of our family, or like trusted friends" (Angell, 1982: 10, 199). And Hall underscores how baseball "connects American males with each other, not only through bleacher friendships and neighbor loyalties, not only through barroom fights, but, most importantly, through generations." He continues:

> Baseball is fathers and sons. Football is brothers beating each other up in the backyard, violent and superficial. Baseball is the generations, looping backward forever with a million apparitions of sticks and balls, cricket and rounders, and the game the Iroquois played in Connecticut before the English came. Baseball is fathers and sons playing catch, lazy and murderous, wild and controlled, the profound archaic song of birth, growth, age, and death. This diamond encloses what we are (Hall, 1985: 49, 30).

In this chapter, I examine one of the ways in which "this diamond encloses what we are," by looking at the historical links between baseball and masculinity in the United States. By focusing on the rise of baseball at the turn of the century, I will develop two themes. First, I look at the ways in which the rise of organized participatory sports was offered as a corrective to a perceived erosion of traditional masculinity in the late 19th century. Second, I explore the rise of mass-level spectator sports as part of the shift in America from a culture of production to a culture of consumption. I argue that baseball—as participatory and spectator sport—was one of the chief institutional vehicles by which masculinity was reconstituted and by which Americans accommodated themselves to shifting structural relations. By specifying the terms on which sports reconstituted American masculinity, I link participation and spectatorship, and explore how baseball provided an institutional nexus by which turn-of-the-century men recreated a manhood that could be experienced as personally powerful while it simultaneously facilitated the emergence of a docile and disciplined labor force. The lyrical eloquence that baseball, above other sports, inspires derives, in part, from the sport's centrality in the effort to reconstitute American masculinity.

I. Forces[2]

The early 19th century provided a fertile environment for an expansive American manhood. Geographic expansion combined with rapid industrial and urban growth to fuel a virile optimism about social possibilities. The Jacksonian assault against "effete" European bankers and the frighteningly "primitive" Native American population grounded identity in a "securely achieved manhood" (Rogin, 1975: 162). But by mid-century, "the walls of the male establishment began to crack," as social and economic changes eroded the foundations of traditional American masculinity. Westward expansion came to an abrupt end at the Pacific coast, and rapid industrialization radically altered men's relationship to their work. The independent artisan, the autonomous small farmer, the small shopkeeper were everywhere disappearing. Before the Civil War, almost nine of every ten American men were farmers or self-employed businessmen; by 1870, that figure had dropped to two of three, and by 1910, less than one of three American men were as economically autonomous. Increased mechanization and the routinization of labor accompanied rapid industrialization; individual workers increasingly were divorced from control over the labor process as well as dispossessed of ownership (see Braverman, 1974).

Simultaneously, social changes further eroded American men's identities. In the burgeoning cities, white men felt threatened by waves of immigrants. In 1870, for example, of the nearly one million people who lived in New York City, 4 of every 9 were foreign born (Adelman, 1986: 21). And the rise of the women's movement in the late 19th century spelled the beginning of the end for men's monopoly over the ballot box, the college classroom, the professional school. The appearance of the New Woman—single, upwardly mobile, sexually active, professionally ambitious, and feminist—also seemed to exacerbate men's insecurity and malaise.

The "crisis" of masculinity in the late 19th century emerged from these structural and social changes, as "the familiar routes to manhood were either washed out or roadblocked." Men

> were jolted by changes in the economic and social order which made them perceive that their superior position in the gender order and their supposedly "natural" male roles and prerogatives were not somehow rooted in the human condition, that they were instead the result of a complex set of relationships subject to change and decay (Hartman, 1984: 13).

The perceived crisis of masculinity was not a generic crisis, experienced by all men in similar ways. Essentially it was a crisis of middle-class white masculinity, a crisis in the dominant paradigm of masculinity that was perceived as threatened by the simultaneous erosion of traditional structural foundations (economic autonomy, the frontier), new gains for women, and the tremendous infusion of non-white immigrants into the major industrial cities. It was a crisis of economic control, a struggle against larger units of capital that eroded workplace autonomy and new workers (immigrants and women) who were seen as displacing traditional American men. And it was also a political crisis, pitting the traditional small town and rural white middle-class masculinity against new contenders for political incorporation. It was a crisis, in this sense, of gender hegemony, of whether or not the traditional white middle-class version of masculinity would continue to prevail over both women and non-white men. To understand how baseball articulated with these various dimensions of crisis in hegemonic masculinity, we will draw on analyses of the relations among various social classes, the relations between whites and non-whites, and the relations between women and men.

Men's responses to the turn-of-the-century crisis of masculinity varied tremendously, especially given the simultaneity of the forces that seemed to be affecting middle-class white men. Some gave vent to angry backlash against the forces that were perceived as threatening men (anti-feminist), while others embraced feminist principles as the grounds for a reconstitution of a new masculinity (pro-feminist). A third response sought to revitalize masculinity, to return to men the vitality and strength which had been slowly draining from American men. This "masculinist" response was not as anti-woman as it was pro-male, attacking the enervation of American manhood, and developing those interpersonal and institutional mechanisms by which masculinity could be retrieved.[3] Often the masculinist response articulated with an anti-modernist rejection of the city as evil den of corruption, where healthy country men were thought to be transformed into effete dandies, and where hordes of unwashed immigrants threatened the racial purity of the nation. "Get your children into the country," one real estate advertisement for Wilmington, Delaware, urged potential buyers in 1905. "The cities murder children. The hot pavements, the dust, the noise are fatal in many cases and harmful always. The history of successful men is nearly always the history of country boys" (cited in Jackson, 1985: 138). Frank Lloyd Wright's tirade against New York City captures part of the anti-urban sentiment, and links it to the perceived feminization of American culture. In *The Future of Architecture*, he described it as:

> A place fit for banking and prostitution and not much else . . . a crime of crimes . . . a vast prison . . . triumph of the herd instinct . . . outgrown and overgrown . . . the greatest mouth in the world . . . humanity preying upon humanity . . . carcass . . . parasite . . . fibrous tumor . . . pig-pile . . . incongruous mantrap of monstrous dimensions . . . Enormity devouring manhood, confusing personality by frustration of individuality. Is this not anti-Christ? the Moloch that knows no God but *more?* (Wright, 1970:136).

Surely the anti-urban sentiments that composed part of the masculinist response were also fueled by a nativist racism that saw cities as the breeders of an immigrant threat.

The masculinist effort to stem the tide of feminization of American manhood included the development of the YMCA and the Boy Scouts, in which young boys could experience the remedial effects of the wilderness away from the feminizing clutches of mothers and teachers. If consumer society had "turned robust, manly, self-reliant boyhood into a lot of flat-chested cigarette smokers with shaky nerves and doubtful vitality," as Chief Scout Ernest Thompson Seton had it (cited in Macleod, 1983: 49), then the BSA could "counter the forces of feminization and maintain traditional manhood" (Hantover, 1980: 293).

Masculinism included the Muscular Christianity movement, in which, through texts like Thomas Hughes's *The Manliness of Christ* (1880) and Carl Case's *The Masculine in Religion* (1906), the image of Jesus was transformed from a beatific, delicate, soft spoken champion of the poor into a musclebound he-man whose message encouraged the strong to dominate the weak. Jesus was no "dough-faced lick-spittle proposition," proclaimed itinerant evangelist Billy Sunday, but "the greatest scrapper who ever lived" (cited in McLoughlin, 1955: 179). A former professional baseball player turned country preacher, Sunday drew enormous crowds to his fiery sermons in which he preached against institutionalized Protestantism. "Lord save us from off-handed, flabby cheeked, brittle boned, weak-kneed, thin-skinned, pliable, plastic, spineless, effeminate, ossified three-karat Christianity" (cited *Ibid.:* 175). Masculinism also promoted a revived martial idealism, and found a new hero in Theodore Roosevelt since "the greatest danger that a long period of profound peace offers to a nation is that of [creating] effeminate tendencies in young men"

(Thompson, 1898: 610). Perhaps masculinity could be retrieved through imperial expansion, since as General Homer Lea put it, "[as] manhood marks the height of physical vigor among mankind, so the militant successes of a nation mark the zenith of its physical greatness" (cited in Roszak and Roszak, 1975: 92).

And masculinism also found institutional expression in the sports craze that swept the nation in the last decade of the century. The first tennis court was built in Boston in 1876, the first basketball court in 1891. The American Bowling Congress was founded in 1895, and the Amateur Athletic Union was established in 1890. Sports offered a counter to the "prosy mediocrity of the latter-day industrial scheme of life," as Thorstein Veblen put it in *The Theory of the Leisure Class* (1899: 206) revitalizing American manhood while it simultaneously "had taken the place of the frontier . . . as the outlet through which the pressure of urban populations was eased" (Green, 1986: 215).

Nowhere was this better expressed than in the rapid rise of baseball, both as a participatory sport and as a spectator sport. Baseball became one of the central mechanisms by which masculinity was reconstituted at the turn of the century, as well as one of the vehicles by which the various classes, races, and ethnicities that were thrown together into the urban melting pot accommodated themselves to industrial class society and developed the temperaments that facilitated the transition to a consumer culture.

II. Playing

> The whole test of the worth of any sport should be the demand
> that sport makes upon those qualities of mind and body which in
> their sum we call manliness—Theodore Roosevelt[4]

In the late 19th century, America went "sports crazy" (Dubbert, 1979: 175). The nation had never been as preoccupied with physical health and exercise, and across the country Americans flocked to health spas, consumed enormous quantities of potions and elixirs (like the 63 imported and 42 domestic bottled waters advertised by one firm in 1900), lifted weights, listened to health reformers extol the tonic virtues of country air and bland, high-fiber diets, raced through urban parks on bicycles, and tried their hands at tennis, golf, boxing, cricket and baseball (see Green, 1986). The search for individual physical perfection indicated a hopelessness about the possibilities of social transformation, as well as the intimately linked fears of the enervation of the culture and individual lethargy and failure of nerve.

Sports were heralded as character-building, and health reformers promised that athletic activity would not only make young men physically healthier, but would instill moral virtues as well. Sports were cast as a central element in the fight against feminization; sports made boys into men. In countless advice books, which counseled concerned parents about proper methods of child rearing, sports were invariably linked with the acquisition of appropriate gender-role behavior for males. Sports were necessary, according to D. A. Sargent, to "counteract the enervating tendency of the times and to improve the health, strength, and vigor of our youth" since they provide the best kind of "general exercise for the body, and develop courage, manliness, and self-control" (cited in Dubbert, 1979: 169). Sports aided youth in "the struggle for manliness," wrote G. Walter Fiske in *Boy Life and Self-Government* (cited in Mrozek, 1983: 207). Sports were especially recommended for boys because, as physical education professor Luther Halsey Gulick, Jr. put it, "athletics do not test womanliness as they test manliness" (cited in Rader, 1983: 165).

Manhood required proof, and sports were a "place where manhood was earned," not as "part of any ceremonial rite of passage but through the visible demonstration of achievement" (Adelman, 1986: 286). Such demonstration was particularly important because lurking beneath the fear of feminization was the fear of the effeminate, the fear of homosexuality, which had emerged in visible subcultures in urban centers. In England, for example, one newspaper championed athletics for substituting the "feats of man for the 'freak of the fop,' hardiness for effeminacy, and dexterity for luxurious indolence" (Adelman, 1986: 284).

Some were less sanguine about sports' curative value. Thorstein Veblen's blistering critique of the nascent consumer culture, *The Theory of the Leisure Class,* suggests that organized sports are an illusory panacea. For the individual man, athletics are no sign of virtue, since "the temperament which inclines men to [sports] is essentially a boyish temperament. The addiction to sports therefore in a peculiar degree marks an arrested development of the man's moral nature" (Veblen, 1899: 200). And culturally, sports may be an evolutionary throwback, as they "afford an exercise for dexterity and for the emulative ferocity and astuteness characteristic of predatory life" (*Ibid.,* p. 203).

But most commentators saw sports as the arena for men to achieve physical manhood, but also believed that organized sports would instill important moral values.[5] Here, especially, the masculinist response to the crisis of masculinity resonated with the anti-urban sentiments of those who feared modern industrial society. Sports could rescue American boys from the "haunts of dissipation" that seduced them in the cities—the taverns, gambling parlors, and brothels, according to the *Brooklyn Eagle* (cited in Adelman, 1986: 277). Youth needs recreation, the *New York Herald* claims, and "if they can't get it healthily and morally, they will seek it unhealthily and immorally at night, in drink saloons or at the gambling tables, and from these dissipations to those of a lower depth, the gradation is easy" (cited in *Ibid.*, 277).

And what was true of sports in general was particularly true of baseball. Theodore Roosevelt listed baseball in his list of "the true sports for a manly race" (along with running, rowing, football, boxing, wrestling, shooting, riding and mountain climbing). Just as horse racing had resulted in better horse breeding, Edward Marshall claimed in 1910, so baseball "resulted in improvement in man breeding" (cited in Spalding, 1911: 534). "No boy can grow to a perfectly normal manhood today without the benefits of at least a small amount of baseball experience and practice," wrote William McKeever in his popular advice manual, *Training the Boy* (McKeever, 1913: 91).

The values that baseball called into play were important to the man and central to the nation. The baseball player was "no thug trained to brutality like the prize fighter." noted baseball pioneer A. G. Spalding, nor was he a "half developed little creature like a jockey" but an exemplar of distinctly "native" American virtues, which Spalding alliteratively enumerated in *America's National Game* (1911):

> American Courage, Confidence, Combativeness; American Dash, Discipline, Determination; American Energy, Eagerness, Enthusiasm; American Pluck, Persistence, Performance; American Spirit, Sagacity, Success; American Vim, Vigor, Virility (Spalding, 1911: 4).

Essayist Addigton Bruce added:

> Physical fitness, courage, honesty, patience, the spirit of initiative combined with due respect for lawful authority, soundness and quickness of judgement, self-confidence, self-control, cheeriness, fairmindedness, and appreciation of the importance of social solidarity, of 'team play'—these are traits requisite as never before for success in the life of an individual and of a nation (Bruce, 1913: 105).

And Henry Chadwick tossed in "courage, nerve, pluck and endurance" (cited in Adelman, 1986: 173).

Such values were not only American, but Christian, replacing the desiccated values of a dissolute life with the healthy vitality of American manhood. Chadwick saw baseball as a "remedy for the many evils resulting from the immoral associations boys and young men of our cities are apt to become connected with" and therefore deserving "the endorsement of every clergyman in the country" (cited in Adelman, 1986: 173). McKeever added that "baseball may be conducted as a clean and uplifting game such as people of true moral refinement may patronize without doing any violence to conscience" (McKeever, 1913: 101). Baseball was good for the body and the soul of men; it was imperative for the health and moral fiber of the body social. From pulpits and advice manuals, the virtues of baseball were sounded. As Adelman notes, baseball "took manliness beyond a mere demonstration of physical prowess and linked it to virtues such as courage, fortitude, discipline, and so on. The argument concluded that if ball games called these virtues into play—as in fact they were critical to doing well at such sports—then ball playing was obviously one way of demonstrating manhood" (Adelman, 1986: 106).

One central feature of the values that were instilled by playing baseball was that they appeared on the surface to stress autonomy and aggressive independence, but they simultaneously reinforced obedience, self-sacrifice, discipline and a rigid hierarchy. This was equally true with other "boy's liberation movements" designed to counter the feminization of the culture. The Boy Scouts instilled a "quest for disciplined vitality" (Green, 1986: 261), in which scouts are taught, in the words of founder Lord Baden-Powell, to "give up everything, their personal comforts and desires, in order to get their work done. They do not do all this for their own amusement, but because it is their duty to their king, fellow country-men, or *employers*" (cited in Rosenthal, 1984: 45–46; emphasis added). The results of this and other efforts were noted with glee by Octavia Hill, the celebrated English social reformer in the 1880s:

> There is no organization which I have found influence so powerfully for good the boys in such a neighborhood. The cadets learn the duty and dignity of obedience; they get a sense of corporate life and of civic duty; they learn to honour the power of endurance and effort; and they come into contact with manly and devoted officers . . . These ideals are in marked contrast with the listless self-indulgence, the pert self-assertion, the selfishness and want of reverence which are so characteristic of the life in the low district (cited in Hargreaves, 1986: 61).

For the boys learning to play baseball, these values were also underscored. Surely the team came first, and one always obeyed one's coaches and manager. What Veblen claimed about football is equally true about baseball:

> The culture . . . gives a product of exotic ferocity and cunning. It is a rehabilitation of the early barbarian temperament, together with a suppression of those details of temperament which, as seen from the standpoint of the social and economic exigencies, are the redeeming features of the savage character.
>
> The physical vigour acquired in the training for athletic games—so far as the training may be said to have this effect—is of advantage both to the individual and to the collectivity, in that, other things being equal, *it conduces to economic serviceability* (Veblen, 1899: 204; emphasis added).

Sports reproduced those character traits required by industrial capitalism, and participation in sports by working class youths was hailed as a mechanism of insuring obedience to authority and acceptance of hierarchy. If the masculinity on the baseball field was exuberant, fiercely competitive, wildly aggressive, it was so only in a controlled and orderly arena, closely supervised by powerful adults. As such, the masculinity reconstituted on the baseball field also facilitated a docility and obedience to authority that would serve the maintenance of the emerging industrial capitalist order.

III. Watching

Just as on the field, so in the stands: baseball as spectator sport facilitated an accommodation to industrial capitalism as a leisure time diversion for the urban lower-middle and working classes. Ballparks were located in the city and admission fees were low, so that "attendance at baseball games was more broadly based than at other spectator sports" (Adelman, 1986: 149).

Baseball did not spring to such popularity overnight, as restorer of both individual virility and national vitality; its emergence as the "national pastime" was deliberately crafted. In fact, in the early half of the 19th century, cricket was hailed for its capacity to instill manly virtues in its players. "Whoever started these boys to practice the game deserves great credit—it is manly, healthy, invigorating exercise and ought to be attended more or less at all schools," waxed the *New York Herald* (cited in Adelman, 1986: 105–106). In 1868, the *Brooklyn Eagle* informed potential spectators of a cricket match that they were about to see a "manly game" (cited *Ibid.*, 169). Baseball was regarded, in fact, as less than fully manly; one letter to the editor of a newspaper contended that:

> You know very well that a man who makes a business of playing
> ball is not a man to be relied upon in a match where great interests
> are centered, or on which large amounts of money is pending (cited
> in Adelman, 1986: 167).

By the late 19th century, the relationship between baseball and
cricket had been reversed. The man who played cricket, Albert Spalding warned, thought that his match was a chance "to drink afternoon
tea, flirt, gossip, smoke [and] take a whiskey and soda at the customary
hour" (Spalding, 1911: 7). How can we explain such a change? In
part, the shift from cricket to baseball can be understood by the
changing class and regional composition of its players and its observers. Whereas earlier in the century baseball had been the domain of
upper-middle-class men, by the end of the century it was played
almost exclusively by lower-middle-class men. Similarly, the rise of
mass spectator sports—the erection of the urban stadium, the profes-
sionalization of teams and leagues, the salaries of players—changed
dramatically the class composition of the baseball fan. The values that
were thought to be instilled by playing baseball had made the imaginative leap to an ability to be instilled by watching baseball. And
values of discipline, self-control, sacrifice for the team, and an acceptance of hierarchy were central to the accommodation of a rapidly
developing working class to the new industrial order.

It was during this period of dramatic economic expansion in the
late 19th century that baseball "conquered" America. In the first few
decades following the Civil War, the baseball diamond was standard-
ized, teams and leagues were organized, rules refined, game schedules instituted, and grand tours undertaken by professional baseball
teams (see Barth, 1980: 159). And though the earliest baseball teams,
like the New York Knickerbockers, were made up of wealthy men,
baseball was soon being played by small town, lower-middle-class men
and watched by their urban counterparts (see Mroze, 1983: 104).

The urban baseball park was one of the new important locations
for social life in the burgeoning late 19th century city. Like the
vaudeville theatre, the department store, and the urban park, the
stadium provided a world of abundance and fantasy, of excitement
and diversion, all carefully circumscribed by the logic of urban capitalism. Here the pain and alienation of urban industrial work life was
soothed, and the routine dull grayness of the urban landscape was
broken up by these manicured patches of green. The baseball park
was a constructed "imitation of a pastoral setting" in the city, in which
identification with one's professional team provided a "feeling of
community" with anonymous neighbors; the ballpark was "a rural

haven of shared sentiments" in the midst of an alienating city (Barth, 1980: 190, 191).[6]

If masculinity had earlier been based on economic autonomy, geographic mobility, and success in a competitive hierarchy, baseball—among the other new social institutions of the turn of the century—allowed the reconstitution of those elements in a controlled and contained location. On the field, baseball promoted values essential to traditional masculinity: courage, initiative, self-control, competitive drive, physical fitness. In the stands, the geographic frontier of the mid-century was replaced by the outfield fences and by the mental frontiers between rival cities. (What we lose in reality we recreate in fantasy, as a Freudian axiom might have it.)

Baseball was fantasy, and it was diversion. "Men anxious to be distracted from their arduous daily routines provided a natural market for the product of the new industry" (Barth, 1980: 151). And baseball was viewed by boosters as a safety valve, allowing the release of potential aggression in a healthy, socially acceptable way; it was a "method of gaining momentary relief from the strain of an intolerable burden, and at the same time finding a harmless outlet for pent-up emotions" which otherwise "might discharge themselves in a dangerous way" (Bruce, 1913: 106). For the fan, baseball was, Bruce noted, "catharsis."

To some supporters, the virtue of spectatorship was analogous to the virtues instilled by participation. Supporters of Sunday baseball extolled the healthy, invigorating and uplifting atmosphere of the ballpark. William Kirk, for example, called baseball "one of the greatest agents for clean living and temperate living." As he explained, "it is far better for the young boys and the old boys to be out in the light and the open air, watching a clean and thrilling struggle that is played where all may see, than to sit with legs crossed under some taproom table, dealing out grimy cards or grimier stories" (Kirk, 1908: 48). In 1912, President William Howard Taft proclaimed himself a baseball fan, linking class, gender, and moral virtue:

> Baseball takes people into the open air—it draws out millions of factory hands, of tradesmen and interior laborers of all kinds, who spend their afternoons whenever possible in a healthful, genuinely inspiring contest in the warm sunshine and fresh air, when many other sports, and in fact all natural tendencies conspire to keep them indoors engaged in various kinds of unwholesome and unhealthful pastime (Murphy, 1912: 3–4).

Like the frontier, the baseball park was also celebrated as "democratic." The experience of spectatorship, baseball's boosters claimed, was a great social leveler:

> The spectator at a ball game is no longer a statesman, lawyer, broker, doctor, merchant, or artisan, but just plain every-day man, with a heart full of fraternity and good will to all his fellow men— except perhaps the umpire. The oftener he sits in grand stand or 'bleachers,' the broader, kindlier, better man and citizen he must tend to become (Bruce, 1913:107).

"The genius of our institutions is democratic," Albert Spalding gushed, and "Baseball is a democratic game" (Spalding, 1911: 6).

Supporters of Sunday baseball celebrated the "real democracy of spirit" that baseball embodied. "One thing in common absorbs us," wrote the Rev. Roland D. Sawyer in 1908, "we rub shoulders, high and low; we speak without waiting for an introduction; we forget everything clannish, all the petty conventionalities being laid aside" (Sawyer, 1908: 31–32). And novelist and former minor league ballplayer Zane Grey echoed these sentiments when he wrote:

> Here is one place where caste is lost. Ragamuffins and velvet-breeched, white collared boys stand in that equality which augurs well for the future of the stars and stripes. Dainty clothes are no bar to the game if their owner is not afraid to soil them (Grey, 1909: 12).

Such mythic egalitarianism, however, ignored the power relationships that made American democracy possible. For the experience of incorporation into community was based on exclusion: the exclusion of non-white men and the exclusion of women. The ballpark was a "haven in a heartless world" for white lower-middle-class men, and the community and solidarity they found there, however based on exclusion, facilitated their accommodation to their position in class society. Professional spectator sports maintained the "rigid gender division and chauvinist masculine identity," as well as the strict separation between whites and non-whites, that provided some of the main cultural supports of class domination (Hargreaves, 1986: 43). While providing the illusion of equality, and offering organized leisure time distraction, as well as by shaping working class masculinity as constituted by its superiority over women, baseball helped white working class men accommodate themselves to the emergent order.

IV. Reproducing

Baseball, as participatory sport and as spectator sport, reconstituted a masculinity whose social foundations had been steadily eroding, and in so doing, served to facilitate the reproduction of a society based upon gender, racial, and class hierarchies. For it was not just "masculinity" that was reconstituted through sports, but a particular kind of masculinity—white and middle class—that was elaborated. And part of the mechanisms of that elaboration was the use of white middle-class masculinity to maintain the social hierarchies between whites and non-whites (including all ethnic immigrants to the cities), between upper classes and working classes, and between men and women.

These mechanisms were developed in the last two decades of the 19th century and the first two decades of the 20th century. In 1919, this world was shaken during the World Series scandal that involved the infamous Chicago "Black Sox," who had apparently "fixed" the Series. The scandal captivated American men, and a certain innocence was lost. Commercialism had "come to dominate the sporting quality of sports" (Filene, 1986: 139); heroes were venal and the pristine pastoral was exposed as corrupt, part of the emergent corporate order and not the alternative to it that people had imagined. But by then it was too late: the corporate order had triumphed and would face little organized opposition from a mobilized and unified working class. The reconstituted masculinity that was encouraged by baseball had replaced traditional definitions of masculinity, and was fully accommodated to the new capitalist order. The geographic frontier where masculinity was demonstrated was replaced by the outfield fence; men's workplace autonomy and control was replaced, in part, by watching a solitary batter squaring off against an opposing pitcher. What had been lost in real experience could be reconstituted through fantasy.

The baseball diamond, as I have argued in this chapter, was more than a verdant patch of pastoral nostalgia; it was a contested terrain. The contestants were invisible to both participant and spectator, and quite separate from the game being played or watched. It was a contest between class cultures in which the hegemony of middle-class culture was reinforced and the emerging industrial urban working class was tamed by consumerism and disciplined by the American values promoted in the game. It was a contest between races, in which the exclusion of non-white and non-European immigrants from participation was reflected in the bleachers, as racial discrimination further assuaged the white working class. And it was a contest between women and men, in which newly mobile women were excluded from equal participation (and most often from spectatorship); the gender hierarchy was maintained by assuming those traits that made for athletic excellence were also those traits that made for exemplary citizenship. The masculinity reconstituted on the ball field or in the bleachers was a masculinity that reinforced the unequal distribution of power based on class, race, and gender. In that sense, also, baseball was truly an American game. And if we continue, as I do, to love both playing and watching baseball, it is also a deeply ambivalent love, which, like the love of family or country, to which it is so intimately linked, binds us to a place of both comfort and cruelty.

Notes

1. An earlier version of this essay was published in M. Messner and D. Sabo, eds., *Critical Perspectives on Sport, Men, and the Gender Order* (Human Kinetics Press, 1990). For critical and supportive readings of this work I am grateful to Ron Berger, Mike Messner, and George Robinson. This essay is dedicated to Norman Elliot Kent and George Robinson who can acknowledge baseball's sexism, racism and venality, and remain devoted fans and loyal friends.

2. The material in this section is adapted from my "Men's Responses to Feminism at the Turn of the Century" in *Gender & Society* (13), 1987.

3. Of course many masculinists were vigorously anti-feminist. But the thrust of masculinism was indifferent to the institutional gains for women, and sought only the preservation of "islands" of masculinity.

4. An editorial advertisement in *Baseball Magazine*, 2(3), 1909.

5. The key term here is, of course, "organized," and I will return to that aspect in the next section.

6. Such experiences of community are reproduced by baseball across generations, so that community with neighbors is linked with a relationship between father and son as fans. I recall vividly, for example, my first ride on the subway to Ebbets Field, when I knew everyone in the train was as adoring of the Dodgers as my father. And, of course, me. I remember reaching up to hold his hand as we walked to that sagging building, and gasping as we entered the stands when I saw how bright and green the field itself was. One needn't be a psychoanalyst to understand how feeling so close to 35,000 neighbors was so intimately linked to feeling so close to that most special person. The memory of community is linked to the memory of family love for generations of American men. And the sinews of that community are the shared idols of boyhood—his Rube Walker and my Sandy Koufax. Such links may help explain my continued passion for the game, both as player and as a spectator. And, perhaps, why I still root for the Dodgers, who, from my perspective, are simply on a very long road trip.

References

Adelman, Melvin L. *A Sporting Time: New York City and the Rise of Modern Athletics, 1820–1870*. Champaign, IL: University of Illinois Press, 1986.

Angell, Roger. *Late Innings: A Baseball Companion*. New York: Simon and Schuster, 1982.

Barth, Gunther. *City People: The Rise of Modern City Culture in Nineteenth Century America*. New York: Oxford University Press, 1980.

Broun, Heywood. "The Happy Days of Baseball" in *Brown's Nutmeg*, May 6, 1939.

Douglass, Ann. *The Feminization of American Culture*. New York: Alfred Knopf, 1977.

Dubbert, Joe. *A Man's Place: Masculinity in Transition*. Englewood Cliffs, NJ: Prentice-Hall, 1979.

Filene, Peter. *Him/Her Self: Sex Roles in America*. Second edition. Baltimore: Johns Hopkins University Press, 1986.

Green, Harvey. *Fit for America: Health, Fitness and Sport in American Society*. New York: Pantheon, 1986.

Grey, Zane. "Inside Baseball" in *Baseball Magazine*, 3(4), 1909.

Hall, Donald. *Fathers Playing Catch with Sons*. San Francisco: North Point Press, 1985.

Hantover, Jeffrey P. "The Boy Scouts and the Validation of Masculinity" in *The American Man* (Elizabeth Pleck and Joseph Pleck, eds.) Englewood Cliffs, NJ: Prentice-Hall, 1980.

Hargreaves, John. *Sport, Power and Culture*. New York: St. Martin's Press, 1986.

Hartman, Mary. "Sexual Crack-Up: The Role of Gender in Western History," unpublished paper, Rutgers University, 1984.

Jackson, Kenneth. *Crabgrass Frontier: The Suburbs in American History*. New York: Oxford University Press, 1985.

Kimmel, Michael. "Men's Responses to Feminism at the Turn of the Century" in *Gender & Society*, 1(3), 1987.

Kirk, William. "Shall We Have Sunday Baseball" in *Baseball Magazine*, 1(3), 1908.

"Know Baseball, Know the American" in *American Magazine*, 76, September, 1913.

Macleod, David. *Building Character in the American Boy: The Boy Scouts, YMCA, and Their Forerunners, 1870–1920*. Madison, WI: University of Wisconsin Press, 1983.

McKeever, William. *Training the Boy*. New York: Macmillan, 1913.

McLoughlin, William G. *Billy Sunday Was His Real Name*. Chicago: University of Chicago Press, 1955.

Mrozek, Donald J. *Sport and American Mentality*. Knoxville, TN: University of Tennessee Press, 1983.

Murphy, Charles. "Taft, the Fan" in *Baseball Magazine*, 9(3), 1912.

Rogin, Michael. *Fathers and Children*. New York: Pantheon, 1975.

Roszak, Theodore and Betty Roszak. *Masculine/Feminine*. New York: Harper and Row, 1975.

Sabo, Donald and Ross Runfola, eds. *Jock: Sports and Male Identity*. Englewood Cliffs, NJ: Prentice-Hall, 1980.

Sawyer, Rev. Roland D. "The Larger Side of Baseball" in *Baseball Magazine*, 1(6), 1908.

Spalding, Albert. *America's National Game*. New York: American Sports Publishing Company, 1911.

Thompson, Maurice. "Vigorous Men, A Vigorous Nation" in *Independent*, 1 September 1898.

Veblen, Thorstein. *The Theory of the Leisure Class*. New York: Funk and Wagnalls, 1899.

Wright, Frank Lloyd. *The Future of Architecture*. New York: Dover, 1970.

Working at the Ballpark

An Ethnographic Study

by Nick Trujillo

Although most fans go to baseball games during their leisure hours to "play," literally thousands of others go to the ballpark to work. And while fans naturally focus on the players on the field, the many nonplaying personnel—including ushers, vendors, announcers, security guards, clubhouse managers, cleanup crews, and countless others—work the stands, suites, and inner sanctums of the stadium. Few pay attention to these mostly invisible workers, but professional baseball would not be possible without them.

This chapter reports the findings of a long-term ethnographic study of ballpark workers in one particular baseball stadium—the Texas Rangers' Arlington Stadium.[1] It begins with an overview of some distinguishing characteristics of work in major league baseball, then examines three key dimensions of ballpark work during the season. It concludes with a discussion of different interpretations of baseball as experienced by those who work at the park. Although this study was conducted in one particular stadium, it examines phenomena enacted in every ballpark each season.

Working in Baseball: Some Distinguishing Characteristics

In some ways, baseball franchises are like other privately owned American organizations, especially those in entertainment and leisure industries. Each franchise has a product (e.g., baseball) and divisions such as research and development (e.g., scouting and minor league instruction), marketing (including advertising and public relations), accounting and finance, and others. So, too, each franchise administers employee payrolls, operating budgets, purchase orders, pension plans, and capital expenditures. And full-time employees work twelve months a year with a two-week (though nonsummer) vacation.

However, there are several features of baseball franchises that make them unique organizations in American society.[2] A sports franchise is perceived not as another bank or department store in the area but as a community institution which engenders a powerful sense of identification (see Lipsky, Novak). Residents consider the team to be "their" team, even though their team is owned by wealthy capitalists who often exercise rigid and unpopular control (e.g., George Steinbrenner). As Margaret Duncan put it, "team loyalties developed over the course of many years provide spectators with a sense of roots, of stability often missing in industrial America" (32).[3] Thus, the Rangers' employee handbook begins with a message from the owner that "our franchise is a 'public trust,' and we want our fans to adopt the Rangers as their team"; this message is also presented in employee orientations.

The perceived status of a franchise as a "public trust"—and the realized status of baseball as our "national pastime"—also engenders a powerful sense of identification for employees. In every franchise, there are so-called "Mr. Baseball" folks who have been in baseball their entire lives—such as the Rangers' special assistant to the president (Bobby Bragan), clubhouse manager (Joe Macko), and spring training director (John Welaj), all of whom started as players and have been in baseball for more than 50 years. But other full-time and part-time employees—many of whom grew up fantasizing about playing major league baseball—also experience a special identification with baseball. As the Rangers' assistant director of media relations disclosed: "When I was about 11 years old, I went to the Hall of Fame and saw an exhibit of Championship rings. That's why I'm working here today, to get one of those rings. I knew I couldn't get one playing but I discovered there was another way." Or, as one part-time security guard put it: "I work eight hours a day in another job but I still get to the ballpark early. This is the only job I've had in over 20 years where I come early."

A sports franchise is also "public" in the sense that it is featured daily in newspapers and on news broadcasts. The Dallas–Fort Worth area has three major dailies, each of which has one or two reporters whose *only* beat is the Texas Rangers Baseball Club. This media attention has positive and negative consequences, often depending on the team's won–loss record. On the *positive* side, the media generate awareness of and interest in games, players, and even promotion items and help the franchise keep a high profile in the community. And as the Rangers' controller explained: "It's nice to work for a high profile organization. When I meet someone on the street and say I'm the controller for the Rangers, they get excited. That's nice. Even though you do the same kind of work, because you're with the Rangers as opposed to ABC Manufacturing, you get instant credibility."

On the *negative* side, sportswriters and columnists also criticize the franchise, especially when the team is down in the standings. Columnists can be quite abusive, scrutinizing every move that is made on and off the field. Unfortunately for the Rangers, some of their past moves—such as the infamous trade of pitching prospects Ron Darling and Walt Terrell for Lee Mazzilli in 1981—did not engender positive coverage. Ranger headlines in years past have included such gems as "Arlington Hillbillies at it again" and "Note to Ranger brass: Losers usually get fired." When Tom Grieve was named general manager in 1984 and hired his previous secretary and fired the previous GM's secretary—a move which occurs in corporate America without notice every day—one writer described the firing as "unnecessarily mean" and said it was another example of "Ranger mismanagement."

Third, the high visibility of and community identification with a baseball franchise poses certain difficulties for franchise employees. Obviously, everyone wants tickets. As one front office employee joked: "You get a lot of people calling you up for tickets. You have to learn to just say no, just like drugs." Others ask for special favors, such as visiting the clubhouse before a game or getting kids in the dugout during a game, both of which are against club and league policy. Outsiders also believe that employees have inside knowledge of player transactions. For example, during the winter of 1987, the Rangers' director of promotions said:

> One of my sponsors called and asked if we're going to sign [free agent] Bob Horner. Well, I didn't even know we were talking to Bob Horner. The guy said, "Come on, you can tell me." People don't understand that I find out about Bob Horner the same way they do—I read it in the newspaper. I love to talk baseball with them but I simply don't have that kind of information.

Finally, there is *the baseball season*. Although many companies have seasonal variations such as financial quarters and pre-Christmas deadlines, there is nothing quite like the season. Hundreds of part-time employees, of course, work only during the season, and they adjust their personal schedules to fit the team's schedule. But even for full-time employees in the front office, the season is a fundamentally different time of year.

There are, of course, duties to perform during the "off-season" such as players to sign and trade, press releases to announce the signings and tradings, winter banquets to organize, promotion schedules to arrange, speaking engagements to perform, fantasy camps to realize, budgets to prepare, ballpark pipes to winterize, and season tickets to sell, sell, sell. And since Ranger players hold winter practice each year at the stadium, there is natural grass to keep in shape and clubhouse laundry to wash and equipment to manage.

As the season approaches, there is job interviewing and training to conduct, especially for the hundreds of part-timers who work the games. The stadium manager and his staff train toll booth operators and ticket takers how to smile at fans and count money (and vice versa). The food services GM and his staff school stand workers about the art (or science?) of making Texas nachos. The head of stadium security teaches in-house guards how to talk in ten-dash codes. The director of parking tutors lot attendants on the illocutionary movements of traffic flow. And, finally, they are ready for the baseball season to begin.

However, once the season begins, baseball is their life. As the Rangers' stadium manager explained:

> From March first until the end of the season, my life *is* the Texas Rangers. On game days, I work a minimum of 14 hours per day. This year [1987] we have ball games for the first three weekends in May so I'll go the entire month without a day off. Then when the season ends, it just stops. You still have duties but there's nothing pressing that has to be done right now. You can't imagine what this does to your personal life. It takes me about a month to get back into my hobbies and get my golf game back in shape. And about the time I finally get back to normal, the season is right around the corner. I know this has caused some problems with a couple of girlfriends [he chuckles] who have a hard time understanding how I could be so free in the winter when I can take off to now in March when time is so valuable.

The baseball season is indeed unique. As Thomas Boswell, quoting former Orioles' manager Earl Weaver, quipped: "This ain't a football game. We do this every day" (3). The next section of this chapter examines some of the every (game) day realities of ballpark work.

Working at the Ballpark: Three Key Dimensions

This section examines a lineup of ballpark workers including ushers, food vendors, parking lot attendants, security guards, special event performers (including the Chicken), cleanup crews, the Diamond

Vision crew, beat reporters, TV news sportscasters, and live TV crews. Obviously, these workers have unique tasks as their titles imply. However, three key elements of ballpark work cut across individual workers: 1) their visibility in the ballpark, (2) their attentiveness to the game, and 3) their effect on the fans' ballpark experience.

"Oh Say Can You See Me": Worker Visibility in the Ballpark

Some ballpark workers—including clubhouse personnel in locker rooms, reporters and sportscasters in press boxes, TV crews in the truck, the crew in the Diamond Vision room, and others—perform their duties *backstage,* invisible to the crowd in the stands. Perhaps the least visible workers are the cleanup crews who pick up trash in an empty stadium after the game, yet who directly affect the fans' ballpark experience. This section focuses on workers who are highly visible and on those who vary their visibility.

Fowl balls and Vendor Comics on Center Stage

The most visible ballpark workers are special event performers such as singers of the national anthem—Charlie Pride is an opening night favorite—and various bands, drill teams, mascots, and first-pitch celebrities. (Tom Landry was a hit on opening night 1989, despite his one-hop throw to the plate.) But as A's pitcher Storm Davis took his warm-ups in June 1987, one unique and very visible visitor performed at the park. That visiting worker was a chicken.

Of course, this was no ordinary poultry. This was the hyperkinetic six-figure "Famous Chicken" who earns his fees by violating every rule of ballpark conduct. On that night, for example, he did a hat dance in the first base coaching box and unceremoniously smashed an A's cap; he ate a warm-up ball taken from shortstop Walt Weiss and discharged two smaller fowl balls from his tail; he held up a pin-up poster of a scantily clad woman (or "chick"?) to distract Davis as he warmed up; and he invited a vendor onto the field to dance, only to throw the vendor's peanuts into the stands behind his back. Perhaps most irreverently, he taught a group of five chicklets—kids of Ranger personnel who were dressed in little chicken suits—how to break wind symbolically on the home plate umpire.

As the crowd applauded every violation of ballpark rules, I wondered how the *children* in the audience interpreted the show. The moralist in me wondered if kids were learning it is acceptable to break rules and abuse authorities if you dress in a costume. The libertarian in me applauded the chicken as a uniquely American entrepreneur who had the right to market himself as a cartoon character, providing comic relief while earning a relatively honest buck. Ultimately, the ethnographer in me decided that both interpretations were plausible and I took more field notes. The chicken's antics do indeed constitute an unusual and visible form of ballpark work.

The roving food and drink vendors in the stands are a group of everyday ballpark workers who also enact visible—though far less dramatic and comedic—performances. Yet, as the personnel director of ARA Services which runs concessions put it, these workers also must be performers: "You have to be a special breed to work the stands. You need to be outgoing and assertive and you need to be a bit of a ham and a stand-up comic."

One roving vendor in the outfield during a dull White Sox game in June 1988 enacted one comedic performance when he served as a walking advertisement throughout the night with a good-natured script: "Peanuts, cotton candy, popcorn . . . Yes, folks, we've got it all. We're ARA, servicing the needs of the fans." Another revealed his (darker) comedic talents during the Rangers' first July rain-out in history in 1989 when ferocious winds swayed light poles and torrential rains saturated the stands; as cold, soaked fans went running toward the concourse for cover, the drenched vendor proclaimed, "Cold beer here, get your cold beer here." Although vendors are not as outrageous as the Chicken, they also must position themselves as visible public characters in order to enjoy personal (and organizationzal) success.

Varying Visibility: Redcoats and Ballpark Blues

At least two sets of workers—ushers and security guards—manage their visibility in the park, sometimes drawing explicit attention to themselves and at other times remaining invisible in the background. These workers vary their impressions of visibility by managing their mobility in the park.

As the Rangers' usher supervisor described, ushers—or "redcoats" as they are called because of their red uniform shirts—are responsible for directing fans to their seats, answering questions (most about locations of restrooms or how to get player autographs), checking on the condition of fans who catch (but usually miss) foul balls, keeping pedestrian traffic flowing, and monitoring the crowd for potential fights and intoxication. These tasks require the ushers to be mobile in the stands, and in their orientation they are instructed to descend to the railing between innings and face the fans, scanning the crowd for disturbances and making eye contact to ensure the fans see them. Ushers also must be assertive yet courteous with fans who are hard to control, enacting what Erich Fromm might have called a "commercialized friendliness" (242–243). Indeed, the toughest job is performed by the redcoat behind the crowded home plate area who must keep onlookers behind the red line on the pavement that parallels the walls and who must keep fans from bottlenecking as they return with their beers. As she put it: "It gets hard because you have to keep people there but you don't want to be a witch. We'll put a sign up but they'll still stand in front."

The second group of workers who manage their visibility in the ballpark are the 30–50 in-house security guards who neither carry guns nor have the power to make an arrest, and the smaller squad of city police officers who do carry such force and power. These ballpark blues are coordinated by the head of security, who sits with his assistant and the stadium manager in the "Command Post," a small upper deck suite with a view of the entire stadium.

Arlington Stadium has one of the lowest ejection and arrest records in baseball, a result of the low crime suburban area in which the stadium is located and the low-key philosophy that is instilled in job training sessions. Thus, most of the incidents to which guards respond are mundane—keys locked in parked cars, upper deck fans throwing ice on season-ticket holders. However, like police forces in any town, stadium security must be ready and able to respond to a potential incident at any moment.

One incident occurred during a Friday night game in May 1988 against, naturally, the Yankees. With an early Ranger lead and cool temperatures, the Command Post was quiet as the head of security and his colleagues responded to minor incidents, enjoyed the game, and took a few curious glances—via the ever-present binoculars—at George Steinbrenner who was with then-owner Eddie Chiles in his suite. But, suddenly, in the top of the seventh, as the Yankees began a rally, Don Mattingly took a decidedly bad pitch that was called strike two. Mattingly complained bitterly, then swung at a worse offering for strike three. As Mattingly yelled at the home plate ump, Yankee manager Billy Martin blazed out of the dugout, offering his perfunctory ritual of umpire dirt-kicking and accepting his perfunctory ejection. For fans it was fun to watch, but for the Command Post, it was time for action.

"Code green at the visitors' dugout," blared the head of security into the mike, watching the area behind the Yankee dugout as fans launched verbal assaults at Martin. Several guards appeared from nowhere and stood on the Yankee dugout, arms crossed rigidly over their chests and heads facing toward the crowd, just as they were trained. As Martin disappeared safely, if frustratedly, into the dugout, the blue-shirts disappeared into the shadows of the stadium. The Command Post had controlled another potential incident by coordinating the mobile—and momentarily very visible—security force.[4]

All in all, the management of mobility and visibility by ushers and security guards defuses most incidents before they heat up. As the head of security boasted, "We can be invisible or make it look like there are thousands of us out there, depending on the situation." Paradoxically, he interprets invisibility as a sign of job success and says that "when someone comes up and says that he didn't see any security guards at the game, I take it as a compliment and tell him thank you."

"What's the Score?": Attending to the Game on the Field

A second element of ballpark work that cuts across various employees is the extent to which they attend to (and understand) the game on the field. Once again, some workers attend to every pitch and play while others are too busy with tasks or are located in areas where they cannot watch the game; others vary their focus on their work and on the field. We begin with workers who watch the game closely but who see it through different lenses.

Producing Plays, Charting Pitches, Announcing At-Bats, and Reporting Games

The workers who focus on the game most intensely are the radio and TV play-by-play announcers and support crews who produce live coverage. The radio and TV announcers, for example, describe each and every action, from *pitch to putout,* and offer nonstop commentary throughout the game, revealing their knowledge about baseball in general and Ranger baseball in particular. But while the play-by-play announcers experience the game in conversational turns of varying degrees of excitement depending on the play, the director and his crew in the truck experience the game in quick, visually-oriented decisions. The director coordinates the show, orchestrating live shots, replays, and graphics with alarming speed and amazing grace: "Ready five—take five—CHYRON in—wipe it—ready four—take four—clean—two—three—ready A—slide in A—freeze it—dissolve. . . . Beautiful, people!"

On the other hand, while the radio and TV crews pay attention to the game from pitch to putout, one worker sits behind home plate with a radar gun, charting the game *pitch-by-pitch* for the Rangers' "Performance Analysis System." He charts each pitch to each home and visiting player for speed, type, location, and result and, thus, he experiences baseball with a focused eye on the A.L. pitchers and their capacity to throw heat. He now uses the "Jugs Supergun II," though he prefers the more conservative "Ragun" he used when he first charted for the Rangers. During games when Nolan Ryan pitches, he also relays the pitch-by-pitch bullets to the sound guy in the TV truck for their "Ryan Radar" inserts during live coverage, as well as to nearby fans who yell (at all games) "How fast was that one?"[5]

The Diamond Vision (DV) control room is an eight-person operation managed by the DV producer (who is also the announcer) and the DV director (who is also the director of promotions). Everyone has a range of duties to perform including announcing, selecting crowd shots from the in-house cameras, taping replays, updating stats, packaging greetings, and updating league scores off the wire. Although the crew attends to every pitch and every play—especially the scoreboard operator, who updates the count—the *at-bat* and the *half-inning* are the meaningful reference units for these workers. During each *at-bat,* for example, the announcer introduces the batter and plays a pre-recorded "organ chop" or other mass-mediated rally cry, the crew generates an electronic page or two of player stats, and the director replays a videotaped highlight of an exciting hit or catch; the routine begins anew with the next at-bat. During each *half-inning* break, then, the DV crew selects and runs the appropriate song (e.g., "Cotton-Eyed Joe" during the seventh inning stretch—this is Texas!), feature (e.g., the sixth inning "Dot Race"), or, in the (post)Ueberroth era of marketing, commercial (e.g., the "IBM Tale of the Tape" and even a network commercial or two).

Finally, newspaper beat writers in the main press box also see the game pitch-by-pitch and play-by-play, but their ultimate unit of analysis is the *game.* After all, they must write the story for the paper, summarizing the plays and pitches and placing the game in a broader perspective. Toward this end, all of the writers score the games—some in their personalized leather-bound game books—and virtually all of them offer commentary and metacommentary—most of it rather sarcastic—throughout the game. After the game, they leave the press box to get quotes from players in the locker room to include in their stories for the next available edition of their papers; they have already fed an early summary of the game, minus quotes, for early editions.

They return to the press box and stay until midnight, working the deadlined oil to complete their stories for last editions.

"Who's on First?" They Don't Know. (But Do They Care?).

A variety of other workers pay little attention to the game because of their job activities or location in the ballpark. For example, most food and drink stands are located in tunnels or on the concourse with restricted or nonexistent views of the field. Many parking lot kids remain in the parking lot, getting the cars in before the game and getting them out during and after the game. Some security guards are stationed outside the stadium, keeping the gates safe from fans who would sneak in. One guard, whose regular position is outside the center field gate underneath the bleachers, can hear the crack of the bat and the roar of the crowd, yet he never sees a single play; instead he listens to the game on the $1.99 AM radio he bought at a thrift shop. For these employees, working at the ballpark does not mean watching ball games. Although some newcomers ill-advisedly apply for jobs so they can watch games, the work can be a disappointing awakening, prompting some—especially the younger parking lot kids—to "retire" after a few weeks because of their lack of (watching) playing time.

Of course, there are some ballpark workers who *choose not* to watch games, such as a minority of parking lot kids, program sellers, or Texas Ranger Ladies Club volunteers who hand out promotion items. Others—like TV sportscasters, who sometimes do their nightly sportscast from the auxiliary box with the field as a backdrop for the report—arrive late for the game and leave early. For example, on one Saturday night in 1988 against Kansas City, the weekend sports anchor from one local affiliate primped himself with his makeup kit as he readied his report of a 6–3 Ranger lead in the ninth inning as Dale Mohorcic tried to save the game for Texas. He arrived at the game in the sixth inning, plenty of time to familiarize himself with the few game details he would highlight. He began his sportscast by noting the 6–3 Texas lead for the viewers before leading to scores and videotaped highlights. But he left the air with two outs and, much to his dismay, the game ended moments after he signed off, prompting a groan to the cameraman: "Damn, if we finish five minutes ago, we beat the traffic."

Finally, ushers, security guards, vendors, and others vary their focus on the game. Their attention is directed to fans in the stands more than actions on the field, yet they respond to certain field actions

such as Billy Martin's dirt-kicking noted earlier. They also attend to
the later innings as the game approaches the eighth inning, the point
at which all beer sales cease—a time for beer vendors to shut down the
kegs and for security to monitor the beer stands. And, quite naturally,
they turn their heads instinctively when they hear the crack of the bat
and enjoy the game during work breaks or when their tasks are
complete.

"What a Nice (Clean) Ballpark": The Impact on the Fans' Experience

Workers in the invisible and inaccessible sanctums, such as clubhouse
personnel in locker rooms, reporters and sportscasters in press boxes,
TV crews in trucks, and announcers in booths, have little or no impact
on the fans' experience. Others have direct impact and varying
effects.

Serving Peanuts and Cleaning Up Peanut Shells

The comic vendors in the stands and the sober concessionaires on the
concourse are crucial to the fans' enjoyment of the game, not because
of how they work but because of what they provide. As Stanton
Delaplane quipped some time ago, "The most important thing about
baseball is the hot dog" (91). In Arlington Stadium, add nachos to the
list and, of course, beer. Indeed, beer sales at the ballpark are consistent and voluminous. In an average six-day period, for example, ARA
will sell 121,000 large beers and pour 10,000 kegs of beer. Such
popularity creates definite security and liability concerns and has
prompted several decisions by ARA and Ranger management including: 1) the termination of beer sales at 10:00 p.m. or after the eighth
inning, whichever comes first; 2) the addition of two non-alcohol
sections, a move adopted by other stadia as well; 3) special major
league "TEAM"—"Techniques for Effective Alcohol Management"—
training in organization; and 4) the use of different colored cups for
beer and soft drinks to monitor minors' purchases.

Food services personnel reflect the tastes of fans in their selections of foods and drinks and then shape fans' experiences by serving
these and other selections. They also influence the fans by intoxicating
them at appropriate levels while, at the same time, monitoring inap-
propriate intoxication.

The cleanup crew also has a direct, if unnoticed, impact on fans.
The crew is comprised of about 40–50 low-income and mostly minority workers who are rounded up by a local labor company for a few

hours' work. They are a tattered lot in frayed jeans who literally crawl across the stands, pitching major league trash into their bags amidst' minor league smells. Crew chiefs prod stragglers to quicken the pace to make way for backpacked blowers who corral the shells and slop into the aisles where it is bagged, dragged to the top of the stairs, and hauled away by suitably banged-up trucks. The ritual is complete when seats are hosed down the following morning.

The post-game cleanup activities offer an eerie contrast to the game-time acts. During the game, the ballpark is alive with fresh smells and a brightly lit stage for the graceful performances of (mostly) shapely ball players who receive musical accompaniment from the DV crew and lively ovations from the audience. After the game, the stadium shrouds a dingy procession of shadowy caricatures who stoop awkwardly in empty stands to the background wheezing of congested airblowers.

As one of the workers walked by that night, I smiled and asked naively, "How's it goin'?" The worker, a disheveled white male about 50 years old, ignored the naivete of the question and smiled a simple but eloquent answer, "I've been better." A few minutes later he ate peanuts from an abandoned bag that had been tossed on the ground an hour earlier. No doubt he had indeed seen better days. For this man and his fellow temps, the ballpark is unmistakably a place for work and not for play. Although few fans see the work of these minimum-wage masses, they have a direct impact, revealed when fans casually remark, "What a nice clean ballpark!"

Enhancing the Fans with Bats, Gloves, and Auto Shades

While the cleanup crew has a direct, if unnoticed, effect on the fans' ballpark experience, the promotions personnel—or, more accurately, the promotion items—have an indirect but more noticeable effect on their experience. Promotion items are handed out quietly by the mostly white-haired volunteers from the Texas Rangers Ladies Club to fans as they enter the park. These items are auxiliary paraphernalia which have an indirect effect on the fans' decisions to attend games and on their ballpark experience. As the director of promotions humbly explained: "You sometimes think your cap night is drawing more fans than the product on the field, and that's just not the case. People aren't coming unless you have that product on the field. And your cap night is just enhancing what's on the field."

On rare occasions, however, promotions appear to do more than indirectly "enhance what's happening on the field." Every now and then, a promotion seems to influence the actions on the field. For example, bat night has a profound impact—mostly on the eardrums—as all kids 13 and under receive bats and pound them mercilessly during the game, creating a thunderingly effective rally cry for the home team. A most impressive use of ballpark promotions, however, came in the sixth inning of a June, 1988 game against Oakland. As the A's continued a two-out rally, the auto shades sponsored by a rent-a-car company and the Rangers entered the game when *everyone* in the outfield bleachers lifted their shades in the air; soon, *everyone* in the infield section followed. Rookie reliever Jose Ceceña, apparently pumped up by the awesomely visible show of support, got Dave Henderson, apparently shaken by the demonstration, to hit into a 3–6 putout. The display was so powerful that one reporter gave the crowd "an assist with the impromptu destruction of Henderson's concentration," adding: "Hundreds, if not thousands, of the white, rectangular car shades that fans had been given began to be held up in the outfield bleachers, presumably to affect Henderson's vision or concentration. They were waved in a manner normally seen behind basketball backboards, and may have had the desired effect."[6]

Interpreting (the Work of) Baseball

The last section examines three key dimensions related to the job performance of ballpark workers by revealing how these workers interpret baseball and the ballpark. Five separate meanings are considered, including baseball: 1) as business, 2) as theater, 3) as fountain of youth(s), 4) as arena for relationships, and 5) as place for storytelling.

Baseball as Business: Stadium Per Capitas and Supplemental Salaries

While baseball laureates such as Roger Angell and W. P. Kinsella enrich our lives with the pastoral pleasures of our national pastime, many employees see baseball as a business and the ballpark as a revenue generator. We attribute such economic visions to front office managers who balance the franchise bottom-lines. And as the Rangers' controller explained:

> You can look at how the bottom-line is going by looking at the stands. The only real variable is game-related income. Our national TV contracts are fixed. Our local TV and radio is fixed until their terms are up. Our advertising is not going to vary much year-to-

year. The thing that makes or breaks the bottom-line is the variable component which is the fans coming to the ballpark to buy tickets, parking, concessions, and novelties.

But front office managers interpret the fans in the stands from a *per capita* perspective—as do the ARA managers who run the food and drink concessions. As the Rangers' former president explained:

> Essentially, the per capita for ticket sales is the gross gate, minus the amusement tax, visitors' share, and league share, divided by the number of people who purchase tickets. Our per capita is next to the lowest in the American League because we have so few high-priced premium seats. Fifty-six percent of the demand is for 8,851 field box seats and the outfield has about 18,900 general admission seats with very little demand. If we draw 1.7 million, that means roughly 950,000 people want to sit in 8,000 seats. Rounding it off, 8,000 times 80 games becomes 640,000 available seats and 950,000 requests. So we're 300,000 premium seats short. That's $3 million gross that we leave on the table. As player costs increase—we could soon be looking at four new millionaires—the capacity of that stadium to generate revenue is limiting to the point where in the mid-1990s, we'll have to draw 2.7, 2.8 million fans to break even. That means a World Series. It's not a good idea to go into a season saying you have to go to the World Series to break even at the bottom line.[7]

Not surprisingly, then, the new Ranger ownership—a group of investors led by George W. Bush (the president's son)—is studying the issue of new stadium sites. And, not surprisingly, published speculation by Dallas officials who want the team to move from Arlington to Dallas has resulted in "stadium wars," as one headline put it, since a ballpark means serious revenue for the city and county in which it is located, as well.

Of course, the economic interpretation of baseball and ballparks is not limited to high ranking front office and city officials. Indeed, many part-timers punch in at the ballpark clock not for the glory of the game but to pocket the bimonthly paycheck. Many retired folks work at the park to supplement their pensions, while some public school teachers work there to earn social security benefits that are excluded from their retirement packages. Others work there simply for extra money. One security guard confessed: "I don't even like baseball. I'm a football man. But I need the money." Ironically, one police officer works at the ballpark to earn money to support the travel expenses he incurs with his softball team.

Baseball as Theater: Staging the "Show"

As Norm Hitzges, the commentator during live TV coverage, readied himself for the camera before his pre-game TV talk show in July, 1989, new owner George W. Bush stuck his head in the well air-conditioned booth for a quick hello. Bush greeted Hitzges warmly, then joked, "You know, you're running up a huge electricity bill in here with that air conditioning cranked up so high." Hitzges smiled and said, "Yeah, we are, but there's nothing worse than sweat on TV."

Although casual and good-natured, this episode reveals how different individuals interpret organizational life at the ballpark. While Bush is no doubt less concerned about the electric bill from Hitzges' studio booth and more concerned with the per capita considerations noted earlier, Hitzges' amusing reply reveals his concern about on-camera presence and suggests that his ballpark booth is a stage for a TV show.

Of course, the stadium is a theater for many ballpark actors, a view that invites dramatistic considerations by baseball analysts (see Combs and Mansfield, Duncan, Goffman). Some workers are "front-stage" performers who enact comedies or dramas for viewing audiences, while others are "backstage" helpers who move props or service audiences but who stay out of sight. For example, the Chicken entertains fans with gags in costume while comic vendors entertain them with bags (of peanuts) in uniforms; the Diamond Vision crew infotains them with stats and songs. And ushers, security guards, parking lot kids, and cleanup crews offer backstage support. As one police officer aptly summarized—no doubt after seeing the movie *Bull Durham:* "They call the major leagues 'the show.' "[8]

Baseball as Fountain of Youth(s)

The ballpark is a domain of youths. There is the smack of hope in gloves brought by little league boys and girls (and a few middle-aged leaguers) who have faith that this may be the season for that foul ball. There are the mostly innocent autograph seekers who ask "Mr. Incaviglia" or "Mr. Witt"—relative youths themselves—for their treasured signatures.[9] And, most strikingly, there was little Jessica McClure— the Midland, Texas, toddler who was rescued from an abandoned well in 1987 after a 58-hour mass-mediated ordeal—who enacted a delightful irony as she sat on the steps of the Ranger dugout before she threw out the first pitch in 1988, playing very soft toss with moon-struck major league stars.

Ballpark workers, too, reveal this youth. There are teen-aged parking lot attendants and program sellers who fall in love despite the parental cautions of supervisors during employee orientation, and who ultimately came of age during their summers of 1988 and 1989. There are kids of coaches and trainers who serve as batboys and clubhouse hands and who literally grow up in the ballpark. Not surprisingly, then, older workers experience their own youth vicariously as they interact with these youngsters and re-enact their glory days. The supervisor of the parking lot kids, for example, shared a recurring dream during a rain delay in May 1989: "I have this dream where I'm dressed in a baseball uniform and I'm batting at home plate. Only the plate is in the parking lot and I'm 16 again, just like the other kids out there." As the spring training director, who is now 75 years old (and quasi-retired), put it: "How can I retire from the ballpark? It keeps me young."

In an oft-quoted passage—one that is even used in the Hall of Fame's video presentation in the new east wing—Roger Angell writes: "Since baseball time is measured only in outs, all you have to do is succeed utterly; keep hitting, keep the rally alive, and you have defeated time. You remain forever young" (25). Actually, rallies come and go. It is the ballpark that keeps fans (and workers) forever young.

Baseball as Arena for Relationships

Ballparks are places where families and friends go on outings and dates. One tour of the tailgate parties in the parking lot suggests that this is a place where families and friends get together to have fun. And, as the director of promotions put it: "From a pure marketing standpoint, it's just got to be fun for a guy to bring his family to the ballpark and have a good time. The music is upbeat, there is the dot race, and they might get a pennant or a ball when they go through the gate."

But the ballpark is also designed to be fun and upbeat for the workers, who develop special friendships that are rekindled at the yearly reunions known officially as employee orientations. As the stadium manager explained:

> We operate under the philosophy that this job has to be fun.
> Nobody is going to get rich out here on a part-time basis. So we try
> to have extracurricular activities like softball games and barbeques
> and form a union with these people. We've got several couples who
> met out here—one couple even got married at home plate.[10]

In short, the interpersonal networks in ballparks are loosely coupled as workers interact in the ballpark with others whom they know on a first name (and a memorized phone or radio number) basis.

On the other hand, from an organizational systems perspective, front offices—like their respective teams on the field—are comprised of relatively autonomous individuals who perform relatively autonomous tasks. For example, even though the Rangers' front office is leaner than most others inasmuch as full-timers wear multiple hats, the franchise is organized into fairly autonomous departments that share limited types of information. As the Rangers' controller—the same person who designs their computer systems—explained:

> There's obviously a need to communicate across departments, but from a systems perspective, accounting, baseball, the ticket office, stadium operations, and field operations are autonomous and don't need to share information. For example, there's no need for the ticket office to have access to the baseball information. So when the lease of our computer system ends, we may get several autonomous systems because there is no need to share that much information.

One special joy of the controller, treasurer, and other financial managers in the front office is their unique opportunity to view the franchise holistically and to understand how all the various informational pieces come together. But it is an opportunity that few full-timers, and virtually no part-timers, experience.

Baseball as Place—or Base—for Storytelling

Scholars from a variety of disciplines agree that storytelling is a powerful vehicle for constructing a sense of place, identity, and history, and for sharing these senses with others (see Bauman, Georges, Turner). And the power of storytelling may be nowhere more apparent than in baseball. As Thomas Boswell wrote: "Conversation is the blood of baseball. It flows through the game, an invigorating system of anecdotes. Ball players are tale tellers who have polished their malarky and winnowed their wisdom for years. The Homeric knack has nothing to do with hitting the long ball" (3).

This "Homeric knack," of course, is not confined to the batting cage (or, for that matter, the luncheon circuit). Indeed, stadium workers share a wide variety of stories, ranging from amusing anecdotes—such as the stadium operations secretary's story about the ladies who saw three "K"s in the outfield during a Nolan Ryan outing and complained that the Ku Klux Klan was demonstrating—to the personal legends of old-timers—such as Bobby Bragan's stories about his initial rejection but ultimate acceptance of teammate Jackie Robinson and his later discovery of minor league shortstop Maury Wills. These and other baseball stories embellish the identities of particular individuals and events but, more importantly, they unite workers of varying ages and races as these workers share in the ongoing narrative drama of the season and add to the oral history of the ballpark.

Baseball and American Culture

> *"Whoever wants to know the heart and mind of America had better learn baseball . . ."*
> Jacques Barzun

Although a variety of sports may reflect and reaffirm cultural values, most observers regard baseball as especially emblematic of American society (see Reiss, Trujillo & Ekdom, Voight, Warshay). For example, Reiss reported that in its early years, baseball was regarded "second only to the public schools as a teacher of American values" (25). Indeed, despite recent changes in the game, baseball continues to be a strong institution for affirming and reaffirming such ideas and ideals as hard work, success, teamwork, individualism, and tradition. And the ballpark is the special place where these and other values are brought to fruition by players and workers alike.

However, the ballpark also reveals other aspects of American society such as class differences and worker stratification. In most ballparks, rich VIPs eat in fancy stadium restaurants served by beautiful waitresses, while season ticket holders in the stands are served by relatively diplomatic vendors. Everyday fans stand in lines to get concessions served by workers who are reminded to bathe and to use deodorant, while the bluest-collar families sit in cheap outfield seats and bring their own food to the game. So, too, players in bright baseball uniforms make guaranteed millions regardless of performance, while part-time workers in red coats or blue shirts punch in time clocks and hope for extra innings to get overtime pay; and lowest class minorities are brought in to clean the park, after hours, for minimum wage. In these and other ways, American ballparks reflect what is good and bad about American society.

This chapter has examined life in the ballpark from the perspectives of the employees who work there whether the team wins or loses. For these workers, it's not whether they win or lose, it's how you work the games. Obviously, the work is more enjoyable when the team is winning because attendance is up (which means sales are up and bonuses may follow), the fans are happier (which means less trouble in the stands), and the workers are prouder to identify themselves as members of the franchise. When the team is losing, workers must, somewhat paradoxically, manage happier faces and enact exaggerated sociabilities in order to satisfy fans, who are inclined to be petulant about the losing product regardless of the winning service. It is a challenge, indeed, and it is one that goes virtually unnoticed and entirely unheralded.

Notes

1. The author conducted interviews with and observations of Ranger personnel for more than two years (October 1987 to January, 1990), covering over 500 hours of field work. Most of the formal interviews with front office personnel were conducted during the off-seasons, though informal interviews were also conducted during observational periods at the ballpark. During the season, the author observed most of the ballpark workers first-hand, sitting or walking with them in their work areas. The author also attended some games as a "mere" fan; in those cases, he chatted informally with nearby fans and vendors and observed the actions of other stadium workers with his binoculars. He thanks the management of the Texas Rangers, especially President Mike Stone, for permission to study the franchise.

2. One set of issues, indirectly related to this study, involves the baseball industry itself, an unusual industry in America, to say the least. Baseball, of course, still has an antitrust exemption, though that will, no doubt, be contested in future court cases. The unusual league structure of baseball is also unlike the corporate marketplace because while each team tries to defeat other teams on the field, the league itself is a cooperative enterprise and each franchise wants (and needs) the competitor franchises to stay in business. Finally, the commissioner is a rather unusual figure in American capitalism; one who exercises czar-like power in the league. In sum, these and other features of the baseball industry affect those who work in management positions in the front office but have few (and indirect) effects on the day-to-day (or game-to-game) activities of most people who work in baseball. For an extended discussion of these issues, see Markham and Teplitz.

3. Of course, the Rangers do not have as long or as venerable a tradition as franchises such as the Dodgers or Yankees. After all, the Rangers came to Texas in 1972—they had been the second Washington Senators—so only young adults have had the opportunity to grow up as Ranger fans. So, too, the Rangers are one of two teams of the current 26 teams—the other being the Seattle Mariners—that have never been in a play-off game. Nonetheless, the Rangers have improved in recent years with a stable management group and an improved team with free agent Nolan Ryan and .300 hitters Julio Franco and Raphael Palmeiro; indeed, after the winter meetings of 1988, which brought Ryan, Franco, and Palmeiro to the team, applications for seasonal

employment skyrocketed. So, too, the Rangers led the A.L. 1989 All-Star team (tied with Oakland) with four members (Ryan, Franco, Ruben Sierra, and Jeff Russell).

4. Later that night, Martin was punched out at a topless bar called "Lace" in a well-publicized incident. The Rangers also went on to sweep that four-game series with the Yanks for the first time ever. Not a great road trip for the Yankee skip, who was fired yet again later in that 1988 season.

5. And who's the fastest gunslinger of them all? In 1988, it was Brewer Dan Plesac with his 97 mph bullet; in 1989, two Rangers hit 97 mph (stopper Jeff Russell and rookie Kevin Brown) as did Royal's ace Bret Saberhagen.

6. Phil Rogers, "Canseco Homer KO's Rangers in 9th," *Dallas Times Herald,* (June 11, 1988). This auto shade performance of the fans was far more positive than the 1986 ball night fiasco when up to 100 fans threw their baseballs on the field in protest of a poor Ranger performance. That particular display created a hazard to Ranger players and served to embarrass the club when the "balls falling from the sky" were covered extensively by local and national sportscasters.

7. These remarks were made before the recent CBS and cable TV packages; nonetheless, the stadium remains a problematic issue for the franchise. The president said that Minnesota has the lowest per capita because of a high city tax.

8. Perhaps fittingly, Arlington Stadium was used as a background for one scene in *Bull Durham.* Remember when the young pitcher, just promoted to the show, unleashed his cliches to a female reporter in a ballpark? That was Arlington Stadium and they were on the first base side in front of the Ranger dugout.

9. Of course, some of these autograph-seeking kids are little entrepreneurs who know the monetary value of—and will use elementary school sabotage and treachery to get—a Nolan Ryan autograph.

10. Ironically, this is the stadium manager who, as quoted earlier, disclosed that some of his own romantic relationships have been disrupted because of the stadium's demands on his time during the season.

References

Angell, Roger. "The Interior Stadium." Rpt. in *The Armchair Book of Baseball II.* John Thorn, ed. New York: Charles Scribner's Sons, 1987.

Barzun, Jacques. *God's Country and Mine.* Little Brown and Company, 1954.

Bauman, Richard. *Verbal Art as Performance.* Prospect Heights, IL: Waveland, 1977.

Boswell, Thomas. *How Life Imitates the World Series.* New York: Penguin, 1983.

Combs, James E., and Michael W. Mansfield, eds. *Drama in Life: The Uses of Communication in Society.* New York: Hastings House, 1976.

Delaplane, Stanton. "The Sporting Way." Rpt. in *The Baseball Reader.* Charles Einstein, ed. New York: McGraw-Hill, (1980): 91–93.

Duncan, Hugh. *Symbols in Society.* New York: Oxford University Press, 1968.

Duncan, Margaret C. "The Symbolic Dimensions of Spectator Sport." *Quest* 35 (1983): 29–36.

Fromm, Erich. *Escape from Freedom.* New York: Rinehart, 1941.

Georges, Robert A. "Toward an Understanding of the Storytelling Event." *Journal of American Folklore* 82 (1969): 313–328.

Goffman, Erving. *The Presentation of Self in Everyday Life.* Garden City: Anchor Doubleday, 1959.

—————. *Frame Analysis.* New York: Harper and Row, 1974.

Lipsky, Richard. *Sports World: An American Dreamland.* New York: Quadrangle, 1975.

Markham, Jesse, and Paul Teplitz. *Baseball Economics and Public Policy.* Lexington, MA: Lexington, 1981.

Novak, Michael. *The Joy of Sports: End Zones, Bases, Baskets, Balls, and the Consecration of the American Spirit.* Lanham, MD: Hamilton, 1988.

Reiss, Stephen A. *Touching Base: Professional Baseball and American Culture in the Progressive Era.* Westport, CT: Greenwood, 1980.

Trujillo, Nick, and Leah R. Ekdom. "Sportswriting and American Cultural Values: The 1984 Chicago Cubs." *Critical Studies in Mass Communication* 2 (1985), 262–281.

Turner, Victor. "Social Dramas and Stories About Them." *Critical Inquiry* 7 (1980): 141–168.

Voight, David Q. *America Through Baseball.* Chicago: Nelson-Hall, 1976.

Warshay, Leon H. "Baseball in Its Social Context." *Social Approaches to Sport.* Robert M. Pankin, ed. East Brunswick, NJ: Associated University Presses, 1982. 225–282.

Shakespeare at Bat, Euclid on the Field

Etymological History of Some Terms in Baseball

by Robert Moynihan

Shakespeare at bat, Euclid on the field? Well, no, the game of baseball, relatively an historical youngster, does not trace its history to either England or to ancient Greece, nor is it as exotic as golf, a game that may trace its history to the pastime, after a meal of haggis, of Scots' hitting stones with clubs. Baseball, like the origin of its home country, is young—so young that the American founding fathers of only two-hundred years ago never played the game, nor was eighteenth-century English used in its service.

Nonetheless, if indeed "America is language" in D. W. Brogan's phrase, it is so because of its inclusive vitality and the national hunting for the new in all its experiences. The founding fathers *could have* played baseball, perhaps, during intersessions of the Constitutional Convention itself. For is not the game of baseball animated and formed through a careful balancing of opposites and rule? Isn't it a sporting reenactment of law and rule in action? Isn't there an interplay between precedent and the attack upon its forms in daily act, legal and sportive? Aren't baseball records as compulsively ordered as the keeping of legal opinions for future precedents?

But to the point of the language of the most common terms of American baseball itself—yes, we shall see if the founding fathers, abetted by earliest English printed sources, had in their possession the terms of baseball. Certainly the founders could realize that their game and its terms were a hybrid, particularly in vocabulary, formed from the two major origins of the language: the Germanic vocabulary of "Old English" or Anglo-Saxon, and the more multisyllabic, legalistic, and usually euphonious (but pompous) terms from Latin and French, reflecting not the dominance of the American Northeast over its more landlocked neighbors of the national interior, but the conquest of the Saxons and Anglos by their foreign and more Latinate victors, who imposed French–Latin as the language(s) of importance and power. The founders knew that this linguistic miscegenation gives English its typical vitality, and that the range from "high" and "low," pompous and vulgar, is itself a persistent linguistic game between the victors and the vanquished.

Now, our umpire in this imagined game is represented by John Jay, the first chief justice of the Supreme Court, and he traces the linguistic lineage of his office, as might be expected, to the "higher" etymological origins of Old French and to Latin. *Umpire* describes the agent who settles disputes between the *non-pare* or uneven, the agent who restores *par*ity or fairness on the fields, who smooths the uneven so that all play is on even ground. Taking his office of umpire, Jay knows that Shakespeare and other less-known users of English had most of the language of the game already in their possession, though not as yet all its nineteenth-century rules. George (Scoop) Washington could indeed have thrown out the very first ball in the history of the game. He could even have said "play ball." Jay could have assertively said "foul" from his position behind the "plate." Thomas (Red) Jefferson might have had a "hit" between first and second "bases," and John (Baldy) Adams might have aggressively argued with the umpire, while Ben (Lightning) Franklin measured the "diamond," or waved toward the left "field," or pointed to the "crowd" as he hit the "ball" over the "fence" to "score" and to then "come home." However, as we shall see, this game will be called for the absence of a mere word. Franklin in the 1780s could not have hit a "homer," which the *Oxford English Dictionary,* c. 1900, defines as 1) a homing pigeon or 2) as a Hebrew measure of capacity. Alas, the lexicographers were not thinking of Hank Greenberg.

But back to the imagined game. What is, of course, striking is the persistence of most of the terms in American baseball from the very origins of English itself, and the terms used in the oldest sources of English are recognizable. *Umpire* for instance, means in its oldest form "one who decides between disputants . . . and whose decision is usually accepted as final; an arbitrator." In Lydgate's 1400 translation of *Aesop's Fables,* Jay may have read that "Among these owmperis was werre none, ne stryf," and in Wyclif's 1430 commentary he found this entry: "the Apostle putte him between as a meene [distinguishing] alle her questions as a good umpire." In the 1450 *Paston Letters,* he found this quizzical but potentially operative definition: "Take ye one, and he another, and if they may not accorde, ye and I to be umpire, for we stand bothe in like cas." Unfortunately, the resulting mayhem is not recorded.

The compound term *base-ball* is itself typical of the complex sources of the English language. The origin of *base* is the Greek *basis,* "a stepping," or that "on which one steps or stands." From this source come dozens of multiply literal and figurative meanings, many of them associated or metonymic. The child's game of *base* in England is defined as "the line or limit from which the start is made in a race, or which serves as the goal for the finish." The British poet of questionable quality, Sir Richard Blackmore, whose list of work is as stinting as his verse is unending, wrote with almost the modern meaning in *King Arthur* (1695):

> While round the Base the Wanton Coursers play,
> The Ambitious riders in just scales they weigh.

Of course the term *base,* with but a twist of vision, becomes geometric, or "that surface of a plane or solid figure on which it stands," so that Sir Henry Billingsley's translation of Euclid, in 1570, defines an elliptical diamond, the geometric foundation of our own baseball "diamond" as "in comparison of two sides of a triangle, the third is called a base." In the next year, Thomas Digges' *A Geometrical Practise Named Pantometria* more generally states that "any one of the Figures wherewith these solides be environed is called the base of that solid."

Ball is unremittingly Germanic, with the etymologies or word origins being Norse, Dutch, and Teutonic. One of its earliest entries is from 1205: "Summe heo drivon ballas wide beyond that feldes." In 1320, the *Seuyn Sag* records "With that bal togider they plaid." Shakespeare's *Henry V* (I, ii, 261) brings the Germanic sphere into more recognizable modern play. "When we have matcht our Rackets to these balles, while the 1611 'King James' Isaiah moralizes and threatens—"He will surely . . . tose thee like a ball." Two relatively modern uses from 1721 and 1783 also bring the sphere into play. Nathan Bailey's *Universal Etymological Dictionary* defines cricket as "a sort of play with bats and a ball, and the poet George Crabbe in *The Village* describes one struck with a passion for sport: "the flying ball, / The bat, the wicket were his labours all." Crabbe nonetheless asks, as we might today in rural New York, with its often economically marginal and dwindling rural life:

> Where are the swains who, daily labour done,
> With rural games play'd down the setting sun;
> Who struck with matchless force the bounding ball[?]

"Pitch" is also Germanic, and, related etymologically to "pick," provides an unwitting pun, as when modern pitchers "pick off" runners. Yet another metonym, or associated generative meaning, "pick" meant "to pitch or fix in the ground," according to Eric Partridge's *Origins,* and the destructive results of a misdirected pitch or beanball hover about this description: "to throw derives from Middle English *pitchen* which strikingly resembles *piken,* . . . or to pierce . . . hence pitchfork." This meaning of "pitch in the ground" gives us the term in cricket: "The Wickets to be pitched by Eleven O-Clock" from the 1745 *Daily Advertiser.* Pitch, "to cast or throw," exists simultaneously, whether it be in Chaucer's 1386 "he pighte hym on the pomel of his heed" or in a 1773 description of sport: "For honest Lumpey did allow He ne'er could pitch but o'er a brow." Presumably Lumpey works in the tradition of cricket, where "the ball which the bowler . . . shall have pitched in a straight line to the wicket."

In baseball, of course, the only wicket known is from a phrase uttered by a displaced British soul at Candlestick or some other park. In baseball, the ball is pitched over the plate to the waiting catcher. The umpires, who have assured both teams that the field is acceptably maintained and flat, that the chances of play are even, dust the plate regularly and keep the other bases in place. Home plate, of course, must be flat or even to the level ground, like the Greek *Platys,* meaning "broad," and the Latin *plattus* or "flat," the terms which provide us with the *plat*-itudes or flatitudes of most commentary on sport, and on both sides of the Platte River. Fortunately, "plate" does exist as a description for the trophies (or the physical representations of *triumph,* a hopelessly Latinate term), sometimes even for baseball victories, and inscribed plates are at times given to represent victory on or off other playing fields. No doubt, however, the Yankees again would like, in Wyclif's 1382 translation of 2 Kings, to capture the "platis of gold, the whiche he had affitchide."

"Home," another Old English Germanic root, in its archaic spellings "ham" or "hame," means a village, town, collection or buildings, one's own country, etc. Certainly this was in the poet Houseman's mind when he imagined:

> Shoulder-high we bring you home,
> And set you at your threshold down,
> Townsman of a stiller town.

Of course, the metonymic sports meaning of "home" or "goal" is also of some age, and in the 1778 *Hoyle's Games* one may read of preventing "*B* from getting his man home."

What of that dread instrument of Ty Cobb, Ruth, and Alex (The Killer) Hamilton, the "bat"? Has it, for instance, anything to do with "bunt"? The latter is another Germanic derivative from "butten," or to "beat" in the sense of "strike." And here, British English fails. Our founding fathers may not bunt. Unless he listened to his Dutch neighbors, Lightning Franklin could not have "bunted." He could, however, have used his "bat," sanctioned as early as the *Ancren Riwle* of 1250, as that "stick or stout piece of wood . . . for support and defence," in its modern paraphrase. In the *Ancren Riwle* "battles heo up hevven," and in another text of 1300 early folk "fyghte with battes." The very nearly modern (and legal) use of bats on the fields of sport appears in 1706 as "a kind of club to strike a ball with." Even earlier, Shakespeare in *Coriolanus* could be speaking to the managers of the Billy Martin stripe, aggressively charging their teams: "Make you ready your stiffe bats and clubs" (I, i, 165).

Was the "catcher" behind the plate the immortal Patrick (Mouthpiece) Henry? From his reading, he knew of the dual origins of the term. Being neither a "captive" of ignorance nor of what he thought to be authoritarian kingly rule, Henry knows that *captare*, the Latin for "strive or seek," becomes in its later French form a term meaning to "chase, run or to hasten," just as Mouthpiece does for hits during the games between the opposing voices of peace or revolution. While "catcher" may sound Germanic, it is a *faux ami*—to mix linguistic metaphor. Reading in the poet John Skelton's *Magnyfycence, a goodly interlude and a mery* (1526), Mouthpiece finds that "Hercules . . . with his stubborne mace, That made to cache Cerberus."

How about the pop-up fly ball just hit behind the plate by Red Jefferson? Lost in thought, Mouthpiece the catcher remembers the oddities of languages, and that in the 1780s the learned books contained no flies in a baseball sense. Racking his memory, Mouthpiece recalls that "fly" means to "move through the air with the aid of "wings" and is related to the Greek *plein,* meaning to swim or to sail. And as Henry ran through the related words from this one root, from pulmonary, to flee, to fluegelhorn, to flutter, to fluster, flood, flow, and to flue, the high fly ball, realizing that it did not in fact exist in the 1780s, simply disappeared. And this game, for all its history in English terminology, was forfeited until a later date in Cooperstown, New York, when the opposing teams of the next century took to Doubleday Field, confident of their poetry and their linguistic history, with, in some sense, Euclid in the field, Shakespeare at bat, and Chaucer pitching the terms we all now know so well on this fiftieth anniversary of The Hall of Fame.

The Country of the Young

The Meaning of Baseball in Early American Culture

by Ronald Story

We know we love it above all others. But why do we? Or rather, since it started a long time ago, why *did* we? Why *baseball* and not some other sport? Or *no* sport? And why baseball with such passionate single-mindedness rather than as one sport among many? How did this come to be?

We can find some tentative answers, I believe, by looking closely at the period when baseball truly began to sweep the country: the years from about 1875 to 1895. Because it was the 1880s (as we'll call them for brevity's sake) with their gaudy promotionalism, kaleidoscopic franchise and league formation, spring training and transcontinental and international barnstorming treks, expanded seasons, city and world series, tobacco cards, product endorsements, knothole gangs, booster clubs, flamboyant daredevil players and weekly baseball newspapers—it was in the '80s that baseball became what can only be described as a mass cultural movement, a large-scale, passionate American affair on the scale and intensity of other mass movements such as revivalism or temperance, and capable, therefore, of creating a bedrock of players and "cranks" on which promoters and sponsors would build.[1]

A mass cultural movement of this kind cannot be accounted for, it seems to me, the way most baseball historians have tried to account for it, by reference to, for example, working-class occupations or Irish ethnicity, or to the masculine subculture or railroad-based entertainment industry, or to promotionalism and sponsorship. These were all significant, the Irish factor particularly so. But they do not explain why the groups, the subculture, the entertainment moguls, and the politicians gravitated so powerfully to baseball rather than to something else. Nor, most importantly, do they explain the intensity and passion, the sudden breathless sweep, of the late 19th century's involvement with the game.[2]

Baseball became so enormously popular in the 1889s for one reason: men loved it. And they loved it, I would argue, because they played it when they were young. Our concentration on the men's clubs and professional teams has misled us. The fact is that for every club or professional player we can identify from the late 1860s to the early 1880s, there were almost certainly a hundred nonprofessional players on organized teams and a thousand on unorganized ad hoc ones, almost all of them boys or young men between the ages of 10 and 20. It was the coming of age during the late 1870s and '80s of these thousands of youthful players that produced the huge critical mass of players, spectators and followers on which the mass baseball movement rested.[3]

Love and passion—strong but appropriate words. Because these boys and young men not only played baseball but played it in the face of adult disinterest and disapproval. This is one of the most important differences between the 19th and 20th century games. Nineteenth century adults did not really want their adolescent sons playing baseball. Stories abound of 19th century fathers tracking down sons and whipping them off the ball field, of mothers throwing iron pots and boiling water at team organizers, of tempestuous quarrels over ball playing instead of chores and serious work. Nor, except for a handful of colleges, did schools sponsor baseball teams; and when school teams did appear, it was the students themselves who organized the teams.

So baseball was not only a mass movement, it was a youth movement, fomented in the face of disapproving authority. It was not only a counterpart to 19th century revivalism and temperance, it was a precursor to 20th century movies and rock and roll. And it left an equally indelible impression.[4]

Mass movements, and mass youth movements especially, arise because they satisfy deep-seated emotional needs among their adherents. Baseball must have been no different. The question, then, that finally addresses the meaning of baseball in early America, and the reason for its fabulous later popularity, is simply this: What needs did this era's adolescent male population have that baseball seemed able to satisfy so powerfully?

First some basics. Baseball was an outdoor activity for the hot months of the year. Nineteenth century houses were places of work and basic bodily functions with poor ventilation and lighting and, until the mid-1880s, no window screens. In summer, a house was "a place to get out of," as were most school buildings and places of work. And houses were crowded, commonly holding eight or more persons in a few small rooms. Front porches and steps were important living and socializing spaces in hot weather. But many houses had the main porch in the rear, and anyway, step and porch activities had to be fairly restrained. That left the streets and vacant lots and fields. Baseball flourished more than "saloon" games such as cards, darts or billiards partly because it gave exuberant young males something exciting and vigorous to do outdoors at a time when staying indoors was agony.[5]

Early baseball was also aggressively physical. It was simple to learn and unlike, say, cricket, easy enough to play to accommodate a range of ages and skills. But the same thing that made the game relatively easy to play—underhand pitching and lenient ball–strike rules—insured lots of hitting and thus lots of fielding and base running, too. There were, therefore, endless bursts of action and limitless quick sprinting with very little dead time in between. And even though agility, speed and reflexes mattered, so did muscle—the capacity to throw the ball swiftly and hit it powerfully.[6]

Baseball, in other words, was a superb outlet for the energies of boisterous young males in a way that languid pursuits—fishing or the saloon games or backyard games such as horseshoes or marbles— were not. Baseball's intensely competitive nature, even in the most casual contests, also led ball players to develop and hone their skills— to exert, that is, even more physical energy and on a more sustained basis. The sport probably never produced enough exertion to trigger the state of ecstasy reported by modern track stars and mountaineers. But the combination of physical exertion and competitive tension could produce tremendous exhilaration, something that even experienced young players called "joy."[7]

This physical side of baseball, the premium it placed on strength, speed, and agility, is especially significant in view of the conditions in the country during the years when it became popular. Nineteenth century America was nothing if not rough, and although the ball field was not the boxing ring, a reputation for baseball excellence carried over into other areas, lending status to players in a brawling era that held physical prowess and "grit" in high regard.[8]

Ball players' pride in their skill, toughness, and physiques must have been acute in the 1860s and '70s because so many men were visibly unfit—frail, disabled, or both. The frail consisted in great measure of Irish immigrants and their offspring, who bore the twin burdens of the potato famine and its aftermath and the harsh poverty of unskilled laborers. Some Irish were, of course, rugged specimens, but many others were not. Their arrival in America lowered the country's average height and held urban life expectancy to under 45. And with this residue of hunger and poverty went the damage of the Civil War. Limbless veterans inhabited every town and city for years after Appomattox, multiplying prosthesis shops as well as pension relief.[9]

Paul Longmore argues that the disabled have been a negative reference group for other Americans just as blacks have been for whites. We define ourselves by what we are not—disabled, black, feminine, and so forth. Conscious of these frail, damaged men, their haler counterparts reacted typically: to display their health and wholeness, they rushed to play a physically demanding, highly visible sport—baseball.[10]

Lastly but perhaps not least, baseball had some sexual significance. Anthropologists have speculated about the phallic symbolism of the ubiquitous bat. But the bat seems no more suggestive than other sporting implements—guns, fishing poles, cricket bats, lacrosse or hockey sticks—and the sport itself no more sexually freighted than games such as football, basketball, or soccer where players "penetrate" the goal with the ball. Yet baseball must have had a sexual dimension. Its players were almost exclusively young males with high testosterone levels and strong sexual urges that did not simply vanish because the sport was all-male. Promoters, in fact, took great pains to stress the game's "manly" and "masculine" qualities, and journalists took careful note of the number of women among the spectators and whether they were young, attractive, and single.[11]

It was, in fact, not the bat but the player that had sexual import, particularly at higher levels where players wore tight-fitting, sometimes colorful, even red, uniforms. Opportunities for male physical display were rare in this era. Ordinary clothing did not enhance distinctive masculine features—broad shoulders, powerful chest, strong thigh and calf—and few activities gave adolescents and young men an opportunity for aggressively physical, therefore implicitly sexual, behavior that everyone, including women, could see. This may have appealed especially to our young Irishmen. Ireland had a heritage of separation, almost segregation, by gender, and the Famine migrants brought this legacy with them to America strengthened by the Great Hunger and reinforced by same-sex schooling. Irish boys had limited occasions to meet girls and gain facility at courtship, and most native-born Americans had it no easier. All-male sports allowed young Irishmen to send sexual signals while remaining safely apart. In this, baseball was a godsend, and not for the Irish alone.[12]

Unfortunately, the basics, interesting as they are, don't really explain baseball's staggering popularity because there were other physical outdoor alternatives that might have satisfied these needs. Walking contests were leading spectator events in the mid-19th century but never captivated the country's youth as baseball did. Young men would watch walkers but only sporadically walk themselves, so an ardent mass following never developed. Important boxing matches drew throngs well into the 20th century, and boxing clubs attracted immigrant members and political patronage. Every 19th century boy had to know how to fight with his hands or take a licking at every corner, and boxing as a sport with commonly accepted rules attracted zealous young participants. Yet neither walking nor fighting swept youthful America save on exceptional occasions when hordes would show up to see who was "fastest" and "toughest."[13]

And there were others. The kicking and/or tackling game of football had been known since colonial times, got frequently touted by the mid-century sporting press as a cool weather sport, and had scattered "clubs" of its own. But it made little headway even after important collegiate matches began; "Irish" football, a soccer-like game played in the 1850s, did no better. Lacrosse, introduced here and there in the 1860s, made even fewer waves, while gymnastics, again widely known, remained almost exclusively a German pastime. Even cricket, which had a significant following before the Civil War, ultimately fared badly.[14]

The question thus recurs. What emotional needs did the young males of this era have that were not met so well by these other sports but that baseball could, and did, meet singularly well? There were, let me suggest, three such needs, intertwined but nonetheless distinctive: comradeship, recognition, and order.

Twentieth century studies indicate that young Americans prefer team sports to individual sports while Europeans and Japanese incline to the opposite. This American preference first manifested itself in the 1860s and '70s, when baseball began to outstrip boxing, footracing, gymnastics and other individualistic physical activities. The young men's clubs that sponsored the earliest organized baseball teams were, in fact, highly "clubbish" affairs even off the field, placing great emphasis on dinners and fetes, and while such fraternal clubbishness declined with the spread of professionalism its aura may have lingered into the '70s.[15]

But far more crucial, similar feelings flowed from the field of play. Not only did "teams"—aggregates of individuals—contest for victory, but the victory itself seemed to require actual "teamwork," a constant working together to blend disparate talents. Warren Goldstein suggests that early artisan players brought this stress on "victory through teamwork" with them from the shop floor and thereby imbued the sport with their particular mode of competitive labor excellence. But the game itself generated "team spirit," too. Teams that won with consistency needed several good players, not just one; even though only one player batted at a time, no one player, however talented, could carry a team. Winning was an inherently collective enterprise, inherently engendering solidarity. So, for that matter, was losing.[16]

Far more than today, moreover, 19th century teams at every level of play used what Bill James calls a "long sequence" offense, scoring by stringing small things together (two singles, two errors, and a single for three runs) rather than by doing fewer, but bigger things (double, single, home run). Historically, long-sequence offenses seem to produce more teamwork and team solidarity than short-sequence offenses because they force players to rely more on one another, thereby producing greater esprit de corps. And this playing-field esprit was intensified by the comradeship of the "bench"—teammates sitting or standing together when their "side" was batting, swapping vulgarities in the summer heat, shouting support in unison, enjoying male closeness.[17]

The collective bonds produced by interdependence, joint contributions, and shared fate were different from the fraternalism of the early baseball clubs. Club members came together on the basis of common interests and attributes to play ball, or at least jointly sponsor ball playing. Teammates, by contrast, felt bound emotionally because they played together. But this esprit then spilled over the boundaries of the ball field to produce an intense camaraderie off it, too—at the adolescent level a tighter neighborhood or ethnic or "street" feeling, at the older level "the boys" singing on the train or in the hotel lobby, seeing new sights together, challenging all comers. The sociability of the club thus fused with the spirit of the team. "We played for love and excitement," they said. "We were a band of brothers, carrying everything before us."[18]

Why did the young males of this era find this dimension of the sport so compelling? Why was the fraternal impulse so powerful among the period's young males? Undoubtedly in part because the rate of urbanization was so high. Urban populations were doubling every 10 years, propelled by a steady migration from country to city. This migration was disorienting under the best of circumstances. Massive war mobilization and demobilization and still more massive immigration, particularly from Famine Ireland, made it especially so. Nor did merely settling in the city mean the moving was over, because the population constantly churned so that boys would often live in three neighborhoods and attend four schools by the age of 15.[19]

Young urbanites of this generation were highly likely, in other words, to have been born elsewhere or to have had parents born elsewhere and therefore to have experienced a dearth of conventional significant others—cousins, grandparents and the like and, even more, familiar faces from their own age cohort. Nineteenth century boys were perpetual "new kids" in town, "green as the verdant prairies," nervous about going outside lest they "be spoken to by someone not a member of the family." Boys created and recreated their own communities all through the 19th century, forming Tom Sawyerish "gangs," shaping streets and blocks into play areas and turfs," finding school "chums." Young men, encountering unfamiliar social landscapes, did much the same with fire companies, reading groups, political clubs and other voluntary associations. But it was not easy for so "scattered" a people to do. Therefore the opportunity to participate in a sport such as baseball, to "break into those crude games of ball" which seemed to create instantaneous community, was irresistible.[20]

Other sports developed facsimiles of this comradely ethos. Racing and fighting exuded a pungent masculine clubbishness, as did early cricket. But they did so almost exclusively at the adult level, where gambling, drinking, and politics helped create the atmosphere, and almost exclusively as spectacle, the comradely ambience deriving from the shared excitement of observing and celebrating, with the contestants' arena more or less delineated from the spectators. Baseball engendered this clubbish aura, too; but it also generated a sense of solidarity among its participants, drew its players together as they played, in a way that fighting and running could not. Further, the dynamic of "the bench" helped produce a sense of comradeship not only by drawing together the players as they played but, as game pictures show, by blurring the line that separated participants and spectators, and rolling players, bench and crowd together into an emotionally unified whole.[21]

But baseball meant more than comradeship. It also, to a degree unique among team sports, meant individual recognition. Lacrosse, soccer, and later basketball and hockey enabled individual players to stand out, chiefly by handling or scoring with the ball. But these sports did not guarantee every player a chance to gain recognition; and particularly at lower skill levels and among youthful players where baseball took strongest root, a handful of players, even a single player, could not only dominate a game but virtually monopolize the ball, leaving other players few ways to excel or even participate.

One player could influence a baseball game, too, especially pitchers; and some positions—pitcher, catcher, first base—got more action than others. But baseball's entire defensive and offensive configuration had individualistic overtones. Each player bore a title corresponding to a specific position—third baseman, rightfielder, and so on; each player bore responsibility for the area indicated by his title; each player himself defended it—caught balls thrown or hit to or through it—alone, out in the open, without aid or hindrance. Some positions had more action than others, but the ball came to every position sooner or later, usually pretty often in the early, high-scoring games. When it did, a single, visibly isolated player had to handle it.

Similarly on offense: A team's players took the offensive in serial fashion, one at a time in prearranged order, for approximately the same length of time—each batter until he reached base or made an out, each team until it made three outs, the game to last until teams made 27 outs or it got dark. Baseball's fundamental structure, that is, guaranteed that every player would have exactly the same offensive opportunity as every other player; that his opportunity would come automatically, without competition or combat for the opportunity; and that in the course of these high-scoring games, teams would bat through their lineups frequently, so that individual opportunities would recur just as frequently.

The offensive structure had other implications, too. By sending one batter to the plate at a time, baseball made every player the team standard-bearer, a personification of the whole team with all eyes on him, teammates' included—a limelight opportunity that the game guaranteed not just occasionally, but frequently during each game. And the rapidity with which teams wheeled their batters to and from the plate insured that offensive players not hitting or on base would keep focused on the field because their turn would soon come again. The sport's structure, rules, and inherent dynamic gave every player an equal chance to play the role of team champion in the offensive spotlight; and it gave him a captive audience while he was there.

Baseball thus brought recognition to its participants by scattering them defensively and bringing them quickly and serially to bat. Early newspaper coverage and the notational formulas devised to summarize the game accentuated these patterns. Organizing a team in the spring meant, among other things, submitting a roster—nine players plus an extra or two, all with their positions—to the press along with an appeal for opponents and sometimes the address of the club's headquarters or captain. Midwestern papers of the 1870s normally published only the rosters of the better young adult teams, but by 1880 they were publishing the rosters of adolescent teams as well. Playing serious baseball was often the best, if not the only way for boys to see their names in print—visible testimony to their individual as well as group identity. Once the season's games began, the papers sometimes announced impending contests by giving the starting line-ups, printing players' positions along with their spot in the batting order, hence doubling the individual recognition. At the professional and semiprofessional levels and for big collegiate and city championship matches, papers would occasionally include a box score consisting of times at bat, runs scored, and some fielding information along with the written account, thereby tripling the recognition factor.[22]

Numbers mean immortality, argues Bill James. Baseball players will live in a way that football or lacrosse players cannot; a player's numbers, compiled from the evidence of the box score, guarantee it.[23] For young players of the 1870s and early '80s, far below the professional level where statistics most mattered, it was not so much the cumulative record of the boxes that counted, although boys may have kept rough track of their own numbers and perceived their games partly through the borrowed lenses of the professional box scores—conceptualized their participation, in other words, according to the portrait of individualized collectivity suggested by the boxes. It was rather that rosters and lineups, and box scores later, publicly acknowledged players' existence not only as *belonging* persons but as *persons.*

Why did the era's young males yearn for recognition? A simple answer is that they resembled young men in most places at most times. The literature of the 18th and 19th centuries is filled with "young men from the provinces" seeking fortune and fame—a little recognition in the world's urban centers. Nineteenth century Americans were no different, though many already lived in cities. They merely had more immediate models than Robinson Crusoe: the older ball players on display at the nearest grounds of whom they "made heroes" and "dreamed of imitating." They even dreamed of becoming heroes themselves.[24]

For baseball, while a collective endeavor, was collective partly in the sense that the sum of a series of individual actions constitutes a collectivity. A team achievement was a statistical construct, the rolling together of many small components. Recognition was comradeship transposed. You were accepted, wanted, for what you yourself, with your own distinctive strengths and idiosyncrasies, could accomplish for your mates. When you failed, then that, too, the downside of responsibility, was glaringly evident. The inherent properties of the game guaranteed it.

Nineteenth century boys may have felt the need for recognition with a special urgency. As family historians are beginning to show, mid-19th century fathers, both immigrant and native-born, commonly related to their sons in two ways: by neglect, if farmers or wage workers; by domination and control, if artisans or clerks. Life, after all, was an ordeal. Security and status as well as survival spurred long hours at work or politics. Long hours meant long stretches when the father was not present, leaving children to feel ignored and neglected—not "recognized" as having value. What they got, instead, was regulated—rigidly directed as to daily regimen, as to schooling, as to fealty, behavior, work. Fathers did what they believed necessary under the alternatively tantalizing and ominous circumstances of the 19th century world. Sons experienced it differently.[25]

Were nineteenth century mothers different? Ball players, like everyone else, remembered their mothers as "friends" and "supporters," full of compassion and concern, and maybe they were. But the typical household was large, with four, five, or more children to make demands on mother's attention and energy. Housework itself was arduous. And consider this: nearly half the total time that a boy might live in his parents' home, his mother was either pregnant or in postpartum recuperation, growing weaker, in many cases, with each pregnancy. Whatever the memories, it hardly seems possible that mothers had much in the way of surplus attention to bestow on a needy son or of surplus energy for meeting the innumerable emotional demands of a bursting household.[26]

A speculation might be in order in this connection with the Irish and baseball. In the "stem" system of Irish families, a single son, usually the eldest, traditionally received what there was by way of patrimony and therefore what existed of concentrated, undivided attention. Favored, usually eldest, sons lived longest at home, got the most advantageous schooling, were introduced earliest to potential patrons or employers. Younger sons—the vast majority of sons—got packed off to work or school. So they sought recognition where they could find it: on the ball field.[27]

Comradeship. Recognition. But also order. Allen Guttmann observes that whereas most team sports—soccer, hockey, rugby, basketball, polo, football, lacrosse—oscillate between the two poles, baseball is circular in its fundamental configuration and flow. This is true because, unlike other sports, where a team scores by moving the ball forward across a line or through a space that the opposing team defends, baseball players score without the ball, which is driven away from the offensive action, thereby enabling an individual player to touch the four points of a square (diamond) for a "run." Guttmann speculates that baseball's rounding of the square perhaps touches fundamental biorhythms related to the transit of the seasons and, by extension, the rhythms of the agricultural world. If so, he reasons, baseball may have served as a mechanism for easing the great transition from rural to urban life that has characterized the U.S.[28]

Guttmann is almost surely right that there was something significant about the geometry and configurations of the game. Before the Civil War, players of ball-and-bat games had three more or less distinct ways to lay out a playing ground. One way was for cricket, with bowler and batsman occupying positions determined by the location of the wicket that the bowler aimed at and the batsman protected; batsmen scored by running along a line to the bowler's area and back. The field itself was oval, extending in every direction to a boundary laid round the outer limits. With "fair" territory defined in this way as anywhere inside the oval, which is to say everywhere, cricket had no fixed defensive posts, and players assumed a sometimes bewildering variety of positions according to their captain's orders.[29]

Another was for baseball New England style, or "town ball," as it was first called. Here the striker stood halfway between home and 1st, then ran to touch markers at the four corners of the square to score before being hit by a thrown ball. The position of the batter meant, however, that there was no good way to demark "fair" from "foul" territory. If lines were drawn along the home–3rd base line and the 1st–2nd line, the field became a rectangle reaching outward from the home–1st line towards the "out" (now left) field, leaving a narrow confining space where crowded fielders jockeyed and jostled for room. As a result, baseball New England style reverted to the cricket mode, a limitless space extending in all directions where players occupied uncertain spots depending on whim, circumstances, or a captain's will. Moreover, with no out-of-bounds there was no particular reason to touch bases in order and, therefore, no need for base paths to control a runner's movement, producing a game that was even more random and willful—disorderly—than cricket. This square-within-an-ovoid New England baseball lasted until the late 1850s when the angular "diamond" New York game supplanted it. When baseball flourished after 1865, it was in this New York form, which then helped it pass cricket in people's affections and thus become *the* model for the sport.[30]

So there was clearly something important about the diamond formed by placing the batter at home plate. In this New York game, three of the right angles formed by lines intersecting the fourth point ("home") were out of bounds. Balls batted there were foul, no good except in a few special instances, and so did not need defending. This definition of "inbounds" as the space inside the single 90-degree arc formed by the diamond thus combined with the four bases of the diamond to determine the logical distribution of defenders—namely, in a double arc, a four-position configuration around the outer limits of the "infield" and a thinner, three-man arc beyond that. And as noted in connection with the recognition factor, from this logical configuration of defenders (fielders), came with equal logic the conventions of fixed and separate positions, each with a name, each name associated with a special space.

Baseball's rules, in other words, and the defensive logic that flowed from the geometry of its diamond-shaped infield, gave its participants fixed defensive positions within discrete spaces. Once the rules and logic became clear, moreover, virtually the same was true for ad hoc contests between odd numbers of players on narrow streets or rooftops or other expanded or smallish areas lacking true squares or a limitless widening of the "fair" angle. The discrete spacing held even under these conditions because of what players had to do to score—touch all bases consecutively without the ball—and how the field was conceived—as a rapidly spreading 90-degree fair territory. Meanwhile, batters who struck the ball had to move along the sides of the square and there only. Baseball, that is, imposed order on its players by sending them to specific areas of the field on defense and down rigidly delimited paths on offense. And it did so automatically by its rules and regulations.

Here is a primary difference between baseball and Guttmann's oscillating sports. In the latter, players' movements were more random and willful, players' paths and spaces less inviolate. There was greater opportunity for conflict, including physical collision, and less clarity of individual opportunity and objective. Sometimes collision was inherent, as with rugby or Irish or collegiate football; or players could perform tasks with little knowledge of how plays developed, again as in football but also sometimes in lacrosse or soccer. Order— the setting of boundaries, trajectories, and responsibilities—could be found in all these sports, but it was a partial order and one largely imposed by a captain's, coach's, or manager's authority. None had baseball's fixity of position, hence inviolability of person, and delineation of pathways, hence clarity of trajectory. Moreover, baseball controlled space and people *automatically*. The rest did so, *if* they did so, by means of external authority.[31]

And observers knew this right away. Baseball was a game "whose regulations are calculated to prevent the ill-feelings engendered by other games." It was a "nonviolent" sport, with "splendid order" and "control," the "most organized of all sports being played." Renderings of 19th century games commonly show the players separated on the field, fixed in distinct spaces, poised for action yet scattered and detached, moving down the narrow paths of the base lines. They stand forth amid the representations of boisterous and uncontrolled 19th century groups, all but frozen in worlds of their own spaces, detached from the welter of ordinary urban life.[32]

Yet the question, as before, is not only what baseball offered—in this case order—but why young men thirsted for it. And explanations lie readily at hand in the period's disorderly, destabilizing mobility and insubordination, particularly as evinced in the brawling cities and experienced by boys in the city streets. Besides seeing their fathers move from job to job, their families from neighborhood to neighborhood, themselves from school to school and boss to boss, males born in the 1850s and 1860s lived through war mobilization and massive waves of immigration, sharp financial panic and deep economic depression, ravenous fires and bitter labor disputes. And disorder's handmaid was raw violence: crime waves, a raucous saloon culture, political combat, turf battles, gang fights.[33]

These young men were tough, make no mistake. They fought continuously to prove and protect themselves, and for thrills. But even the toughest young men, Robert Coles shows, need respite, "time out," if they can find it without losing face, and the not-so-tough-beneath-the-surface majority need it especially. Lacking adult authority figures to furnish safety and sanctuary, in the 1860s and '70s they found their own: on the ball field.[34]

Richard Sennett argues that in the absence of powerful overarching institutions—a standing army, a national church, a corporate economy, a rigorous system of national schooling—a chief 19th century refuge from danger and disorder was the family. But this is not wholly persuasive for our period. Consider the household from the standpoint of a boy growing up there: perpetually crowded with little room for consolation or order; the mother distracted, fatigued, "sick" with childbirth; the father remote, often absent, but when at home severe and critical and a conveyor, too, of the angry social and political passions of the world outside, a bearer sometimes of its physical wounds, always of its anxieties.[35]

We may surmise, then, as follows. Young males of this generation needed security and order—breathing space, respite—in a world where violence and chaos seemed the norm. But families, which might have been a refuge, were often microcosms of the outside world, fecund sources of their own forms of unhappiness and insecurity; schools and gangs helped but brought uncertainties of their own. Still needing security, young men sought it where they could, especially in the surrogate family ambience of team sports. And of the available team sports, baseball, after the adoption of New York rules, served best. It constrained willfulness and assault better, and ordered space better, and it did so automatically and spontaneously, without adult aid or intervention.

This was, finally, an encompassing national movement because all of America was in turmoil in the 1860s and '70s. And baseball, which carried the seeds of security and control, of comradeship and recognition, within itself, was there to scatter them in identical ways all across the country. Because adolescent boys of that generation needed them, baseball became their salvation and their love. And they never forgot it. In partial payment, they made it the American game.

Notes

1. For baseball in the 1880s, see e.g., Harold Seymour, *Baseball: The Early Years* (New York, 1960), 94–239; David Quentin Voigt, *American Baseball: From Gentlemen's Sport to the Commissioner System* (Norman, 1966), 99–221; Dale A. Somers, *The Rise of Sports in New Orleans, 1850–1900* (Baton Rouge, 1972), 115–139; Donald Mrozek, *Sport and American Mentality, 1880–1910* (Knoxville, 1983), 67–102. See also the undocumented but insightful coverage in Ted Vincent, *Mudville's Revenge: The Rise and Fall of American Sport* (New York, 1981), 87–223; Bill James, *The Bill James Historical Baseball Abstract* (New York, 1986), 3–21; and Robert Smith, *Baseball* (New York, 1947), 84–135. My understanding of the 1880s, as well as earlier years, comes partly from perusal of the *Chicago Tribune* and *St. Louis Post-Dispatch* from 1860 to 1900 and, more spottily, the *Milwaukee Sentinel, Dubuque Herald, Cincinnati Inquirer,* and *St. Paul Dispatch* from 1870 to 1890.

2. For the masculine subculture or "subculture of sensuality," see Benjamin G. Rader, *American Sports from the Age of Folk Games to the Age of Spectators* (Englewood Cliffs, 1983), 88–122; Lois Banner, *American Beauty* (Chicago and London, 1983), 112 ff. For the significance of the railroad and telegraph, see John R. Betts, *America's Sporting Heritage, 1850–1950* (Lexington, Mass., 1974); Somers, *Sports in New Orleans.* Most studies of 19th century baseball stress the importance of promotionalism and political patronage, but see, in particular, Vincent, *Mudville's Revenge;* Melvin Adelman, "The Development of Modern Athletics: Sport in New York, 1820–1970 (Ph.D. diss., University of Illinois-Urbana, 1980), 349–355, 390–417, passim.

3. The evidence for this is of course impressionistic. Much of it lies buried in the sports columns of the daily press and in casual references from contemporary and historical works. One bit of hard evidence as to how young men began to play ball is perhaps that the average age for National Association players upon their entry into the league was about 22; three were 17.

Ages are computed from Joseph Reichler, ed., *The Baseball Enclopedia* (6th ed., New York and London, 1985). The average age of all traceable Northwestern League (Illinois and Iowa) players, entering or otherwise, in 1878 and 1879 was 22; the five whose age when they started playing baseball is traceable (Charles Comiskey, Ted Sullivan, Bill Gleason, Tom Loftus, Charles Radbourn) seem to have begun at about age 12.

4. Ted Sullivan's *Humorous Stories of the Ballfield* (Chicago, 1903), is full of relevant anecdotal information, but see also Gustav Axelson, *"Commy": The Life Story of Charles A. Comiskey* (Chicago, 1919) for a full version of a classic (and oft-repeated by baseball writers) father–son conflict over baseball. For schoolboy games, see Stephen Hardy, *How Boston Played* (Boston, 1982), 107 ff; Donald Mrozek, *Sport and American Mentality, 1880–1910* (Knoxville, 1983), 67–102. Schoolboy baseball, football, and track teams were all student-run even after school administrators and teachers adopted them as representatives of the school in interscholastic contests.

5. On 19th century houses, see e.g., Kenneth Jackson, *Crabgrass Frontier* (New York and London, 1985), 280, passim; Barbara Mercedes Posadas, "Community Structures of Chicago's Northwest Side: The Transition from Rural to Urban, 1830–1889" (Ph.D. diss., Northwestern University, 1976), figures v-1 and v-2, passim; Peter Hales, *Silver Cities* (Philadelphia, 1984), 266, passim.

6. By vigorous and physical, I mean simply that there was a lot of hitting and base running, that pitchers threw the ball to the batter pretty much as soon as they got it, and that batters swung rather than waiting for a base on balls that would only arrive after 7, 8 or 9 called balls. *The Bill James Historical Baseball Abstract* gives in brief the main features of this early, fast-paced, quick-moving game. Had baseball been as ponderous in the 1870s and 1880s as it sometimes is today, when batters step out of the box after every pitch and pitchers frequently walk around the mound when they're not being changed, young males of the period would not, I'm convinced, have taken it up so eagerly.

7. On the sports "high," see e.g., Michael Murphy and Rhea White, *The Psychic Side of Sports* (Reading, 1978). Baseball could nonetheless generate enough tension to cause crowds not only to whoop it up but to discharge revolvers over an exciting play. Cf. Carter Harrison, *Growing Up With Chicago* (Chicago, 1944), 72–74, 227–228; Carter Harrison, *Stormy Years: The Autobiography of Carter H. Harrison* (Indianapolis and New York, 1935), 28–29, 78–79, 193. The atmosphere suggests what some observers find at games in the modern Caribbean (except Cuba). Cf. Thomas Boswell, "A Country for Old Pitchers," in *How Life Imitates the World Series* (Garden City, 1982).

8. For the brawling side of 19th century America, see Elliott Gorn, " 'Good-Bye Boys, I Die a True American': Homicide, Nativism, and Working-Class Culture in Antebellum New York City," *Journal of American History* 74 (Sept. 1987), 388–410; Elliott J. Gorn, *The Manly Art: Bare-Knuckle Prize Fighting in America* (Ithaca, 1986); Roger Lane, *Violent Death in the City* (Cambridge, Mass., 1979). Anecdotal evidence for this point is everywhere in the daily and weekly press, which regaled readers with stories of steel-toed shin-kicking bouts, walking contestants with bleeding and damaged feet, and brutal boxing matches. See e.g., Otto L. Bettmann, *The Good Old Days—They*

Were Terrible! (New York, 1974). Ball players, even though they were not boxers, were respected participants in this roughhouse world and in fact crossed the line into the boxing and wrestling ring with ease.

9. The literature on the Irish immigrants of the 1840s and 1850s is voluminous. Most of it stresses suffering, hardship, survival and, eventually, triumph. Reading extensively on the ravages of the Famine years, however, reminds one of nothing so much as the ravages in modern Bangladesh or Ethiopia, where famine survivors are visibly weakened and shrunk and newborns are underweight and susceptible to illness and thus unlikely to grow to "normal" height or weight. I cannot conceive that even Famine Irish who escaped to America bore no physical trace of this gruesome ordeal or, more importantly, bore children with no physical trace. As late as 1890, only about 5 percent of Chicagoans were 55 or more, and only 13 percent were 45. Bessie Pierce, *A History of Chicago: The Rise of a Modern City, 1871–1893* (New York, 1957), 519.

10. For a brilliant discussion of the significance of disability in American history, see Paul Longmore, "The Life of Randolph Bourne and the Need for a History of Disabled People," *Reviews in American History* 13 (Dec. 1985), 581–587. No one, to my knowledge, has surveyed postbellum cities for the presence of disabled veterans, although the task is feasible with the help of the published lists of federal pension recipients. I counted prosthesis shops in Boston and Chicago city directories for the years 1865 and 1870.

11. Anthropological speculations, some of them silly, include George Gmelch, "Baseball Magic: Professional Taboos, Totems, and Rituals" *Transaction* 8 (June 1961), 39–41; Richard Grossinger, "Baseball Variants," in Kevin Kerrane and Richard Grossinger, eds., *baseball i gave you all the best years of my life* (Richmond, Calif., 1980), 21–22; Robert Kelly, "A Pastoral Dialogue on the Game of the Quadrature," *ibid.*, 181; Peter Gardella, "The Tao of Baseball," *Harper's Magazine* (May 1986), 28–29. For baseball and masculinity, see Adelman, "Modern Athletics," 685 ff.

12. On men's dress, see Valerie Steele, *Fashion and Eroticism* (New York and Oxford, 1985), 17–19, 102–104. For Irish patterns, cf. Hasia Diner, *Erin's Daughters in America* (Baltimore and London, 1983), xiv, 16–25.

13. Cf. Vincent, *Mudville's Revenge*, 30–57; Somers, *Sports in New Orleans*, 159–236; Gorn, *The Manly Art*, 194–206. Though for a slightly later date, Randy Roberts's *Jack Dempsey: The Manassa Mauler* (Baton Rouge and London, 1979), 1–10, is a wonderful evocation of the brawling late 19th century.

14. Adelman, "Modern Athletics," 257–318, 530–650; Somers, *Sports in New Orleans*, 72; Raymond Smith, "Sports and Games in Western Iowa in the Early 1880s," *The Palimpsest* 65 (Jan/Feb. 1984), 9–18; Vincent, *Mudville's Revenge*, 13–83; Betty Spears and Richard A. Swanson, *History of Sport and Physical Activity in the United States* (Dubuque, 1978), 67–98; Stephen Freedman, "The Baseball Fad in Chicago, 1865–70: An Exploration of the Role of Sport in the Nineteenth-Century City," *Journal of Sports History* 5 (summer 1978), 52; Henry Roxborough, *One Hundred-Not Out: The Story of Nineteenth-Century Canadian Sport* (Toronto, 1966), 1–9; George B. Kirsch, *The Creation of American Team Sports: Baseball & Cricket, 1838–72* (Urbana and Chicago, 1989), 201–256.

15. Warren Goldstein, "Playing for Keeps: A History of American Base-

ball, 1857–1876" (Ph.D. diss., Yale University, 1983), 42 ff.; Allen Guttmann, *From Ritual to Record: The Nature of Modern Sports* (New York, 1978), 151; Adelman, "Modern Athletics," 335 ff.

16. On artisans, victory, and teamwork, see Goldstein, "Playing for Keeps," 146–147.

17. Bill James, *The Bill James Baseball Abstract,* 1983 (New York, 1983), 66. James is talking about 20th century big league teams—specifically the Houston Astros, whose park forces them to become a long-sequence offensive team, versus the Boston Red Sox, whose park induces the opposite. The observation holds true for other times and levels as well.

18. For instances of these emotions, see e.g., *Dubuque Times* 6/28/77, 6/5/79; *Dubuque Herald* 6/8/77, 8/16/78, 7/28/78; *Sporting News* 2/27/97; Smith, "Sports and Games," 9–18. The quotation is Charles Comiskey's. *Sporting News* 1/24/1918.

19. For 19th century migrations and "churning," see e.g., Caroline Golab, *Immigrant Destinations* (1977); Stephan Thernstrom, *The Other Bostonians: Poverty and Progress in the American Metropolis, 1880–1970* (Cambridge, Mass., 1973)

20. Peter Levine, *A. G. Spalding and the Rise of Baseball: The Promise of American Sport* (New York and Oxford, 1985), 5. The phrase is from Gerald McFarland, *A Scattered People* (New York, 1987). For a romantic view of urban children forming their own communities, see David Nasaw, *Children of the City* (New York, 1985).

21. For the racing and fighting atmosphere, see Somers, *Sports in New Orleans,* 91–114, 159–191. For views of the interaction of bench and audience, see, e.g., John Thorn and Mark Rucker, *The National Pastime: The Nineteenth Century* (Cooperstown, 1984), 7, 23–24, 48, 51, 61.

22. For early notational formulas, see John Thorn and Pete Palmer, *The Hidden Game of Baseball* (Garden City, 1984) 1–36. My sense of the nature of early newspaper coverage comes chiefly from extensive reading in the *Chicago Tribune* and *St. Louis Post-Dispatch.*

23. Bill James, *The Bill James Baseball Abstract, 1982* (New York, 1982).

24. The classic account of this theme in literature is Lionel Trilling, "The Young Man from the Provinces," in Trilling, *The Liberal Imagination* (New York, 1950). The quotation is Charles Comiskey's. *Sporting News* 12/28/1918.

25. The scholarly literature on how 19th century boys were reared is comparatively skimpy, but cf. Robert Kennedy, Jr., *The Irish: Emigration, Marriage and Fertility* (Berkeley, Los Angeles, London, 1973); Diner, *Erin's Daughters;* Elizabeth Pleck, "Challenges to Traditional Authority in Immigrant Families," in Michael Gordon, ed., *The American Family in Social–Historical Perspective* (3rd ed., New York, 1983), 504–517; Linda Gordon, "Child Abuse, Gender, and the Myth of Family Independence: A Historical Critique," *Child Welfare* 64 (May–June 1985); Edward Shorter, *The Making of the Modern Family* (New York, 1975); Linda Pollock, *Forgotten Children: Parent–Child Relations from 1500 to 1900* (Cambridge, 1983).

26. For the image and reality of 19th century mothers, cf. Steven Mintz and Susan Kellogg, *Domestic Revolutions: A Social History of American Family Life* (New York and London, 1988), 55–65; Ruth Schwartz Cowen, *More Work for Mother: The Ironies of Household Technology* (New York, 1983); Susan Strasser, *Never Done: A History of American Housework* (New York, 1982); James Mohr,

Abortion in America: The Origins and Evolution of National Policy, 1800–1900 (New York, 1978); Peter Uhlenberg, "Changing Configurations of the Life Course," in Tamara Hareven, ed., *Transitions: The Family and the Life Course in Historical Perspective* (New York, 1978), 94 ff.

27. For Irish family patterns, cf. Kennedy, *The Irish,* chapter 1; Diner, *Erin's Daughters,* chapter 1.

28. Guttmann, *From Ritual to Record,* 107–116.

29. A serviceable view of cricket's defensive complexities is Patrick Barclay, *The Puffin Book of Cricket* (Middlesex, 1986), 42–48. There is no substitute, however, for actually seeing a cricket match.

30. For the New England, or Massachusetts, game, see Seymour, *Baseball, The Early Years,* 26–29; Jacob Morse, *Sphere and Ash* (Boston, 1888), 6–7.

31. C.L.R. James argues in *Beyond a Boundary* (London, 1963) that colonial cricketeers internalized the rage for self-restraint and adherence to established rules that were a part of the game as it was introduced by the British, thereby helping the empire to perpetuate itself. But this kind of order, flowing as it did from the immense prestige and power of the English, is quite different from the inherent order of the early baseball grounds. For a different view of why baseball surpassed cricket in the U.S., see Adelman, "Modern Athletics," 283–284.

32. Seymour, *Baseball, The Early Years,* 45; Adelman, "Modern Athletics," 328–329; Mrozek, *Sport and American Mentality,* 166–167; Goldstein, "Playing for Keeps," 42–45; Guttmann, *From Ritual to Record,* 107–111; Freedman, "The Baseball Fad," 59–60. For pictorial representations, see Thorn and Rucker, *The National Pastime: The Nineteenth Century,* 6–7, 19, 23–24, 48–51, 78–79.

33. Eric Monkonnen, argues that drunken and disorderly behavior has trended downward since 1860, but his data underscore the extreme disorder of the entire 19th century as compared to the 20th; and the repeated outbursts of disorderly behavior—in the mid-1860s, the mid-1870s, and the 1890s—attendant on the rowdy, footloose bachelor subculture produced by war and depression. "A Disorderly People? Urban Order in the Nineteenth and Twentieth Centuries," *Journal of American History* 68 (Dec. 1981), 543–546. See also David R. Johnson, *Policing the Urban Underworld* (Philadelphia, 1979).

34. Robert Coles, *Children of Crisis: A Study of Courage and Fear* (Boston and Toronto, 1964), 323–326, passim.

35. Richard Sennett, *Families Against the City* (Cambridge, Mass., 1970). See also Kirk Jeffrey, "The Family as Utopian Retreat from the City," in Sallie Teselle, ed., *The Family, Communes, and Utopian Societies* (New York, 1972), 21–41. Eric Monkonnen writes: "The nuclear family, jobs, and the military located men in private space, thus removing them from risk of observation and arrest, as well as from opportunity for drunken and disorderly conduct." "A Disorderly People?", 546. For immigrant families, see Laurence Glasco, "The Life Cycles and Household Structure of American Ethnic Groups," in Nancy F. Cott and Elizabeth H. Pleck, *A Heritage of Her Own: Toward a New Social History of American Women* (New York, 1979), 273–277; Paul Gilje, "Infant Abandonment in Early Nineteenth Century New York City," in Ray Hiner and Joseph Hawes, eds., *Growing Up in America* (Urbana and Chicago, 1985), 109–118; Elizabeth Pleck, *Domestic Tyranny* (New York and Oxford,

1987), 69–123. As a case study, Charles Comiskey's mother was either pregnant or recovering from pregnancy for more than half of the 13 years from 1859 to 1872 that Charles was at home; she died giving birth to her seventh child, Charles's brother Ignatius, who was congenitally deaf. *Sporting News* 12/28/1916, 1/4/1917, 1/11/1917; Cook County, Illinois, manuscript census returns for 1860, 1870, 1880; Comiskey plot list, Calvary Cemetery, Cook County, Illinois.

You *Can* Blame the Media

The Role of the Press in Creating Baseball Villains

by Peter Williams

I f we were to begin at the beginning, we would need to identify the ancient and anonymous tribal tale-tellers who first recorded the exploits and treacheries of Achilles, Goliath, Mad Sweeney and Alberich the gnome. In the millennia when our only form of media was the oral tradition, these storytellers were the only reporters in town. Post-Gutenberg man views them as myth-makers, of course; however, we do not as automatically recognize that contemporary journalists are their direct heirs. Like the ancient oral historian, the modern reporter embellishes and alters fact in order to create characters who are heightened, oversimplified and quasi-fictional.

Classical psychologists like Jung and Rank, as well as more recent social scientists like Joseph Campbell, have emphasized the importance of archetypes in human culture and in the human mind. If humans think in terms of archetypes, as these and other thinkers contend, we are likely to demand, era by era, individual manifestations of universal types: to borrow terms from sociology, the archetypes are general "slots" into which we feel a continuing need to place individual "fillers." We "fill" archetypal "slots" with real individuals, whether or not the process is completely fair to the individual—was Gerald Ford really an inept klutz? was Helen really much more than a zoftig little Greek girl?—and we do it in sport as surely as in any other area of public life.

There is no orthodox number of categories, or archetypal "slots," in sport, but the three most usually discussed are *hero, villain* and *fool,* to which might be added Tristram Coffin's *trickster.* Thus, baseball's wily managers (Stengel, Weaver, Martin, Herzog) are tricksters; Babe Herman and Yogi Berra, though the judgment is very unfair in both cases, are fools; Ruth is a hero, his unsavory behavior unreported in the press, and Joe Jackson, who led all batters and made no errors in the 1919 world series, is a villain, no matter what Gropman or Kinsella can do about it. In all of this, the sportswriter, the representative and voice of the fan, plays a crucial role—take Hughey Fullerton, who invented the kid who asked Jackson to say it warn't so.

Modern sports journalists appear to have different motives for their revisionist versions of actual people and events. The most frequent motive is likely the one which prompted the old tale-tellers: the need for a good story. The oral historians knew that their listeners wanted to hear about unambiguous heroes and villains, and they obliged. The same goes for the contemporary journalist. This form of journalistic invention normally takes one aspect of an athlete's persona and exaggerates it, in the manner of a Mullin cartoon: the most famous example may well be Ruth's "called" home run in the '32 series, an event reported by only one witness to the game and later denied by many (Creamer, 304), but a story so appealing that many otherwise mature and intelligent observers (Gallico and Kieran are only two) became convinced they'd seen Tinker Bell in full flight.

For a second example, let me offer the story of Pea Ridge Day. Al Lopez, who caught him in the famous game during which Day gave his hog call from the mound, told me that, one slow afternoon, the Dodger reporters were pleading with the players for something, anything, that they could use for copy. After some time, Pea Ridge said he'd once won a hog-calling contest back in Arkansas, when he was 18 or so. The writers pounced. Pea Ridge became the certified and unquestioned hog-calling champ of the entire state of Arkansas, and on the day he finally yelled "SOO-EY!" on the mound in Ebbets Field, he did so in response to a wild crowd that had been egging him on for several minutes. Lopez, who was breaking up when he told me this, said Ruth was at the plate when Day gave the call. Lopez said he never saw Ruth laugh so hard, that the tears were streaming down his face. Incapacitated by laughter and possibly blinded with his own tears, Ruth took two strikes. Then he hit one over the right field wall into Bedford Avenue.

While the natural impulse to create archetypes out of individuals is undoubtedly the most common of the writers' motives, there are others, and at least one is equally familiar and just as documentable: the desire to defame a fallen hero. Heroes defamed by the press are inevitably ones who have in some way let that press down. Most commonly, they have been shown to be, not Gods, but humans. They have made it plain that they have some flaw, some ordinary human vulnerability, and the writer, with his flaming sword, drives them out of the paradise he created for them in the first place. Most often the hero's flaw is ethical, involving a lapse in character; we are, after all, still a Puritan nation. Gooden used coke, and it seems not to have mattered to Dick Young, himself quite a beer-drinker, that Gooden was never a severe user. The verdict on Pete Rose will be in by the time you read this, but whatever the Commissioner decides, Rose's heroism is already permanently tarnished. And in the famous case of Joe Jackson, we can see journalistic piety at its most vicious when Fullerton provides the country with his Dickensian, heartbroken little boy:

> After an hour, a man, guarded like a felon by other men, emerged from the [courthouse] door. He did not swagger. He slunk along between his guardians, and the kids, with wide eyes and tightened throats, watched, and one, bolder than the others, pressed forward and said "It ain't so, Joe, is it?" Jackson gulped back a sob, the shame of utter shame flushed his brown face. He choked an instant, "Yes Kid, I'm afraid it is," and the world of faith lay crashed around the heads of the kids. Their idol lay in dust, their faith destroyed. Nothing was true, nothing was honest. There was no Santa Claus. Then, and not until then, did Jackson, hurrying away to escape the sight of the faces of the kids, understand the enormity of the thing he had done. (Gropman, 191)

It should be noted not only that this is the only recorded instance of Jackson admitting his guilt, but that Fullerton candidly admitted he'd never spoken to Jackson, and therefore very likely was nowhere near that courthouse door; he was a good reporter, and it would take a bad reporter indeed to refrain from asking Shoeless Joe a question or two as he left court on that particular day.

Heroes can let the press down in another way: by remaining silent. Since the modern tale-teller who has no tale to tell is obviously out of work, the press does not take kindly to silence. In our era, Steve Carlton is the hero most guilty of this sort of hubris, and the press seems unaware that their inaccurate reporting of his comments led him to stop granting interviews.

One more thing must be said about the function of sports journalists before we get down to the specific business at hand: like the old tale-tellers, modern reporters are a bridge between the heroes and the people, the fans. The archetypes they create are the archetypes required by the public; and, in fact, a journalist who does not provide the fans with the heroes, villains, goats and con artists they require will not do well in his syndicate or on his network.[1]

Finally, archetypes come in two flavors: universal, and local or regional. The universal villain, like Joe Jackson, becomes anathema to *every* fan; the local or regional villain is usually a hero in a different venue—even in an adjacent borough of the same city.[2] Leo Durocher is primarily a universal villain; Bill Terry is mainly a regional one.

Durocher was Brooklyn's hero and the Giants' villain in 1946 when his famous remark was recorded, and so he was, to an extent, a regional villain. But he was also The Lip, a player who blurred the distinction between hustle and hostile, one of those who, we were told, "associated with known gamblers"—in other words, a much better candidate for universal than for regional villainy. "Nice guys finish last" exaggerated a basic aspect of his character, and Leo's villainy was created by caricature, in the same manner as was the divinity of Ruth. In any event, exaggeration and caricature it was, and, as is so often the case, the myth has outlasted the reality. Leo tells his side in the 1975 book whose title lets you know what a valuable commodity the myth has become for him:

> The Nice Guys Finish Last line . . . came about during batting practice at the Polo Grounds while I was managing the Dodgers. I was sitting in the dugout with Frank Graham of the old *Journal-American,* and several other newspapermen, having one of those freewheeling bull sessions. Frankie pointed to Eddie Stanky in the batting cage and said very quietly, "Leo, what makes you like this fellow so much? Why are you so crazy about this fellow?
>
> I started by quoting the famous Rickey statement: "He can't hit, he can't run, he can't field, he can't throw. He can't do a goddam thing, Frank—but beat you. . . . Sure, they call him the Brat and the Mobile Muskrat and all of that," I was saying, and just at that point, the Giants, led by Mel Ott, began to come out of their dugout to take their warm-up. Without missing a beat, I said, "Take a look at that Number Four there. A nicer guy never drew breath than that man there." I called off his players' names as they came marching up the steps behind him, "Walker Cooper, Mize, Marshall, Kerr, Gordon, Thomson. Take a look at them. All nice guys. They'll finish last. Nice guys. Finish last."
>
> That was the context. To explain why Eddie Stanky was so valuable to me by comparing him to a group of far more talented players who were—in fact—in last place. Frankie Graham did write it up that way. . . . But the other writers who picked it up ran the two sentences together to make it sound as if I were saying you couldn't be a decent person and succeed. (Durocher, 13–14)

Last year, one writer told the story this way. Red Barber was interrogating Durocher:

> "Leo," said the soft-spoken redhead, "how about those five home runs yesterday? Your guys were lucky to split."
>
> "Home runs?" snapped Durocher, taking the bait. "*Home runs?* Line drives and pop-ups that would have been caught in any other park! That's what they were!"
>
> Barber continued, "Why don't you admit they were real home runs? Why don't you be a nice guy for a change?"
>
> The suggestion of his being a nice guy ignited Leo. He

launched into a soliloquy that probably could have been heard across the Harlem River in Yankee Stadium. . . .

"A nice guy?" he roared. "A nice guy! I never saw a nice guy who was any good when you needed him. :

Leo paused and heated up, his voice becoming more shrill : "I'll take the guys who ain't nice. . . .

Eventually, Durocher pointed across the field to the Giant bench. "Look over there. Do you know a nicer guy than Mel Ott? Or any of the other Giants? Why, they're the nicest guys in the world. And where are they? In last place!"

Now Leo was in full gear. He looked at the batting cage where Eddie Stanky was taking his final swings. "Look at that little bastard," Leo said approvingly. "Think he's a nice guy? The hell he is. He'll knock you down and pick you up and say, 'I'm sorry.' That's the kind of guys I want on my ball club. He can't run, he can't hit, he can't do nothing. But what a ball player!" (Hynd, 337–338)

That was from *The Giants of the Polo Grounds* by Noel Hynd, a regular contributor to *Sports Illustrated,* and it is largely an uncredited pastiche based ultimately on the Frank Graham column which both Hynd and Durocher identify as the original source. Here is part of the original column of July 6, 1946:

It was twilight at the Polo Grounds and, in the Dodgers' dugout, Red Barber was needling Leo Durocher about the home runs the Giants had hit the day before. "Home runs!" Leo said. "Some home runs! Line drives and pop flies that would be caught on a bigger field! That's what they were!"

"Why don't you admit they were real home runs?" Red asked, sticking the needle in a little deeper. "Why don't you be a nice guy for a change?" . . .

He walked up and down the dugout for a moment, then whirled suddenly and pointed toward the Giants' dugout.

"Nice guys!" he said. "Look over there. Do you know a nicer guy than Mel Ott? Or any of the other Giants? Why, they're the nicest guys in the world! And where are they? In seventh place!" . . .

The bell rang and the Dodgers were streaming into the dugout. A reporter who had been sitting on the bench got up.

"All up, boys," he said. "Make room for some nice guys."

"Not in this dugout," Leo said.

He waved toward the Giants' dugout again.

"The nice guys are all over there," he said. "In seventh place."

The column ends there. The word "last," in fact, appears nowhere in it, not even in the caption, which reads, "LEO DOESN'T LIKE NICE GUYS—Isn't One Himself, He Loudly Admits; Says They Wind Up In Seventh Place." And even those afflicted, like myself, with math anxiety, will have trouble figuring that "seventh" equals" last" if there are eight teams in the league.

Then how did Leo break into the stuffy confines of *Bartlett's Familiar Quotations,* considering he never said what they said he said? No other New York reporter quoted his remarks on that day, and there is no further reference to them in any of the papers for two weeks thereafter. The interest of the writers turns to the All-Star game on July 9 (it was the 12–zip A.L. romp in which Ted Williams hit two homers) and to the death of Jack Johnson in a car crash on July 11. The big Dodger news is a potentially serious injury to Reese, there are pictures of DiMag in a hospital bed with his bad knee wrapped in ace bandages, and nothing much at all is said about Ott's Giants. Durocher is forgotten, at least until September.

In September, *Baseball Digest* printed "Leo Says, 'Phooey On Nice Guys,'" a shortened version of Graham's column; and Herb Simon, that magazine's editor, made a change which turned out to have some small significance. He changed Graham's language, probably in the interest of gaining greater dramatic impact, and no sober hindsight can possibly question his journalistic savvy in so doing. Here are the most pertinent parts of his version:

> "Nice guys!" he said. "Look over there. Do you know a nicer guy than Mel Ott? Or any of the other Giants? Why, they're the nicest guys in the world! And where are they? Buried in the second division!"
>
> "The nice guys are over there in last place. Well, let them come and get me!"
>
> "The nice guys are all over there," he said. "In the second division!" (Simon, 59–60)

It's Simon's version that is picked up both by John Kuenstler in his 1975 anthology, *From Cobb to Catfish,* and in 1981 by Frank Graham, Jr., in *A Farewell to Heroes,* where it appears as follows:

Red Barber . . . was needling Durocher about the home runs the Giants had hit the day before.

> "Home runs!" Leo said. "Some home runs! Line drives and pop flies that would have been caught on a bigger field! That's what they were!"
> "Why don't you admit they were real home runs?" Red asked. "Why don't you be a nice guy for a change?"
> Leo had been reclining on the bench. Now he leaped to his feet.

"A nice guy!" he yelled. "A nice guy! I been around baseball for a long time and I've known a lot of nice guys."

He walked up and down the dugout, then whirled and pointed toward the Giants' dugout.

"Nice guys!" he said. "Look over there. Do you know a nicer guy than their manager, Mel Ott? Or any of the other Giants? Why, they're the nicest guys in the world! And where are they? In last place!" . . .

He waved a hand toward the Giant dugout.

"The nice guys are over there in last place. Well, let them come and get me!"

The Dodgers were at batting practice and Eddie Stanky, the second baseman, was at the plate.

"Look at that little ————!" Leo said. "Think he's a nice guy? The hell he is! He'll knock you down to make a play, if he has to. That's the kind of guys I want on my ball club."

He spoke warmly now.

"Look at him," he said. "The little ————. He can't run, he can't hit, he can't throw, he can't do nothing. But what a ball player! . . .

The bell rang and the Dodgers were streaming into the dugout. A reporter who had been sitting on the bench got up.

"All right, boys," he said. "Make rooms for some nice guys."

"Not in this dugout," Leo said.

He waved toward the Giants' dugout again.

"The nice guys are all over there," he said. "In last place."
(Graham, 208–209)

According to the written record, then, Durocher was never reported as having said "nice guys finished last," although he seems to have come very close to saying "nice guys finish next-to-last." According to the written record, credit for this immortal baseball *riposte* belongs to Herb Simon, the editor of *Baseball Digest.* But there is still another puzzling inconsistency in the story.

Frank Graham, perhaps the most accurate and reliable reporter ever to write sports, described a scene immediately before the Dodgers–Giants night game of July 5; his column, of course, came out on July 6. The Dodgers won that night game, and on July 6 the Bums *were* in seventh—but on July 5, while Graham was interviewing Leo, they were in last, tied with the Pirates, who had lost that afternoon. Is it possible that a copy editor for the *Journal-American* altered Graham's original column, since by press time any reference to the Dodgers being in last place would have been inaccurate? Then Leo *could* have said it, and Simon's version would be more correction than revision.

Finally, however, all we have to go on is what has been recorded in print, and what happened in Durocher's case was, as I've suggested, simply this: a mythical figure of a certain kind was required, and one was created. The vivid detail of Graham's story, particularly after it was revised by the editor of a national magazine, helped the myth along, and as surely as some barbaric Achaen who was probably a little bigger and smarter than most became the wily Odysseus, Leo was transformed into the one and only unfeeling tough guy of sport, a position he was to hold without challenge until a remark of Vince Lombardi was similarly misinterpreted.

Bill Terry, too, was a villain both universal and regional. As a universal villain, however, he was obviously not the Durocher type— no fast living, no flashy women, no associations with high-rollers. In fact, Terry once told me the thing he disliked most about Rogers Hornsby—shades of Pete Rose—was the fact that he'd use the dugout phone to call his bookie. Terry was an upright man, religious, strictly monogamous, honored by the Kiwanis as a great role model after inheriting the manager's job from McGraw. Above all he was a family man, and his refusal to give out his home phone number (he was afraid the ringing would wake his young kids) was what got the press down on him. Ironically, his feud with the press didn't truly explode until some time after his famous comment. But Terry, who wouldn't make himself available for post-game interviews because he wanted to get back home to be with the aforementioned family, was probably in hot journalistic water after mid-'32, when he took the manager's job. As a regional villain—well, need anything be said? After he asked if Brooklyn was still in the league, he became, as the phrase went, "the most hated man in Brooklyn,"[3] and even Bob Thomson (who is, incidentally, a great admirer of his) may not have displaced him there. As the taciturn type, he was easy for the sportswriters to hate; as the epitome of the arrogant, efficient, relatively colorless Giants, he was a cinch for the Brooklyn fans.

The source of Terry's comment is a news conference he gave on January 24, 1934. Again working backwards, here's the version of Noel Hynd, author of several popular thrillers and a confirmed baseball addict:

> "What about Brooklyn, Bill?" asked Roscoe McGowen, who covered the Dodgers for the *New York Times*.
> "Brooklyn?" asked Terry, gently teasing McGowen. "I haven't heard anything from them lately. Are they still in the league?"
> The writers laughed. The writers reported the remark. But in

print the next day the question didn't have the playful tone in which it had been spoken. (292)

And Lee Allen's account:

> "What about Brooklyn, Bill?" Roscoe McGowen, of the *Times,* wanted to know.
> "Brooklyn?" Terry asked. "Gee, I haven't heard a peep out of there. Is Brooklyn still in the league?" (154–155)

And Frank Graham's, the opening paragraph of a chapter titled, "Gibe That Cost A Pennant":

> In February of 1934, the major league meetings were on in New York, and one afternoon, in the lobby of the Hotel Roosevelt, Terry was talking with some newspapermen. They asked him about his own club, about this club, about that. Roscoe McGowen of the *Times* asked, "How about Brooklyn, Bill?"
> Brooklyn had finished sixth in 1933.
> Terry, in mock wonderment at the question, countered with, "Brooklyn? Is Brooklyn still in the league?"
> It was a fateful moment in the history of the National League but none present could know that. Everybody just laughed, and everybody printed the question and answer. (*Giants,* 210)

Graham's photographic memory failed him here, by the way; as I've said, the date was January 24, and in fact the story was very poorly covered. On January 25, there was no mention at all of Terry's crack in the *Journal,* the *Post,* the *Sun,* the *American,* the *World-Telegram,* the *Mirror* or even the *Brooklyn Eagle.* But two papers did print the remark. Rud Rennie, in the *Trib,* said this:

> "Do you fear the Dodgers?" he was asked.
> "I was just wondering," said Terry, "whether they were still in the league."
> Terry thinks that the Cubs have been strengthened . . .

And Marshall Hunt, in the *News,* had it this way:

> The Dodgers? Will they give trouble? Mr. Terry grinned. He said he hadn't heard much about that outfit in a long while and he wondered whether they're still in the league. He's had letters from Travis Jackson and William Watson Clarke. Both have put on plenty of weight . . .

You'll note that Hunt suggests the remark was humorously

meant, and that both Rennie and Hunt make so little of it that they immediately turn to other matters. Still, it was one of these columns—Hunt's—that started this particular mythical ball rolling.

Bob Quinn was the new Brooklyn business manager, and he appears to have read the *News* in preference to the *Herald Tribune,* because Hunt was the writer Quinn phoned after the story came out. Hunt picked up the phone in his office and Quinn identified himself. Hunt said, "What's on on your mind?" and Quinn, according to Hunt's story on January 26, went on as follows:

> "Why, dammit, in your paper this morning you had a paragraph about Bill Terry saying that he didn't have any use for the Dodgers. You quoted him wondering whether the Dodgers are still in the league.
>
> "I've found out that you didn't misquote Terry. I called him up this afternoon and he verified everything.
>
> "But I still think that the Brooklyn club has been maligned unnecessarily by Terry. That's a terrible way for a manager of a championship club to talk. Especially one who is as thin-skinned as he proved to be last year.
>
> "I told Terry that I think we have grounds for action. His statements will ruin our business and times are especially tough right now. Terry should try to steam up business between the Dodgers and Giants which will benefit both clubs at the gates.
>
> "If Terry persists in ridiculing the Brooklyn club the element of competition will vanish. No one will come either to Ebbets Field or to the Polo Grounds if they think the games are a breeze.
>
> "We in Brooklyn are doing our best. You can't make trades out of a clear sky. Perhaps the Dodgers don't look so hot. Neither did the Giants a year ago. The writers picked them for sixth place, didn't they? Terry didn't like it, did he? But he wound up in first place. Give the Dodgers a break.
>
> "Not only do the Dodgers need good will, Lord knows, but Terry is in far greater need of good will. Tell Terry that as a manager he is a great success. But as a man he is a woeful flop and empty seats at the Polo Grounds all last season prove that something is lacking. I do not intend that Terry's insolent statements to the press or his ill-mannered reference to the Dodgers shall keep our seats in Ebbets Field empty."

At this point some reference should probably be made to floodgates. A chance, facetious remark had been reported in an offhand manner by only two of nine major metropolitan dailies, but it suddenly became one of the major stories of the year. It seems certain that nothing would have come of it had Bob Quinn not leapt like a cougar attacking a mouse. At any rate, the writers obliged Quinn by keeping the story alive for the rest of the week. Herewith, a day-by-day summary of highlights:

January 26

Dan Daniel, *World Telegram:* The offices of the Brooklyn club, otherwise quiet and calm, today were not well disposed toward William Harold Terry, manager of the Giants. When asked about the Dodgers in an interview yesterday, Terry naively asked, "Gosh, are they still in the league?" Of course, Memphis Bill knew that Brooklyn had not left the circuit.

But Bob Quinn took up the issue today and, in so many words, indicated that Terry was the last bird in the world to spoof a second-division club. "Where was Terry at this time last year?" asked Mr. Quinn, his acerbity reaching a Matterhorn peak.

"I will bet you a hat that the Dodgers will spring the surprise of 1934," volunteered Mr. Quinn. . . .

In the meantime, Mr. Terry is advised not to visit Brooklyn. The Gowanus Vigilantes are looking for him.

Harry Nash, *Post:* Chance remarks with concomitant reverberations are nothing new in the charmed life of William Harold Terry. The good Colonel has spoken out of turn before. He probably will do it again. You can't stop the irrepressible Colonel. But he happened to take an unkind cut at the Dodgers and Colonel Terry is in for a ride.

When those Brooklyn jockeys get through with Memphis Bill, he'll feel like a spavined nag that has hauled one load too many.

It is amusing how quickly a Brooklynite can be aroused by a slur against the Dodgers. Terry happened to remark, "I was just wondering whether they were still in the league."

Bob Quinn, Dodger business manger, lost no time in slapping back. The cudgels will be snatched up by every loyal fan, not to mention a number whose loyalty has been only lukewarm lately. And, if the good Colonel is as thin-skinned as Quinn says he is, he is due for a miserable season, so far as Giant–Dodger series are concerned.

Garry Schumacher, *Journal:* Is Bob Quinn angry? Oh me, oh my—the man is steaming.

And all because Bill Terry, in answer to a newspaperman's query about the Dodgers, countered with one of his own—"Are the Dodgers still in the league? I haven't heard much about them lately.". . . .

Tut, tut, Mr. Quinn, don't take it to heart that way. Being new to Brooklyn, you probably don't realize it, but Terry, when he made that crack, did you a bigger favor than if he'd picked the Dodgers to win the pennant.

Wait till April. Your fans will storm the gates when the Giants play over at Ebbets Field, just on the chance that they might get the opportunity to turn the laugh back on Terry.

January 27

Nat Gerstenzang, *Post:* And now fuel has been added to the heated Brooklyn–Giant warfare. Bill Terry wants to know if the Dodgers still are in the National League. The Flatbush fans will answer this insult with deep-throated catcalls whenever the Giants cross the bay next summer.

This state of affairs will whet the fans' interest in a game that is one of our national customs. Of course, all connected with the business will profit. That is, all but the umpires, whose lot will be an unhappy one indeed.

Keen competition [makes] the turnstiles click. They'll click even more merrily next summer.

Marshall Hunt, *News:* "Plenty of hell!"

That's what the Dodgers will give the Giants next summer, Robert Quinn, business manager of the Brooklyn baseball corporation, promised yesterday as he continued to nurse a deep-seated grudge against Bill Terry, manager of the world champions. . . .

"That man Terry," fumed Quinn yesterday, "is burning me up . . . the Brooklyn club will give the Giants plenty of hell next summer. That New York team will have a tough time winning the pennant.

"We've gone about the job of rebuilding the Brooklyn club in a rather silent manner. . . . We don't sound off every time we get our hands on new players. . . . I know the Dodgers didn't get very much publicity this winter. But wait."

January 29

Garry Schumacher, *Journal:* Terry's crack has fanned into a blaze a feud that has been smouldering for a couple of years.

Sid Mercer, *American:* The righteous indignation vented by Bobby Quinn, director general of the Brooklyn baseball club, over a chance remark dropped last week by Till Terry, manager of the Giants, has reached the ears of [Dodger manager] Max Carey away out in St. Louis.

Max will be here at the end of this week to personally answer Terry's query: "What has become of the Dodgers? Are they still in the league?"

Mr. Quinn arose in high dudgeon to announce that the Dodgers were doing all right and would prove it next summer when the Giants call on them at Ebbets Field.

Dan Daniel, *World-Telegram:* It doesn't take much to start a baseball war in Brooklyn.

While being interviewed on his arrival here the other day, Bill Terry was asked what he thought of the Dodgers. In the spirit of levity, Memphis Bill exclaimed: "Is Brooklyn still in the league?"

In so far as Flatbush, Red Hook, Gowanus, Brownsville, Bushwick, Coney Island and Bath Beach were concerned, that remark was like the shot that rang out on the bridge at Concord. Brooklyn fans have taken pen in hand. Brooklyn papers have fanned the flames of furious resentment against Terry. Bob Quinn has made the retort courteous for the Dodger front office, and Joe Gilleaudeau has made diplomatic representations in Charley Stoneham's headquarters.

Chagrined over this strange interpretation of what he regarded as an innocent and comic interjection, Terry has headed for the wilds of Arkansas until the war blows over. But Bill will have to wait a long time for the fans of Brooklyn to forget. He will hear his exclamations thrown back at him many an afternoon during the twenty-two games which the Giants and Dodgers will play with each other next season. . . .

If Terry has started a real war between the Giants and the Dodgers, more power to Memphis Bill's flair for comic commentary on the Brooklyn situation.

Since the passing of Wilbert Robinson from the leadership of the Dodgers, the old feeling of animosity between the New York and Brooklyn clubs has been disappearing gradually. . . We hope Terry has rekindled it to the white heat of its Washington Park flame. . . .

The late Charley Ebbets had the correct idea. . . . In every way Charley fanned the flame of rivalry between the two clubs and made their annual series the most vitriolic, the most keenly contested and, let us not forget, the most profitable financially of all the competitive amenities in the National League.

January 30

Clair Hare, *Post:* You have to hand it to Bill Terry for helping out a sad situation. He has assured a return of "the good old days" every time the Giants and Dodgers clash on the diamond in the season that soon will be with us. . . .

There was a time, long before Terry ever played for the Polo Grounds ensemble, when every Giants–Dodgers game was an event to be remembered. More intense rivalry never existed. . . . It was great while it lasted, but it eventually died out to almost nothing and reached a new low last year. . . .

Despite this, Terry took some of the subtlety out of the Dodgers' mien by asking "Is Brooklyn still in the league?" when queried as to what he thought of the Dodgers. To which Quinn, on behalf of the Brooklyns, answers "He'll find out."

This gentle repartee is certain to be taken up by the two teams' supporters, particularly by the Brooklyns. They're sure to make their field and Coogan's bluff ring with the good old Bronx cheer, missing all too much in the past.

Won't they have fun! And won't we have fun! "Happy days are here again."

George E. Phair, *American:* The Giant–Dodger war showed signs of petering out last season. So what if the boys strive to inject new venom into the interborough strife? As the old gambler said about the phony wheel game, "it's the only one in town":

> Though Ebbets Field is cold and still
> And Coogan's Bluff is bleak and chill
>   And wintry winds are rude,
>
> The Dodgers and the Giants rise
> With flames of battle in their eyes
>   To fight the ancient feud.
>
> Though Brooklyn fans are wrapped in furs,
> They take exception to the slurs
>   Of William Harold Terry,
>
> And now we see some glowing sparks
> Proceeding from the hot remarks
>   Of Maximilian Carey.

As you can see, the tone is often one of amusement, as though the writers are not entirely convinced that Quinn's rage is genuine, and there are frequent references to a probable improvement at the gate. The temptation to conjecture here is truly hard to resist. While Terry never discussed Quinn with me, he never referred to his famous remark and its aftereffects without laughing. I would love to have wiretapped their conversation in January of 1934. Did they cook the whole think up between them? One was a business manager, the other an acknowledged business wizard who was already, and in the Depression, a millionaire. Terry's remark was obviously jocular. If Quinn didn't understand that before talking to Terry, Terry would have made it clear to him; Terry, remember, was a man less deceitful than George Washington. And however he said it, what Terry said about the Dodgers had certainly been said before. In fact, the *Post*'s Nat Gerstenzang had this to say on January 24, and it's even conceivable that Terry had read it before going to his news conference that afternoon:

> Some one smuggled a telephone directory into The Dugout, and thus we were able to check the fact that there is a Brooklyn baseball club.
> Ever hear of it? Many years ago there was such an organiza-

tion. . . . Reference to dusty files indicates that the Dodgers
clinched sixth place last summer and promptly went to sleep. They
haven't been awakened yet. Compared with them Rip Van Winkle
was an insomniac. . . . Apparently they don't think much about
keeping the fans' interest in the team during the winter over in
Brooklyn. While the Yankees, Giants and out-of-town teams have
been popping items of interest into the sports pages, the Dodgers
sleep soundly.

You can't blame Business Manager Bob Quinn for that. The
other officials are doing nothing to prevent the fans from dozing.
Even an extended snooze like the Dodgers' isn't news any more.

If it's not impossible that Terry read Gerstenzang's piece on the 24th,
it's equally tempting to imagine that Quinn read it, too, and that it
prompted his extreme reaction to Hunt's column on the 25th.

Well. If Durocher's comment was misrepresented by the writers,
Terry's was misheard, and primarily (and doubtless intentionally) by
Bob Quinn. And what Quinn had prompted the writers to start, no
retraction could stop. The anger of the Flatbush partisans had been
aroused. When the *Brooklyn Eagle* finally got around to addressing the
question, Tommy Holmes joined earlier writers who had predicted an
increase in revenue; and later on, Lee Allen poetically imagined that
the boos of the paying fans would constitute, to Terry's ears, "a chorus
as sweet as the music of Guy Lombardo" (155), a reference to the band
with which Terry traveled in the winter when he was working for
Standard Oil.

Both Durocher and Terry, then, were misrepresented by the
press. Durocher's language was changed; Terry's ironic tone was ignored, at least after Quinn made an issue of Terry's remark. Durocher
was made into a universal villain, Terry into a regional one. Neither
man, however, had cause to regret the misrepresentation, and neither
did. Durocher, the only athlete before Ali to bear a nickname suggestive of his fondness for speech, used his comment as material for
endless interviews and as the title of his autobiography. Terry, the
deadpan ironist and laconic businessman, relished the boost at the
gate in quiet amusement. When he demanded police protection before he'd take the Giants to Ebbets Field, I think he knew exactly what
he was doing. In any event, here's what each man said last year when I
asked for comments on their famous remarks, with Durocher adding
a few points about Terry:

Durocher on His Own Remark

I made a remark, and they took it out of context, took it out of
context. "Nice," I said, "Nice guys finish last." And then I went on to
explain, gimme some Stankys. He's a scratcher, and a diver, he likes

to win—he can't, you know, run, can't do—I said, and I prefaced my remark by saying it's an old Rickey remark, Branch Rickey remark: "He can't run, he can't throw, he can't hit, he can't do anything but beat you." Now I said—and about that time the Giants were coming out of the dugout to warm up. I said, see that Number Four? Mr. Ott? One of the nicest men that ever put a shoe on, I said, but he has surrounded himself with a lot of fifty, sixty thousand dollar ball players, and I'm not so sure that they care too much whether they win or lose. They get a couple of hits, they go home, go to sleep. But Mel Ott doesn't. He worries. He likes to win.

And so they took that out of context. I said, that's another Rickey remark, put that in there. And they never mentioned it. I said, Mr. Rickey said to me once, Leo, if you put me on a boat with a lot of hungry players, ten thousand dollar players, fifteen at the most, and you take the fifty, sixty thousand ball players, and you drop off at an island and drop me off at an island and I'll be better off than you will at the end of six months. 'Cause my players get hungry. And yours are self-satisfied, self-sufficient. I don't want the guy that's makin' sixty, seventy, and—that's enough in those days, plenty—I want some guys that are *hungry*. And Stanky's a hungry player, likes to play, comes to play, comes to win. And he'll do anything to win. He's that type of player.

Durocher on Terry's Remark

They still talk about—anybody, anybody's liable to make a re-mark, you know, and I think it's a little unfair to be holding that, you know, every time you look up they're writing something about Bill Terry saying, "Is Brooklyn still in the league?" That's a little bit unfair for the media to continuously do that. And, and he was joking anyway; I mean, yeah, it was just a, an off-the-cuff remark, a throwaway, he wasn't—he wasn't mad at anybody. You can't explain it.

Terry on His Own Remark

That day they asked me what I thought about Brooklyn, and I—"I don't know," I said. "Are they still in the league?"

That—that made a lot of money for us. The whole team.

Oh, I got a lot of angry letters on it. I told Jack [Terry's personal secretary] to read 'em all and throw 'em away.

I didn't get up until around noon [presumably on the 25th], and I got downstairs about four or five o'clock, and it was in blank letters in the *Sun*—TERRY WANTS TO KNOW: IS BROOKLYN STILL IN THE LEAGUE?

That was a nice paper. I'd buy it all the time. I bought it *that* time—

That made a lot of money.

Interestingly, neither man has a clear and flawless recollection of the event. Terry, in particular, seems to have imagined a banner headline in a paper which carried no mention of the remark until well after it was made, and Durocher seems convinced he said "last," not "seventh."

The postscript I'd like to add now has little to do with the press coverage of these two famous quotes, but much to do with the respective characters of Durocher and Terry, so at the risk of abandoning academic symmetry I'll share it with you. When I spoke with Leo he told me what a wonderful man Mr. Terry was, universally admired and respected, a gentleman of the first water, possibly the man in baseball of whom he thought most. He said he "never heard of one bad word" about Terry, that he was "one of the finest men [he'd] ever met," that when he saw him a while back he "was never so, so happy just to see a man again," that Terry was a "tremendously nice person" and "some kind of man." Leo went *on.*

When I said I was on my way to Jacksonville and volunteered to give Mr. Terry his best, Leo said, "no, don't give him my best—give him my *love.*"

Naively, I swallowed Leo's effusions whole. I couldn't wait to get to Florida to tell Terry how the acknowledged tough guy of baseball felt about him. When I got there I told the story—how Leo had said many warm things, how he sent, not his best, but his *love,* how he had continued in that vein for quite a while. Mr. Terry was patient enough, but he hardly let me finish before he answered me. He looked at me, and this look had no touch of his usual subtle irony.

"You know what *that's* worth," he said.

Notes

1. For a discussion of writer as extension of fan, see Judith Cramer et al, "Athletic Heroes and Heroines: The Role of the Press in Their Creation." *Journal of Sports Behavior,* IV, 4 (1979).

2. The regional villain can become a hero simply by changing jobs: think of Sal Maglie, and of Durocher himself.

3. He was already one of the most hated, as Lee Allen points out: "In Brooklyn they hated him more than they had McGraw. . . . And secretly Terry loved it" (152). After The Wisecrack, however, it's Douglas Wallop's understatement to say Terry "sufficed nicely as a villain" in Brooklyn (209).

References

Allen, Lee. *The Giants and the Dodgers.* New York: Putnam's, 1964.
Coffin, Tristram. *The Old Ball Game.* New York: Herder & Herder, 1971.

Cramer, Judith, et al. "Athletic Heroes and Heroines: The Role of the Press in Their Creation." *Journal of Sports Behavior.* IV, 4 (1979).

Creamer, Robert. *Babe.* New York: Simon & Schuster, 1974.

Durocher, Leo. *Nice Guys Finish Last.* New York: Simon & Schuster, 1975.

Graham, Frank. *The New York Giants.* New York: Putnam's, 1952.

———. "'Phooey On Nice Guys,' Says Leo." *Baseball Digest,* V (September 1946).

Graham, Frank Jr. *A Farewell to Heroes.* New York: Viking, 1981.

Gropman, Donald. *Say It Ain't So!.* Boston: Little, Brown, 1979.

Hynd, Noel. *The Giants of the Polo Grounds.* New York: Doubleday, 1988.

Kuenster, John. *From Cobb to Catfish.* Chicago: Rand McNally, 1975.

Wallop, Douglas. *Baseball: An Informal History.* New York: Norton, 1979.

About the Authors

Alvin L. Hall is dean of continuing education and director of summer sessions at the State University of New York College at Oneonta. He holds a Ph.D. in history from the University of Virginia.

James A. Vlasich is associate professor of history at Southern Utah University. He holds a Ph.D. in history from the University of Utah.

Marty Appel is executive producer of New York Yankee baseball for WPIX-TV in New York City. He holds a B.S. in political science from the State University of New York College at Oneonta.

Peter C. Bjarkman is a free-lance writer specializing in baseball. He holds a Ph.D. in linguistics from the University of Florida.

Thomas L. Altherr is professor of history and American studies at Metropolitan State College. He holds a Ph.D. in history from Ohio State University.

Shelly M. Dinhofer is coordinator of museum programs at the City University of New York. She has an M.A. in art history from the Graduate Center of CUNY.

Maggi E. Sokolik is lecturer in English at Texas A & M University. At the time her paper was presented, she was visiting assistant professor of foreign languages and literature at the Massachusetts Institute of Technology. She holds a Ph.D. in applied linguistics from UCLA.

Gai Berlage is professor of sociology at Iona College. She holds a Ph.D. in sociology from New York University.

Mark W. Clark is assistant dean of the graduate school and associate professor of research, evaluation and development at the University of Northern Colorado. He holds a Ph.D. in education from Stanford University.

Phil Mullen is director of the evening division and summer session at the University of Northern Colorado. He holds an M.A. in English from the University of Northern Illinois.

J. Michael Lillich is University Editor at De Pauw University. At the time his paper was presented, he was a public information specialist at Southern Illinois University. He holds a Ph.D. in English Literature from Southern Illinois University.

Paul L. Gaston is dean of the college of arts and sciences at the University of Tennessee at Chattanooga. He holds a Ph.D. in English from the University of Virginia.

Carl F. Ojala is professor of geography at Eastern Michigan University. He holds a Ph.D. in geography from the University of Georgia.

Michael T. Gadwood is a student assistant and graduate student in the department of geography and geology at Eastern Michigan University. He holds a B.S. in geography from Eastern Michigan.

Richard Gaughran is visiting assistant professor of English at Lehigh University. He holds a Ph.D. in English from Lehigh University.

Linda A. Kittell is instructor of English at Washington State University and the University of Idaho. She holds a master of fine arts in creative writing from the University of Montana.

Monty E. Nielsen is director of admissions and records and adjunct assistant professor of higher education at the University of North Dakota. He holds an Ed.D. from the University of Nebraska.

George W. Schubert is dean of the University College and summer sessions and professor of communication disorders at the University of North Dakota. He holds a Ph.D. in communication disorders from the University of Washington.

Sally A. Canapa is assistant professor of the humanities at Concordia University in Wisconsin. She holds a Ph.D. in English from the University of Wisconsin–Milwaukee.

Michael S. Kimmel is associate professor of sociology at the State University of New York at Stony Brook. He holds a Ph.D. in sociology from the University of California at Berkeley.

Nick Trujillo is associate professor of communication studies at the California State University–Sacramento. At the time his paper was presented, he was assistant professor in the Center for Communication Arts at Southern Methodist University. He holds a Ph.D. in communications from the University of Utah.

Robert Moynihan is professor of English at the State University of New York College at Oneonta. He holds a Ph.D. in English from the University of Arizona.

Ronald Story is professor of history at the University of Massachusetts at Amherst. He holds a Ph.D. in history from the State University of New York at Stony Brook.

Peter Williams is on the faculty of the County College of Morris in New Jersey. He holds a Ph.D. in English from the University of Michigan.